*'Tis our college on the hill,
Stately standing, grandly, still,
As a trusty guardian true,
O'er past memories and the new,
That around its wall entwined,
Till its noble form, enshrined,
Stands a monument to fame –
S.D.A.C. is its name.*

November 1903 Industrial Collegian

For our families

The College *on the* Hill

A SENSE OF SOUTH DAKOTA
STATE UNIVERSITY HISTORY

By Amy Dunkle
with V.J. Smith

Copyright © 2003 by
South Dakota State University Alumni Association

All rights reserved. Published 2003

Library of Congress Control Number: 2003111811

ISBN: 1-57579-271-0 (cloth)
ISBN: 1-57579-270-2 (pbk.)

All stories are the responsibility and property of the South Dakota State University Alumni Association. The SDSU Alumni Association is a private non-profit entity and does not fall under the auspices of South Dakota State University. The material presented does not reflect the view or views of South Dakota State University. Requests for reproduction of any material in this book must be sent to: SDSU Alumni Association, P.O. Box 515, Brookings, SD 57007

Printed in the United States of America
Pine Hill Press, Sioux Falls, SD 57106

Table of Contents

The Early Years
1. Born in Politics — 1
2. A Pioneer's Diary — 9
3. 'First Pure, Then Peaceable' — 21
4. Great Legacies — 33
5. A Dangerous Game — 45

Traditions
6. School Songs — 55
7. School Cheers — 65
8. Becoming Jackrabbits — 73
9. Hobo Day — 79
10. Cowbells — 93
11. The Blue Key Smoker — 99

Campus Landmarks
12. Coughlin Campanile — 105
13. Coolidge Sylvan Theatre — 113
14. Clock Tower — 117
15. Memorial Gateway — 121
16. Old Central Archway — 125
17. Woodbine Cottage — 129

Student Voices
18. Power Play — 133
19. Food Fight! — 143
20. Stadium for State — 151
21. 1971 Engineering Crisis — 161
22. A Decade of Unrest — 171

Athletics
- 23 Cleve Abbott — 183
- 24 The Great Weert Engelmann — 191
- 25 A Great Road Trip — 195
- 26 Winning Silk Pants — 201
- 27 The First National Championship — 207
- 28 Tragedy and Triumph — 211
- 29 Détente with a Round Ball — 221
- 30 Oh, How it Hurt(s) — 227
- 31 A Run for Glory — 233
- 32 Tossing Critters — 243
- 33 The Best — 249

And the Band Played On
- 34 1904 St. Louis World's Fair — 253
- 35 A Brush with Royalty — 257
- 36 Playing for the Gipper — 263
- 37 The Smell of Roses — 269

Oh, Those Students!
- 38 Peace Pacts Meant to be Broken — 277
- 39 In Quest of Lingerie — 285
- 40 The Fictitious Candidate — 289
- 41 Whipping to White — 295
- 42 Streaking — 301
- 43 1990 Hobo Day Incident — 307

War Times
- 44 The War to End All Wars — 315
- 45 Omar Bradley — 321
- 46 December 7, 1941 — 325
- 47 Hobo Day Lost — 331
- 48 The '44 Kings — 339
- 49 A University Honors a Hero — 347
- 50 The Heartache of Vietnam — 357
- 51 'They Were All So Young' — 365

Those Were the Days, My Friend
  52 The Little Engine That Did 371
  53 President Coolidge Visits 375
  54 Campus Life 383
  55 Those Nasty Blizzards 393
  56 A Family Affair 399
  57 The Day President Kennedy Died 405
  58 When the College Became a University 411
  59 The Rules Have Changed 417
  60 Olivia's Kiss 431
  61 The Humble Beginnings of Prairie Rep 435
  62 Dr. Wagner's Marriage Class 441
  63 Dance for Dystrophy 449
  64 Horatio's 455
  65 Odds, Ends and Jackrabbit Tales 461
  66 Raymond, S.D. 471

Presidents and Places
  The Presidents 481
  The Places 487

The rabbit caricatures following each chapter in this book appeared in the 1940 Jack Rabbit yearbook.

Foreword

When V.J. Smith first asked me about writing a history of South Dakota State University, his vision was broad and the details were sketchy. The only thing he was certain about was that the project had to be done.

I eagerly bought into the dream. It seemed like a good idea. I needed work. And, of course, what writer doesn't dream of publishing a book?

As the project evolved, my perspective changed radically. But, not just because V.J. handed me two file boxes full of research and a few piles of Jack Rabbit yearbooks.

Rather, it was the stories of the people — both living and long gone — that drew me in and gave me a deep sense of appreciation for South Dakota State. Not every school inspires such intense loyalty in its students.

Former men's basketball coach Gene Zulk best summed up the State experience after I interviewed him about the 1984-85 championship run. He talked first about growing up in Spencer, S.D., a town of 500 people, and what an opportunity it was when then-basketball coach Jim Marking brought him to State to play ball. After college, Zulk returned to SDSU to coach.

"I look at how my life unfolded, first playing and then coaching at State," Zulk told me. "The things I learned, the opportunities I was given — they made whatever my life is now."

Zulk largely credits Marking and former Athletic Director Stan Marshall for giving a small-town kid like himself the chance of a lifetime.

"When I think about South Dakota State," Zulk said, "it gives me chills. I look back on having played there, having gone to school there, having coached there, and I wish everybody could have that experience. It's really a blessing."

Before "The College on the Hill," I always thought it didn't matter where you went to college — that all schools were pretty much the same. Now, I know better.

Having finished the book, I find myself returning to Zulk's words along with the many other wonderful stories people have passed along. And I think, yes, it truly is a blessing to go to a school that has such an imprint on individuals' lives.

To all of you who let me into your memories, your thoughts and your wisdom — I thank you. This book could not have happened without you.

I am also forever grateful to my family and friends, who with unfailing good humor supplied encouragement and support, and listened with interest (or so it seemed) to the telling and retelling of so many chapters along the way.

Amy Dunkle

In Appreciation

The idea for this book was born on a day when I was signing sympathy cards. As I surveyed the graduation dates of those recently departed State alumni, I was intrigued by one who had graduated in 1927. "That was before the Coughlin Campanile," I muttered to myself. I then began to wonder how many of our living alumni had graduated before 1930.

Barb Koenders, assistant director of the SDSU Alumni Association, quickly produced a list that included the names of approximately 30 people. As I read through the names, I noted Russa Osborne, class of 1926. He lived in Mitchell.

Russa Osborne, class of 1926.

The spelling of the last name and the fact that Mr. Osborne lived in Mitchell caught my attention. A friend of mine, Kurt Osborne, is a Mitchell native who now lives in Brookings. I called Kurt and asked if he knew Russa Osborne. Kurt replied, "He's my grandpa." He then told me his grandpa wasn't feeling well at the time but he'd be better in a couple of weeks, and invited me to go with him to Mitchell sometime to talk to him.

Kurt then revealed a Russa Osborne tale. He said his grandpa loved to tell the story of the all-college picture taken on the campus green in 1924. The photographer had the camera mounted on a tripod. "Nobody move!" the photographer yelled as the camera panned the assembled group, beginning on the right and sweeping to the left. "After the camera went by him, Grandpa jumped up and ran to the other side of the group and the camera went by him again," Kurt told me. "Grandpa really enjoyed telling the story about how he was in the picture two times."

I was eager to meet Grandpa Osborne and find out what other things he could share about the pre-Campanile days. It was a meeting that would never take place. A little over a week after our conversation, Kurt sent me an e-mail that said, "Grandpa died last night."

It was at that moment I knew something had to be done to record the personal history of South Dakota State University. Each time I signed a sympathy card I realized stories were being lost — forever. I was determined there would be no more delays; it was time to get on with it.

For a few weeks I gave serious thought to the project. There was no way I was going to write the book as I lacked the proper writing skills. By chance, I met Amy Dunkle at the Post Office. We spoke for a few minutes and set up a time to talk about the possibility of her writing the book. The book had neither a title nor an outline. All I knew is that we had to do something.

Amy said she would do it. As I reflect on it now, I can't believe how fortunate it was that our paths crossed at the Post Office. Amy Dunkle has done a great service for all of us who share a fondness for SDSU. She is a graduate of the University of New Hampshire but soon after beginning this project, she began referring to SDSU as any proud alumna would.

My job was to identify appropriate topics for the almost 70 chapters and to do research. I read through every student newspaper from 1885 to the late 1990s. I read every yearbook, twice, and noted important events and interesting pictures. I also talked to a lot of people.

Dr. J.P. Hendrickson

One of those individuals was Dr. J.P. Hendrickson, former head of the SDSU department of political science. My visit took place in January 2002 at McKennan Hospital in Sioux Falls. 'Phil,' as he was known by family and friends, had been hospitalized for several months. Susie Hendrickson, Phil's wife, said he would enjoy a visit.

Before entering his hospital room, I had to wash my hands, put on a sterilized gown, and don a surgical mask. After doing this, I walked into his room. Phil was sitting in a wheelchair beside his bed. He was connected to a variety of wires and tubes. He smiled, stuck out his hand, gave me a firm handshake, and said, "Hello, Vincent." Teachers, from grade school through college, always called me by birth name. Phil Hendrickson was forever the teacher.

For the next hour we talked about his time at South Dakota State. He was proud that many of his former students had done so well. Phil had a keen intellect and great sense of humor. Both of those qualities were present as he sat in his chair and reminisced about the past. As I sat and listened, I couldn't help but think about all his former students — lives he had touched. I'd like to think that those individuals, like me, absorbed the lessons that seemed to be his themes. First, be ethical in your life's pursuits, but don't brag about it. Second, be compassionate and seek understanding. Third, humility is a great virtue and too often in short supply.

Phil left us on March 17, 2002. His lessons remain.

As the research continued and Amy Dunkle began to churn out chapters, I tried to envision who would want to read this book. I concluded that a lot of people would. Why? Because over the years, I had met so many people who were passionate about this place. I suppose most colleges claim to have a host of passionate alumni. Our alumni have proven it and many people notice it.

I recall a conversation I had with former Governor William Janklow. He said: "What is it about your place? I've met so many people who flunked out of there after a semester or two, but will stand up and sing the college song as if they were the valedictorian of their classes!" Yes, people are passionate about this place.

Wanda and Les Roberts, both from the class of 1948.

In December 2002, I went pheasant hunting at the Roberts family farm, which is 17 miles northeast of Redfield. Les Roberts, class of 1948, lives on the farm homesteaded by his grandfather in 1881. He was born on the farm in 1922. Les's wife, Wanda, also a 1948 graduate, died in 1999. They raised four children and each of them enrolled at SDSU. Grandchildren have come this way, too.

Truly, SDSU passion runs deep in the Roberts family. Stepping into their home, you immediately discover that you are in "Jackrabbit Country." In the kitchen hangs a clock bearing the name of the SDSU Foundation. Les served on the SDSU Foundation board for several years. He also served as a member of the SDSU Alumni Council. When you walk out of the kitchen and into the living room, looking straight ahead, you see a large framed picture of the Coughlin Campanile.

Those displayed symbols are outright signs of affection for their alma mater. But, the real testimony of love for this place can best be measured by what Les, Wanda and their children have given back to SDSU. All told, Les and Wanda Roberts have funded about a dozen scholarships. Music students, nursing students and student athletes have benefited from their kindness. When new scholarship programs like Leaders for Tomorrow and the Jackrabbit Guarantee were proposed, they quickly responded to the call. Season tickets for athletic and theater events were purchased; tens of thousands of miles were driven between their home and State's campus. On several occasions, Les has responded to the call of doing fund raising on behalf of SDSU.

I'd like to think this book will find a place on the coffee table or bookshelf of the Roberts' home. It would add to a cup that is already overflowing with love for this place.

Even as this book is being prepared for printing, another event has reinforced the reason for the project. John Bibby, class of 1942, died on July 26, 2003. John, especially through his work in the South Dakota Legislature, had an enormous impact on this university. He was interviewed several times during the past two years and many of his quotes are recorded in this book. We are grateful for his life and his memories.

My apologies to the people who feel we have slighted anyone by failing to mention their name, or another person's name, in this book. Never have we claimed this to be a complete history of South Dakota State University. That is the reason for the subtitle, "A Sense of South Dakota State University History." To write a complete history of SDSU would require a tremendous amount of time and money. We tried to do the best we could with what we had.

I would like to acknowledge the wonderful work of three individuals: Crystal Gamradt, Kristi Schelhaas and Sherry Fuller Bordewyk. Crystal serves as an archives associate in the SDSU Archives and Special Collections at the H.M. Briggs Library. She offered advice and gave invaluable assistance in acquiring more than 1,500 articles and pictures. Plus, she always laughed at my stupid stories. Kristi designed the book and did a great job. What I liked best about working with her is that she truly cared about the project and it shows. Sherry had the daunting task of editing the copy. I knew we had selected the right person when she revealed that she had tears in her eyes while reading the chapter titled, "Stadium for State." Each of these individuals has earned my undying respect and gratitude.

A very special thank you is owed to Bob Fishback of Brookings. Early in the project I went to him requesting financial support. He didn't hesitate for a moment. This book would not have been possible without his very kind assistance.

Finally, I want to thank the history professors of SDSU who were a part of my collegiate experience. Drs. Rodney Bell, John Miller, Jerry Sweeney, Michael Funchion, and David Crain instilled in me the importance of understanding and recording history. I was one of John Miller's first advisees when he came to SDSU in 1974. It's ironic, I suppose, that this book be published in the same year as his retirement.

Early in this project, Dr. Miller reminded me of the importance of being thorough in my research. One day I sent him an e-mail because I was excited to find a piece of information courtesy of the famous South Dakota historian, Doane Robinson. In his reply message, Dr. Miller simply wrote, "This merits further research." I was stunned. How could the great Doane Robinson be wrong? Digging deeper, I discovered Robinson was wrong. Thank you for reminding me about the importance of being thorough, Dr. Miller.

This book has taken me on a great journey. I learned so much along the way. My affection and respect for South Dakota State University deepened. It truly became a labor of love.

It is my hope that the following pages take you on a great journey as well.

V.J. Smith

Chapter 1

Born in Politics

If everything had gone the way it was intended, Brookings just as easily could have become home to the state penitentiary. The Dakota Agricultural College essentially was a consolation prize. And even then, not everyone saw the value in a campus of higher education.

Had it not been for one man — John O'Brien Scobey — South Dakota State, and all that has followed in its wake, might never have been. Yet, despite playing such a pivotal role, Scobey and his contribution soon faded into oblivion.

There are few scattered details about what Scobey did and where he went after leaving Brookings. What is left of him — a building and history books — reveals that history didn't always record his name right. In some instances he is referred to as J. O. B. Scobey; in others, as in the plaque in the building named after him, James O'Bryan Scobey.

Pictured above, John O'Brien Scobey.

Scobey typified the pioneers who settled the Midwest. He and University of Iowa law school buddy George A. Mathews rode into the town with a pair of mules and a covered wagon on March 31, 1879, looking for adventure in the new country. Along with several other local men, the pair had big ideas for their future as well as the town, which at that point was Fountain.

Once the early arrivals realized that the railroad was not going to make it to Fountain, they picked up and moved to the railroad. Brookings was born.

This small anecdote in Brookings' past offers a clear picture of what life demanded in those early days. As pointed out in the Brookings County History Book, "Success came to those with a purpose and vision of how to obtain it, and it came to those who were quick to adapt to the particular circumstances in which they found themselves."

Scobey's ability to do just that is why South Dakota State University exists today.

In addition to practicing law and selling land, Scobey was a member of the territorial Legislature during the session of 1881. He traveled to Yankton to fulfill his legislative duties in the midst of what was recorded as a winter of big snow. Scobey's prime objective, according to the history books, was to convince Gov. Nehemiah Ordway to appoint Mathews to the post of superintendent of public instruction.

Ordway, however, had already decided to appoint someone else. So, Scobey turned his attention to another prize. As the story goes, Scobey's constituents wanted him to bring home the penitentiary, which promised jobs and economic vitality. But, Sioux Falls laid claim to that. Scobey instead settled for the college.

And yet, South Dakota State was a long way from becoming a reality.

According to Charles Sewrey's history of the early Dakota Agricultural College years, the state was ready for higher education by the time the land-grant movement reached the Dakotas in 1881. These were the boom years, which saw the population in the eastern half of the territory jump from 82,000 in 1880 to 248,000 in 1885.

Twenty years earlier, in 1862, Congress had paved the way for both westward expansion and the education of the common man. The Homestead Act gave any citizen — or any person who intended to become a citizen — 160 acres of public land, with the potential to purchase it after living on the land for five years.

That same year, the Morrill Act, sponsored by Congressman Justin Morrill of Vermont and signed by President Abraham Lincoln on July 2, gave every state in the union a grant of 30,000 acres of public land for every member of its congressional delegation. For South Dakota, with two senators and one representative, that meant 90,000 acres. The states, in turn, were to sell the land and use the proceeds to establish colleges in engineering, agriculture and military science.

These institutions would become known as the "land-grant colleges," and their role in the future of states as well as their citizens cannot be overstated. Originally intended to be agricultural and technical schools, many of the colleges (South Dakota State included) evolved into large public universities that have, throughout the years, made education affordable and attainable to millions of Americans.

In that sense, the institutions of the Morrill Act put into practice the democratic ideal that everyone, regardless of social standing, could pursue a higher education. The Morrill Act also shifted the emphasis of higher education from classical studies to a more practical course that would prepare students for life in the real world. The measure pioneered the concept of government support for education.

Gov. Ordway signed off on Scobey's legislation providing for the Brookings location, but no funding was appropriated. Instead, the community had to fulfill the condition to come up with no less than 80 acres.

Ultimately, but not until after delay and debate, the citizens of Brookings agreed to purchase a tract northeast of town for $600. At a meeting, the amount of pooled funds totaled $400. By the next morning, another $200 was raised. The first tract of land that would give way to the SDSU of today belonged to Mrs. Randi Peterson. Fifty-eight townspeople pledged $647.50 toward the purchase price, but only $602 was collected, with donations ranging from $1 to $50.

Following the initial investment by local residents, Scobey sponsored a bill in February 1883, seeking $25,000 in bonds to pay for the campus building. In exchange for backing of his measure, Scobey aligned himself with the faction that was seeking to relocate the capital to Pierre.

To ensure support, Gov. Ordway withheld his signature from the bill until the capital legislation was passed and his son was approved for the position of territorial auditor.

"Facing the inevitable cry of 'politics,'" writes Sewrey, "the Governor defended his consistency in signing the 'Brookings college' measure while turning down a number of allegedly similar college projects in other communities. The difference between the 'Brookings bill' and these, Ordway contended, was that the latter involved mostly normal schools, of which a sufficient number were already planned, and were also sheer 'giveaways.'

Brookings, on the other hand, had demonstrated its willingness to assume part of the cost and responsibility itself."

Although Scobey's bill asked for $25,000 and received support in the Council, the House trimmed the amount to $20,000. The Dakota Territory, however, did not generate enough revenue to cover expenses and fund all the special appropriations approved in the 1883 session. To compensate, lawmakers passed a bill to authorize the issuance of $25,000 worth of agricultural college bonds. The bonds carried 5 percent interest and would run for up to 20 years. The cost of the college building was not to exceed $20,000 and it was to be enclosed on or before July 1, 1884.

A bid opening in May awarded the project to architect C.H. Lee of Winona, Minn. His plan called for a large building facing the west, with a large central structure and more modest north and south wings. Old Central, as it was known by generations of faculty and students, actually was intended to be the south wing, which explains what one historical account described as the building's "sawed off" appearance.

On July 4, 1883, the contract for the south wing went to I.H. Baldridge of Des Moines, Iowa, for $19,750. A groundbreaking took place the next day, complete with prayer, speeches and the ceremonial spade-turning of soil. The celebration, however, was short-lived and work ceased.

Bonds were issued, but failed to attract enough buyers. So, again, the people of Brookings stepped forward and contributed another $1,000 to help dispose of the bonds. By Aug. 1, a new contractor — O.R. Mather of Mankato, Minn. — was on the job and construction resumed. The building was enclosed before winter, but not enough to prevent snow from drifting into the basement and damaging the foundation walls. By spring, all the funding allotted for the project had been used, leaving the interior unfinished.

According to legislative provisions, the governor appointed a six-member Board of Regents and made himself the seventh, ex-officio, member. The board met and organized in early June 1884. The salary of college president was set at $1,500 for the first year. The position was offered to Dr. George Lilley of Corning, Iowa, and he accepted. Nine chairs of instruction were established: agriculture, science, mathematics and English, English literature, modern languages, military tactics, veterinary science, practical business, and political and domestic economy.

The regents also set up a so-called preparatory department, which was slated to open Sept. 10. But the building was unfinished with no end in sight for the fall term. President Lilley came to the rescue, advancing $500 of his own salary to finish three rooms. The opening of the preparatory school was shifted to Sept. 24 and then delayed again by two weeks. The course of study was limited to grammar, arithmetic, geography, physiology and United States history.

According to "A History of South Dakota State College, 1881-1931," admission requirements were that "a student must not be less than 12 years of age, and be able to intelligently render specimens of the grade of Swinton's Fifth Reader, etc. ... and they must be thoroughly acquainted with the four fundamental operations of arithmetic. Such applicants must be able to write simple English sentences, to capitalize and punctuate the same, and write a fair letter." Tuition was free for Dakota students and $8 a year in advance for others.

The opening of the college was delayed until funding was secured to finish the main building and pay off expenses already accrued.

"The first preparatory year passed without particular incident," R.F. Kerr, one of the early professors, recounted in the college history book. "The students from outside boarded in town and each school day the faithful of all classes wended their way across the then three quarters of a mile of bleak prairie to the lone building on College Hill in search of knowledge ... They entered their work with enthusiasm for they were pioneers. They were also makers of precedents. We read of their separating into divisions and holding literary exercises, their observing the day of prayer for colleges, the celebrating of Arbor Day,

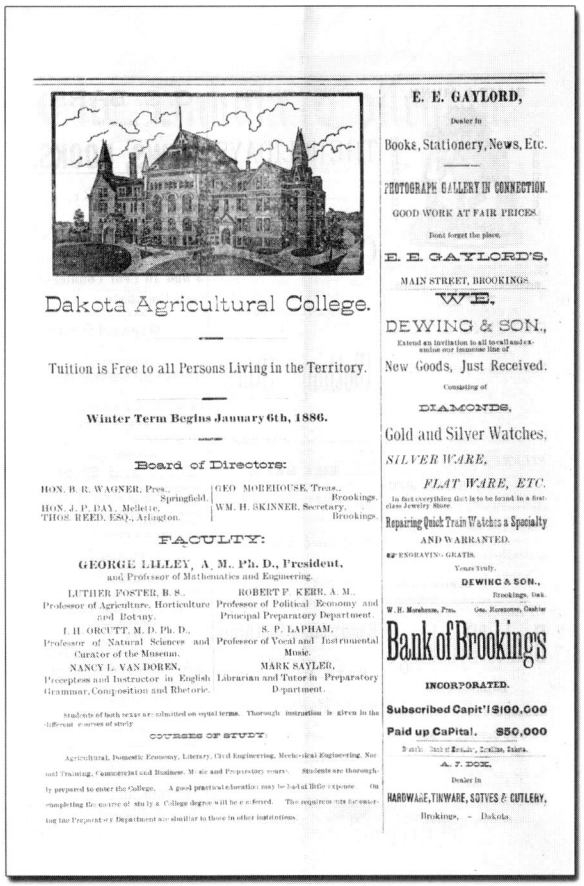

Advertisement about the college in the Dakota Collegian, December 1885.

Members of the Dakota Collegian staff in 1886.

and conducting a college paper. The latter was called 'College Sheaves,' an appropriate name for a to-be-agricultural-college paper."

In January 1885, the 16th territorial assembly met in Bismark and, among other actions, authorized issuing $20,000 in bonds — $12,000 was earmarked for finishing, furnishing and heating the incomplete college building and $6,000 would be spent on a dormitory. The total appropriations bill amounted to $45,000, of which $25,000 was for maintenance.

Nothing indicated, however, that the unsettled nature of the college's founding was about to change.

Instead, the Board of Regents and the building committee were disbanded and a five-member board of directors was established, bringing about the third administrative change in four years. And, college classes hadn't even begun. Teachers came, went and were brought back. Work on the South Building began. A course of study was adopted for a bachelor of science degree — agriculture, agriculture and domestic science, literary, civil engineering and mechanical engineering.

Finally, fall term for the college was advertised to begin on Oct. 7, 1885. All activities — eating, sleeping and learning — would take place in the one college building as workers continued construction. Central's upper floor was finished off to accommodate living quarters for the boys. The girls' dormitory was incomplete, so they were housed temporarily in a large room on the second floor. The kitchen and dining room were on the first floor. Although there were 62 students, the dining room could fit only 24 at a time. So, they ate in shifts.

Professor Kerr wrote that students were kept busy with exams for the first week because classrooms were not ready for use. "It was about the only thing to do under the circumstances." Of the 62 students, Kerr wrote, "only twelve were last year's (preparatory school) students and they had no credits. The others were in like condition; for we must remember that the common schools were not very well graded in the early '80s and pupils did not receive grade cards. To illustrate how new we were, out of over 200 enrolled that school year, only one gave his birth place as Dakota Territory."

Within two years of its start, the college experienced the first of many upheavals. President Lilley, it turned out, had only an honorary degree. He was dismissed from the presidency, but allowed to stay on as a professor of mathematics. After a few years, though, he was let go in one of the periodic purges that marked the administration of his successor, Lewis McLouth.

The agricultural college in Pullman, Wa., selected Lilley as its first president in 1890. Scobey and another purged member of the DAC faculty, Nancy Van Doren, followed Lilley to Washington. Scobey signed on as an ag professor. Lilley's tenure, as in South Dakota, was short. After two years in Washington, he was gone. His successor there, John W. Heston, would serve as president of DAC from 1896-1903.

Scobey went on to Olympia, Wa., where he became a newspaper publisher. He also served in the state legislature there. The closest he apparently ever came to returning to the Brookings campus was in 1932, when his former law partner, George A. Mathews, then living in Los Angeles, Calif., gave a photograph of Scobey to the college. At the time, the Collegian reported that the picture was to hang with those of presidents of the institution, "as one who provided for its establishment."

In hindsight, the efforts to turn the dream of South Dakota State into reality clearly were tenuous at best. Many points along the way left the process open to failure. Had it not been for a few determined visionaries who were willing to take risks, history as we know it — and Brookings along with it — easily could have played out very differently.

Thus was the inauspicious start of the Dakota Agricultural College. The financial and political struggles were emblematic of the early stages and would persist for many years to come. Still, whenever conflict or controversy arose, putting higher education in jeopardy, Brookings citizens characteristically rallied around the cause for the greater good.

As settlers of the Dakota Territory, they would not have survived otherwise.

In search of a good life, they journeyed here sight unseen to an often unforgiving and harsh prairie. Yet, undaunted by hardship, they risked and sacrificed, failed and thrived. And had they not dared to dream, those 80 acres on the northwest side of Brookings might never have given birth to the dreams of countless others.

Chapter 2

A Pioneer's Diary

The modern-day campus of South Dakota State University offers few, if any, signs of the school's birth in 1884.

Gone is Old Central, the first structure to rise on the College on the Hill. More than a century has passed since one or two buildings were sufficient to house, feed and educate the students. Trees rustle their leaves in the prairie winds where land once stood barren. Footpaths have given way to a sprawling system of sidewalks and roadways.

Imagine, though, through the eyes of John Merton Aldrich, one of the first three students to graduate from Dakota Agricultural College in 1888, what it must have been like to pursue higher education in pioneer times.

Eager to have a graduating class, DAC President Lewis McLouth, who took office in Aldrich's sophomore year, changed the standards. Aldrich, along with classmates Aubrey Lawrence and Lulah Wellman, achieved his degree in

Pictured above, John Merton Aldrich. (Courtesy SDSU Archives and Special Collections)

three years by taking a heavy course load his last year and working through the summer term.

In some ways, college then was much the same as it is today — going to class, studying for exams, working to put yourself through school, going on dates and roughhousing in the dorm. The key difference, though, was life in the late 1800s lacked all of the comforts we take for granted today.

A college degree was a highly sought commodity and carried great status, but the process of securing it posed a formidable challenge. Simply getting to campus was an ordeal. Aldrich recorded all the trials and tribulations of his college years in a daily diary, which is kept today in the archives room of the Briggs Library.

On Sunday, Oct. 4, 1885, Aldrich, his younger sister, Nellie, and their father, L.O. Aldrich, set out for the Brookings campus from their Grant County home on the eastern border of Dakota Territory. Preparatory level, or high school, classes at DAC had been under way for a year. It took the Aldrich family two days to make the trip. Although opening day for the first fall semester was only days away, the one-building campus was not ready.

"We saw the college about 14 miles before we got to it," Aldrich wrote on Monday, Oct. 5, 1885. "When we got there we found they had not quite finished the buildings, so the scholars will have to board in town for a week."

The steam heat would not be on until Saturday, but Aldrich accepted the offer to stay in a third-floor room, where the male students would live. The college provided "cheap new beds and wire springs" and the students took care of the covering and mattress.

Downtown to see what meals would cost, Aldrich said he "could not find a place where they were less than 25 cents."

That Monday night, Aldrich was the first student to sleep on campus: "My feet were rather cold, but otherwise I was comfortable." With opening day set for Wednesday, Oct. 7, other students soon started to arrive. That first semester, there were 19 freshmen, 43 prep students and five teachers. By the end of the year, DAC boasted 252 students and eight faculty members.

The first week was slow going as students crowded in and exams determined their placement. Only three rooms were finished on the first floor, and the new scholars gathered in one with a stove. The group listened to a speech from the first president, George Lilley, and filled out paperwork. By the second week, lectures had begun, but schedules, textbooks and other details, including construction, continued to evolve.

"Missed the agricultural lecture, on account of their having a new programme (sic) which I thought went into effect today, but which did not really until Monday," Aldrich noted on Friday, Oct. 16. "After this ag. comes Tuesdays and Thursdays. German class came today, but as we have no books yet nothing was done except to give us 15 nouns to learn and to find out how many books were needed."

Sunday, Oct. 18, was the first time the boys had any heat: "Pretty cold to sit in our room. About four o'clock they turned on the steam for a while, but soon stopped it again. ... Steam came up some time in the night, and when we got up it was nice and warm, but in one place it leaked almost a stream."

After being on campus two weeks, the students met Wednesday, Oct. 21, with professor Robert Kerr, who lived in the college building and had drawn up dormitory regulations. That same day, they also raised the bell for Old Central.

"It was quite an operation, as it weighs 750 pounds," wrote Aldrich. "I carried the clapper up through the inside, and struck the first tap on the bell with it. Charley Aurick, one of the carpenters, struck it first of all with the toller."

The next day, Thursday, Oct. 22, was as typical as any of the days Aldrich spent at college: "School as usual. Agricultural lecture today and nothing else till 3:45. Put in a good deal of time writing letters. Nellie (his sister) came up and visited me a little while in the afternoon. At 3:45 we had military drill for the first time. We liked it first rate. This evening went with Miss Jenness to 'An evening with Longfellow' at the Presbyterian church. Had a good time. The entertainment was pretty good, and the house was packed full. I didn't get permission, as Kerr was eating supper when I went. We were the first ones there. A whole lot went without permission. Got in about 9:30."

Friday, Oct. 23: "Just as I was posting my diary for yesterday, about noon, a lot of boys came in, carrying John Day, who had a fall while scuffling and broke his leg. It was his wooden one, but his real one was strained too. They put him on his bed and went off with his leg to repair it. I don't know how seriously he is hurt. Went to the Baptist church to hear a Huron preacher, Mr. Barker who is trying to start a revival."

Church played a strong role in student life. Aldrich frequented the Baptist and Methodist services and Sunday school programs. Occasionally, he ventured to other churches: "Went to Presbyterian church this morning. Thought it the most tiresome sermon I had ever listened to."

Mealtime and all its social aspects also drew considerable attention. The dining room was too small for all the students to eat at one time, so they ate in two shifts at assigned tables. First seating, of course, was preferred. Back on campus for the second semester, Aldrich griped: "Have to eat at the second table right along. Spoke to Mr. Kerr about it, when they get the dishes that are ordered they can set two more tables, and he will then see that all last-term students get in at the first table." A few days later, on Jan. 13, Aldrich happily recorded his new meal status: "Got a permanent place at table, at Mr. Kerr's left."

About a month and a half into the first semester, the dormitory South Building was ready for the girls, who had been rooming in local boarding houses. Within weeks, there was a new rule — "that young ladies receive no young gentlemen, except their brothers, in their rooms, under any circumstances." Typing a copy of his diary more than 40 years later, Aldrich quipped that despite the seeming severity of the regulation, it offered "great possibilities for a fellow lucky enough to have a sister in the dormitory."

Thursday, Dec. 10, after a faculty meeting, Alrdich recorded: "President Lilley announced this morning that there would be an hour appointed on Saturdays, when the young ladies could come over to the chapel and have a social time with the young men. Gosh, was all we could say. They won't come, it would look silly. They are not so anxious to see the boys."

A common date involved asking a girl — usually Miss Jenness, in his first year — to attend a church service. Even then, rejection was tough to take. Sunday, Jan. 24, 1886, Aldrich lamented: "Did not go to Church at all. Went to prayer meeting this afternoon, and walking with some of the girls afterward. Asked Miss Jenness to go to church, and she refused. Told her I was getting discouraged, and she said I'd have to stay discouraged. Don't know

GENERAL CONDUCT.
The following are strictly forbidden.
1. The use of intoxicating liquors.
2. The frequenting of saloons.
3. The use of tobacco in any of its forms about the buildings or on the grounds.
4. The use of profane language, all indecency of speech or behavior and all immorality of any kind.
5. Card playing in or about the college buildings.

ATTENDANCE.
1. It is of the utmost importance, both in the formation of correct habits, and in the successful prosecution of college work, that students maintain regular attendance at recitations and other general exercises.
2. Excuses for absence from class and chapel should be rendered without delay to the President.
3. Unexcused absences from recitation are entered as failures.
4. Students are not permitted to absent themselves from the college in term time without permission of the President.

LITERARY SOCIETIES.
1. No societies shall be organized by the students except by consent of the Faculty.
2. The constitutions of all societies organized, and all subsequent amendments to these constitutions must be submitted to the Faculty for its approval.

LIBRARY AND READING ROOM.
1. The Library shall be open to members of the Faculty, students and employes of the College for reading and study, at such hours as the Faculty may prescribe, and, in these hours, conversation or other conduct which may divert attention, or otherwise annoy, shall not be allowed.
2. Any one wishing any book or periodical (dictionaries excepted) must apply to the librarian for it, and before leaving the room, the same must be returned to the librarian, if not regularly drawn.
3. Reference books, current periodicals and papers cannot be taken from the library room.
4. It is the duty of the librarian to enforce the above regulations.

When a student has once entered the College he is subject to all its laws until his connection is formally severed by graduation or otherwise.

The Faculty reserve the right of determining by proper rules all the relations of the young men and women socially, and of prescribing at what times and under what conditions they may, and may not, enjoy the benefits of each other's society.

College rules for the 1885-86 school year from the records of professor R.F. Kerr. (Courtesy SDSU Archives and Special Collections)

what's the matter."

In his sophomore year, Aldrich pursued a Miss Campbell until she decided it was time to change company: "Got a note this morning from Miss C. She said she did not think it advisable to go too long with one fellow, or words to that effect. It was a pretty decent note."

The students formed literary societies (one male, one female and one coed), often debating such topics as "Resolved, that Chinese immigration should be abolished in the United States;" "Resolved, that the government of the United States should own and control the railroads;" or "Resolved, that the United States should proceed at once to build an extensive navy." Society gatherings also offered the opportunity to entertain each other with music and oratory.

College then also had its share of lighter moments, which were remarkably tame in comparison to modern-day activities.

"Tonight," wrote Aldrich on Friday, Dec. 18, "when part of us in Room 4 went to bed, we put a trunk out in the middle of the floor where those who got home later, would fall over it. Austin fell, but the others didn't."

Other times, as they would do for decades to follow, students sought diversion downtown: "A few days ago Nash, House and Wagner got drunk and the (student) Council recommended a pretty severe punishment, but the faculty have decided that Wagner and Nash will only have to ask permission for a month when they want to go down town, while they let Elson off entirely. It makes the Council and most of the students pretty mad."

In another incident, Aldrich recounted: "The boys got to tearing around after ten o'clock, and ended by pitching the dustbox down over the banisters to the landing in front of the library. At the faculty meeting last night ever so many boys were called up and questioned about it, but the faculty didn't find out very much."

About 80 years before the infamous food protests of the late 1960s, Dakota Ag College students laid the foundation of culinary unrest. One day, after "some awful bread for supper," Aldrich said they put a sample in the museum and labeled it "Remarkable Petrification. Brookings Co." They circulated a petition demanding better cooking.

Pies, however, were the exception. Aldrich and three others made a bet with English teacher and girls' dorm matron Nancy Van Doren that they could eat pie every day for 30 days. "If we finish the 30 days, she pays for the pie; if we fail, we pay — but that is impossible." From Jan. 19 on, Aldrich recorded the daily pie intake, saying "we boys are much pleased with the situation."

Wednesday, Feb. 17, was the final pie day. But the young men were hardly sick of the daily routine.

"We all ate our two pieces like little men, have not had the slightest difficulty or got tired of apple pie at all. In fact I like apple pie better than when we began," Aldrich wrote.

The next day's journal entry recounted how the foursome ordered one pie per person from a local eatery "just to demonstrate what we could do. ...

"At dinner we partook sparingly till time for dessert, then we each had a whole big uncut apple pie brought in. And each ate his without any apparent difficulty; it was however about all the pie I wanted just then."

Winters on the prairie — particularly in the days before buildings and trees helped block the wind — were incredibly harsh. Aldrich recorded temperatures of 25 to 35 degrees below zero. Although similar to today's drops of mercury, such cold weather is tougher to take when your feet are your only mode of transportation and there is no steam heat in your room.

A walk from downtown to the campus once left Aldrich with a foot so sore he could not wear a shoe for several days. Or, consider this account from Monday, Dec. 5: "This morning awoke at 3:15 and thought it was pretty cold for our plants. Got up, lit lamp, and found thermometer at 34, and wind rushing in through cracks around our south windows. ... (D)idn't get steam until after we had gone to breakfast."

Blizzards were a common, often daily occurrence. Diary entries from a six-week period early in 1887 were typical: "Blizzard like old times," "Best blizzard of the year," "Quite a blizzard," "Blizzard tonight, about as bad as we have had this winter," "Raging old blizzard from the south," "Bliz this morning from the northeast," "Blizzard from the northwest this morning," and "Good big healthy blizzard this morning."

The worst blizzard of Aldrich's school days, and one of the worst in the history of Dakota Territory, hit on Jan. 12, 1888. In the next days, temperatures would hover around minus 40. Trains stopped and, consequently, so did the delivery of mail, food and fuel.

Tuesday, Jan. 24: "Blizzard from the south. Cold in our room. No mail."

Wednesday, Jan. 25: "Went down town just after dinner and got a half a ton of coal. ... There is no wood in town and only a little coal. The college has hardly enough to last a week. ... I got all the sugar that could be spared in five places in town, about ninety pounds."

Friday, Jan. 27: "Storm King No. 2, with three engines, plowed up from the east today (and opened the railroad)."

Sunday, Jan. 29: "Went down to the (post) office before church. Had two letters from home, one two weeks old and one three weeks old."

The cost of an education in those days, by current standards, sounds ridiculously affordable. Tuition was free for residents of the Dakota Territory and Aldrich's expenses for his first year, from Oct. 4, 1885 to June 24, 1886, totaled $139.39. Among his costs were: $71.40, board; $16.05, travel; $10.12, books; entertainment, $2.85; washing, $2.45; and church collection, 57 cents.

Still, money was tight and Aldrich continually was on the lookout for odd jobs to help cover his school expenses. Initially, he had hoped to deliver the campus mail from downtown, but that didn't work out. He sawed wood, often more than a cord at a time, reporting in his diary that he worked "till I was pretty tired." He wrote for professors (earning about 25 cents per hour), taught prep classes, fed the press at the local print shops, worked on a farm and did odd jobs such as cleaning windows.

One day, Aldrich recorded working 12 and a half hours on the farm, stopping only 30 minutes for dinner and 25 minutes for supper: "Shoveled dirt and hoed alfalfa for the rest of the day ... and worked until 8:45 this evening — till it was too dark to see the little stuff any longer. ... The reason I worked so hard is that I haven't enough money to go home on, and won't have unless I rustle."

After the start of his second semester, professor Kerr and President Lilley asked Aldrich if he wanted to take charge of the reading room for $10 to $15 a month. "I jumped at the offer," Aldrich wrote. "Now I'm going to sublet the woodpile."

But, shortly after Aldrich returned the following year, the plum job turned

	LOW.	AVERAGE.	LIBERAL.
Tuition,	$ 6.00	$ 6.00	$ 6.00
Incidental Fees,	6.00	6.00	6.00
Board and Room,	75.00	90.00	120.00
Clothes, including Military Uniform	30.00	45.00	65.00
Laundry,	12.50	15.00	25.00
Books and Stationery,	15.00	25.00	35.00
Laboratory Fees,	0.00	2.00	5.00
Traveling Expenses	0.00	10.00	25.00
Total,	$144.50	$199.00	$287.00

Any fairly prudent student can pay all his expenses with $165.00 per year.

College expenses listed in an advertisement in the Dakota Collegian.

out to be short-lived: "Professor (James) Lewis called me into Mr. Kerr's room today. I supposed he was to pay me $20, as he said a few days ago that he would give me the two months' pay when his salary for the month came in."

There was no money budgeted for the library position, so the local board of directors for the college was supposed to be paying Lewis an extra $10 a month for Aldrich's work. Lewis informed Aldrich that he had spoken with board member and local businessman W.H. Skinner.

"Mr. Skinner had said that he — Mr. Lewis — had entire control of the reading room, and might hire whom he pleased and pay what he liked. He proceeded to say that he had always thought ten dollars a month was too much, as there was really no work to do in the reading room. He said he thought I ought to have a per cent on the books sold, and that I ought to take care of the reading room for the privilege."

For Aldrich, who was always enthusiastic about college and enjoyed positive relations with the faculty, this episode was troubling. He felt Lewis was treating him unfairly and worried about the financial consequences.

"He asked if my coming to school depended on my staying in the reading room. I replied that I had to earn my expenses some way. He gave me ten dollars and said he would talk the matter over with the other members of the faculty. He said I need not worry about my board, as he would see that I did not get into serious difficulty about it. Then he left. I don't like the outlook at all. He can't give me a cent, if I know it. He seems to want to patronize me."

What Aldrich couldn't have known at the time was that he was merely a pawn in a greater scheme of campus politics. At the end of his freshman year, Aldrich noted that President Lilley had resigned and accepted a professorship of mathematics. The students were told that "Mr. Lilley had never claimed to be the proper leader for several hundred students, and as the school had grown altogether beyond his expectations he thought it best to resign. ... Mr. Lilley's place would not be filled by anyone now in the institution, as they did not wish it to appear that he had been crowded out, but they would select some new man, probably from the East."

The explanation satisfied the students and they headed home for the summer. At the beginning of the fall term, Aldrich's sophomore year, professors Kerr and Lewis revealed more to the story: "They say that during the last week of last year the board called each instructor up before them and examined his or her qualifications and credentials. Mr. Lilley acknowledged, so a member of the board said, that he was not a graduate of any college, and therefore had no degree but honorary ones; that he had never studied higher mathematics than trigonometry; and that he had never taught. They make the case look bad against Mr. Lilley."

Ultimately, this dissension spilled into the reading room. Aldrich went to see Lewis: "He said he would give me five dollars a month, and I couldn't make him think otherwise. He thinks that Professor Lilley is doubling my work there by imposing the selling of books on me, and he wants to be very careful not to pay for anything to accommodate Prof. Lilley. He didn't say it in just that way, but I understood. So my term's work comes to just $17.50 — half of what I expected. Then I can't go home for Christmas, and will have to look sharp or I shall get behind in my board bill next term. ... I am going to see Prof. Lilley about it, and see what I can get out of him, for book-selling."

Aldrich made it home for Christmas break, but when he returned, he discovered that Lilley was selling books, "thereby admitting that it is his business, but still he don't want to pay me anything. He claims he just takes it off my hands this term because he don't like to see me do it for nothing."

And yet, the students managed to make their fun amid the upheaval.

The newly installed President Lewis McLouth welcomed students when they arrived in the fall of 1886. He then headed back to Michigan until moving to Brookings in December. In the meantime, Stephen Updyke of Watertown filled in as acting president.

"Prof. Updyke has some daughters and so has Pres. McLouth," Aldrich wrote in his Sept. 18 diary entry. "Both will move here this fall. Clarence has bet treats with Will Allan for the room that Updyke's daughters are the better-looking. I am to be the judge for Clarence and Rob for Will. We select a third."

On Sept. 20, Aldrich noted, "Saw Mr. Updyke's daughters. They are about average." Months later, when McLouth arrived without his family, the concern was that the two who made the wager would be gone before seeing the daughters.

Sept. 29, Aldrich was downtown and "met a lot of the college boys who were going to be weighed and have the average man pay the treats. I joined them. There were ten of us. The average was 145 pounds." At 119 pounds, Aldrich figured it was safe for him to join in.

Enrollment was small enough that when there was a meeting to discuss bringing the mail to campus and setting up the Collegian staff, everyone attended. That fall of 1886, the student body decided that the last year's editors would solicit subscriptions for the Collegian and the subscribers would "elect the rest of the officers" to run the paper. Aldrich earned the position of editor that year, and often took pride in reporting that the edition got out on time.

On Saturday, April 23, however, he lamented: "The Collegian got out this afternoon. It is the latest, and also the poorest job, that we have had yet."

As the spring semester came to a close in 1887, the waters of political turmoil on campus started to churn again, sending a vague signal of the storm on the horizon. Both Professor Lewis and a Miss Daniels were fired. "It was some scheming on the part of Lilley and Updyke that made the change in the faculty," wrote Aldrich.

Academically, Aldrich found his niche in the sciences. Although he did not write much about his classes, other than an occasional mention of tests, labs always seemed to generate excitement: "Had laboratory botany. Looked at mould (sic) from a fly that had fallen in water. It was boss. Beat anything we have seen yet." Another entry reported: "Jake came into the room, and we looked at blood corpuscles and a section of a fly's eye with the microscope."

On Monday, Oct. 24, McLouth returned from Washington, D.C., with news of $15,000 for the college experiment station: "It made the faculty very happy. It will help out with their salaries very much besides doing a good deal else." By March 1888, the $15,000 had arrived and Aldrich signed up to participate in experimental work.

The Wednesday, May 16, diary entry was typical: "Put in 4 1/2 hours this p.m. on experimental work. They put up the meteorological instruments today. Eno and I went out after breakfast and he snared two gophers. I got four fleas and two or three lice off them for entomology slides."

Thursday, May 24, Aldrich wrote: "Put in 4 hours at experimental work. Caught some gophers in a trap. ... Prof. wants me to count all the hills of corn that the gophers have taken. It will be a big job."

As he neared the end of his college years, Aldrich toyed with the idea of going to divinity school, but soon found his life's calling in entomology. In his diary notes from 1930, he noted, "Prof. I.H. Orcutt, M.D., taught the entomology, and wisely turned us loose to get acquainted with the insects. The institution had no collection, nor any library, beyond Packard's Guide to the Study of Insects; and the prof. was innocent of any knowledge of the subject until about the time we began. Nonetheless I am under obligation to him for introducing me to this fascinating field, in which I have worked ever since except for a few months just after my graduation."

On Tuesday, Aug. 7, the night before his graduation, Aldrich asked classmate Nellie Roe to marry him and she accepted. Decades later, he summed up his launch into the world beyond Dakota Agricultural College:

"When I finished my course at Brookings, Aug. 8, 1888, I had no idea what my life work might turn out to be. I had decided not to undertake preaching, though much interested in religion as I have always been, from the liberal viewpoint. There seemed to be no way to get a start. Everybody was poor, and it was very hard to accumulate even a few dollars. Teaching seemed a possibility, but I did not succeed in getting a town school — which I am thankful for now. I had a brief experience selling books, and came home to help my father in his harvest.

"Looking back now, my father seems heroic in that he did not ask me to give up any plans of my own to help him on the farm, though he needed me. He hoped all the time that I would be able by education to accomplish something worth while in the world."

Aldrich was in his father's field, though, shocking corn, when the idea hit him that Professor Orcutt might need an assistant for the increasing amount of experimental work. Had it not been for the course in entomology Orcutt gave that summer of 1888, Aldrich said, he likely never would have found his niche.

Orcutt told Aldrich to study entomology through the winter and then they would see what was available in spring 1889. When the time arrived, Aldrich accepted an offer to work at the college for three months at a rate of $40 a month. In the fall, he was put on staff with an annual salary of $500 and the understanding that he would devote his winters to study in his field.

Nov. 23, 1930, after copying over his diary for the college's collection of faculty papers, Aldrich reflected on how most of the students in his time had been in Dakota Territory for only four years when they enrolled in school in 1885. They had arrived in the region with the "great wave of 1881."

Aldrich mused: "It is really remarkable how much education we got with facilities which would seem ridiculous in these later days. But they were far from ridiculous to us, and they served their purpose very well. Our zeal for learning overcame all difficulties."

Chapter 3

'First Pure, Then Peaceable'

T he student revolt of April 1893 got its start with a bang — the deafening bang of a Civil War cannon, to be exact — on Halloween 1892. By the time the proverbial smoke cleared six months later, the hard-fought, bitter upheaval had left many casualties — professors were dismissed, students were expelled and more than half the student body defected to other schools. It took 19 years for enrollment to fully rebound.

There also was the immeasurable consequence of damage to the college's reputation and its ability to attract faculty.

Like other Morrill Act institutions, the early days of South Dakota State played out under the constant threat of instability. The state instituted a two-board system in 1890, giving the nine members of the Board of Regents broad

Artist's drawing from 1909 Jack Rabbit depicting flag flown at outset of the student rebellion. Latin phrase Me Taedit Vitae translates to "my weary life."

control over the state's schools. Five-member local Boards of Trustees oversaw the individual campuses. Ultimately, this system was abandoned, but not before wreaking havoc in Brookings.

Factional power struggles, financial crises and self-serving political interests ruled the day and led to justified fears of job insecurity. The all-too-real joke was that every time the boards met someone's position was at stake. College history traces the troubles of 1892-93 to the inherent flaws of the two-board system, coupled with an unfortunate chain of events.

William Howard Powers, who served as college librarian from 1905-1931, calculated in his faculty papers the continual upheaval at the board level, which ultimately trickled down to the campus:

"During the first two years, on a board of six members, nine different men served at different times. Late in the winter of 1889, Gov. Louis K. Church appointed an entire new board. This board, however, never had a meeting. In March, Church was succeeded by Gov. (Arthur) Mellette, who appointed a board of new men (except one) who served until the spring of 1890. In the first three years, 14 different men served on the governing board which never had more than six at a time."

The stage was set with heightened tensions under the administration of President Lewis McLouth, who endured strained relations with the governor and both boards during his tenure from 1887-1896. It was not unusual for personality clashes to play out with the firing of professors and the giving of their positions to unqualified trustees or regents, or their friends.

Powers writes: "It was at the first meeting of the trustees under the new double board system imposed by the new state constitution that the real trouble began. At this time, 9 May 1890, were dropped both the former executives, Lilley and Updyke. 'The first,' says Dr. McLouth, 'without my knowledge or advice, the second contrary to my advice.'"

Lilley was former Dakota Agricultural College President George Lilley, who served two years, from 1884-1886, before it was discovered that his only degree was honorary. He stayed on as a professor of mathematics. Updyke was Stephen Updyke of Watertown, who served as acting president before McLouth arrived on campus from Michigan.

To be sure, this situation was fraught with potential trouble. Not only had Lilley been demoted, but another man had been brought in to serve as acting president. Then, McLouth arrived and was in charge of a faculty that included two ex-presidents, neither of whom was particularly qualified for his faculty position.

R.F. Kerr, professor of history and political economy, maintained in meticulous cursive a running diary of events: "The faculty was reasonably harmonious. Profs. U. (Updyke) and L. (Lilley) began to be half way courteous. ... At the close of the term the two surly members were unceremoniously dropped. This caused quite a commotion among their friends. Their work was divided among the members of the faculty. I get history again, which had been taken from me to give Prof. U. enough work to justify a place in the college."

McLouth also stirred controversy by his interpretation of the Morrill Act and his efforts to abide by it. Believing in the strict interpretation of the law — that the federal funds could be used only for clearly specified subjects — McLouth cut liberal arts and civil and mechanical engineering. The courses were reinstated after a couple of years, but only to the bare minimum.

The spring of 1891 saw another bout of controversy. McLouth asked for an assistant in the mathematics department, hoping to hire a young graduate of the college for $500 a year. Instead, the president reported, "the governing boards, doubtless with a purpose of doing better for us than we asked them to do, proceeded to elect, at a salary of $1200.00 per year, a worthy, elderly gentleman who did not claim to be specialized in mathematics and who had been preaching several years since he had taught."

When Curtis R. Waters, a bookkeeper from Plankinton, arrived to assume his duties in April 1891, McLouth wrote, "he hardly knew for what work he had been chosen."

The worst incident, however, was the September 1891 dismissal of Dr. Cary, a popular professor of veterinary science, to make room for a Dr. Cormack. The Collegian described Cormack as "not a man of science, but an ordinary horse doctor. He has no culture, no general education and his speech betrays his utter ignorance of even the elements of English grammar."

In the fall of 1892, the student payroll for campus jobs failed to arrive on time. Joseph Freudenfeld, treasurer of the Board of Regents, was blamed, although the money actually had been sidelined in the college secretary's office. McLouth thought it was an attempt to discredit Freudenfeld, but the explanation came too late.

The 1909 yearbook recounts what happened:

"On Halloween in '92, great plans were made for a celebration. Some of the young people holding details had failed to receive their pay and as the Secretary of the Board of Regents was the first person they thought of who would be apt to be responsible, they decided to hang him in effigy. But this was not enough, so the girls made a large black flag, which cost the boys two dollars. On this flag in white, were a skull and cross bones and the motto, "Me taedit vitae" (My weary life). Sometime after midnight, the boys gathered near

North and planned their campaign. They collected all the combustible material within a large radius and after making a pile some fifteen feet high in the drive near the flagstaff, poured a half a barrel of kerosene over it. At exactly two o'clock A.M. at a signal from one of the leaders, the flag and effigy were run up, the bell was rung, the cannon shot, and the bonfire lighted. The noise was deafening, but was continued until Dr. McLouth was seen approaching. Before he came into the circle of light around the fire every boy had disappeared and no one could be seen except the girls peering eagerly from the windows of the dormitory. The ring-leaders were never discovered but woe unto them if they had been."

In truth, Freudenfeld was not at fault. But, he was not well-liked and made for a popular target. Powers wrote: "The dominant figure on the controlling boards appears to have been Joseph Freudenfeld of Plankinton, appointed a regent in 1890 and serving until about the beginning of 1894. A German, perhaps a jew (sic), moderate, forceful, 6 ft. 2 in., of broken speech, without much education, a big man and rather coarse in appearance, he was the object of much bitter denunciation as an unprincipled politician."

Freudenfeld's friendship with Waters, the math assistant, was a classic example of the political patronage that took place. So, too, was the appointment of A.H. Wheaton, president of the Board of Trustees, as dairyman at the college. Before Wheaton left the board, the trustees successfully lobbied the Legislature for — surprise — funding for a dairy department and a building.

When Freudenfeld entered office, controversy simmered over the college funds, the ongoing rivalry among local banks for custody of the funds, and charges and counter-charges of misappropriation or, at least, poor bookkeeping.

Worried that the trouble would continue as long as the funds were under control of the local Board of Trustees, Freudenfeld convinced the regents to move the funds to a bank in Plankinton, where Freudenfeld coincidentally held some interest.

The strife between the boards forced everyone to take a side. Among the locals in Brookings, anti-McLouth-Freudenfeld sentiment was popular. In an attempt to discipline the trustees, the regents ousted one by the last name of Hitchcock.

Writes Powers: "He was fearless, incorruptible, well-educated — the only educated man on the trustees board, but very set in his opinions."

Hitchcock appeared at the Jan. 20, 1892, meeting, but was not admitted. He filed a protest and took the matter to the Supreme Court, which said the regents had no power to dismiss him. The boards were deadlocked.

"It was impossible for anyone to be on friendly terms with both," Powers quotes McLouth as saying. "Whoever tried to be neutral was quite sure to incur the displeasure, or at least, the distrust of both."

Throughout all of this, a funding battle ensued, with the regents and trustees staking out opposing ground. At issue was the $15,000 per year in federal funds that came from the Hatch Act's establishment of experiment stations. The trustees argued that the funds were distributed to the college, so the college should maintain control. The regents, however, thought the funds were their domain and ultimately emerged victorious in the dispute.

According to Powers' history of events, the two boards met in early autumn 1892 in joint session in Huron, behind closed doors, with their attorneys. (One of the attorneys happened to be G.A. Mathews, the law partner of John O'Brien Scobey, who as a Dakota Territory legislator was responsible for bringing the ag college to Brookings.)

Under some unknown arrangement, the trustees resigned. The regents met weeks later in November 1892 in Aberdeen and elected a new slate of trustees, who quickly fell in line and supported the election of Freudenfeld as treasurer of the Board of Regents and "Custodian of all the moneys granted by act of Congress known as the Morrill Fund and of all other funds."

At the same meeting, seven faculty members were dismissed and one reassigned. The dismissed were: Mr. and Mrs. Stephen P. Lapham, music; L.H. Orcutt, zoology professor; John M. Aldrich, class of 1887, zoology assistant; Nellie Berkey, drawing; W.S. Frost, secretary and professor of civil government, commercial law and bookkeeping; and professor Kerr. George E. Dawson, professor of English and literature at State, was transferred from English (which was given to Waters) to history (which had been Kerr's job).

This was the so-called great clearing of 1892. Powers sums up the incredible mess:

"A college of a new sort in a new state, without standards, without clearly defined aims, an experiment itself in education; two ex-presidents as heads of departments, themselves almost a majority of the small faculty; a Scotch-Irishman (McLouth), scholarly, uncompromising, domineering, heady, chosen to bring order and peace, to preside over his two predecessors and a few others; compelled to work under the authority of boards who came to their task of directing the educational destiny and who were so frequently superseded in office as to have little opportunity to acquire any thorough experience; a common sentiment that teaching positions in state schools were plums for politicians; a jealous local constituency forming cliques with this or that teacher or group of teachers and regarding the school as their social perquisite.

... It seems doubtful whether anyone could have succeeded."

Kerr and Dawson received the grim news while studying at the University of Chicago for the winter break of 1892. Prior to their departure in November, Kerr summed up the atmosphere on campus: "College matters not satisfactory."

The breach widened irreparably during those fall months.

"There were strained relations between the two factions in the faculty all term," Kerr explained. "By the close of the term it was evident that one side or the other would have to go. ... At the close of the term I was uncertain about my tenure of office. I went to see (S.H.) Elrod at Clark Nov. 8th but he did not have any certain knowledge. I had planned to go to the University of Chicago and started out before I knew my fate."

Kerr wrote in his diary:

"In the evening I had a rumor that I had not been confirmed at Brookings. Nov. 21 a telegram confirmed the report and eight of us were laid on the shelf. I was not greatly surprised but there was a momentary disappointment. ...

"On the 22nd Dawson came. He had been confirmed and given my place. No knowledge of it on his part. Angry. News of dissatisfaction came by mail and papers. Too much of it sometimes. It interfered with our work."

In February 1893, with college classes still in recess, the state Legislature launched an investigation into charges of preferential appointments and financial impropriety. According to critics, the probe found evidence to support the claims. Still, President McLouth came out clean in the official report. The accusers were deemed troublemakers and two more professors were asked to resign.

Kerr returned to Brookings on Feb. 18: "When I arrived in Brookings I heard the results of the investigation. Adverse to our side. Opinion of nearly everyone that it was a 'whitewash' The town was indignant. Sympathy was with the 'outs.'

"Monday the 20th I went to the college and packed up my effects preparatory to moving out. I had been connected with the institution for so long that I felt a paternal interest in it. I regretted giving up my old associations, that is the pleasant side of them. I had no desire to remain while Dr. McLouth presided over its destinies with some of his assistants."

Kerr spent March 2 and 3 in Pierre and "heard the last attempts to clear up some unfinished matters in regard to the college controversy. The whole thing was an acknowledged farce as viewed by my friends."

On March 10, Dawson and Luther Foster, head of the agricultural department and director of the experiment station, were removed. Regent Ed Hewitt replaced Professor Frost, and E.C. Chilcott, the member of the Senate investigating committee that recommended Foster's removal, filled Foster's position.

"New excitement to watch," reports Kerr.

Students returned for the spring semester, but the atmosphere was dismal. On March 17, 1893, more than 100 students held a reception and banquet for the departing faculty members.

The Collegian account of the event reflected: "It was a very enjoyable occasion, and was full of the love and confidence which always marked the connection of the students with these teachers. We have nothing but praise and heartfelt thanks to give these for their labors for us, and the banquet was the least we could do to express these feelings to them. We wish them all success in the future, and assure them they cannot find warmer friends than their student friends who remain behind them at the SDAC."

At the time, there were two local papers in Brookings — the Press, which sympathized with the students and faculty, and the Register, which sided with the administration. The Press gave its entire front page over to coverage of the event. The Register called it "a nice little affair."

A.S. Harding, class of 1892, arrived by train in Brookings the night of April 8 and quickly learned about the unfolding events. The previous week, on Thursday night, more than 100 students — more than half the student body at the time — had gathered in Old Central and crafted a statement of grievances to be published in newspapers across the state. The students, said Harding, were "peeved by statement in the Watertown Public Opinion and other papers, that everything was now lovely at the college after a necessary house cleaning, and that the student body had settled down to work."

McLouth heard about the student meeting in progress and tried to talk with the group. He asked if he could read the statement and perhaps sign onto it, but the students refused. After McLouth left, the statement was adopted. The following week, on Friday night, April 7, the faculty detained the ringleaders — N.D. Talcott, Leon Aylsworth, Willard Lusk, Earl Douglass, William Meinzer, John Maguire and Phil Maguire — but got nowhere.

At about 6 p.m. Saturday, the disenfranchised students wired their 1,200 word statement, with 90 signatures, to the Evening Argus-Leader in Sioux Falls. Several hours later, the group of seven was suspended for the remainder of the semester, and ordered to leave town by Monday night or lose their academic status. At midnight, students gathered en masse, agreeing not to attend chapel or classes until the seven were reinstated.

Picture of the 44 members of the sophomore class who opted not to return to the college. They were referred to as 'outs.'

Sunday morning, the statement appeared in the Argus. The goal was to give the people of South Dakota the facts and set the record straight. According to Harding, the statement "was 'strong medicine' but dignified in form."

The statement read:

"Scarcely had we left school last fall when we learned that a number of our best teachers had been discharged. Why was this done? No satisfactory reasons have ever been given. These removals seriously injured the college. When the spring term opened many of us were undecided whether to return and finish our courses or go to some other college. ... About two weeks after our return Profs. Dawson and Foster were also removed.

"Half our faculty has now been cut off. On the whole, it was the better half. ... These last removals were an outrage which aroused the indignation of every student in the institution, but we hoped the positions would be filled with good and competent men as had been promised" by a letter circulated among students by seven faculty members.

"Let us see how the promises have been fulfilled. Three of these places were given to men who are a disgrace to the college and an insult to the intelligence of the students."

There was Cormack, the horse doctor; Chilcott, the new teacher of agriculture, deemed "woefully ignorant of the subject which he is trying to teach"; Wheaton, the dairy professor, "a man utterly unfit to hold a position in a college" and "an ignorant man and unscrupulous politician"; and Waters, the Plankinton insurance company bookkeeper brought in for the English department, "whom even the president of the college is unwilling to trust with the supervision of the chapel rhetoricals."

The students laid complete blame on the shoulders of President McLouth. His policy, they said, was "to surround himself by men over whom he could exercise absolute control."

The students concluded: "There is, perhaps, hardly a school in the whole country where students would have been as quiet and conservative as we have been under the wrongs which we have suffered but if we are true to our manhood we cannot keep still any longer. We have determined that the people shall know the truth as far as it is in our power to make the truth known, be the consequences to us what they may."

In Harding's account, more than 100 students stayed away from their classrooms Monday, April 10. Brookings residents met and decided to remain neutral. On Tuesday, April 11, most of the college's students gathered at the county courthouse, leaving only 30 to attend chapel. Also that day, Board of Regents President J.W. Shannon arrived in town.

At the same time, the Argus-Leader called for the regents to step down: "The high-handed proceedings of last winter have born their legitimate fruit and if the State Agricultural college is to escape destruction there must be prompt, vigorous and patriotic action.

"The first thing required is the resignation of the board of regents. The members have disgraced an office which should from its nature be lifted above political deals and personal feuds. ... Themselves mostly men of little education and unaccustomed to methods of instruction and to qualifications required in instructors, they have managed the college partly haphazardly, partly in the interest of themselves or friends and partly at the dictation of political manipulators. They have dismissed the men whose scholarship, experience and instructing ability had raised high the name of the college and have filled their places with people who have demonstrated their incompetence. ...

"The young men and young women of the agricultural college have in their love for the institution and their desire to submit to any hardship rather than to forfeit their standing there, endured patiently the long course of evil management which was undermining the college and they spoke only when the radical changes recently made have reduced its standard below the level of toleration.

"The agricultural college is one of the valued possessions of the people of South Dakota. They have a right to demand that it be purified from the deteriorating influences which have lately been in control. And the people are in no temper for a repetition of the farcical proceedings at Pierre."

Other newspapers were equally harsh, particularly the Yankton Press & Dakotan, which thought the college's tumultuous state of affairs was simply pay-back time. About a decade earlier, Yankton had been slated to receive the state capital, but lost it to Pierre, thanks in part to Brookings County delegate Scobey, who supported the capital removal bill in exchange for the college.

"The mess began about 13 years ago," the Press & Dakotan concluded after McLouth was removed from office in 1896. "It broke out at the time Councilman Scobey sold out to the capital removal gang for one Agricultural College. Conceived in sin and brought forth in iniquity, what besides trouble can you look for?"

On April 12, wearing badges that proclaimed "First pure, then peaceable," a phrase adopted from an Argus editorial, 115 students voted to stay true to their cause. The faculty, too, stood its ground. The so-called bolters were warned to end their strike by April 14 or risk suspension. The deadline passed and some students went home. Gov. Charles H. Sheldon arrived on Friday, April 15. He spoke at the college, telling students they were acting childishly and urging them to return to classes the following Monday.

Sunday evening, however, Sheldon met with representatives of the students and, according to the Collegian: "for the first time heard the students' side of the case. The charges against Dr. McLouth and other members of the faculty were reviewed and substantiated. It transpired here that Gov. Sheldon had been grossly deceived; that facts had been withheld which should have been placed before him.

"The governor, seeing that he had been led through misrepresentation to take unjust action, sought to make amends. He promised a fair hearing before the regents at their June meeting and requested the president to reinstate the suspended students."

Monday morning, 102 students boarded the same train that was heading west to Pierre with Sheldon. The college faculty met and refused to reinstate the students. About 80 students remained on campus to finish out the year.

Kerr reflects in his diary: "Blue day for the college. Tues. 18th Dawson left S. Dak for good and I was homeless in my cottage."

Epilogue

The ex-students had their final say with a souvenir edition of the Collegian published in June 1893. Along with class pictures of the senior, junior and sophomore "outs," they reprinted the statement that had been sent to the Argus in April. The students also recounted Gov. Sheldon's efforts and the

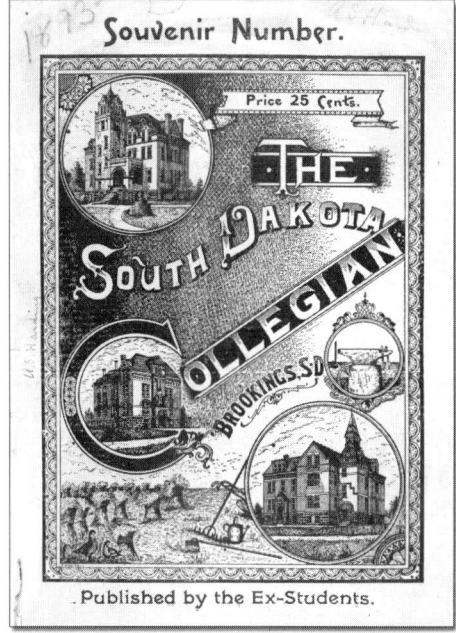 

Souvenir publication produced in the spring of 1893 by former students giving their version of the events leading to their decision to leave the college.

problems with the regents and trustees.

They took issue with the Register, charging the editorial staff with "sending forth from their infernal machine bombs of destruction, in the shape of a country newspaper, containing some of the most outrageous statements about the citizens of the city ever exposed by printer's ink." Regent Shannon also earned harsh criticism for his insistence in blaming students for the college's woes.

Biographies of the ousted faculty members detailed their individual achievements and explained why they were so popular with the students.

Aldrich moved on to Lawrence, Kan., where he entered the graduate program. Shortly after his removal from State, Foster was hired as a professor of agriculture and acting president at Montana Agricultural College. Orcutt, for the time being, remained in Brookings, pursuing his special studies and experimenting with the effects of alcohol on the nervous system.

Dawson left for Chicago and was reportedly "ruminating over the material for a novel, which he collected in South Dakota. He thinks he has found a modern Machiavelli, and a South Dakota Uriah Heep." There was no information on where the Laphams headed.

Kerr stayed in Brookings until May 19, when he received a telegram to meet with a representative of a book company. Kerr signed on to work for three months at $75 per month and traveled throughout the Dakotas and Minnesota, selling school books.

"The great 'Panic' which commenced in the east soon after the inauguration of Cleveland Mar. 4 did not reach this section till after Jun. 1st or later," wrote Kerr. "I was successful till after October when times grew so bad that it was uphill work. The last month I was not satisfied with my work but I finished all that could be done in the state and then notified the company that I was ready to quit. It was accepted.

"I arrived in Brookings on the 22nd (of December), built a fire in my own house and settled down to reading and recreation, and general self-improvement while awaiting something to do again. New Years Eve of '94 found me with as few prospects for work as I ever had."

Kerr served as Brookings County superintendent of schools from 1895-99. In the fall of 1898, he was hired as librarian and principal of the college's preparatory department, a position he held until 1906, when he resigned to become private secretary to Gov. Samuel K. Elrod. Kerr died at home, in Brookings, on Oct. 16, 1921.

In July 1894, the regents requested McLouth's resignation and he agreed. But McLouth managed to hang on until 1896. According to Charles Sewrey's history of the college, McLouth remained in Brookings through the middle of 1897 and then left for the East, where he presided over two correspondence schools. He also did editorial work for an encyclopedia. McLouth returned to the State campus one last time in 1908 for a reunion, and died the following year.

John W. Heston, president of Washington Agricultural College, came on board in 1896 as McLouth's replacement. Although his years at the helm were comparatively more peaceful, Sewrey writes: "Like his predecessor, he had the reputation of being suspicious, a quality which may well have been an occupational disease of land-grant college personnel."

The first year of Heston's presidency, the dual regent-trustee board system was abolished and the new Board of Regents decided to end the micromanaging of campus affairs.

Chapter 4

Great Legacies

Picture of Dr. George Brown from the 1907 Jack Rabbit.

George Lincoln Brown
Jan. 25, 1869 – Aug. 8, 1950

Born on a Missouri farm and educated in a country school, George L. Brown arrived at State College on Feb. 1, 1897, with a master's and doctorate magna cum laude in mathematics. He was hired to teach math and astronomy, and was immediately selected by his peers to be secretary of the faculty.

In what would become standard practice, Brown also was assigned administrative duties. By the time he retired 48 years later, Brown had served as professor of mathematics, dean of faculty, vice president, dean of general science, acting president and president.

Brown endeared himself to generations of students with an unfailing sense of humor and a much admired love and understanding of humanity. He encouraged and then organized the Early Rural Life Conference, which

The campus in 1888.

became the campus' Farm and Home Week.

Brown left a lasting legacy in helping to organize the Students' Association, a form of campus government that gives students democratic control over their activities. He also was instrumental in the organization of the South Dakota Extension Service. Brown set up the first summer session in 1914. In 1917, Congress passed the Smith-Hughes Act, providing for the training of teachers in agriculture and home economics. Brown, when acting president, worked with the federal government to institute the program at State.

As testimony to his leadership abilities, Brown was called upon five separate times in a 32-year period to serve as acting president for State. Yet, he was more than an impressive list of administrative credentials.

"He is remembered by former students and alumni because of the twinkle in his eyes, his warm, firm handshake, his slow, quiet manner of speech, his gentlemanly way of always greeting a student, and his way of talking least about himself and most about you," wrote the May 1950 Alumnus. "He is remembered because of his keen interest and understanding of students. ... Probably one of his outstanding characteristics was his ability to handle students and his success in guiding them in their work."

At Brown's funeral service, Dr. Harold M. Crothers — class of 1910, dean of engineering and vice president — commented that both the college and the state of South Dakota had reaped substantial rewards from Brown's life of service. The college Brown arrived at in 1897 was considerably different than the one it was when he left, and Brown had played a key role in the changes. State, in the early years, was not well-established, the atmosphere was often less than harmonious and its purpose as a land-grant college was poorly understood.

By the time Brown left State, said Crothers, "its purposes and possibilities were becoming more clearly understood throughout the state, and its organization had been adapted and expanded to fit these purposes. ... The spirit of an institution is molded by individuals, and few men have done more in any institution than Dr. Brown did in State College to mold a strong institutional character."

Portrait of Dr. Brown painted by Harvey Dunn. (Courtesy of S.D. Art Museum)

Great Legacies

Ada B. Caldwell
Sept. 28, 1869 – Nov. 8, 1938

Ada Bertha Caldwell picture from the 1911 Jack Rabbit.

Each of the visionary, dedicated individuals who helped make South Dakota State University what it is today carried an impressive pedigree — dean, world famous horticulturist, interim president and beloved longtime band director.

So, it seems odd — but only at first glance — that someone like Ada B. Caldwell, an art professor and a woman, would be counted among such distinguished company. Yet, campus history indicates Caldwell well deserves the accolades.

Born in Lincoln, Neb., on Sept. 28, 1869, Caldwell spent one year at the University of Nebraska before enrolling in the Chicago Institute of Art. She spent one year as head of the art department at Yankton College and then, in 1899, accepted a professorship at State College. She held her position in Brookings until retiring in 1936. She died two years later, on Nov. 8, at age 69.

People best know Caldwell for having instructed Harvey Dunn and Hubert Mathieu, but her legacy far surpassed her two most famous students. Among her accomplishments was her dedication to teaching. Contending that one could be either a creator or a teacher — but, not both — she opted to teach. Still, Caldwell cannot be defined by the classroom alone. She contributed to the design and decoration of Wenona Hall, the first women's residence hall on campus, and designed the art department when it was moved into the Administration Building in 1917. She also designed the Coolidge Sylvan Theatre. From 1907-1917, Caldwell took on the unpaid and unofficial position of dean of women. She also lived in and acted as supervisor of Wenona from 1908-1911.

Sandwiched between her teaching, faculty and dormitory duties, Caldwell devoted herself to causes beyond campus. At the time of her death, the 1938 State College Alumnus wrote: "Miss Caldwell gave unstintingly to her community, to her state in the promotions of exhibitions, of Y.W.C.A. activities, of club work."

Although physically frail, Caldwell was a strong presence, insisting on high scholarly standards and morals. She shared her time as well as her money. Those who worked alongside of her or received her instruction, described her quiet power and infinite patience.

Helma Hutton Keil, class of 1925, wrote in the 1938 Alumnus that her life had been immeasurably enriched by Caldwell: "Her teaching seemed to be as natural to her as breathing, and no one could emerge from her classes without a love of beauty."

On a grander scale, Dean George Brown said of Caldwell: "If a complete history of the South Dakota State College should be written, Ada B. Caldwell will have an important place in it. Coming to the college while it was small and just entering upon a new period of growth, she has done much during her long period of service to shape the spirit of the institution."

Portrait of Ada Caldwell painted by Harvey Dunn. (Courtesy of S.D. Art Museum)

Carl Christensen picture from the 1908 Jack Rabbit.

Carl Christensen
Aug. 26, 1881 – Feb. 21, 1965

"All I want to do is direct the band."
— Carl Christensen at the 1961 dedication of the Christy Ballroom in his honor

Marching band to orchestra, chorus to concerts — music at South Dakota State University bears the stamp of Carl Christensen.

The man who directed State bands and orchestras for more than 40 years started playing the violin at age 6 in his homeland of Denmark. Christy, as he popularly became known in Brookings, was 13 years old in 1894 when he and his family emigrated to Minnesota.

State College hired him in 1906 to teach violin and direct the school's orchestra. Five years later, Christy was named director of the band. The next year, in 1912, Christy's 26-piece group marched in the first Hobo Day parade. By 1918, Christy was head of the music department — a position he held until 1951, when he retired at age 70. Still, he continued to direct both marching and concert bands until 1954.

Christy's achievements during his tenure at State were nothing short of spectacular. One of the highlights was the band's 1939 invitation to play in Winnipeg for the king and queen of England. As if that weren't compliment enough, the band took first prize as the most outstanding marching band in the parade.

Other honors for the legendary musician and bandmaster included an honorary bachelor of music degree from McPhail School of Music in 1929. South Dakota State presented him with the first $1,000 Lincoln Brown award for able and inspired teaching in 1950. The 1952 yearbook was dedicated to Christy. And, Karl L. King, one of the country's foremost march composers, wrote the "SDSC March" in 1932 and dedicated it to Christy.

On Hobo Day 1950, SDSC alumni wanted to do something for Christy. Upon discovering that the great band leader was driving a 1940 Buick with more than 100,000 miles on it, they decided to present him with a new Buick at halftime of the Hobo Day game.

In 1961, in perhaps the most lasting honor, SDSC named the Christy Ballroom in the then-Pugsley Student Union after Christensen. Among all the heartfelt tributes were these simple words of Ben Reifel, 1932 SDSC alumnus and South Dakota congressman: "The real meaning of life on a college campus does not spring from its buildings but rather from its great teachers. And Christy, you are one of those great teachers."

Portrait of Carl Christensen painted by Hubert Mathieu. (Courtesy of S.D. Art Museum)

Picture of Hubert Mathews from the 1907 Jack Rabbit.

Hubert Berton Mathews
April 10, 1868 – March 18, 1936

Every single person who has passed through the halls of State has in some way, large or small, contributed to the institution. But, would they have had that opportunity without Hubert Berton Mathews?

The January 1936 Alumnus pondered life in the absence of the pioneer educator and beloved dean: "When we look at the man, and think of his work, we sometimes wonder to ourselves, what might have been if he had gone some place else? What would have been the losses to the people of South Dakota? It would have been tremendous."

Mathews was born near Muscoda, Wis. A precocious youngster, he started attending country school before age 4. He began teaching at a school just east of Willow Lake, S.D., in 1885, when he was 17. Mathews enrolled at SDAC in 1889 as a freshman, less than five years after classes first started on campus. At the time of his death, he had been either a student or teacher under every president of the college (there were already eight by 1936).

As a student, Mathews also racked up the accomplishment of being on the first football team to play the University of South Dakota. It was 1889 and there were 225 students at State. Years later, at taller than 6 feet and weighing 200 pounds, Mathews was said to still look the part of an athlete. In 1912, Mathews marched in the first Hobo Day parade as the king of the hobos.

In his 42 years of teaching physics at State, Mathews instructed more than 9,000 students in his classroom. In its entirety, his teaching career spanned more than half a century. Mathews served State in various administrative capacities — vice president, acting president, head of the electrical engineering department and acting head of the engineering division. He also held several civic offices, including mayor of Brookings and serving on the City Commission.

For the 19th Annual Dakota History Conference in 1988, Marian Cramer wrote "A Study of the Development of Electrical Engineering Department at State," in which she summed up the results of Mathews' efforts: "Time is one measure of accomplishment. One hundred and three years have passed since the establishment of Dakota Agricultural College. Ninety two years have been marked since H.B. Mathews began his college teaching career in Brookings. The electrical engineering department which he founded has been operational for seventy six years."

Mathews died doing what he liked best — teaching. He missed one month of school prior to his death, which came after surgery in Rochester for an internal goiter.

The Collegian eulogized him as one of the most important parts of the college. Under Mathews, physics became enjoyable rather than torturous. He was a human encyclopedia concerning State's past. And, he had the uncanny ability to remember names and faces.

Portrait of Mathews painted by Harvey Dunn. (Courtesy of S.D. Art Museum)

Mathews' popularity on and off campus was evident in the two funeral services held for him — one in the college auditorium with students, alumni and faculty and another at the Presbyterian Church with the community. In his tribute, fellow professor A.S. Harding said Mathews' impact on others rippled beyond the classroom:

"Hubert B. Mathews was a great soul. He was great in the simplicity and honesty of his character, in his democracy, in his invincible resolution, in his willingness to bear heavy burdens cheerfully, in his kindly spirit of helpfulness, in his genial philosophy of life. He rang true always."

James H. Shepard
April 4, 1850 – Feb. 22, 1918

Picture of Dr. James Shepard from the 1910 Jack Rabbit.

As with many of the pioneering members of South Dakota State University's faculty, James. H. Shepard was both beloved by the student body and noted worldwide for his academic accomplishments.

Shepard, a chemist, was born in Lyons, Mich., and graduated from the University of Michigan in 1873. After teaching at an Ypsilanti, Mich., high school, he arrived on the Brookings campus in 1888, just four years after classes started.

During his 30 years at State, Shepard (also called Uncle Jimmy on campus) earned an international reputation as a technical writer and investigator of bleached flour, bad whiskey and pure food violations. He also developed a super-strain of sugar beets. His first contribution to his field was the publication of "Shepard's Elements of Chemistry," which was groundbreaking in that it introduced the laboratory method of teaching chemistry as opposed to the early classroom lecture practice.

Working as the chemist for the South Dakota Pure Food Commission for nine years, Shepard investigated the effects of preservatives and coal tar dyes on digestion. His exhibit of adulterated foods at the 1904 St. Louis World's Fair attracted worldwide attention. No one, it was said at the time, did more to advance the cause of pure food than Shepard.

Shepard's bleached flour investigations added to his international reputation. His probes into nitrogen peroxide, the agent used in bleaching flour, revealed that it was a powerful antiseptic. A paper on his findings was presented to a national meeting of the State Food and Dairy Commission. Prosecution of bleaching trusts followed and Shepard served as a key witness in a Fargo lawsuit. His expertise also was called on in other bleaching cases, both in the United States and abroad.

In 1908, the federal Board of Food and Drug Inspection deemed that the bleaching of flour was illegal. The decision was hailed as important news on the State campus, where Shepard had conducted elaborate artificial digestion experiments.

Shepard was the first to analyze whiskey and his findings were published in a 1906 pamphlet, "The Constants of Whiskey." The report ended a long-standing controversy over the components of whiskey and laid a foundation for judging the brew. In that capacity, Shepard served as an important witness in several different lawsuits between the government and whiskey trusts.

In 1909, along with a Pennsylvania professor, Shepard was delegated by the State Food and Dairy Commission of the United States to represent the pure food interests in a famous hearing before President William Taft. The attempt focused on solving the question "What is Whiskey?"

Shepard's expertise led to such frequent travel that a 1909 yearbook cartoon shows him standing at the train station, suitcase at his side, and holding up a long strip of tickets to the conductor. The caption below reads: "Pittsburg, Chicago, St. Paul, Minneapolis, and all farther west." A year later, the 1910 annual depicts Shepard with his head atop a chemistry beaker.

As the second director of the Dakota Experiment Station, Shepard investigated the water supply of the Dakotas. He discovered that little or no true alkali occurred in eastern Dakota, but that the water contained the neutral salts of calcium, magnesium, iron and sodium. That explained troubles experienced by early settlers, who reported that water turned coffee color, foamed and emitted a strong odor of sulphurated hydrogen. Shepard found that this was caused by the action of organic matter on iron pyrites, or fool's gold, which was present in the soil.

Dr. Shepard with world-record sugar beet. (Picture from 1917 Jack Rabbit)

And ultimately, after a quarter of a century of selection based on chemical analyses of mother beets, Shepard developed a strain of beets producing 25 percent sugar, having started with beets of less than 10 percent sugar content. Shepard also demonstrated that sugar beets could be grown for substantial profit throughout South Dakota.

But, as Charles Coughlin, class of 1909, once noted, Shepard's work with whiskey was most memorable among his students.

Writing from Milwaukee, Wis., where the Briggs & Stratton Co. was headquartered, Coughlin said: "As to the fund for our memorial tablet for Professor Jimmie Shepard, I really feel that everyone that attended his classes and has since gone through the era of the 18th Amendment enforcement should feel indebted to him for the advice that he gave us, which was — 'If you are going to drink whiskey, boys, for God's sake drink good whiskey.'"

Portrait of Dr. Shepard by Harvey Dunn. (Courtesy of S.D. Art Museum)

Niels E. Hansen picture from 1910 Jack Rabbit.

Niels Ebbesen Hansen
Jan. 4, 1866 – Oct. 5, 1950

N.E. Hansen traveled the world over in search of hardy crops and varieties that could survive the harsh life of the northern plains. A transplant himself, Hansen was born in Ribe, Denmark, and arrived in the United States in 1873. He became a professor of horticulture at South Dakota State College in 1895 and professor emeritus in 1937, his tenure on campus encompassing 55 years.

Hansen's contributions to both horticulture and State in that time were extraordinary, particularly in the sense that his work forever changed the way people lived, worked and ate. From researchers in the lab to farmers in the field and families at the dinner table, Hansen's efforts in the field brought him not only worldwide acclaim, but also gave South Dakota and the northwest dozens of new plant varieties that grew the wealth and productivity of an entire region.

The 1936 Department of Agriculture yearbook named Hansen as one of three men who played important roles in the introduction of wheat into the United States. His name was inscribed in the wall of the American Common Hall of Honor at the New York World Fair and he earned many medals for his work. Hansen's most appropriate nickname came from a Danish authority — "The Banebryder," or trailbreaker.

Overshadowed by his science was Hansen's love for music and poetry, which he said were "two great essentials in life." In addition to writing poems, Hansen also is credited with penning State's school song, "The Yellow and the Blue," originally called "To the Colors."

In 1949, Hansen was honored with a monument on the State campus. Then-Gov. George T. Mickelson called the recognition long past due and said, "The honor given him today, acknowledges he is, above all, a creator, humanitarian and benefactor of those who toil through the years to produce more and better food for the earth's teeming millions."

Responding to the dedication address by Frank Cundill of the Board of Regents, Hansen remarked: "The idea is to leave the land in a more profitable condition than you have found it."

Often called "The Burbank of the Plains," in reference to the famous horticulturist Luther Burbank, Hansen traveled to Europe, Asia, Russia and many points in-between for his work with plums, cherries, wheat, apples, apricots, pears and roses. His work in Siberia yielded invaluable results with hardy grains and grasses.

Taking seeds from literally the ends of the earth and bringing them back to the Brookings campus, Hansen crossed and bred thousands of plants in the quest for suitable varieties. In his ornamental plant work, Hansen imported more than 500 species of shrubs from many countries to determine their hardiness under prairie conditions. Explaining his work to the

Professor Hansen outfitted in Russian clothing obtained on one of his numerous trips abroad. (Courtesy South Dakota Ag Heritage Museum)

1907 yearbook, Hansen said: "From the ashes of millions of seedlings will rise, Phoenixlike, the new creations which will dominate our future prairie pomology."

"Monumental," says Kevin Kephart, director of the S.D. Agricultural Experiment Station, characterizing the impact of Hansen's work. "Truly monumental. He gave us the tools to conserve soils. He gave us the tools to add productivity to the land, to help keep people out on the land."

Hansen brought back alfalfa from Russia, including the hardy and disease-resistant Cossack line. In turn, Cossack led to the historic variety, Vernal, which dominated the northern United States for 30 to 40 years. Then, Vernal became an important genetic source for modern-day alfalfa breeding. He also brought back smooth brome grass and crested wheat grass from Russia.

Explains Kephart: "His mission was to bring back plants useful to homesteaders, to find very productive forages."

What's more, Kephart notes, traveling to Russia in Hansen's time was an enormous investment of time. The trip by train, boat and horse-drawn wagon took a month. Today, SDSU researchers travel to Russia in 24 hours.

Chapter 5

A Dangerous Game

There was a time, in the early days of the ag college, when your years on campus meant more than a countdown to graduation and gaining entry into the "real world."

Back when the College on the Hill was just that — a few buildings and a couple hundred students — class membership inspired intense loyalty and a deep sense of pride, not to mention annual fights to determine superiority and bragging rights.

The rite of passage began when students arrived on campus each fall. There would be a flurry of meetings with substantial debate over class colors, cheers and a flag. For some unaccounted-for reason, the class of 1903 initiated a spectacular and daring game called "Flag Rush," a literally high-stakes rendition of the popular children's game, Capture the Flag.

The danger involved — climbing to the highest points on campus, hoist-

Members of the class of 1911 on top of the old water tower defending their flag. Note students climbing the tower.

ing your class flag and then defending it from removal — made Flag Rush a short-lived tradition. The administration put an end to it about 10 years later.

Class spirit was a serious matter, as pointed out in the March 1910 Industrial Collegian:

"You cannot define it, artists fail in trying to portray it and writers are at a loss for terms to describe it, but there's an added gleam in the eye, the blood flows faster and up and down the spinal column a series of chills follow each other in quick succession, when class patriotism is in possession of a man."

Having risen through the ranks from lowly freshmen, each class turned around and railed on those who followed. The spirited exchange of intellectual barbs and physical contest fueled the solidarity of students and cemented an undying devotion to their class. In a parting shot before graduation in 1910, the senior class felt it necessary to pass on advice to the class of 1911:

"We hesitate to leave our dear old college in the hands of such a class of bunglers, but it cannot be avoided. ... When you first appeared on campus as Freshmen we had many hopes for you. And had you but followed the advice we so generously tendered you; you would have bid fair to be at least respectable. But no! You chose another course and have grown steadily worse from your very first appearance. Yet such a mob of brainless humanity as you have proven yourself to be; could hardly do otherwise. You have only yourself to blame, for time after time we set before you worthy examples which you would not follow. Your mistakes have indeed been many and one evening would not suffice to tell all of them."

Three years earlier, the class of 1907 had been equally harsh to its successors, calling the juniors "that peculiar and treacherous species of the human race." The writer went on to talk about a calamity greater than any earthquake or flood, when the sun would cease to shine and the earth suddenly halt on its axis:

"The waters of the lakes and rivers will boil and their vapors, mixed with the awful gasses issuing from the earth will force men and animals alike to seek shelter with the snakes, lizards and reptiles in the bowels of the earth only to be scorched and forced to the surface again."

The cause of all the chaos? The juniors making the transition to the seniors, fueling the unbroken cycle of class warfare.

Under the original rules of Flag Rush, the sophomores flew their class flag from the most prominent place on campus. In the fall of 1902, the options were few — the water tower, the smokestack for the old heat plant or the top of Old Central. The freshmen were then charged with locating the flag and retrieving it. If the flag was still flying at 10 the next morning, the sophomores reigned as the victors.

According to Collegian accounts, however, other classes also tried to keep their flags flying high and untouched over campus.

In 1903, three freshmen from the class of 1907 — Stephen Briggs, Eugene Corbin and George Haven — hoisted their flag on the chimney of the new heating plant, the night before Halloween. But that wasn't all. On the way down, they cut away 13 rungs from the iron ladder to prevent other classes from retrieving the flag. They were fined $20 for damages.

George L. Brown, who arrived on campus in 1897 and served in various faculty and administrative positions for 48 years, witnessed many of the flag fights. In his papers, Brown recounted a humorous incident that involved then-President James Chalmers chasing down students to retrieve a flag.

After the class of 1907 freshmen raised their flag and sawed off the ladder rungs, Chalmers persuaded the students to take the flag down and talked the two fighting classes into declaring a truce.

"A morning or two later, the president must have been chagrined when he looked out across the campus to see that the flag that had been removed from the chimney (was) floating on the tower used for the display of the national flag," Brown wrote. "However, he called in the leaders of the class and induced

Members of the class of 1909 on top of Old North showing off their trophy — the 1910 flag.

them to take down their flag a second time. Proceeding to the flag tower with a group of students, he waited for the flag to be handed to him. Just as he reached out to take it from the student who was descending with it, one of the fastest sprinters of the college grabbed it and ran.

"Dr. Chalmers prided himself on being something of a sprinter himself and started after the student, calling on him to stop, but the student kept running."

The chase continued, with Chalmers losing ground. The student ran past the corner of the heating plant, where another student, also a sprinter, was waiting to take the flag.

"Seeing that he was racing with a relay team," concluded Brown, "Dr. Chalmers discontinued the chase in a very great rage."

In the aftermath, the first student who was on the run claimed that he thought another student was chasing him — not the president. Chalmers accepted the explanation and the matter was concluded.

The fall of 1905 was a contentious one. In what the October 1905 Collegian called "Scrap Number One," the seniors were the first ones to flaunt their flag colors:

"The flag floated proudly in the breeze until about 10:30 Tuesday morning when the crafty Juniors burned it down. The scrap which followed was fierce, but a good natured one. Dr. Chalmers said it was the best conducted class fight that he had ever witnessed."

The morning of Oct. 16 saw "Scrap Number Two" unfold:

"The Sophomores awoke to find to their surprise that the Freshmen, by daring feat, had floated their colors of blue and white high above the top of the military flag staff. The Freshies were over confident, which is the general rule in regard to the efficiency of their work, and over-slept a few minutes. When they arrived on campus the Sophomores were assembled in goodly numbers. The nervy lad of the class, having climbed the flag staff, was busy loosening two tenpenny nails being all that was between the nervy little Sophomore and the ground, one hundred feet below."

Unable to hold onto the unfastened flag, the student dropped the flag and "three or four Sophomore warriors seized it and started off. The Freshmen were on deck, however, and there was something doing. Sam Hanson was given a respectable eye full just for a starter — a wild tussle ensued for the next ten minutes, at the end of which Sperb, the Sophomore race horse, and Standly, the Freshman, each had about half of the flag. The Freshies soon had their capture hidden and even went so far as to go after Sperb with horses. The plucky Soph was too much for them and much to the chagrin of the

Freshmen, the Sophomores have a large slice of their pennant."

Sure enough, yearbooks in those years typically feature drawings and photographs of students climbing flagpoles, flags waving high above the smokestack and entire classes posing atop Old Central with their flag and wearing their class sweater. The 1907 yearbook, in a display of campus sights, shows the smokestack with scaffolding around it and the caption underneath reads: "Junior flag staff under construction."

Hoisting the flag to new heights was only part of the battle. Freshman classes often agonized over which colors to choose. Consider this account in the June 1905 Collegian, when members of the class of 1905 detailed a meeting from their sophomore year:

"… the girls proposed changing the class colors and it was decided to do so. Some of the prominent members of the class who evidently wanted to be seen as well as heard, made very eloquent speeches in favor of various colors. … Finally we hit upon the happy plan of simply dropping the black from our former colors and adopting the red and yellow, as they embodied many of the tints and shades suggested and once more harmony reigned supreme."

The next year, as juniors, the class of 1905 realized that its college years were waning and decided to go out with a flourish. Instead of just one flag, the students flew two.

"… while gazing at the unwritten pages of our orations in the vain hope of inspiration until our heads grew dizzy and our eyes grew dim, it was then that we threw down our blank pages in disgust, went out one night about midnight, and noiselessly made our way up to the Miltonian hall."

As the girls waited, one group of boys placed a flag on the heating plant smokestack as another scaled the tower of Old Central and attached a second flag.

"After this was accomplished, which was no easy task, all repaired to the Miltonian hall and joined the girls who were awaiting them with refreshments. Finally at an early hour a tired but jolly crowd wended its way homeward with clear heads and no thoughts of oratory. The loss of sleep occasioned by these night prowlings was, as is usual, made up in that very appropriate class — Oratory."

Often, with the colors flying so high overhead, opposition classes had to devise creative methods of lowering the flags. As freshmen in the fall of 1904, the class of 1908 found that the sight of the sophomore flag flapping high above the heating plant smokestack stirred feelings of defiance. The flag had to come down: "Sam Newton, our famous marksman, came upon the scene, took careful aim and fired. The aim was true, the flag came fluttering into the

Artist's rendition of class fight, taken from the 1909 Jack Rabbit.

outstretched arms of the two classes. After a fierce scrap we got possession of the flag and thus our stock went above par."

In the fall of 1906, the 64-member class of 1910 got its first taste of campus life when scaling the fire escapes of Old Central early one morning to secure the blue and white sophomore flag. A few weeks later, the freshmen returned to the scene to hoist their maroon and cream flag. They rang the bell to signal an attack by the sophomores, and a "battle among the clouds" ensued. The '09s enlisted a secret weapon — "the entire college fire apparatus" — and secured the freshman flag: "We had lost not in a fight with the students, but in a battle with the elements."

A drawing in the yearbook, sketched from the North chimney, illustrates the annual war playing out on top of Central. It is titled "Fresh-Soph Battle Among the Clouds. Fall of 1906." The scene depicts a free-for-all, complete with someone chopping the flag down and a firehose trained on freshmen trying to block the flag's removal.

These long and drawn-out fights continued into the Robert L. Slagle administration, Brown said, and often consumed considerable amounts of time. There also was a lot of danger involved. The battle on top of Central, for example, raged all night and almost resulted in a student falling from the roof. He was caught by another student.

Another tragedy nearly occurred when a flag was placed on the chimney of the heating plant. Brown said a student almost suffocated in the chimney from inhaling the smoke generated in the furnace by "the enemy."

"I have often wondered why college and universities tolerated such practices as class fights and others equally bad that were so wasteful of the students' time and also dangerous to life and limb," wrote Brown. "It can be explained, I think, in connection with our institution, by the fact that at that time we had very few athletic events and no dancing on campus."

As sophomores, the class of 1912 raised its flag from Old Central and then rang the bell to awaken the freshmen. The class colors proudly waved above campus, withstanding a skirmish that involved Roman candles and shotgun fire.

The 1907 freshman class soared to even greater heights, as detailed in its 1909 yearbook account: "One night, while the Sophomores were slumbering sweetly after their many, long, night vigils, our boys put up our beautiful flag, the Yellow and Brown of nineteen eleven, over the water tank."

Yes, the water tank.

"The following morning, as the girls could neither climb the water tank nor pour water on the Sophomores, they stayed away from classes to bring sandwiches and coffee to the boys, and help them by their very presence. Our flag did not wave more than half a day, but it was unharmed, and our dignity unruffled as we gently lowered our flag, and, all marching in a body, bore it to a place of safety.

"Class spirit was born that morning, and is still growing and thriving in every Freshman heart. For her age she is very great in this class, so much so that she is an object of envy and admiration."

A new silo offered another option for displaying class colors. And at some point, the students discovered that tying up and disabling their opponents greatly aided the fight. Various accounts tell of wrestling one another to the ground, binding opponents with rope and making off with the class flag. Other attempts involved leaving kidnap victims at a farm and under guard.

By the fall of 1910, the Collegian was heralding a new era of combat, saying that the time had come to abandon the flag fighting. Other schools had long since done away with flag rushes, the paper reasoned, and replaced them with something better: "Flags have been raised on every accessible point on the college grounds and each class from year to year has followed in the footsteps of former classes. It is thus just the same thing over and over again. The progress of the school demands a change."

A picture of the lone '12 senior class flag in the 1912 yearbook, with the description "The last victim of aerial warfare," signaled the end of flag rushing and SDSC ushered in the era of bag rushing.

According to Brown, he was responsible for finding a substitute for the flag rushing. Two students approached him after an all-night battle on top of the North building, saying that the classes would not stop unless the administration stepped in.

Brown said he went to a room with windows that opened up to the roof of North and called a conference of the students: "I explained to them the bad effects on the public if any of them should be killed or seriously injured during such a fight and suggested that they should try to find some substitute in which the contest would be conducted on an orderly basis, and mentioned the push ball as a possibility."

The students embraced Brown's suggestion.

The regulation push ball, which was used at larger schools, was too expensive for the Students' Association budget. As a substitute, three big bags were filled with straw and cement until they weighed 800 pounds apiece.

The bags were placed in the middle of the football field, with the freshmen and sophomores lined up on opposing ends. The contest lasted 15 minutes until one team pushed the bag over the other's goal line, typically leaving both sides battered and bruised, and according to the Sept. 25, 1928, Collegian, sporting "bloody noses, nakedness and broken ribs." Football players (called foot ball men), however, were barred from the contest.

Recounting its freshman victory, the class of 1915 wrote in its yearbook history:

"The bag rush was to all of us the greatest event of the year. Picture us now with a field cleared for action, three mammoth bags in the center, the two classes lined up at ends of the field, stripped for the fray — a signal, a rush, a collision, rival grapples with rival. There is a momentary lull; then freshmen reserves rush in and the bags begin to move, the Sophs throw themselves in front of the bags and try to keep them from the dreaded Freshmen goal. It is in vain, slowly one goes over then the next and finally the last. Over the field men are locked in each other's embraces; as the last bag goes over they slowly relax. The bag rush is finished, and the 1915s go down in history as the winners of the first bag rush."

It didn't take long for students to realize that out-manning their opponents just by sheer numbers was a dependable tactic. The annual sophomore-freshman fight was soon preceded by kidnapping efforts. The class that succeeded in otherwise occupying most of its rivals was bound to win the bag rush.

"The bag rush has done away with the class fights which were staged on the roof of Old Central," reported the Sept. 28, 1915, Collegian, "yet it has fostered the custom of capturing the members of the opposite class and stowing them away in barns, silo pits or any other convenient place. Such procedure is within the rules and nothing can be done about it, but are we to let this continue until the outcome of the bag rush depends on nothing but the ability of a class to capture the most of the opposing side?

"In such case the fight proper is not staged on the gridiron, but in the streets, alleys, and barns of the city and surrounding country. ... We are gradually slipping back to the traditional class fight."

Sure enough, having lost about 30 potential warriors, the freshmen that year suffered defeat at the hands of the sophomores:

"The Sophs numbered 48 men while the freshmen, while showing an enrollment of 75 boys, were represented by only 39 on the field of battle, the remainder whiling away their time in the barns and woodsheds where the thoughtful sophs had placed them out of danger's way. An exchange of prisoners immediately before the rush gave each class five more men."

The fighting was fierce as the sophomores moved the bags to the freshman goal. The bags moved slowly — 26 yards in 15 minutes — and then, the Collegian story said, "At about this time the clothes began to fly, and one by one the contestants discarded their cumbersome garments so that they might fight more effectively."

Fearing another round of kidnappings the next year, for the clash of 1916, both freshmen and sophomore classes took precautions to protect themselves. The freshmen, according to a Collegian report, sought refuge at the county jail: "The jail, however, was not built with sleeping apartments for such a great number, therefore, some slept on tables, some under tables, some sitting up in chairs, some on the floor of the padded cell, and some in the regular bunks, but the greatest number slept in the aisles and corridors on the cement floors."

By 1923, rules were drawn up to prevent "premature hostilities," the most important of which was limiting the number of participants to 45 from each class. The students also upped the ante, using the wearing of the freshman green beanie as inspiration. If the freshmen won, they had to wear the beanie only until Hobo Day. Lose, and the beanies stayed on until Thanksgiving. The senior honor society, the Tradition Club, served as the rules enforcer.

Ultimately, the bag rush and the spirit of interclass warfare died. Brown wrote that after the initial thrill, the game held little interest for spectators and soon was discontinued. Although, in 1928, that idea seemed far-fetched to the Collegian staff:

"Because the fight and bag rush are State College traditions they are to be preserved, and because it seems almost instinctive for the two lower classes to get together in a general scrap there are no indications that the tradition will die out for a great length of time."

Chapter 6

School Songs

Sheet music for the school song sold for 10 cents, circa 1915.

In the November 1904 Industrial Collegian, editors waxed eloquently about both the purpose and the importance of a college song:

"Perhaps there is nothing around which sentiment plays more exultingly than does it around song. We all of us, as we page through some old familiar hymn book, become aware of the strange manner in which memory has associated facts of bygone days to the songs we used to sing. ... The songs we sing while in college are ... apt to become the nucleus around which will gather the memories of college days."

To be sure, college songs in the early days played a big role in campus life. Whether the intention was to rouse the fighting spirit or pledge your loyalty true, singing the school song evoked a great sense of pride and a surge of emotion.

According to Keith Jensen, class of 1956 and former Alumni Association

N.E. Hansen   A.N. Haynes

director, the one and only true school song for SDSU is "The Yellow and the Blue."

"At some point later, 'Ring the Bells for South Dakota' came along," Jensen explains. "The school song is more like 'I love my alma mater.' That went to 'Ring the Bells,' which is the rouser song, the fight song. It came to be more well-known. It's played more, like at the Festival of Champions. I think today's kids know 'Ring the Bells' more."

Penned in 1908 by the great horticulturist N.E. Hansen, who wrote the lyrics, and music professor A.N. Haynes, who wrote the refrain and music, "The Yellow and the Blue" tells the story of the SDSU student. The two professors wrote the song after Haynes offered a prize to any student who could create the best college song.

However, the April 1908 Collegian reported, "as yet there is no evidence that anyone is taking advantage of his offer. It seems somewhat strange that among the numerous talented students of the SDSC, no one can be found competent to write a college song. Or is it simply indifference?"

When Haynes' plan failed to produce the hoped-for results, Hansen challenged Haynes to a duel of pens. After several nights of struggle, the pair came up with "To the Colors," which evolved later into "The Yellow and the Blue":

We come from the Sioux and the Missouri
The Cheyenne and the Jim
From the pine clad peaks of the Black Hills
Brimful of vigor and vim;
We sing the song of the prairie
The home of the yellow and blue
The gleaming gold of the cornfield
The flax of azure hue.

(Refrain)
Oh, SDSC
Hurrah for the yellow and blue

School Songs

Old SDSC
All honor and glory to you
Forever raise the song
In praise both loud and long
With loyal hearts and true, so true. (Repeat)

Rejoicing behold we the sunset
O'er waving plains of wheat
And Paradise portals of sunrise
Aglow with glory replete;
Oh joyous life of the prairie
More free than oe'r mountain and vale
To SDSC thou callest
Whose honored name we hail.

Then forth to a bold life of action
Both stirring and grand for all;
As knights of old battled evil,
so we are heeding the call;
We scorn the faint-hearted coward
A slave for the galley is he.
We cheer the knights of the present
And fight on to victory.

At the start of classes in the fall of 1959, Ken Carpenter, director of the State College band at the time, gave student composers a chance to exercise their talents and come up with the last line to "Ring the Bells," the new pep song he had written. The inspiration, of course, was the ringing cowbells at State games:

Ring the bell for South Da-ko-ta,
The Yellow and the Blue.
Cheer the team from South Da-ko-ta,
The Jack Rab-bits so true.
Win the game for South Da-ko-ta,
The school that serves us all.
We will fight for South Da-ko-ta,

According to the Collegian explanation in the Sept. 24, 1959, edition, the new song was to be sung to the tune of "Wave the Flag," which was copyrighted in 1929 by the University of Chicago: "Students will have chances to hear and familiarize themselves with the tune during the Augustana game and the Kansas State game when it will be played both on the field and the sidelines during halftime. The last line must contain exactly seven syllables. Reasonable alterations of the song words to make the last line suitable will be allowed."

Carpenter set Oct. 5 as the deadline for entries, with the winner to be announced in the Oct. 8 Collegian. All registered undergraduate students were eligible to participate in the contest. Entries were judged by the music department faculty. The bookstore offered a Sheaffer cartridge pen and pencil set to the winner, and the song was slated to be used as a supplementary pep song for SDSC's 75th anniversary celebration.

The winning last line was supplied by music student Stan Schleuter: "Ring, ring, ring those bells."

Forty years later, Carpenter says he doesn't remember the contest for creating the last line for the song, but he clearly recalls the motivating factor.

"The cowbells were quite a major thing," says Carpenter. "At basketball games, they about took the roof down. Why were we not singing ring the bell for South Dakota? Furthermore, 'The Yellow and the Blue' was a rather droll pep song. We didn't have a fight song."

Kenton Frohrip was on campus in the early 1950s and then again from 1957-61, when he was a graduate student in the music department. He, too, assesses "The Yellow and the Blue" as lacking in terms of rousing the troops for battle.

"We stole the song," Frohrip laughs. "It was like, 'Hey, we need a fight song. Let's find a fight song.' 'Wave the Flag for Old Chicago' was the one we picked. Really high-tech stuff. ... I think that 'Ring the Bells' captured people's imagination better. It was easier to sing, a simple song."

"Ring the Bells" was truly a collaborative effort, from the concept of needing a fight song to stealing "Wave the Flag" and writing the arrangement for a 100-piece pep band. Every instrument was manufactured with different keys, but the song had to come out with a uniform sound. First, Carpenter, and then his successor, Warren Hatfield, wrote the band arrangements.

Hatfield, band director from 1961-73, came to South Dakota State from the University of Iowa. For the arrangement of "Ring the Bells," he says, "I just wrote it in the style of Big 10 bands. I just gave it more power, more kick."

As for "The Yellow and the Blue," Hatfield adds, "It's a six-eight march, not a real powerfully exciting march. 'Ring the Bells' fit the bill for a more rah-

rah song, with faster tempo and more excitement to it. You play 'The Yellow and the Blue' for a more traditional school song. But, following a touchdown, you need something exciting."

South Dakota State, however, did not limit itself to just a school song and a fight song. There also was "Far Across the Plains of Brookings."

The song, like "Ring the Bells," came from another campus, notes Brookings native Bob Fishback, not an SDSU grad, but an SDSU preschool alum. "Far Across the Plains of Brookings" is modeled after Cornell University's "Alma Mater," a melody that enjoyed great popularity at many other schools. The Cornell song offered easy inspiration:

Far above Cayuga's waters,
With its waves of blue,
Stands our noble Alma mater,
Glorious to view.

"Oh, what a great memory," sighs Don Barnett, class of 1964, before trailing off into song: "Far across the plains of Brookings, as far as the eye can see, stands an old abandoned outhouse called the University."

Laughing at the memory, Barnett adds: "That was almost the fight song. We would sing that song, especially if we were playing the U. The whole crowd would sing and the band would play it. It was really our theme song."

Of course, USD students had to come back with something, typically singing "Old McDonald Had a Farm."

Hatfield, in his tenure, also wrote several short songs that the cheerleaders used. And, he says: "I did the drum cadence. First the drums play, then the S, then the drums, then the D, then the drums, then the S, then the drums, and then the U. Then, it starts picking up and goes faster and faster."

In its Oct. 15, 1930, edition, the Collegian reported that there would be a new song, "The Song of the Hobo," written especially for Hobo Day:

"It is promised that the new song will be heard for the first time at the pep meeting held in the college auditorium the evening of Oct. 24. Free copies will be distributed to students, faculty and alumni at this time and at the bonfire following, so that all may learn the words and music and be ready to sing Hobo Day proper. ... If the new song meets with general approval, it is expected that it will become a regular feature of Hobo Day and help make this celebration even more unique than it has become in the 17 years observed."

If historical accounts — or the lack thereof — are any indication, however, the song never managed to catch on. The Collegian made one more mention of the song and then it was never heard of again. The same seems to have happened with the college song of 1898:

> *Sing to the colors that float in the light,*
> *Hurrah for the yellow and blue!*
> *Yellow the stars as they ride through the night,*
> *And reel in a rollicking crew.*
> *Yellow the fields where ripens the grain,*
> *And yellow the moon on the harvest wane, — Hail!*
> *Hail to the colors that float in the light!*
> *Hurrah for the yellow and blue!*
>
> *Blue are the billows that bow to the sun*
> *When yellow-robed morning is due;*
> *Blue are the curtains that evening has spun,*
> *The slumbers of Phoebus to woo.*
> *Blue are the blossoms to memory dear,*
> *And blue is the sapphire that gleams like tear, — Hail!*
> *Hail to the ribbons that nature has spun!*
> *Hurrah for the yellow and blue!*
>
> *Here's to the College whose colors we wear;*
> *Here's to the hearts that are true;*
> *Here's to the maid of the golden hair,*
> *And the eyes that are brimming with blue.*
> *Garlands of bluebells and maize intertwine,*
> *Hearts that are true and voices combine; — Hail!*
> *Hail to the college whose colors we wear!*
> *Hurrah for the yellow and blue!*

As important as the words of the songs are to stir emotions, even greater are their purpose. There was a time when the Collegian ran "The Yellow and the Blue" on the front page in the first edition of the school year so students would know the words. Throughout the years, Collegian editors bemoaned the fact that not all students knew the college song and urged everyone to fall in line.

In a November 1909 Collegian essay on college spirit, the editors wrote about the stirring impact of "S.D.S.C. Hurrah for the Yellow and Blue" ringing in the ears during the early tradition of the nightshirt parade:

"There is something inspiring in marching together side by side 'neath the colors we love to honor. Class rank is forgotten. None of the scores who joined the nightshirt parade can forget that thrill of patriotism which instilled us all.

"We were out for a common purpose, for on the morrow we were to meet a common foe. Our hopes were centered on our gridiron warriors. We strove to aide them from the sidelines, and when the strife was over and we had lost, we were prouder than ever of the team that played the game and played it well — our team.

"Time may dim the recollections of buoyant youth, but college spirit will ever live in our memories. It is a patriotism that does not wane."

Far Across the Plains of Brookings

The "unofficial" college song of SDSU.

The bronchos we break for the round-up,
And ride the range all day;
We kill the coyote and gray wolf
As snarling they sneak away.
The peace-pipe smoke with the red-man,
And listen to legends of gore,
The loud tum-tum of the Siouxs' drum,
The tomahawk dance of war.

The Yellow and Blue
Continued

Yellow and Blue

Arrangement written by Assistant Director of Bands Jim Coull.
This arrangement is typically played at SDSU athletic events.

Ring The Bell

Arrangement written by Assistant Director of Bands Jim Coull.
This arrangement is typically played at SDSU athletic events.

Chapter 7

School Cheers

Time was when there was more to demonstrating your school spirit than cheering on the Jacks at a football or basketball game and lining the parade route on Hobo Day.

In the early years of the SDSU campus and well into the 1940s and 1950s, the student body was a creative bunch, generating cheers, poems and mottoes, either for the glory of a particular class or the college as a whole.

That is not to say, however, that the literary efforts were genius. More typically, they were simple, rhyming and full of exclamation points. Consider the college yell in 1894:

> *Hurrah! — Hurroo!!!*
> *The yellow and blue,*
> *Haw-Gee — Haw-Gee!!!*
> *S. D. A. C.*
> *Whoo-o-o-ah!!!!!!*

State College pep depicted by R.H. Smith in the 1927 Jack Rabbit.

By 1907, that had changed slightly:
> *Hurrah! Hurroo!*
> *The Yellow! The Blue!*
> *Haw Gee! Haw Gee!*
> *S.D.A.C.*
> *Woo-o-o-o*

Another version from May 1897:
> *Hoo-ra Hoo-ra*
> *Zip Bom Ba*
> *S. D. A. C.*
> *Ra Ra Ra*

The early cheers also used words and phrases that seemingly had the sole intention of rhyming rather than making sense:
> *With a Vevo! With a Vivo!*
> *With a Vevo Vivo Vum!*
> *Bum Get a Rat Trap Bigger Than A Cat Trap*
> *Bum Get a Rat Trap Bigger Than A Cat Trap*
> *Bum*
> *Cannon Ball*
> *Zip Boom Bah*
> *S.D.A.C.*
> *Rah! Rah! Rah!*

Three years later, the Nov. 1, 1910, Industrial Collegian published a specific cheer for a U game. Again, spirit overwhelmed creativity and exclamation points reigned:
> *Give 'em the ax! the ax! the ax!*
> *Give 'em the ax! the ax! the ax!*
> *Give 'em the ax! Give 'em the ax!*
> *Where!!!!!!*
> *Right in the neck the neck the neck!*
> *Right in the neck the neck the neck!*
> *Right in the neck Right in the neck!*
> *There!!!!!!*

These two were published in the 1919 Collegian:
> *1. Our name is S.D. State,*
> *We win as sure as fate.*

School Cheers

When we get through
With these guys, too,
They hardly will see straight.
The others envy us,
'Cause they're not worth a cuss.
And when we play (trombones)
We all shout GO YOU STATE.

2. Brookings will shine tonight,
Brookings will shine!
Brookings will shine tonight,
Brookings will shine!
When the sun goes down and the moon comes up,
Brookings will shine!

A third cheer carried the instructions of "snappy like":

Yay, team; Yay, team; Yay, team;
Fight-'em! Fight-'em! Fight-'em!
Yay, band; Yay, band; Yay, band;
Blow! Blow! Blow!

By 1933, college spirit had evolved little. But, clearly, the agricultural ties of SDSC had become a source of great pride rather than a slam as opponents likely intended:

S-O-U-T-H D-A-K-O-T-A
(faster)
South Da-ko-ta
South Da-ko-ta
STATE!

M-O-O-O
M-O-O-O
M-O-O-O
Beat the "U"
STATE!

Yea, State!
Yea, State!
Yea, State!
Fight 'em, Fight 'em, Fight 'em

The 1925-1926 cheer squad included the first State female cheerleader, Virginia Breed. An account written in the 1927 yearbook stated, " ...who may say that ... Virginia Breed didn't possess all the 'pep,' 'fire,' and 'pull' of any of the other boys on the squad?"

Urging newcomers to prepare their lungs for the Saturday football game, the Sept. 18, 1935, Industrial Collegian published another version of the yell on Page 1. It seemed to combine both the new and old elements of State cheers:

S-O-U-T-H D-A-K-O-T-A
(faster)
South Da-ko-ta
South Da-ko-ta
STATE!

M-O-O-O
M-O-O-O
M-O-O-O
Beat the "U"
STATE!

Hurrah! H'roo!
The Yellow! The Blue!
Hagee! Hagee!
S.D.S.C.
State!

School Cheers

Wah-wah! Wah-wah!
STA-STA—STATE!
Wah-wah! Wah-wah!
S-T-A-T-E
State! State! State!

The "Yell Column" in the Oct.13, 1943, Collegian published a series of four cheers with a stern reminder to the youngest class. "Freshmen: Learn these yells! We'll need them on Hobo Day. Remember — to take off those green caps, you've got to know SDSC cheers."

1. South Dakota Locomotive
S-o-u-t-h D-a-k-o-t-a
South Da-ko-ta
South Da-ko-ta
STATE!

2. Sizzling State
(Whistle) State!
(Whistle) State!
(Whistle) State!
South Da-ko-ta
South Da-ko-ta
(Whistle) State!

3. U-Rah-Rah-Rah-Rah
U-rah-rah-rah-rah
S-D-S-C
U-rah-rah-rah-rah
S-D-S-C
U-rah-rah-rah-rah
S-D-S-C STATE!

4. YEA-A-A-A-A Jacks
Yea-a-a-a-a Jacks
rah-rah-rah-rah
YEA-A-A-A-A Jacks
Yea-a-a-a-a Jacks

According to the December 1909 Industrial Collegian, class yells and mottoes were essential in cultivating class spirit. The paper recorded the following:

Class of 1910 cheer
We are it, that's no dream!
Rah! Rah! Rah! Maroon and cream.

1910 class motto (football slogan)
Don't flinch. Don't foul, but hit the line hard.

Class of 1911 cheer
Brown and yellow
Sis! Boom! Bah!
Nineteen eleven!
Rah! Rah! Rah!

Class of 1912 cheer
Hurrah! Huroo!
One nine! One two!

The class of 1913, however, had its work cut out for it. The December 1909 Collegian stated: "Inquiry reveals the fact that the Freshmen have no motto or yell. The girls are hard at work however and we predict that a yell and motto of genuine merit will soon be brought forth."

These cheers had nothing on the class of 1902:
Ching-a-ling, ching-a-ling, chow, chow, chow
Bing-a-ling, bing-a-ling, bow, wow, wow
One zip, two zip, zip-a-zip, zu
S.D.A.C. nineteen two.

There were also dueling class cheers:
Rickety Zip!
Zip! Boom! Bah!
1905
Rah! Rah! Rah!
Hurrah! Horroo!
Dippala! Dippaloo!
Rah! Si Ki Yu!
Hot, cold, wet or dry!
Sophomores!

School Cheers

The junior class responded with its version:
Go-less
Know-less
Work-less
Brain-less
Sophomores.

Chapter 8

Becoming Jackrabbits

At some point in the early years of South Dakota Agricultural College, someone or some group of people decided that the school's mascot would be the Jackrabbit. More than a century later, though, that single decision — a decision that has played a role in the lives of a multitude of students — remains elusive.

The question begs to be asked: Why did SDAC switch from the Barn Yard Cadets to the Jackrabbits? Fifteen years into the school's history, according to an October 1899 account in the Industrial Collegian, the Cadets reigned mightily:

"Since the game with Madison, the students have taken quite an interest

---

Artist's sketch in the May 1906 edition of the Industrial Collegian, in which a jackrabbit, associated with an SDSC athletic team, made its debut.

in football and now have two full teams, which are able to hold their own in the state.

"We have made many challenges but few have been accepted. We once thought we had a game with the Mitchell University team but we hear nothing more from them. Their teams of Sunday-School boys are either too nice to give us a game or they lack the courage. We hardly understand why they should feel so timid, but evidently they have no desire to rub up against the 'Barn Yard Cadets.'"

Four years later, Barn Yard became one word instead of two. The May 1903 Collegian paid homage to the track team, starting off with this little refrain:

> *"Barnyard cadets,*
> *Well, I don't know,*
> *Us farmer boys*
> *Are now so slow."*

The campus paper went on to laud the team's accomplishments:

> *"Who says our athletes ain't all right;*
> *They're a jolly good bunch of boys.*
> *They've skun 'em all — what came in sight.*
> *Why shouldn't we make a noise?*
> *They beat Vermillion and killed off Ames,*
> *At the meet they earned immortal names.*
>
> *"Our track team, this of nineteen-three,*
> *The best we've ever had —*
> *That's why we are so glad;*
> *Hurrah! huroo!! the yellow, the blue!*
> *Haw-gee, haw-gee, SDAC Roo-o-o!!"*

A 1904 Collegian commentary offers the first hint of change or, at least, the potential need to change:

"Although Barnyard Cadets is a title that we as students of SDAC have never had reason to feel ashamed, still we do not desire to give people the impression that we constitute the whole barnyard menagerie. The tendency of a few in this direction is manifested by the unearthly noises and rude scraping and stamping of feet during the different gatherings in the chapel."

That same edition of the Collegian also includes a vague reference, involving local editor R. Adams Dutcher, the father of Hobo Day, that some kind of push for a name switch may have been in the works:

"Adams has jack rabbit on the brain and was unable to write locals this month. Poor boy, with burnside and jack rabbit he is liable to have some complications."

One year later, when the 1905 football team played and lost 81-0 to the Minnesota Gophers, the talk again turned to jackrabbits. The November 1905 Collegian reported the thoughts of one SDAC alumnus, who reasoned: "It was a frightful score, but in the language of the poet paraphrased, 'tis better to have played and lost than never to have played at all.' The papers report that the 'jack-rabbits' put up a plucky fight from start to finish. We feel proud of them for that. Some day the old SDAC squad may turn the tables on the Ski-u-moles. It will be only with pleasure when we look back and note the improvement."

Sure enough, the Minneapolis Tribune account of the game, beneath a simple headline that read "SWAMPED," included a jackrabbit reference.

"In one of the most uninteresting contests ever played at Northrop Field, Minnesota yesterday defeated the ... South Dakota Agricultural College in two halves of twenty minutes each by a score of 81 to 0. At no time during the contest was the Minnesota goal in danger and the game was simply a succession of Gopher gains which resulted in a total of fourteen touchdowns, with the visitors unable to stop the Minnesota offense at any stage of the contest. ...

"It was a shame to send the varsity first eleven against the Aggies for the visitors were very light and knew but little football. They had no attack and could not gain an inch, while their linebackers were not heavy or experienced enough to make any show of holding Minnesota's rushes."

And yet, there was some admiration: "In spite of the terrific pounding they received, the South Dakota forwards stuck to their colors through the game, and played nervily all the time."

The jackrabbit connection, although not in the text of the story, appeared in a cartoon sketch of the week's sporting events. The panel on the SDAC game depicts a rabbit hitting a wall, with the description, "The South Dakota Jackrabbit football team runs into the Minnesota stonewall and is bumped."

Then, in May 1906, along with a story about the 12th annual state track meet, there appears an illustration of a runner alongside a jackrabbit.

The first sense of any formal name change, however, does not appear until the April 1907 Collegian, when an editorial talked about the legislative meas-

Sketch taken from Minneapolis-based The Sunday Tribune on Nov. 12, 1905. The artist depicted the State team as a jackrabbit.

ure that renamed SDAC the South Dakota State College of Agriculture and Mechanic Arts.

"Hereafter we will be known as the 'South Dakota State College,'" the editorial stated. "This action was the result of a long-felt want as the word 'Agricultural' was misleading in that it gave the impression that agriculture was the only branch taught. We will miss our pet name of 'Barn-yard Cadets,' but the loss will be more than made up by the recognition of our courses in the Mechanic Arts."

In their junior year, members of the class of 1907, sought to make a name for themselves in campus history. A poem titled "How the Jack-Rabbit Came to Be" details how the new name for the college yearbook evolved, but mentions nothing about the mascot:

> *"Slowly down the horizon,*
> *Sunk the golden autumn sun;*
> *And the library clock a striking,*
> *Showed the day was almost done.*
>
> *When a band of merry Juniors,*
> *Met in thirty-five that day,*

Becoming Jackrabbits

*And whispered how they'd make them famous
In an intellectual way*

*Then a tall good-natured fellow,
Rose from out the Junior mass,
And addressed his fellow students,
Of that most industrious class.*

*"Fellow Juniors, we've decided
A new stunt to introduce,
That we'll edit a 'Jack Rabbit,'
Which we'll very soon turn loose.*

*Soon the news was circulated,
And it ceased to be a jest,
For '07's Jack Rabbit,
Took its place among the best.*

*And now each year the Junior class,
In this agricultural school,
Point with pride to the precept,
And try to follow the rule.*

*And forever and forever
Tho others take their place,
They'll all acknowledge freely,
That '07 set the pace."*

Based on this poem, conjecture throughout the decades points to the class of 1907 as the source of the Jackrabbit mascot. But, the earlier references from 1904-06 poke holes in that theory.

The origin of the logo is equally difficult to pin down. Although, the yearbooks show an interesting progression from caricature to cartoon and a variety of mutations in-between. The 1908 yearbook pictured a rabbit walking, football in arm and wearing football pants. Nearly 20 years later, the 1927 yearbook depicted a drawing of a realistic-looking rabbit on the run. The 1938 annual saw a shift toward a more cartoonish character.

During the 1960s, there was an effort to create a rabbit that looked more mean and vicious, but the search for a suitable logo failed. In 1971, there was a student contest to come up with a new design. The winner was a burly looking rabbit, with protruding front teeth and what looks to be bloodshot eyes. The design was never adopted.

The task of finding a logo next fell to a committee. According to Dave Martin, then sports information officer, former University Relations staffer Larry Westall created what is so well-known today as the running rabbit, complete with teeth bared in a full grin.

Running rabbit logo created by Larry Westall.

Clearly, South Dakota State's mascot has seen its fair share of change over the decades. The one constant, however, remains the pride and loyalty of the State family, friends and fans. And nothing — not Barn Yard Cadet, nor Jackrabbit — can alter those emotions.

Chapter 9

Hobo Day

G iven the serendipitous origin of South Dakota State, it's only fitting that the university's greatest tradition — Hobo Day — evolved purely by chance as well. Had the sequence of events been altered in any small part, the celebration would not be as we know it today.

What's more, a look at how Hobo Day unfolded reveals just how close we came to a totally different tradition.

"The night of November thirteenth is one that will be set down as a historic date in the annals of the State College."

That was the prediction of the 1909 yearbook staff. Little did those students know how true their words would ring nearly a century later.

In the fall of 1907, the student body unknowingly set in motion the chain of events. The football season opened with a loss against Huron. Oct. 18, the team racked up a decisive win, 48-0, against the Flandreau Indians only to face

---

This 60-foot-tall hobo greeted visitors to the campus during Hobo Day activities in the 1960s.

defeat Nov. 1 in Grand Forks. Beaten, but not discouraged, State girded itself for the next game:

"With a ginger that did not desert them, and spirits that did not falter, they prepared for the battle with Dakota Wesleyan, a week later," the May 1908 Collegian reflected on the fall football season. "The SDSC student body resolved to do all in their power to make this game a decisive victory, for the strength of the visiting team was fully realized.

"New college yells were practiced and the night before the game nearly every college man marched through the streets, helped kindle a bonfire on the campus, and participated in an event that will go down as college history, the Nightshirt Parade."

Four years later, through seeming happenstance and the vision of one State student, the festivities mutated into Hobo Day, the time-honored homecoming tradition of South Dakota State University.

"It was the eve of the game with Dakota Wesleyan," read the 1909 yearbook, "and in order to stir up enthusiasm among some of the dormant members of the college and the people of Brookings, a Nightshirt Parade was decided upon."

There is no explanation offered of what inspired the nightshirt theme, other than perhaps the hour at which the event took place:

"(T)hey certainly were a queer looking aggregation — nightshirts of every description. ... Branches were stripped from the trees in the grove to make a roaring bonfire. Songs and speeches were rendered in a fitting manner and one after another the college yells were given. ... As the fire began to die down torches were prepared, a line of march was formed, and headed by the band, started for the city."

According to the yearbook account, it was a spectacular sight — hundreds clad in white, winding their way into town beneath the flickering of torches. They stopped along the way at the homes of SDSC football players and cheered them on.

"Arriving downtown they gently removed from the opera house a few lukewarm students and forced them to don nightshirts and get in line," the yearbook description continues. "A grand march was enacted on Main Street and the noise shook the buildings.

"The town was voluntarily turned over to the students and they wielded their power in no unjust way.

"They assembled at the depot to give the incoming football team a warm reception, but here they met with the first disappointment of the evening. The Wesleyan eleven was accidentally delayed and did not arrive until the following morning.

"The final object of the parade was thwarted, but the fundamental purpose, that of arousing interest in town and college, was gloriously successful. At the game the next day, the sidelines were crowded with patriotic rooters, and victory was ours."

Such were the modest, yet spirited beginnings of Hobo Day, which never would have happened without first the death of the Nightshirt Parade. The Hobo Day special edition of the Oct. 28, 1924, Industrial Collegian chronicled the demise of the Nightshirt Parade on Oct. 12, 1911.

As had been the custom, the men wore nightshirts and the women dressed in sheets. They danced through the streets to meet the arrival of the night train and then visited the rooming houses of football team members, stopping to sing and cheer. The evening's activities wrapped up with a bonfire, which witnesses said typically were 150 feet across and 100 feet high.

And then, a 1924 campus paper reported: "The college authorities rang the knell of doom for the fairer sex of S.D.S.C. by announcing that it was undignified and unseemly for college women to roam the streets of Brookings draped in sheets. This not only plunged the girls into the slough of despond, but the men also missed the better half of their numbers. Much discussion followed, and finally a group of men, consisting of Roy Nord, Adams Dutcher, Ben Schaphorst, and Harry Rilling, canvassed the possibilities of a substitute."

Ultimately, Dutcher brought the Hobo Day concept to the Brookings campus. Now lost in the shuffle of decades of State history, Dutcher had seen a Hobo Day celebration at the University of Missouri. The event failed there because too many authentic hobos turned out and scared off the college students.

At SDSC, however, the students figured Hobo Day would work with the proper precautions: "With the assistance of the town law enforcers, who promptly 'jugged' any unlooked-for visitors, the day was put over with great credit to all concerned in the fall of 1912. The problem of providing eats for the crowd of merrymakers was met by the Women's Clubs of the city, who offered to feed the students in true hobo style."

With no shortage of enthusiasm, the campus paper declared Hobo Day a huge success. Given the intense preparation and serious attention to detail, that shouldn't have come as any surprise. Mass meetings were held and rules adopted to govern the day's proceedings.

Any man who risked shaving after Monday morning would be voted into the Bull Moose club "with a barrel, an oak lath, and a white hope as the agents of initiation." Classes after 10 a.m. were canceled. Students attending the first

A float carrying students in the first Hobo Day parade in 1912. (Courtesy of South Dakota Ag Heritage Museum)

two classes of the morning had to wear appropriate costumes — boys as hobos and girls as "fair Indian maids." Girls who failed to dress appropriately were to be painted with red ink and have their hair braided by "Big Chief's wife."

That Friday morning, according to the Nov. 5, 1912, Collegian, "the campus was transformed into a Hobo jungle and an Indian reservation. ... The onlooker could not have told whether he was in an 1849 Indian village or a Twentieth Century division point on the Northwestern railroad."

At 10 a.m., the hobos and Indian maidens met in the chapel and then marched to the train depot to meet the Yankton football team. Professor Carl Christensen's hobo band led the way, the band being so large itself that it required two drum majors:

"The members of the band were almost beyond recognition by even their friends. ... Rufe Simpson resembled a chimney sweep who had just finished a bad job, and Pratt looked like a fugitive from Yankton, who had 'bummed' his way in on the rods. 'Pudge' Sherwood was taken for a cross between a third-rate prizefighter and a sack of wheat. Close behind the band was carried the Hobo flag of peace, which consisted of four bandana handkerchiefs sewed together and tied to a fish pole. This was borne by George Philips, as Old Father Grimes, who wore a coat which was excavated from grandfather's woodpile twenty years ago."

The motley procession marched to Kendall's corner at the intersection of Fourth and Main streets, the band playing on, and then up Fourth Street to serenade the high school. From there, "a rush was made ... for the meat markets, bakeries and grocery stores and then walked to the jungles in the college grove to prepare dinner. ... By half past twelve all had arrived at the jungles and were busy getting ready for their Hobo or Indian dinner. No restrictions were made against the hobos and Indian girls eating together, and strange as it may seem, the Aborigines mingled with the Twentieth Centurists and were seen in mixed groups scattered through the jungle."

Janet Keysser of Golden Valley, Minn., says her grandparents, Ralph Johnston and Blanche (Avery) Johnston, both class of 1916, participated in the first Hobo Day parade.

"Grandma told of how they all wrapped in blankets to dress like Indians," recalls Keysser. "The girls wore braids of black yarn." And the rest, as they say, is history.

The first Hobo Day stirred this retrospective in the Nov. 12, 1912, Collegian:

Hobo Day
The college bell is silent
The books are stored away,
The girls are feeling jubilant,
The boys, happy and gay.
And the teachers hear no classes,
For this is Hobo Day.

See the Indian maidens
In beads and blankets arrayed,
They like the flowers' fragrance;
Of mice they're not afraid.
And they'd like some strong young brave,
Who'd like an Indian maid.

Who cares for learning's crown?
Much less a crown in a hat,
Fashions at them frown
They want to be plump and fat.
And say, boys, isn't it jolly?
Being a hobo for a day.

We are happy-go-lucky,

All cares are driven away,
We all are jolly, but plucky,
We'll work some other day,
And we like the college routine,
But, O, you Hobo Day.

The following fall of 1913, the Hobo Day tradition took firm root. Boys were to dress as hobos and girls as Indian maidens. They would march in two lines — "as straight as possible" — behind the band and the hobo flag of peace. The parade route started at the campus, going south to Eighth Street, west to Main and then south to the depot. From there, the procession would head to Kendall's corner, where the band would play, with the hobos forming a circle around the band and the Indian maidens forming a circle around the hobos.

Two years into Hobo Day, however, the celebration nearly lost the hobo. After the 1913 festivities, the Collegian called for a change in names and a shift toward a more meaningful and historically correct focus than bums.

"Now is the time — while the subject is fresh in our minds," the campus paper said in the Nov. 18, 1913, issue, "for the suggestions of our future Hobo Days. When the faculty granted this day, they had in mind a day somewhat historical. The two Hobo Days so far have been very successful. No one can honestly criticize the students for crudeness or disorderly conduct. ...

"But why not have something a little more compatible than Hobos and Squaws? If next year, for example, we could have Cowboys and Squaws we could introduce pageants into our parade which would be unique, historical and attract much more attention. It would get out over the state better. In fact a 'Dakota Day' as we might call it, would be reported throughout the North West.

"It would draw visitors and in time set a precedence which might encourage a statewide holiday, sanctioned by the Governor. Keep a 'Dakota Day' in mind. Plan for it."

State President Ellwood C. Perisho took up the fight for a name change after his appointment in 1914. He championed a more dignified title for the event, wanting to call it "Dakota Day."

But, it was too late. Hobo Day was stuck in the student body consciousness. Soon after, Dakota Day found a home at SDSU's greatest instate rival — the University of South Dakota campus. Yankton began Pioneer Day and Northern State Teacher's College in Aberdeen initiated Gypsy Day.

Throughout the history of Hobo Day, however, doubts resurfaced about the celebration and efforts continued to fine-tune the festivities.

Then-student and future congressman Ben Reifel dressed in appropriate costume for Hobo Day, Oct. 17, 1931.

The May 2, 1922, edition of the Collegian listed the many attributes of Hobo Day, saying that on this glorious day "the 'Spirit' of State College, though robed in hobo attire, stalks exultingly throughout the city. … Everything personal and petty is forgotten now; the heart vibrates with enthusiasm, and the bewhiskered and bedaubed faces fairly radiate the good will and the joy of partaking."

However, the editors noted, each year three questions become more acute:

1) Should we continue to celebrate Hobo Day as we have in recent years, each year making it more of a pageant day and spending more time and money on our floats?

2) Should we offer prizes for the best floats in the parade, thereby causing keen competition between the various departments or groups and, incidentally, perhaps just a little ill feeling?

3) Should we go back to the original Hobo Day when everyone appeared either as an Indian maiden or hobo?

"At least," the Collegian mused, "we want to remember that it is a day when everyone should forget his worldly cares and just be happy."

In the beginning, the men let their beards grow for one week, then two and three, and finally four by the late 1930s. Float building began modestly and grew increasingly elaborate until its heyday in the 1940s and '50s. Throughout most of the 1920s, Dr. N.E. Hansen continued the tradition of a spectacular chrysanthemum show, drawing thousands of visitors to see the flower's varieties and all the curios he collected on his trips to Japan.

"In marked contrast to the glitter and activity of the other Hobo Day celebration," reported the Oct. 24, 1925, Collegian, "the 'mum' show is an oasis of refreshing quietness. Colorful flowers, rare specimens of plant life, rippling water fountains and entrancing music, all invite the Homecoming visitors to stop and linger over their beauty and charm."

Two years later, the Oct. 23, 1928, Collegian reported that a new feature — table decorations representing about 60 countries — would replace the annual mum show. Much of the material for the international show came from items Hansen had collected during his trips abroad. Red-fleshed apples, one of the latest hybrids Hansen developed, were the central display of the 1928 show.

The 1928 Hobo Day also featured a football match-up between State and the U. Professor Carl Christensen took his State military band on the road for a three-state, 22-town booster trip to advertise the game. It was an ambitious schedule, starting in Elkton and then spending 15 minutes per town as the band made its way through southwestern Minnesota, northern Iowa and then back up to campus.

In 1929, authorities put a dent in the drinking supply when they raided a Brookings area farmhouse and seized 600 gallons of grape and rhubarb wine with an alcoholic content of nearly 9 percent. The stash was in town for Hobo Day, noted the Nov. 2, 1929, Collegian, "but the liquor is safely reposing in the Brookings County jail."

The early Hobo Days also featured huge barbecues. In 1922, 7,000 people feasted on two large steers plus the hindquarters of two more steers, boiled potatoes and six barrels of coffee. The first 5,000 were fed within an hour during the noon meal.

The late 1920s and early 1930s saw a return of an occasional Nightshirt or Torchlight parade. As their predecessors had nearly 25 years before, hundreds

Pharmacy students dominated float competitions throughout the years as demonstrated by this 1946 entrant to the Hobo Day parade.

On Oct. 4, 1952, presidential candidate Dwight Eisenhower visited the campus and gave a speech to 12,000 people at the Coolidge Sylvan Theatre. He had his picture taken with Grand Pooba John Young, class of 1953. Hobo Day was still 14 days away. In response to the visit, the modest Collegian headline read "Ike Reaches Peak in Career."

of coeds snake-danced their way through the streets of Brookings for the 1931 Hobo Day, carrying flaming torches and colored flares and ringing cowbells. At the corner of Fourth Street and Main Avenue, the girls threw their torches on a bonfire, led the group in cheers for the Jacks and then rushed the Grand Theatre.

John Bibby, class of 1942, remembers as a young boy watching the men march in the Nightshirt Parade and the women in the Torchlight Parade.

In fact, laughs Bibby, the Hobo Day parade posed an annual problem for his family's dairy business: "We had milk routes around town, and we couldn't deliver during the parade. So, we'd start delivering milk around midnight Friday. It was kind of a pain."

Years passed, classes came and went, yet Hobo Day in all its many forms and varied traditions prevailed. The pushball contest, which had been an annual game in the early 1920s, reappeared in the 1930s. Students in 1934 refused to attend classes the Monday after the Hobo Day football victory — it was the second annual skip day.

In 1939, Frank Weazel, "an admirer of State College," gave the Students' Association a 1912 Model T Ford with the understanding that it appear each year in the Hobo Day Parade. The year the car was made, of course, was the same year the Hobo Day tradition began. The Collegian noted, "At last, Hobo Day royalty of State College will have transportation befitting the dignity of their exalted station, for the car is complete in every detail including a set of genuine acetylene headlights."

According to the Oct. 2, 1941, Collegian, the 1931 Hobo Day was unprecedented in the number (100) of floats and stunts — a figure that steadi-

Hobomobiles were a common part of Hobo Day parades until 1984, when safety issues brought an end to the tradition.

ly declined over the years. By 1955, it dropped to 55. Beards and pigtails prevailed throughout the 1940s. And, bums still went knocking on local doors.

Bob Karolevitz, who attended State from 1940-43 and graduated in 1947, says that in his day "we went and knocked on the doors and got our lunch from the housewives of Brookings. We had to grow beards — it seemed like weeks. We also put out the 'Bum,' the football program."

In the 1947 yearbook, Hobo Week festivities inspired the following poem, attributed to Shakespeare. Some State traditions — obviously — have withstood the test of time:

> *When a Stater sees a whisker*
> *Or a dirty stack of clothes,*
> *Or a cowbell or a burlap bag,*
> *Or guys enroute to Joe's,*
> *Then his mind goes back to Hobo Week,*
> *To sleepless nights and days —*
> *To the foll'wing Sunday morning*
> *And a mind engulfed in haze.*

By the late 1940s, instate rivalries had added to the Hobo Day rites of passage. Walt Conahan, class of 1952, recalls an incident from 1948 or '49 involving the bummobile: "There were a pair of brothers, Steinmetz, Bob and Chuck, from Watertown. The story is, the U people stole it and had the bummobile down in Vermillion. It was down there during the summer. The story goes that Chuck Steinmetz went down there as an enrolled student, he passed himself off as a student, found out where the bummobile was. Then people went down and got it, and brought it back."

The rivalry also played out in other suspected ways. On more than one occasion, Hobo Day has coincided with the opening of pheasant season. In 1954, that predicament led the Collegian editors to wonder about the source of the continued conflict.

"Is there a subversive in the South Dakota Game, Fish and Parks Commission?" asked the Sept. 23, 1954, Collegian editorial. "Is it possible there may be a Communist in this above-mentioned Commission? Or, do you suppose the man or men in charge of the opening of pheasant season in South Dakota is a graduate from the University of South Dakota?"

Chuck Cecil, class of 1959, notes, "Hobo Day, when I was a student, there was a lot more creativity. Maybe it was because of finances. Kids didn't have a whole lot to do. There were beautiful floats. And the stunt cars actually performed stunts. They reared up on their back tires, or they'd spin around."

The 1953 Hobo Day saw the big controversy over Miss Biffy, described by the Oct. 22 Collegian as a "breathtaking float done in contrasting colors and elaborate accessories." Driven by John T. Schluenz, Miss Biffy took first place in the stunt division. The car had an outhouse on the back, with a big picture of Miss Biffy, a scantily clad woman, posted on the outhouse. The outhouse

Vivian Volstorff, former dean of women, judges the whisker growth of student Walter Johnson during 1956 Hobo Day activities.

door was open and, says Cecil, inside was a "guy with his pants down around his ankles. It was just a simple little float."

The Sioux Falls Argus Leader, however, lambasted the float, called it vulgar and said "it belongs in the same classification as livery stable stories."

"In the next years," laughs Cecil, "the trailers got bigger, the outhouses got bigger, there were more stunt cars and they kept getting larger and wider. The kids driving 'em had a few beers. They were three stories up, double-deckers, held together with two-by-fours. One tipped over. It was really scary. It turned the corner too quickly and some of the structure fell. Kids fell off. There were two-by-fours with big spikes sticking up. That started a movement to do away with stunt cars. The floats were also getting obscene. They would be inspected, the judges would check all the words. They'd block that one word out with spray paint, but the kids would spray paint it back on by the time it got another block down the street."

When Margie Fiedler, class of 1977, came back as Dirty Lil she found a changed Hobo Day atmosphere.

"People didn't dress up like hobos," Fiedler says. "They didn't know all the old songs. They didn't know all the traditions, like the burying of the razor ... or freshmen wearing the green beanies."

She laughs at the memory of another tradition: "Every time an upperclassman asked you, you had to be carrying candy to give them. My roommate and I, we bought all this ExLax. They looked like chocolate candies. We wrapped them up in cellophane to hand out. Like an idiot, I licked the container, thinking all the chocolate would be on the side. I got so sick. I spent homecoming night sick in bed."

Bibby, who was born in 1920, has seen his share of Hobo Days and reflects on the changes the celebration has seen.

"It's not nearly as big a deal as it used to be," he says. "It was a unique kind of homecoming. Lots of people did come back. As young adults, we'd have guests from out of town, former students, bringing their families back. They'd join us for a meal or two. I suppose some of that goes on now, but I don't know if it's as much as it used to be."

Like others of his generation, Bibby talks about the spectacular floats and the hundreds of students who marched in hobo attire.

"They spent a lot more time in construction of the floats," he says. "Pharmacy students always were good float-builders. Of course, in pharmacy, they had a course in window decorating."

Today, despite the decrease in student involvement and the disappearance of hobos, Bibby says he still enjoys watching the parade.

Hobo Day

"Oh, yeah," he chuckles, when asked if he takes in the annual event. "I don't get all shook up about it as I used to. I just walk over two blocks and sit down and watch it."

Chapter 10

Cowbells

No history of South Dakota State University would be complete without a look at the cowbell-ringing lore.

By today's standards, the quaint tradition is tame — one, two, perhaps a handful of bell ringers swallowed up in Frost Arena or strategically stationed in the grandstand of Coughlin Alumni Stadium.

But, go back 50, 60, 70 years and there was a time when nearly every fan in attendance arrived with cowbell in hand. At the Barn, they literally filled the place to the rafters.

"Back in the old Barn, it was cowbell time," recalls LaVerne Kortan, class of 1942. "It was a tremendous amount of noise, of course. And people sat right on the edge of the bleachers, almost on the edge of the floor. You had to pull your toes back when the players came by."

The spectacle of hundreds of fans, sitting or standing in every possible

---

Pictured above, an original cowbell presented to the 1926 State cheerleaders by the Students' Association. (Photo courtesy of Eric Landwehr)

Father of the State cowbell tradition, Robert Bloedel.

space, ringing bells, was a sight and sound to behold — especially for University of South Dakota and Augustana games.

"I remember when the U brought their whole band in uniform," says Phyllis Bartling of Brookings. "The place was so jammed pack, legs were hanging down from the rafters. And the cowbells. Oh, it was loud."

Exactly who launched the tradition depends on which version of history you subscribe to. There is, however, no question as to why the tradition started. Of course, it stems from State's rivalry with the U. What else?

Writing for the Sept. 25, 1935, edition of the Collegian, John M. Ryan recounted: "It was back in 1926, when Robert Bloedel of the class of 1928, now an engineer in Chicago, was captain of the cheer squad. Students of the University of South Dakota for several years had been derisively referring to State as the 'cow college.' Bloedel got the idea that if they were to be known as the cow college, they might as well be proud of it and he asked Pres. C.W. Pugsley if State rooters might not carry cowbells to the game and ring them in answer to the taunts of the Coyotes. He also cooked up the 'Mo-o-o-o-o, beat the U' yell.

"The Board of Regents thought that the idea was okay and on Hobo Day in 1926, President Pugsley presented Bloedel with a real he-man's cowbell, almost a foot high, which Major Bloedel now has on exhibition in the military supply room."

After the presentation of the bell, Bloedel turned around to the crowd and led the "Mo-o-o-o-o, beat the U" cheer. He concluded with the tolling of the huge bell, but "was drowned out by the racket of a thousand cowbells swung from the hands of howling State rooters."

A Nov. 2, 1926, front page note in the Industrial Collegian reports that Stephen Jones, president of the Students' Association, presented President and Mrs. Pugsley with a matching set of his-and-her cowbells before a football game.

Several weeks earlier, in the Oct. 19, 1926, edition, a story penned by an anonymous freshman had noted that "the college is suffering from a severe attack of 'cowbellitis.' Cowbells on sale at the book store have been purchased by many. At the game last Saturday approximately half of the crowd were possessed by them."

The ensuing racket, made at a football game, was loud — even by college standards: "One good-sized cowbell vigorously shaken by an enthusiastic rooter runs a close second to a fire engine in the amount of noise made. When this is multiplied two or three hundred times over, the clamor is earsplitting. Cowbells were originally intended to show the location of a herd of cattle. Last Saturday, if noise is any indication, they showed a large amount of school spirit."

Clyde "Buck" Starbeck, a colorful character of North Central Conference football fame, also took credit for initiating the cowbell ringing. In a series of articles written about him at the start of his 20th coaching season at Iowa State Teachers College (now the University of Northern Iowa), Starbeck talked about his years of playing football for the Jacks and how the U students referred to State as Cow College:

"I decided to fight fire with fire, and shortly before one of our games with the University, I ordered five barrels of cowbells from a mail-order house. The idea was to sell them to as many students and fans as possible to use at our game. I got rid of all five barrels, all right, and during the game the noise from our cheering section was out of this world. The fans liked them so well, they used the cowbells from then on."

What Starbeck didn't know then was that years later, when he was coaching at Iowa, those cowbells would come back to haunt him when his team traveled to play in Brookings. And, regardless of who started the custom, the cowbells were well-received by everyone except, of course, the U.

The Nov. 2, 1926, USD Volante gave the bells a — shall we say — less than ringing endorsement: "The morning attraction at Brookings Saturday seemed to be the parade — perhaps it was. The parade, after being pushed to the edge of the campus and then shoved off, arrived on Main Street at exactly 11:44 that morning.

"A little bull led the parade, symbolic of the journalism department. Following were the cheerleaders, attractively dressed and wearing small cowbells around their necks. ... The freshmen put on several stunts, one of them carrying out the problem of recovering lost or stolen cattle. They solved the problem by putting a cowbell around the neck of each of their cows, then if they were stolen or lost they could locate them by the sound of the cowbells — very clever indeed. ...

"There were also several groups of students in the parade well armed with cowbells. State College might call their fair sex cow-eds or probably cow-belles would be an appropriate name."

The snide comments ran both ways. After a visit to Vermillion, a Nov. 13,

1927, column in the Industrial Collegian quoted a "University style" news story: "The Howling Hundred carried horns ... which assisted them in offsetting that country effect produced by the Jackrabbits with their cowbells."

But the intended slam only entrenched the State mindset and drew further attack.

"By gee, that's right," snapped the Collegian. "We were down at Vermillion that day and we almost got lost in their magnificent one block of main street, and our adenoids are all sunburned from looking at the sky scrapers. Citified is no description for the U and its surroundings. We'll have to apologize for those cowbells. They had no place down at that aristocratic little school, nestled comfortably among the cornfields and pastures of southern South Dakota."

After the first year of cowbell ringing, the practice sparked some criticism. The enthusiasm turned annoying when fans started ringing the bells on their own instead of waiting for guidance from cheerleaders. An Oct. 4, 1927, Collegian editorial decried the "spasmodic outbursts" and noted that the announcer in the radio booth had a tough time making himself heard over the constant clanging.

"Of course, we want pep and lots of it," the paper stated. "But this pep, so far as the cowbells are concerned, should be generated when the cheerleaders call for it."

The bell-ringing fans took the hint and got their act together. Later reports indicate hundreds of bells being sold. An Oct. 5, 1932, Collegian story announced the big bookstore sale of 700 bells at reduced rates to fill the demand of students intending to ring them at a North Dakota State game. That fall, there were five sizes of bells, ranging from 3 to 7 inches in height, and selling for 25 to 35 cents each.

By 1934, students were being urged to buy all their necessary equipment for Hobo Day, and particularly the bells. Pep squad members had to have a cowbell in order to join the group. The following year, all the high school seniors in South Dakota were invited to State. Part of the visit involved the football game against St. Olaf. Each student received a miniature bell, which bore the inscription "Ring for State."

The only unforeseen hitch in the tradition was cowbells fell into disuse for their intended purpose. That left it up to the book store manager to round up enough bells for the student body. The Sept. 25, 1935, edition of the Collegian explained the complicated process:

"Miss Mae B. Austin ... experiences a great deal of difficulty each fall in stocking up for the demand that always comes just before Hobo Day. She gets in touch with a maker of the tinklers and orders all that they have of all sizes up to a certain amount, and feels lucky if they are able to ship more than five or six dozen. Almost invariably the shipments come in split dozens, a few having been sold out of each case. She continues this process, calling upon several different firms until she feels that she has enough to meet the rushing sale afforded by Hobo Day enthusiasm."

Such a tiresome, and probably thankless, task did not endear the poor Miss Austin to the cowbell ringing tradition.

"If you ask me," she told the student paper, "I don't think much of this cowbell business. There is no money in it and I have never yet sold a cowbell to a student unless he insisted on trying it out on everyone in the store. And the night before Hobo Day — oh, my head."

Try as Miss Austin and her successors did to stock up with the bells, some of the ringers often went missing.

Bob Karolevitz, who attended State in the early 1940s and then graduated in 1947, remembers a U game at the old armory when a Vermillion fan stole a cowbell.

"We all came off the bench," Karolevitz says of the basketball team. "The ball game was stopped. It was a real riot. ... We got the cowbell back and the game was renewed."

The mayhem in the stands — particularly for home games in the Barn — added a new challenge to the coaching experience.

From his vantage point on the court, Jim Marking, former men's basketball coach, says simply, "It was very loud."

Daktronics, the Brookings-based electronic message and scoreboard company, made an earphone and speaker system for the coach and his players. That was how Marking communicated with the team during timeouts.

"That's how loud it was," Marking says. "We played in a regional tournament here and the other coach laughed at me. The next night he had placards."

SDSU Athletic Director Fred Oien, class of 1968, describes the cowbell noise level as deafening.

"I grew up in the Barn," he says. "In those days, it was tradition for everybody to bring a cowbell."

NCAA rules — which govern the North Central Conference — do not permit artificial noisemakers. But, Oien says it wasn't until the 1980s that the NCC got serious about enforcing the regulation.

"There was some real concern with us having cowbells," says Oien, noting, however, that there are schools in other conferences who share the cowbell tradition.

Handing out technicals to teams with cowbell-ringing fans, however, did not bring an end to the noise.

Marking says: "Then, there were the drums. They were worse than the cowbells. They drummed the whole game. It was so loud one timeout that the players got mixed up."

To capture the crowd atmosphere in the Barn, explains Marking, you have to realize that people came to games not just to watch, but to participate.

"It was such an emotional thing," he says. "They would chant 'Bring on the Jacks' before we came out to play. There would be this rising crescendo. It'd make your hair stand on edge. We'd let 'em do it 10 or 12 times before we came out. That noise was deafening. The other teams couldn't believe it."

As loud as they were, the fans were invaluable in terms of pumping up the players. Says Marking, "After the cowbells, I never coached a basketball game without the band."

Keith Jensen, class of 1956 and former Alumni Association director, remains one of a handful of cowbell-ringing diehards who keep the tradition alive. Fans can't miss him — he sits in the front row at home basketball games and rings his cowbell.

Taking the bells on the road to away games can mean taking a stand, Jensen says, because schools interpret the rules differently.

"You can ring 'em when the ball's not in play," he says. "We sometimes have to fight that battle. Down at the U last year, we got heck from a lot of people. ... But, as long as the ball's not in play, it's OK."

Not coming from an ag background, Jensen, in his student days, did not make the connection between cowbells and State's "Moo U" nickname.

"Cowbells were big when I was in school," Jensen explains. "When I came back in 1971 as alumni director, I just got a bell and started ringing. Nobody else was doing it except Jerry Busick. I'd hear him down below and I was way up above then. I think we were the only two.

"It was just a way you could show your enthusiasm. Some people are concerned about being called 'Moo U,' but it never bothered me too much. We're in an ag state; ag is the main industry. It's nothing to be shameful about. It's just a tradition."

Chapter 11

The Blue Key Smoker

Throughout the years, school traditions at South Dakota State have come and gone. Some, like the hoisting of class colors, died because they were too dangerous. Others simply fell by the wayside, a sign of changing times.

The Blue Key Smoker came to an end after four decades because society had advanced and the Smoker had not. The night of dinner, smoking and raunchy jokes was for men only — except for the scantily clad Smoker Girls, who were selected to hand out the smokes.

"The Blue Key Smoker?" laughs Bob Karolevitz, who graduated in 1947. "That was one of the reasons I went to State. I went up there as a high school senior and got to go to the Blue Key Smoker. They told risqué jokes, although nothing compared to today's television. ... That was a good recruiting tool."

Pictured above, the crest of the Blue Key National Honor Fraternity.

SDSU graduate Jim Woster serves as emcee during the 1964 Blue Key Smoker. The caption from the 1965 Jack Rabbit reads, "Jim Woster tells a joke as he introduces the shapely cigarette girls at the Smoker."

Walt Conahan, class of 1952, remembers the Smoker being held in what used to be the old stock pavilion, which today is the Agricultural Heritage Museum:

"It was still a working pavilion. They used to run livestock through there when they were working with them. They would get it all cleared out, put big tables up, with a stage on one end where they'd have the band. It'd be Christie's band, or maybe the pep band. And, they had cigarette girls with trays, selling cigarettes and cigars. Everyone was smoking one or the other. It'd just be blue with smoke."

Blue Key was an honorary service fraternity, which according to an old yearbook had evolved from the Tradition Club, commonly known as the Thirteen Club. The SDSC Blue Key chapter started in 1927, with its first members installed on May 2. The evolution from a campus group was significant in that Blue Key was a national organization.

According to the Jack Rabbit yearbook: "This membership afforded each person a chance to join in with a nationwide group and thereby offers distinction formerly lacking at State. Blue Key is a new and rapidly growing college and university organization. When South Dakota State entered there were forty-three chapters, some of which included representation at some of the largest educational institutions in the United States."

The first Smoker took place in October 1936 and was intended to be part of the pep events scheduled for the week preceding Hobo Day. Football players attended as honored guests with Blue Key picking up the tab for their dinner.

The Blue Key Smoker

The Oct. 28, 1936, Collegian reported: "The initial dinner-smoker at State sponsored by Blue Key was carried out Monday evening with a marked degree of success. By count there were approximately 225 men in attendance.

"The spirit of the evening was well-sustained by toastmaster Lyle Cheever, student president Maurice Vick, and cheerleaders Carol Comstock and Eleanor Nelson. Many familiar songs appropriate to a men's gathering were quite spontaneously indulged in and several times the cheerleaders were called forth to conduct yells."

A men's night out was not a trailblazing event for Brookings. There are records dating back to at least 1912 that document such festivities.

"The Stag Party was a success," reported the Dec. 17, 1912, Collegian. "The Commercial Club, businessmen, S.D.S.C. Alumni, and all well-wishers of State College were the guests of the men of State College. In an evening of entertainment and informality, the men downtown and at college were brought into closer touch and the feeling of good fellowship that has always existed was brought into greater prominence.

"It is hoped that the Stag Party will be made an annual affair. ... With the experience gained this year the party next year should be much more of a success. It brings the city and college closer together. ... It would be well to take immediate steps to make permanent a custom of annual stag parties such as the one held Friday night."

On Jan. 13, 1914, the Collegian recounted events of the Stag Party the week prior: "One of the largest gatherings of men the Hill has ever experienced enjoyed an evening of informal program consisting of music, athletic stunts, refreshments and toasts."

Professor Carl Christensen and his band "were up to usual standards" and the athletic stunts "took exceptionally well." In addition to boxing and wrestling, the faculty and students played tug of war:

"During the first moments that the rope was made tense, a deadly stillness overtook the crowd and a breathless silence awaited the first movement of the handkerchief that marked its center. It gave a slight lurch toward the professors, then stopped; then a slow creeping movement away from them and in less than two minutes the boys were leading their 'instructors along the flowery path of knowledge' off the floor mid yells of 'down with the faculty,' 'out with the kids,' 'they soaped our shoes' and other discordant sounds."

Ultimately, despite protests on behalf of the faculty, the students were declared the victors. Lunch was served, speeches and toasts were made, and "the best of spirit was exhibited throughout the evening between the businessmen and students."

When exactly the stag party died and whether it played any role in spawning the Smoker is unclear. There is some reference to the Smoker replacing the Nightshirt Parade, which was the precursor to Hobo Day. Whatever the connection, it wasn't so much the tradition as what took place at the Smoker that sparked debate through the years.

Even as early as 1940 — just four years into the annual Smoker — the night of male bonding fell under attack. An anonymous student, in a letter to the Oct. 30, 1940, Collegian questioned whether the Smoker accomplished its original intent.

"Wasn't the original purpose of the smoker supposed to be that of honoring the football men, and having a chance to meet and talk with them face to face, and person to person in the light, of course, of the coming Hobo Day game?" the student asked. "But those men who attended the affair must surely have had a tough time to strain out the real significance of the occasion, if they did get it, through the haze caused by satisfying Chesterfields, and the steady and rapid barrage of smutty 'illustrations.'

"As for the spirit it stirs up, isn't that just a bit artificial? There seems to be considerable more spirit aroused over the meaning of some of the smut than over the enthusiasm aroused for the forthcoming game. ... Truly we do have a great pride in our institution and its social functions, and it is for the continuation and betterment of this moral standard, prestige and school pride that we are struggling. Must we stand idly by and watch it fall?"

Dave Pearson, 1938 Students' Association president, was quick to reply in the next edition of the Collegian, which was careful to point out that "the ideas contributed by these readers do not necessarily reflect the attitude" of the student paper.

Pearson launched into his rebuttal, saying that he was privileged to be the "roastmaster" of the 1940 Blue Key Smoker and was willing to take responsibility for the evening's events.

Wrote Pearson: "The nameless red-eyed patriot who wrote so loquaciously, if unintelligently, in your last issue is entitled to an answer for his heart-rending appeal."

Extolling the virtues of the Smokers, Pearson wondered whether it was "poor psychology, poor technique, and indescribable ignorance, to attempt to keep the pent-up emotion and hell-raising urge confined for one night to the controlled — if somewhat uncensored — surroundings of the Smoker."

The Smoker, added Pearson, "is advertised as a stag affair at which we let our hair down and have a lot of harmless fun — and we had it."

The Blue Key Smoker

Joe Foss, former governor of South Dakota and World War II hero, was the headliner at the 1961 Blue Key Smoker.

In 1952, Collegian editors questioned the behavior that took place and chastised the audience for not giving the speaker his due respect. Programs printed for the evening were fashioned into paper airplanes and flown at the podium; some people talked during the speech.

"It is definitely disappointing to see how barbaric man can be on certain occasions," the college newspaper editorialized.

The event persevered, with various luminaries serving as masters of ceremonies and guest speakers headlining the night. One custom involved awarding the Smoker Girls as door prizes. Entrants wrote their names on the back of their ticket and names were drawn. The winners got to take off the garter of a Smoker Girl and receive a kiss from her.

In 1972, then-Rapid City mayor Don Barnett, class of 1964, was the event's speaker. That night, about 250 people attended — an estimated 30 percent of whom were women, including the cheerleaders who put on a skit.

"The girls dressed up wearing real scant outfits, like the cigarette girls in Vegas, just looking like 10 million bucks," recalls Barnett from his days on campus. "It would not be politically correct today."

Clare Denton, who was a faculty member from 1956-91, served as master of ceremonies for the 1961 Smoker, when former South Dakota Gov. Joe Foss was the speaker. Introducing Foss was a huge honor, says Denton, "both of us being World War II veterans. I was in Europe; he was in the Pacific. He was the ace — an incredible fighter pilot."

By allowing the Smoker to continue, Denton surmises, the administration played two sides of the coin — not necessarily endorsing it, but not stopping it either.

"We all thought we were pretty daring," laughs Denton today. "We thought we were very vulgar, but by today's standards, it was a pretty mild thing."

That women were not allowed — except for the Smoker girls — was not seen as anything to protest. In fact, the night of the Smoker, the women held the Torchlight Parade. Torches for the 1946 parade were handed out in front of Wecota Hall. From there, the girls marched down Eighth Street to Main Avenue and then down to the Fourth Street intersection where they held a pep rally.

Following the rally, everyone headed to State Theatre for a movie. State students were admitted free and Blue Key members acted as ushers, the Collegian reported, "giving the girls first chance at the seats so they can make it back to the dorm before the curfew hour."

Jim Woster, class of 1962, emceed the Smoker in 1964. Echoing others' thoughts, Woster says the event was mild by modern-day standards, but could be considered demeaning — particularly in hindsight.

"A whole lot of people smoked," he says. "Smoking was accepted. ... It was pretty raunchy. Then, people started realizing we were not supposed to be doing these things."

By 1975, Blue Key membership was down. Interest in being a Smoker Girl also had waned as some came to realize the honor might have been a dubious one.

Still, LaVerne Kortan, class of 1942, says he enjoyed attending the Smoker during the years he was at State and thought it was a night of harmless fun.

"It was kind of a humor, comedy-type program," he recalls. "They told stories and jokes. I don't know why it went out of existence."

Keith Jensen, class of 1956, says plainly: "It was a male thing. The speaker would make ribald jokes — for the times. We'd have a good time, smoke a cigar. The women, they had their Maypole Dance and Torchlight Parade. They would have their different events and nobody thought it was a big deal."

Chapter 12

Coughlin Campanile

South Dakota State alums are typically passionate about their alma mater. Charles Coughlin, class of 1909, was no exception.

However, the lengths to which the electrical engineering grad from Carthage, S.D., went to express his love for State literally tower above the rest.

In 1928, Coughlin, then treasurer and general manager of the Briggs & Stratton company of Milwaukee, Wis., donated the money to build a bell tower, or campanile, on the southwest corner of the Brookings campus — an anniversary gift to State, 20 years after his graduation.

The dream, according to longtime history professor John Miller, began with SDSC President Charles W. Pugsley, who oversaw the extensive campus beautification efforts of the 1920s. Pugsley's vision was a campanile to be located near the campus gateway, and Miller credits him with working almost

Picture of Charles Coughlin from the 1909 Jack Rabbit.

Collegian announces laying of the Coughlin Campanile cornerstone in this June 1929 headline.

single-handedly behind the scenes to get the project going.

"Even so," Miller writes in a historical piece on the Coughlin Campanile, "the man who deserves credit for first suggesting the idea to its eventual sponsor was long-time physics and engineering professor Hubert B. Mathews.

"No doubt operating on instructions from the president, Professor Mathews suggested the bell-tower idea to 1909 graduate Charles L. Coughlin while visiting with members of the State College Club of Milwaukee, Wisconsin, in early 1928."

Coughlin had been an electrical engineering student of Mathews and he was as ardent a stater as they come. Class president, he enjoyed a stellar career on campus, both as a student and athlete. He was a standout in every sport, including football, baseball, basketball and track. He also was a champion bowler. The 1910 yearbook lauded Coughlin as Collegian sports editor, who "writes his articles with a stick of lunar caustic dipped in a dynamite cartridge filled with nitroglycerine and blood."

In his graduation address, Coughlin spoke lovingly of his four years at SDSC: "How sweet are the memories which keep rushing in our minds as we are gathered here and realize that it is the last time we will be together as students. We are loathe to leave the old walls that have guarded us so well. It is hard to break away from our student friends. With bowed heads we bid our instructors adieu and listen to their wishes of Godspeed. ...

"Together we toiled and played and won and lost. Always in unity. Now we separate. Each one must take up his work and fill his niche, making the world better for having lived in it."

Closing his remarks, Coughlin recited a short poem:

Coughlin Campanile

I would it were possible,
After years of grief and pain;
To find the arms of my Alma Mater
Around my neck again.

Decades later, Coughlin's gift stands as testament to his and, in turn, others' undying affection for State. The project was estimated to cost $15,000 to $20,000, and Coughlin gave SDSC the authority to pick the architect, call for bids and do the building. Construction was to start in the fall of 1928 and finish during the summer of 1929.

The Campanile, explained a story in the Sept. 18, 1928, Collegian, "will harmonize in architecture with the campus entrance, the Sylvan Theatre and the Lincoln Memorial Library. These three structures are of red brick trimmed with Bedford stone. The tower will be of a height that will dominate the campus, town and surrounding country. In addition to providing elevation for the electric chimes and clock, the Campanile will have an open side toward the Sylvan Theatre for a moving picture machine and flood lights that will reach the stage."

As the plans evolved, specifications for the Campanile called for a tower 165 feet high and 30 feet wide at the base. To match the new library, the structure was built of red brick and Bedford stone. The first 24 feet were constructed entirely of stone, with four approaches and one entrance door on each side and eight steps measuring 8 feet wide leading to the approaches.

The next 94 feet were built of red brick. Two casement windows were located at each side of the structure. At the top, casement doors were made to open out on iron and stone balconies at each side. Above those features was the 37-foot chimes chamber built of Bedford stone. Topping off the Campanile was a copper cap, or crown, 8 feet high, with four leaded glass openings, behind which was placed a 1,000-watt light. An iron stairway 110 feet long led to the observation room, located just below the chimes room at the top.

For the chimes, Coughlin chose a set of 18 tones to be electrically operated from a keyboard in the control room at the base of the tower. He also opted for an automatic Westminster chime device to sound each quarter-hour and strike the hours in the same tones and manner as the famous Westminster clock in London. In addition, he ordered an electric concert player, which operated with perforated rolls similar to a player piano, with each roll playing a concert that ran from 10 to 30 minutes before automatically rewinding.

Placed atop the Campanile's light-flooded dome was an 8,000,000-candle-power airplane beacon light to revolve at a rate of six revolutions per minute, throwing out a beam of light visible at night to planes 100 miles away and at an altitude of about 5,000 feet. In the daytime, it was anticipated that the tower could be seen from 20 miles away. Months after the building was completed, President Pugsley announced that P.R. Crothers, father of Dean Harold Crothers, reported seeing the beacon light of the Campanile at his farm near Badger, 35 miles from Brookings.

The low bid — $50,679 — was awarded to a Brookings company, Wold-Mark Construction. Aberdeen Engineering did the wiring. The design came from architects Perkins & McWayne of Sioux Falls. The final cost of the project totaled nearly $75,000.

During construction, which went at a pace of two and a half feet a day, Coughlin wrote in a letter: "I forget what the Campanile was going to cost when we started and I am sure we are going to forget what it costs when it is finished, if it pleases my old friends and does some good for the student body."

June 10, 1929, as part of commencement exercises, Coughlin laid the cornerstone of the Campanile, using the same trowel President Calvin Coolidge had used two years earlier for the memorial stone at Sylvan Theatre. A sealed metal box placed in a recess in the stone included a copy of the latest State College catalog; copies of the Industrial Collegian, containing stories on the tower and commencement exercises; information on Coughlin; and other information deemed to be of historical importance.

Chiseled into the Bedford stone above each of the four entrances were the inscriptions: "Louisiana Territory Purchased April 30," "Land Grant Colleges Established July 2, 1862," "South Dakota State College Founded February 21, 1881," and "State of South Dakota Admitted February 22, 1889."

But the Campanile was more than a mere building. Said Coughlin of the grand plan: "... the dignity of the structure might symbolize the majesty and the dignity of the state, that the notes of its beautiful chimes might be understood as a call to the student sons and daughters of the state to avail themselves of the educational opportunities afforded by the generosity of the people of the state ... and that the beacon light might point always toward the realization of the dream that was in the hearts of the pioneers."

The Coughlin Campanile was set for completion by the 1929 Hobo Day on Nov. 2. "Old Faithful," the 650-pound bell purchased for the college by the Dakota Territories in 1885, was mounted in the chimes tower dome and was ready to announce football victories. But, delays in shipment of the white Bedford stone for the top of the tower pushed the final date back a few weeks.

Constance Mark Goodwillie, class of 1938, was about 10 years old when her father's company, Wold-Mark Construction, built the Campanile.

"It was a very important event in Brookings and at the college," Goodwillie says of the Campanile construction. "Nothing like it had been done before. ... To have this structure going up out in the prairie, it looked very high."

Goodwillie, whose family's home was on the southwest corner of Fourth Street and 11th Avenue, remembers the pride she felt as her father took on such a grand project: "I used to ride my bicycle up and look up and here he was, standing way up near the top. I was pretty impressed."

Asked whether her father talked about the project at home, she laughs: "We probably didn't talk about anything else. It was just a big event. People who had never seen one were intrigued with it. And most people had not seen one. I had not seen one until long after that one was built. I just thought it was the only one in the world."

On Dec. 18, 1929, the Collegian reported an audience of more than 5,000 people for the inaugural concert of the Charles Coughlin Campanile chimes. The program consisted of three units — the first was church hymns; the second, Christmas songs; and the third, favorite selections. The following spring, the Campanile welcomed its first visitors,

The 165-foot-tall Coughlin Campanile graces the campus of South Dakota State University.

with more than 1,500 ascending the 180 steps.

Troy Bouman, class of 1994, holds the fastest record for climbing the Campanile. In 1992, he raced up the 180 steps in 32 seconds.

Robert Burris, class of 1936, grew up close to campus at 915 Ninth St. He was 15 when the Campanile was built.

"It was just one-half block east of our house," says Burris, who was born in 1914. "We watched that thing go up. Of course, it was quite a structure. It was visible from all over the place."

With a laugh, Burris adds: "When they finally got the Campanile up, you know, they had bells in it. They started the chimes every quarter of an hour and ran 'em all night long. It kept everybody in town awake until there was enough screaming that they terminated the chimes at 10 at night."

Still, the Campanile inspires great loyalty and a deep sense of pride. Miller explains that in addition to the universal ideals the building represents, individuals also find their own sense of meaning. He cites a poem written by an SDSC faculty member and published in the Nov. 13, 1929, Collegian:

> *And now in the bell-tower are musical chimes,*
> *the symbols of loyalty, beauty, and peace,*
> *Singing their message to hearts turned to hear,*
> *An uplifting message that never shall cease*
> *To call to endeavor, to cheer, and inspire;*
> *This gift of the old world, at home in the new.*
> *Each day will remind us that all that is best*
> *Shall live on forever, the lovely, the true.*

In October 1930, the Collegian reported that Coughlin arrived to inspect his tower, but the guard on duty refused to let him into the locked control room that operated the chimes.

"When Mr. Coughlin found the room locked, he asked, without introducing himself, if he might have the keys to gain entrance. The guard explained the situation, and no amount of persuasive talk would turn the guard from his duty."

A member of Coughlin's party asked, "You would let a friend of President Pugsley's in, wouldn't you?"

The guard shook his head and responded, "No, I wouldn't even if Charles Coughlin asked it."

"Well, this is Mr. Coughlin," the friend replied.

Unmoved, the guard asked: "How do I know who he is, maybe it is his brother or somebody else?"

As time passed, the Campanile became a symbolic fixture, towering over the changing campus and the surrounding prairie. Although, 30 years later, area birds continued to have trouble navigating around the obstruction.

Reporting that the building was a night hazard for feathered friends, the Collegian noted on May 3, 1950: "The imposing brick structure has snuffed out the life of at least three birds, apparently migrating through this area, and found dead at the base of the Campanile the next morning."

The worst casualty was a mallard duck, the campus paper said, which "probably worrying about his income tax statement, smashed into the side of the Campanile so hard one night he mushed about an inch and a half of his bill as if it were a dried cracker. The poor mallard didn't have a chance."

The Campanile's original 18 tubular bell chimes have been removed and replaced with a state-of-the-art "Americana" 318 Digital Auto-Bell Carillon. The digital technology uses encoded cards and pre-programmed functions, and a keyboard for manual playing of the carillon is located in Lincoln Music Hall. The carillon follows a set playing schedule with an early morning weather bell, late morning and early afternoon musical selections, and Westminster chimes on the half hour.

Nearly 70 years after the Campanile rose on the State campus, a fund drive began for a major restoration project that would return Coughlin's gift to its original glory. The effort, co-chaired by 1964 grad Sid Bostic and his wife Bonnie, class of 1967, drew more than $600,000 in donations from 3,500 people.

Once again, birds made the news. Crews working atop the Campanile found themselves knee-deep — really — in pigeon poop.

Writing for the Sioux Falls Argus Leader, Chuck Cecil reported that workers had to clear away about five cubic yards of pigeon droppings before they could tuck-point joints and remove damaged limestone blocks.

On Sept. 22, 2001, members of the Brookings and SDSU communities, including distinguished alumni and special guests, gathered for the rededication. The ceremony, which had been planned for months, called for the Pride of the Dakotas Marching Band to play "God Bless America." Just days after the tragedy of the 9/11 terrorist attack on the United States, the performance was more fitting than event organizers could have imagined.

Alumni Association president Denny Everson, class of 1973, told the crowd of about 800: "The repairs were desperately needed and they came none too soon. I'm confident the restoration project will maintain her as a significant and famous landmark for a long period of time. Without question, the Campanile will always be the icon of SDSU."

In addition to the extensive restoration work, the project also fixed a longstanding error etched in the base of the building — South Dakota formally was admitted to statehood on Nov. 2, 1889. The earlier date in February marked congressional passage of an enabling act that set the statehood process in motion. Oddly, though, the original box filled with items to withstand the passage of history remained unfound.

Chapter 13

Coolidge Sylvan Theatre

Coolidge Sylvan Theatre, more than any other spot on campus, symbolizes the extraordinary bond between South Dakota State and its many generations of students.

A combination of gifts from several classes, the outdoor theater began as a vision of the beloved art teacher Ada B. Caldwell. It was designed to take advantage of the natural slope of the land just west of where the Lincoln Memorial Library was built.

The Sioux Falls architecture firm of Perkins & McWayne, which had designed the library, prepared and donated the plans for the theater. The front stage wall and stage steps used a ruble stone design. Red brick and imitation stone formed the gateways and stage entrances to harmonize with the brick and Bedford stone of the library and main campus gateway.

On campus to dedicate the new library Sept. 10, 1927, President Calvin Coolidge and his wife, Grace, laid the cornerstone for Sylvan Theatre, which

First lady Grace Coolidge and President Calvin Coolidge apply finishing touches to the Coolidge Sylvan Theatre on Sept. 10, 1927.

resulted in renaming it Coolidge Sylvan Theatre. The 9-by-2-foot granite stone was etched with an inscription to commemorate the Coolidge visit.

"It polishes to a dark mahogany, which blends perfectly with the ruble stone wall of the theater," reported the Sept. 1 edition of The Brookings Register. "The inscription in sunken letters will stand out strikingly in white on the mahognay background."

How the name Sylvan was given is not recorded. However, the dictionary definition — living or located in a wooded area or abounding in woods or trees — offers a fitting description. An undated account explains that the original developers "planted trees, shurbs and vines to evoke the sylvan effect of this amphitheater."

Quiet and peaceful, the theater has been the setting for many outdoor campus activities throughout the decades — graduations, concerts, plays, summer school lectures and May Day celebrations.

"My commencement was held in the Sylvan Theatre," recalls Mary Louise DeLong, class of 1929, the first class to enjoy outdoor commencement exercises at Sylvan Theatre.

Years later during another graduation ceremony, DeLong notes, "One of the newscasters, Chet Huntley, was to give a talk. He just got started and it rained hard. Everybody either left or went to the library."

The unpredictability of the weather was largely responsible for chasing commencement exercises indoors after more than 40 years. From about 1928 to 1973, Coolidge Sylvan Theatre hosted the event. The potential for rain as graduation dates moved earlier into May, along with increasingly bigger crowds, led to the switch to Frost Arena.

Sylvan Theatre's iron gate was a gift from the class of 1921, the East wall from the class of 1926, the South wall from the class of 1927, and the center wall from the class of 1928.

In the years that followed, the class of 1929 added the balcony with a $750 donation. Located at the back of the stage, the balcony was built with the same color brick as the theater and trimmed in Bedford stone. The class of 1930 pitched in with four concrete benches.

The class of 1931 presented the 5-foot statue of Tetonkaha, a Sioux Indian maiden, to incorporate in the theater design. State grad M. Krete Kendall Miller carved the statue out of Bedford stone to match its surroundings. The class of 1932 provided the lighting.

The story told is that a soldier found Tetonkaha lost in the prairie and returned her to her tribe. She repaid the kindness by warning him of a pending attack by the Indians. It was also said that she had fallen in love with the

Gifts from the classes of 1921 (a), 1926 (b), 1927 (c), 1928 (d), 1929 (e), 1930 (f), and 1931 (g). (Photo courtesy of Eric Landwehr)

soldier, who was with a detachment at a fort on Oakwood Lakes. When her people discovered that she had aided the soldiers, they cast Tetonkaha into the lake and she drowned.

Retired history professor John Miller writes in the Brookings County History Book that details are hazy about the relationship between Native Americans and Oakwood Lakes.

"Before the white people arrived," explains Miller, "Native Americans had often made the lakes, which they called 'Te-tan-Ka-hoak' or 'Tetonkaha,' their headquarters or a stopping point."

Other than that, however, Native American activities around Tetonkaha were sometimes shrouded in mystery and legend, according to Miller. Where legend leaves off and reality begins is unclear.

A.B. Crane, an early faculty member of SDSC, told Tetonkaha's story in a poem. The last verse details how her spirit lives on at Oakwood:

> ... time has wrought many changes,
> The Indian no longer roams,
> The valiant victorious soldiers,
> Have returned to their wives and homes.
> And now the settlers' cabins,
> Rest near Tetonkaha's shores.
> And oft on a wild autum evening
> When the west winds whistle and roar,

A cry sounds over the water
A weird and tremulous cry,
'Tis a heron, says the settler,
Tis a loon, the children reply.
But what is the sound that disturbs them
Coming so shrill o'er the wave?
'Tis the Indian maiden's warning
Her pale face hero to save,
For oft on a moonless evening
When the winds are blowing bleak
Thither returns her brave spirit
Its earthly hero to seek.

On June 3, 1963, South Dakota State College unveiled a plaque that was mounted on the south side of Coolidge Sylvan Theatre, paying tribute to Caldwell:

"Hers was the vision which brought this theatre to us. A devoted and inspiring teacher, a skillful and courageous administrator, and an artist who created lasting beauty."

Chapter 14

Clock Tower

The graduating classes of 1922 and 1923 combined their memorial funds and presented South Dakota State College with a clock.

Placed in the tower of Old North, the gift overlooked the campus to the south and west until Old North was torn down in the 1960s. For generations of students, the clock served as a constant reminder of how much time they had to get to their next class or return to the dorm before the doors closed for the night.

In fact, according to the March 30, 1949, Collegian, the convenient excuse of not knowing what time it was led to the gift of the clock:

"It all started back in 1923 and the years before. The gay young blades of that time seemed to find as much trouble getting the ladies into the dorms on time as they do today. In those days they had trouble getting to class on time, too. There was no campanile so the logical excuse for being late was the delin-

---

Aggie School Clock Tower on the grounds of Tompkins Alumni Center.

quent did not know what time it was."

Collegian files revealed that one student in particular, Lorenz Lippert, was the most time-challenged. But, he was not the only one. The solution, everyone agreed, was a clock big enough and high enough to be seen by all. To prevent excuses that the clock couldn't be seen, they decided to light it.

A box at the top of the tower held the working parts of the clock. A shaft, which ran through the tower, was turned by a system of weights and pulleys that made the clock's hands move. The clock had to be wound once a week and was set to the master clock in the Administration Building.

Yet, the Old North clock wasn't always so reliable — as one unfortunate fellow opined in his "Ode to the Campus Clock" in the May 4, 1926, Collegian:

> *Moonlight and her*
> *Beside me,*
> *How lovely*
> *Everything is*
> *At eight o'clock.*
> *"Tempus fugit"*
> *So the Latins say.*
> *Moonlight and her*
> *At nine o'clock*
> *What a pleasant*
> *Evening to*
> *Remember.*
> *Again we forget*
> *That tower clock*
> *Until the dorm is locked.*
> *How oft in the*
> *Evening the*
> *Lowly freshman*
> *And the senior too*
> *Has been fooled by*
> *That campus clock.*

The third building to rise on the State campus, Old North was built in 1887. It was razed in 1962 to make way for Shepard Hall. At that time, the clock faces were dismantled and stored. In 1981, thanks to the foresight of longtime college registrar David Doner who suggested saving the clock faces

Old North, home to clock faces for almost 40 years. (Courtesy South Dakota Ag Heritage Museum)

at the time Old North was torn down, the clock was restored as part of an exhibit in the Agricultural Heritage Museum for the university's centennial celebration.

A year earlier, Chad Kono, class of 1970, had been hired as the executive director of the Alumni Association. When he arrived on the job, Kono says the new alumni building, which had been built in 1976, still lacked a finished courtyard. The council wanted to see that project completed. The first design proposed a 10-foot-high brick wall intended to block the view of the parking lot to the west.

"That didn't meet with much enthusiasm," recalls Kono. "At the same time, they were going to restore the clock as part of the exhibit at the Ag Museum."

However, the 1922 and 1923 grads, who had been approached for funding to restore the clock, wanted to know what the plans were beyond the exhibit.

Says Kono: "They gave the clock once and now we were asking them to restore it. The university didn't have any permanent plans but to put it back in storage. They (the grads) said that was not good enough."

During the discussions, Kono happened to stop by the storage area west of Coughlin Alumni Stadium and found the bell from Old Central, the first and only building on campus in 1884. In its days, the bell was used to start and end classes.

"So we had a clock coming out of the Ag Heritage Museum, we had this old bell, and we had this courtyard with a 10-foot wall that nobody wanted," Kono says. "So, I said, if we're going to build a wall, why not make it a little taller and put these two old pieces of memorabilia in a clock tower. The idea caught on."

Kono laughs and adds: "The wall was forgotten about and we did a patio with sunken berms. What started out as a cement patio got out of hand."

The top section features the clock in a reproduction of the Old North tower. The center section is a belfry from Old Central and contains the Victory Bell — also known as Old Faithful. The clock mechanism sits in full view through a window in the bottom level of the tower.

Despite the new location, the hands of time remain no match for Mother Nature. All it takes is a strong prairie wind to wreak havoc with the best of scheduling intentions.

One of the three major contributors to the project was Millie Bylander, who donated to the cause as a memorial for her son, John, a 1943 engineering graduate. Bylander, a lieutenant in the Air Force, was killed on Aug. 10, 1949, in an airplane crash near Whitehorse, Yukon, Canada, while leading a squadron of F-51 fighters to an airfield in Michigan. The courtyard is named after him.

Also pitching in were alumni from the "aggie school." (From 1911-1961, the SDSC agriculture school served as a high school for area farm children.)

"They had a very loyal bunch of alumni," says Kono, noting that the bell tower was named after the "aggies." (Old North had been home to the aggie school for a period of time.)

The third major contributors were the Richards brothers — Ernest, class of 1943, and Morgan, class of 1953. Ernest also was a member of the math faculty at SDSU. The brothers made a donation as a memorial for parents had who made sacrifices to send their children through school.

Chapter 15

Memorial Gateway

Understated and quietly dignified, the Memorial Gateway has watched over decades of campus traffic while getting little recognition in return.

The Gateway — built in 1923 with funds from the class of 1924 — is older than both Coughlin Campanile and Coolidge Sylvan Theatre. Yet, the gift received only a fraction of the fanfare and notoriety of its more prominent counterparts.

In fact, the Gateway is not even in its initial spot nor does it span its original width. It was relocated only four years after being built. Scant information exists about the first location, but the best estimate available is that the Gateway was moved about 60 to 100 feet south along Medary Avenue to where it sits today.

This much, however, is known.

Construction on the Gateway began in early September 1923 by Wold-Mark, the same company that built the Campanile. The class memorial was planned and designed by Herold Palmer, class of 1924, who, the Sept. 18,

---

The Memorial Gateway, a gift from the class of 1924, as it is seen today.

The original site of the Memorial Gateway which stood from 1923 to 1927. A dirt road ran through the center of campus past Old Central and the Administration Building.

1923, Collegian said, "should be highly congratulated for his work."

"The college has long felt the lack of an appropriate entrance to the large and beautiful campus," reported the Collegian, "so this Memorial Gateway will add considerably to the improvement of the college grounds."

That entrance location was fleeting. Barely four years later, the Aug. 18, 1927, Brookings County Press noted: "Following the recommendations of the officers of the Alumni Association and friends of State college in Brookings, the main pedestrian entrance to the college campus is being placed at the end of Ninth Street."

The group that had studied the issue determined that the old road through campus marred the beauty of the landscape and, with the increase in motorist traffic and student body numbers, had evolved into a dangerous driveway. The new location would be for pedestrians only and the old road running diagonally across campus would be removed.

The Press reported: "The new location of the entrance and gateway is ideal in that it faces down Ninth Street, one of the main approaches to campus from downtown. There is also an ideal natural opening in the trees at that point."

The new plans for pedestrian traffic put the start of the sidewalk at the relocated Memorial Gateway and ran the walk along the outskirts of the newly built Sylvan Theatre. One walk branched off to the then-new Lincoln Library before extending to the engineering building. Another walk headed off to meet the one that ran between the Administration Building and the dormitories.

Memorial Gateway

Although little-noticed and not well-documented, the Memorial Gateway has withstood the passage of time and campus growth. In doing so, the class of 1924 achieved what Collegian editors in 1923 deemed the noble purpose of a class gift.

"A class memorial should typify faith, hope, loyalty and charity," the editors wrote in the Feb. 13, 1923, edition, urging the class of 1925 to come up with a worthy legacy. "Its faith in the institution should be suggested by its very permanency; faith in the endurance of the alma mater, which is a lasting one. The hope that a memory of deeds well done and lessons will not fail to profit him who enters here."

The proper memorial, continued the editors, "should signify a class well-united in loyalty by the unanimity of the gift of each student, the only permanent thing we leave to point to those who follow that we passed this way. It (indicates) charity in the usefulness which it performs, in the service which it renders to those who may use it in years to come. With these points in mind, a memorial cannot be a failure."

Chapter 16

Old Central Archway

Old Central

When virgin was the soil, and all around
there stretched unbroken prairie, fields untilled,
Where plow had never stirred the mellow ground,
Thy stately walls were reared upon the sod
By men whose minds with hope were ever filled

From out thy halls to deeds with trials fraught,
Have passed the winners of a people's praise,
Each in his place his task has nobly wrought.
In hamlet, far or near, where e'er he dwells,
His thoughts are oft of thee and college days.

Still stand! and may thy tributes e'er be raised,
Thy name inspire to deeds of valor true,
And may thy form, whereon we oft have gazed,

Pictured above, the pediment taken from Old Central when it was razed in 1962 now adorns the lobby of the Northern Plains Biostress Laboratory. (Photo courtesy of Eric Landwehr)

> *Bid welcome unto coming eager throngs*
> *And yield to us a memory ever new.*
> — 1910 Jack Rabbit

The first building to rise up on the prairie campus of South Dakota State is long gone. Old Central — deemed an "eyesore" by 1929 — was torn down in 1962 to make way for the future.

The only vestige is the triangle that sat above the arched front door. Rescued from a coal pile north of the rodeo grounds, the triangle, or pediment, found new life in the Northern Plains Biostress Lab, where it was integrated into the lobby exhibit.

Construction started on Central in the fall of 1883, two and a half years after Dakota Territory legislators endorsed the concept of an agricultural college. For its time, the four-story building was impressive — cream-colored bricks, Mankato cut freestone trim and iron cornice.

Under the original plans, Central was to be the north wing of a larger building. But, that vision never came to pass. The $20,000 allotted ran out before the interior was finished.

Central, which finally was completed in 1885, first housed the entire school, from the janitor's room and laboratories in the basement to the boys' dorm on the top floor. On the floors in-between were the president's and matron's rooms, chapel, library, reading room, classrooms, and a professor's room. As State's campus grew, Central served as a boys' dorm, class building and Extension service building.

By the time Central was 40 years old, however, its luster was lost. The Jan. 22, 1929, Collegian editorialized that Old Central and its dated counterpart Old North were "pretentious old edifices in their day, but now nothing but worn-out shells amid structures of modern architecture."

The two buildings, said the Collegian, were "truly eyesores in comparison with the other buildings."

Old Central was razed in 1962 and in its place rose a new science building — Shepard Hall. Nearly 30 years later, when the Biostress lab was built in 1993, John Awald, director of the Agricultural Heritage Museum, saw an opportunity to integrate the old with the new.

Awald was working with Barb Hartinger, director of ag communications, on the lobby exhibit for the state-of-the-art lab building.

"I knew that the pediment and some of the stonework for Central were stored out in the old coal pile," says Awald. "I thought the pediment would

Old Central Archway

1910 Jack Rabbit photograph of Old Central, the first building on the campus.

fit into the structure of the Biostress. ... I think it reminds people of the first building, which is no longer here."

Awald says the museum also owns some of Central's original stonework, which eventually will be used in landscaping at Woodbine Cottage, home to the university's president.

Chapter 17

Woodbine Cottage

I f the walls of Woodbine Cottage could talk, there would be few details lost in the history of the State campus.

Lewis McLouth, the second president of Dakota Agricultural College, had Woodbine built in 1887. In the 116 years since, Woodbine has been home to nearly all of the school's presidents. Substantially larger than the typical "cottage," it is one of the last early structures to remain standing.

The home sits at the corner of Medary Avenue and Harvey Dunn Street and offers a showcase of South Dakota turn-of-the-century architecture. The style is referred to as Queen Anne.

McLouth sold Woodbine in 1896 to a holding company of Brookings citizens, who sold the house to the state of South Dakota. For a brief period, a converted Woodbine served as a girls' dormitory and took on the identity of the Girls' Cottage. For the 1901-02 school year, Woodbine was transformed

Pictured above, the front door of Woodbine Cottage in 2003. (Photo courtesy of Eric Landwehr)

Picture of Woodbine Cottage taken from the 1907 Jack Rabbit yearbook.

into a campus music facility.

James Chalmers, the fourth college president serving from 1903-06, brought the presidency back to the residence. Since then, nearly all of the institution's presidents — current President Peggy Gordon Miller is the 16th — have lived in Woodbine for all or part of their tenures.

Woodbine also has hosted an impressive array of guests, from foreign dignitaries and politicians to famous artists, poets, writers and musicians. From her vantage point, Miller says living in the presidential home is a wonderful existence.

"You begin to feel that you are the front room of the campus," she says. "There is a lot of sense of history living in it."

Miller is particularly delighted to have secured an original pattern book, from which Woodbine was ordered. Palliser's American Cottage Homes, based in Bridgeport, Conn., came out with two catalog editions — 1878 and 1888.

When McLouth built Woodbine, says Miller, "there were only two ways you could get a house on the prairie. If you had $2,500, you could get it from Sears and they sent (the pieces) by train. Or, you could order from a pattern book for $750."

In a special 1981 centennial publication, the late Hilton Briggs, who served as president from 1958-75, said Ellwood C. Perisho, the sixth president, took a leave of absence from his duties in 1918 after falling ill. A serious flu epidemic spread across the campus and six students died. Woodbine was used as an infirmary to care for the sick.

Albert Pugsley, the architect son of president C.W. Pugsley, designed a remodeling project for the residence in 1930, adding an upstairs bedroom and bath on the north side and a first-floor sunroom on the west side. After World War II, a utility room and small living area were added to the north rear side of the home.

On Saturday, Dec. 26, 1931, local contractor Matt Heslopp was driving by Woodbine shortly after 7 a.m. and saw flames through a living room window. He woke the Pugsley family and helped Albert Pugsley douse the flames with a fire extinguisher. The blaze caused about $1,500 in damage.

In 1984, after outgoing President Sherwood Berg moved out and before his successor, Ray Hoops, moved in, Woodbine went through a badly needed overhaul. SDSU physical plant employees and community volunteers pitched in and carried out a year's worth of restoration work in two months. New hot water heat was installed, electrical wiring and wallpaper were replaced, plaster was removed and new windows and carpet were put in.

Today, as Miller — the university's first female president — wraps up her sixth year in office, Woodbine is on the verge of another round of renovations.

Chapter 18

Power Play

In the spring of 1951, after several decades of relative calm, South Dakota State College slipped back into an abyss of campus politics. This round of unrest had started three years earlier, in 1948, when all the members of the agronomy department refused to sign their contracts for the coming school year.

According to a brief summary of the events, SDSC President Fred Leinbach then met with department head W.W. Worzella and fired him. At Leinbach's request, the Board of Regents called Worzella and Dean of Agriculture A. M. Eberle to appear before the board.

Worzella argued at the meeting that each man in his department played a key role. He demanded universal raises for all his employees at a time when funding, as is often the case, wasn't in abundance.

Worzella later apologized to Leinbach, and the president withheld his

---

A student's sign posted to a tree in response to the resignation of President Leinbach.

recommendation for dismissal. Any resolution, however, was short-lived.

At the March 7, 1951, regents meeting, a plan was presented and approved to reorganize the college's agricultural division. In tandem with the plan, Leinbach offered his resignation "to place the issues involved above personalities ... rather than to attempt to lead a disorganized and uncooperative organization."

Fueling the dispute were the recommended dismissals of Worzella, Extension Director George Gilbertson and College Experiment Station Director I.B. Johnson. The notice was effective June 30.

"This action was taken," Leinbach said in a special Collegian Extra edition published April 2, 1951, "because they had repeatedly refused to cooperate with each other or the college administration."

Leinbach was pushing a reorganization plan that put both the Extension and College Experiment Station under the dean of agriculture instead of having the three report individually to the college president. The new hierarchy was known as the Purdue Plan, a form of organization typically found at land-grant colleges.

"The former directors were recommended for dismissal not only because they could not fit under the proposed plan, but also because of their insidious and underhanded tactics in trying to undermine the institution through creating dissent, in interfering with the legislative proposals which had been approved by the State Board of Regents and the State Board of Finance, in attempting to instill their staffs with a spirit of defiance of state and college regulations," Leinbach explained.

However, the men would not be dismissed without a hearing before the regents. That session was set for April 14, 1951, at 9 a.m. on the University of South Dakota campus. About a week prior to the hearing, Johnson, Gilbertson and Leinbach reached a compromise and Leinbach withdrew the charges against the pair.

The session was slated to focus on Worzella, but few of the individuals involved were left unscathed. In anticipation of the hearing, Gov. Sigurd Anderson said he might make a recommendation, but ultimately it was a matter for the regents to decide.

Others would not bow out so easily.

On April 4, angry farm groups descended on Pierre and adopted four resolutions: Have lawmakers investigate the situation at State; have the regents delay any reorganization until the probe is complete; reinstate the three department heads; and send a delegation to the April 14 meeting at USD.

An estimated 400 people showed up for the regents hearing in Vermillion, including farm group representatives who demanded that Leinbach, Eberle and Charles Dalthorp, the college finance officer, resign. And at one point, Johnson declared: "We have all been tarred by the same brush; let us be cleared with the same brush." Gilbertson echoed his sentiment.

Leinbach was the first to appear in the Saturday morning lineup. He read a prepared statement, citing specific incidents to support Worzella's termination. Among the accusations was the 1948 refusal to sign contracts.

"It is my sincere belief that this man has not rendered my office in the administration of South Dakota State College, the support, cooperation and loyalty to which the President and administration are entitled," stated Leinbach. "There are some instances of insubordination cited. The situation which has resulted as a result of the dismissal has not been pleasant and it is always regrettable when certain matters must be aired in public to the detriment of all concerned."

Other points of contention included a report from the Midwest Barley Association that it had not been able to obtain cooperation from South Dakota as it had the other Midwestern states. Leinbach also said that in November 1950 Worzella submitted three requisitions for out-of-state trips. Two were approved. Eberle turned down the third because it was against school policy to approve more than two such requisitions for any one trip.

Following that decision, Leinbach said, he received letters from outside groups objecting to the refusal to grant the travel requisitions: "Only three men knew this. Worzella, Eberle and Johnson, and it still got out."

Leinbach said the tensions of the relationship were obvious: "When we visit agronomy, we are met with an air of aloofness and lack of cordiality."

Finally, Leinbach blamed Worzella for delaying completion of the new ag hall because he had demanded that one entire floor be devoted to agronomy.

Next, H. M. Crothers, SDSC vice president and engineering dean, took the stand and supported Leinbach. According to the Collegian report, Crothers said the problems had been going on for at least five years and likely longer. After Crothers, the regents called upon Worzella to answer the charges.

In regard to the 1948 raise standoff, Worzella said only he held out his contract: "I withheld mine and asked for a conference with Leinbach to discuss adjustments of contracts of agronomy department members. This conference was denied and I was dismissed. Some ethics were involved in my dismissal. I was just told that my services were no longer needed but was never told my work was unsatisfactory.

"On June 1 pressure was brought on Dr. J. E. Grafius by Dean Eberle and President Leinbach to accept the position as acting head of the agronomy department. Two days later we had a conference. The statements of Dr. Leinbach indicate that at this conference I apologized. I did not apologize. However, our differences were settled."

On the matter of the travel requisitions, Worzella maintained that he did not leak the information. The building delay, he said, was a trivial matter and the blame did not rest on his office. Worzella also refuted the characterization of the "air of aloofness and lack of cordiality."

"My leadership can best be judged by the respect of members of the agronomy department," Worzella said. "Before today few knew of this air of aloofness and lack of cordiality."

Dean Eberle followed Worzella's testimony with support for both Leinbach and the farmers of South Dakota: "You people don't think for a minute that I'd sell you down the river. I'll fight for you."

The Collegian reported that Grafius appeared on behalf of Worzella and admitted that he had been offered the position of acting head of the agronomy department.

However, Grafius said: "Had I taken that job, I would have been a one-man department, I'm afraid. The rest of the department would have resigned."

The holdup of signing contracts happened, conceded Grafius, "But were we the only department on campus that withheld contracts?"

Leinbach drew considerable support, as did Worzella. Those who lined up behind the president included: Walter Conahan, student body president-elect; Orlin Walder, director of student affairs; R. B. Frost, head of the athletic department; George Phillips, head of the journalism department; and a few state legislators. Worzella had the farmers on his side.

Speaking for a seven-man committee chosen to represent the farm groups in the state, E. B. Hubbard said of Worzella, Johnson and Gilbertson: "If we lose these three men we'll be set back many years. If we lose any one of them we'll be set back many years."

The Collegian also quoted Art Thelin of Sioux Falls, who asked about the long-term impact: "How far will the ax swing after today? How many more of the State College faculty will have to go?"

Conahan, class of 1952, recalls heading to Vermillion with fellow classmates Larry Wagner and Bill Blankenburg, who shot photos for the Collegian.

SOUTH DAKOTA COLLEGIAN
Leinbach Resignation Follows Regents' Decision
Students Strike in Protest

Headline from the April 26, 1951, edition of the South Dakota Collegian.

"We sat in the front row," says Conahan. "The Board of Regents was up on the stage. The president was there, the dean of ag. Both were under fire with the Worzella deal. ... The president spoke, and then he said, 'There are some people who want to speak on my behalf.' There were other administrators and citizens. I don't know how it came about, but all of the sudden, I hear, 'Walter Conahan, president of the student body.' In effect, they called on me, so I went up and testified on his behalf. I think the students were behind him. ... He was a wonderful man."

In a stunning reversal of where events appeared to be headed, the Board of Regents met a week later in Huron on April 20 and 21 and offered Worzella a contract on the condition that "he will, in the future, give his full, willing and continuing cooperation to State College and its administrative head." The vote was 3-2 in favor of the contract. The regents unanimously declined to cede completely to the farm groups and asked for the resignation of Leinbach, Eberle and Dalthorp.

President Leinbach, having had the proverbial rug yanked out from under his feet, decided it was time to quit. Leinbach's notice touched off another round of controversy, this time with students striking in support of the president.

"An unofficial strike kept the majority of students out of classes Tuesday and whitewash signs decorated sidewalks in all quarters," reported the April 26 Collegian. "Cries of protest and appreciation echoed around the campus as members of the student body at State College held a mass demonstration to proclaim 'Dr. Leinbach day.' Posters indicated the desire of some students for the continued administration of President Leinbach."

The sentiment was not unanimous, though.

The Collegian story noted: "Disapproval of the action came from some members of the agriculture division. Paid political announcements were broadcast to counteract the announcement Monday night concerning the strike and Tuesday's activities. New signs appeared on the campus during the day, urging disapproval of the strike and petitions."

Tuesday morning, the campus awoke to whitewashed signs on sidewalks reading "Fred — the Students' Friend," "We're with you Fred" and "One College Head." More than 1,500 students, businessmen and residents gathered at Sylvan Theatre for an all-college assembly to honor Leinbach.

Student body president-elect Conahan praised Leinbach's work at State and proclaimed, "We are dedicating this day to Dr. Leinbach — the friend of the South Dakota State College students."

Leinbach received a standing ovation as he approached the microphone. He was presented with two scrolls — one with signatures of 65 local businessmen and one with signatures of more than 700 State students. Leinbach responded with appreciation and said he was honored that students felt close enough to call him by his first name. He also urged calm and rational thought.

"Be honorable and thoughtful," he said, "and act accordingly to these dictates. ... Let's not stoop. Let's uphold the dignity and honor of this student body, let's not degrade it. This institution has to go on; you're going to help it go on."

In closing, Leinbach added, to another standing ovation, "I cannot help but say I love you."

Despite Leinbach's departure, the so-called Worzella Affair was far from over. In the immediate days that followed, five SDSC students visited with Gov. Anderson. They said the regents' decision was not based on facts and called on the governor to air the reasons behind the decision. Anderson said he would write a letter to the chairman of the board, conveying the students' sentiments, but he would not get involved.

Seven years later, another Worzella controversy exploded. This time, Dr. Ephriam Hixson, who had been hired to head the dean-director system of administrating the agricultural divisions of the college, lit the fuse.

Hixson submitted a 41-page report to the regents and then-Gov. Joe Foss, detailing charges of maladministration and "character assassination" at the college. He called for a major housecleaning and urged firing then-SDSC President John Headley, Worzella, Gilbertson, Eberle, Joe Hill (district Extension supervisor), Jim O'Connell (Extension animal husbandman), and Bob Plyman (Deuel County agent).

To be sure, Hixson had some axes to grind. He had been hired to head the dean-director system for the ag college — the same system that Leinbach had proposed back in 1951 and the same system the regents directed to be instituted in 1956. However, the organization failed to materialize, as allegedly did other agreements made with Hixson when he was hired in May 1956. The Hixson report set into motion a probe by the regents.

To further complicate matters, President Headley was killed Nov. 29, 1957, in a hunting accident. Vice President Crothers, also dean of engineering, moved into the role of acting president as the regents searched for a new president.

According to Argus Leader stories published in January 1958, as the Worzella debacle continued to unfold, the regents determined that Hixson's appointment as chief of agriculture was "ill-advised, both as to Dr. Hixson and the college.

"The board finds that in the hiring of Dr. Hixson certain written commitments were not fulfilled, particularly in reference to furnishing him with a certain house upon his taking up his duties … and other commitments and agreements with him were not met."

Hixson reportedly complained bitterly that he had been promised a place to live, but the dwelling never became a reality. What's more, Headley removed Hixson from his position without, the regents said, "the sanction or approval of this board."

Citing insubordination as the cause, the regents fired Worzella and handed down a slate of administrative measures, starting with the institution of the dean-director system for all of SDSC's agriculture divisions. Under that plan, a dean would be in charge of all agricultural programs, including the directors of the Extension, the experiment station and the ag department. Dean Eberle and Extension Director Gilbertson were effectively a moot point, with both men set to retire June 30.

The board also ruled that all officials and staff members of the college refrain from making "personal, castigating or derogatory remarks" and conduct themselves "in a manner befitting their status." And, the regents demanded that county Extension agents and other personnel cease engaging in "pressure group activities" and obey college authorities or "seek employment elsewhere."

The board reminded the Extension agents that it was their duty to carry out programs as prescribed by their superiors. "It is not," the report said, "their function to engage in pressure group activities or to indulge in a quest for power … in which they have become tools in many cases, or in some cases at least, of individuals who are seeking to rise at the expense of others."

In addition, the regents found that the office of comptroller at the college had not "exercised proper control of the fiscal affairs thereof" and ordered that the office should be reorganized so that it would advise the president and assist in the financial affairs of the school.

Contrary to accusations, the regent report also said SDSC did not restrict academic freedom, no threats or reprisals were lodged against individuals testifying about conditions on campus, and there was no evidence of Headley having slandered anyone. Nor, reported the Argus, had the administration "violated the sacredness of human dignity."

The regents concluded that except for the disputes in the agricultural divisions and comptroller office, there existed a "wholesome attitude of cooperation and good feeling" at SDSC and the board commended the faculty for maintaining such a positive atmosphere.

As had been the case in 1951, the farm groups came to Worzella's aid.

A seven-man committee formed the Organization for the Advancement of Agriculture, with the slogan "A Non-Political Organization With No Political Motive." The group started publication of a "newspaper," called Fair Play. The first edition trumpeted the headline, What One South Dakota Newspaper Finds After Objective Study of State College Affair, and published editorials from the Hamlin County Herald-Enterprise of Hayti:

"Like most laymen, the editor had been disposed to credit the Board of Regents with sincerity in its efforts to clear up the dispute precipitated by Dr. Ephriam Hixson last summer. But its final disposition of the case that resulted in the summary discharge of Dr. Worzella ... for no good reason, and then its almost hysterical insistence that the public refrain from criticism or speculation placed a rather different aspect on the picture. ...

"As matters stand, the three men (Worzella, Eberle and Gilbertson) directly under fire of the board are pictured to the public as a group of petty, selfish troublemakers, with whose services South Dakota can well dispense in the interest of harmony. Nothing could be more wrong or misleading."

Fair Play called for a full and public airing of the facts: "Let's break this thing wide open even if it does disturb the folk who would have good men do nothing while evil is permitted."

The paper berated the regents for firing "the one man whose competence and fitness for his post are proved; a man who commands national acclaim for his scientific ability; and a man of the type South Dakota constantly seeks — in vain."

Next, continued the Fair Play editorial, the Board of Regents "coldly maligned ... the now deceased SDSC president, no longer here to defend himself. Then in Hitlerian gesture, it summarily ordered extension agents to keep their mouths shut. And finally, as a crowning insult, it demanded that the public forget the mess (and) allow peace and quiet to descend."

Months later, in the spring of 1958, the issue remained unresolved — at least in the minds of some in the state's agricultural sector. Claiming that Worzella, Eberle and Gilbertson were denied a fair hearing and the regents' investigation was rigged, the Organization for Advancement of Agriculture published a third edition of Fair Play.

The implications of what took place ran deeper than the three ousted ag leaders, the grass-roots paper insisted: "There is grave danger that both State and the University may well be downgraded to third-rate institutions, staffed only with mediocre teaching talent and low-level research personnel. ...

"This downgrading would be the direct result of this injection of politics in our college management by the state regents board. Political control in our schools is both hateful and fearsome, and the South Dakota board's action has aroused resentment and apprehensions everywhere — not just at State and the University. The action may well lose our proud schools their accreditation."

If accreditation was withdrawn, the Fair Play editorial said: "South Dakota could find itself in a bad way for qualified teachers. Without recognized accreditation only third-raters and misfits will apply for posts here, while competent teachers will shun our state."

Worzella took his dismissal to court. He contended that he had permanent tenure, and that he could be dismissed only in compliance with tenure policy provisions. The Board of Regents maintained that the tenure policy did not abrogate its power to dismiss all officers, instructors and employees under its control. The state Supreme Court upheld the dismissal.

In 1960, two years after Worzella left for the American University of Beirut in Lebanon, the American Association of University Professors (AAUP) launched an investigation. In 1961, the group issued its finding that academic freedom and tenure were not secure on the Brookings campus. The AAUP censured the regents in 1962 for the Worzella case, putting the board on its blacklist of academic freedom violators.

After three decades, the Worzella affair was finally put to rest. It took the passage of time, people and a few new regental policies. In 1991, after two years of work by regents Executive Director Howell Todd and general counsel James Shekelton, the AAUP voted to remove the South Dakota Board of Regents from its blacklist.

"Academic freedom is fundamental to contemporary education, and the South Dakota Board of Regents has made it clear that the policies of the Board recognize and protect it through the Regental system," Todd said in a prepared statement released June 17, 1991. "It is important for the academy to know that academic freedom is protected in South Dakota and that there is no blemish on our record."

Chapter 19

Food Fight!

Long before the days of cappuccino, veggie burgers and salad bars, State students had no choice about what they ate and how much. They paid a lump sum and took what they got.

In turn, the student body routinely voiced increasingly rabid complaints about the College Food Plan, targeting both the quality and the quantity. It wasn't until massive protests in 1969, however, that the campus-run food service was dumped and private companies were allowed to bid on a contract to feed university students.

"I was on the 20-meal plan," recalls Wes Tschetter, class of 1969. "That was 20 meals a week. The only meal we did not eat on campus was Sunday evening. Food service was closed. There were very few restaurants in Brookings that could handle the college crowd. You either foraged or went to some restaurant. You kind of got by. The church groups used it as an oppor-

---

Pictured above, a cartoon from a sign held by a student protesting campus food service in 1967.

tunity to serve youth groups."

The issue of quantity left students with little option. Tschetter says: "You filled up on bread. Guys walked through and took six slices of bread. That was how people usually compensated."

It also helped to have a student worker at the end of the line tending the dessert table. Adds Tschetter, "She wasn't going to say anything if you took seconds."

The quality of the food was debatable.

Jerry Fiedler, class of 1970, says: "I didn't think it was that bad. I remember the food service director was real concerned about having all the food groups on your plate. She was a home economist and concerned about nutrition."

A little less charitable in his review, Tschetter comments: "Friday night was notorious. Fish was served. We Protestants, we just accepted it. But, it was not cooked. Fish needs to be properly prepared."

Jerry DeWald, class of 1969, was a resident assistant in Mathews Hall, and clearly remembers the dissatisfaction that swelled among the ranks of the student body and fueled a massive protest that ultimately brought about change.

"We were very dissatisfied with how the food service was being managed between Mathews and Brown," says DeWald. "The quantities were not fair. You could go through the line, for example, and a get a hot dog or a hamburger — not both, and not two. And, even if the person next to you in line didn't want one, you couldn't get theirs. It didn't seem fair to us and we were hungry, young people."

DeWald had a five-day meal ticket for each week, which meant he had to eat enough to last him through the weekend. Hungry, he would often head to his roommate's house in Aberdeen or his home in Watertown. His roommate lived on a farm, supplementing the pair's food intake with fresh bacon and eggs, which they would cook up illegally on a hot plate in their dorm room.

Civil disobedience sounds like the perfect antidote today, but it wasn't that easy in the late 1960s.

Tschetter says: "The big deal was, when you went through the line, they crossed off your number. Mine was 17363. That way, you couldn't go through twice."

This process worked against the students who planned one protest to leave their plates on the table.

"Then," says Tschetter, "they knew, among who left their plate, who was part of the protest. You were scared of being thrown out of school by Hilton Briggs with no due process."

Food Fight!

Headline from the April 8, 1965, South Dakota Collegian.

DeWald points out: "We were all pretty nervous. Those were the early days. All the men were eligible for the draft. If you got kicked out, you lost your deferment status."

Dissatisfaction with the food service, though, was nothing new. And, in all likelihood, that contributed to the problem. Any dissent — from the administrative perspective — was nothing more than the typical griping.

In 1958, the plan was simple. Students eating under the College Meal Plan received three "well-balanced" meals a day for $1.75. Seconds were allowed on milk, bread, butter and most of the main courses. That was considered to be a much better deal than students eating off campus for about $2 a day — no seconds, but they did have a choice of what to eat and when to eat it.

In defense of the food service, the program was entirely self-supporting. Electricity, heating, equipment and maintenance costs were shouldered by the College Cafeteria.

The students, however, were not sympathetic. In one anonymous letter to the Collegian editor, someone complained: "The $1.75 that I paid for 'three well-balanced meals' is an understatement. Yes, we got enough milk and ascorbic acid, but many times we didn't get the amount of meat it is reported we got. For an 85-cent supper we should have had good quality meat.

"Maybe people not eating on the Food Plan aren't acquainted with veal drumsticks, but they appear frequently on the plates going out the line — and later — show up uneaten in the garbage can. They are dipped in hot grease and are known to the freshmen as 'fried popsicles.' This low-protein, high-fat meat has little value to us. Warmed over liver also has little food value."

Salad servings were so small, the writer alleged, they must have been measured on a gram scale. There was, however, plenty of starch, "many times in the form of instant whipped potatoes, which made my mother comment, 'You appear well-fed.'"

By 1963, food continued to make front page news of the Collegian. Sophomores were being required to eat on the college food plan to keep the service from losing money. Then-food service director Ann Little rejected student complaints, telling the Collegian: "Students are and should be proud of such a unit as the Men's Dining Hall. Our meals are designed to provide a satisfactory balance of nutrition and taste."

In response to accusations of skimpy servings, she said, "Most students are satisfied with the amount of food." If greater portions were offered, Little added, the price of meals would increase. She also discounted the idea of a pay-as-you-go system, saying that it would discourage students from eating regular, well-balanced meals.

Although the Jungle offered variety and options, the union eatery also was subjected to criticism. The coffee price — 10 cents a cup in 1964 — was deemed too high. A student attempt at boycotting, however, failed. On the day they were supposed to forgo coffee, the Jungle reported washing the usual number of cups.

The spring of 1965 arrived without any appeasement. By this time, in addition to other issues, students were complaining that meal tickets were not transferrable. They also continued to battle against the food plan being mandatory and the lack of variety. Responding to complaints that students were not able to get more meat when they didn't take vegetables or potatoes, Miss Little explained: "The price of meat prohibits this, although twice the vegetable is permitted when the student doesn't take potatoes."

On Nov. 18, 1965, the Collegian reported that the "Annual I Hate Food Service" campaign was well under way. "Students eating in the Jungle upset at least three trays of food Nov. 10 and then dumped at least two tables again the next day in what was apparently the umpteenth annual protest against food service."

The assistant director of the Jungle food service, Mrs. Cassie O. Davis, told the student paper that anything could have sparked the protest.

"Students don't like to be told 'You have to do this,'" she said. "It was a normal reaction, even though it was a bit childish."

Food Fight!

> **ay-tipping latest fad**
>
> ## Annual 'I Hate Food Service' campaign begins
>
> By JANET WARREN
> Collegian Reporter
>
> ...udents eating in the Jungle upset at least ... trays of food Nov. 10 and then dumped ... at two tables again the next day in what was ...rently the umpteenth annual protest against ... service.
>
> ...rs. Cassie O. Davis, assistant director and ... manager at the Jungle, reported that the stu-...s' actions could have been spurred by any of ... things.
>
> ...RST, Mrs. Davis suggested that the students ... demonstrating against the newly-initiated ...ract food service program.
>
> "Students don't like to be told 'You have to do this,'" said Mrs. Davis. "It was a normal reaction, even though it was a bit childish."
>
> SECOND, problems with some new equipment recently installed in the Jungle may have initiated the action.
>
> "The Jungle just put in some new equipment and has had problems with its operation," said Mrs. Davis. "New ovens and french friers are being used and it will take a little while to learn how to use this equipment."
>
> FINALLY, she cited the breakdown of food service's budget as a possible reason.
>
> According to Mrs. Davis, only half of the $1.50 daily cost of food service is used for buying food. "The rest," she said, "is used to pay for employee wages, sales tax and lost silver, salt shakers, glasses and other dishes."
>
> "The protesting students don't hurt the food service administrators. We can provide more food if there is less wasted. When we no longer have to pay for extra items, food service will probably improve."
>
> THE MEN'S Residence Association plans to discuss food service during a regular meeting of the MRA executive council Tuesday, Nov. 23.
>
> The meeting will be open to all voting and non-voting members of MRA. Those attending the meeting will be asked to provide constructive criticism of each food service complex.
>
> FOOD SERVICE Committees have been established in all but West, Harding and Development Halls, where the committees are being planned. Representatives from each hall attend the regular meeting of the University Food Service Committee, which formulates food service policy.
>
> Men students with complaints for the committee may contact Bill Eisingson, Stan Michaelson A4, Bill Goddard E3 or Larry Kramer E3. Women students may present their complaints to Annette Belkonen S4, Corrine Frerichs S4 or Joyce Hodgson S3.

The Nov. 18, 1965 South Dakota Collegian announces new fad concerning the campus food service.

The Collegian weighed in with an editorial on Nov. 25, placing the blame for the "annual student-food service feud" on both sides.

"Students no doubt have some legitimate reasons for complaints about the quality — or lack of it — and the preparation of food," the editors wrote. "But tray-tipping, food-throwing and other childish actions are carrying the act of protest too far."

The paper also criticized the food service, pointing out, "Remaining aloof from the students' complaints, whether they are legitimate or not, will not solve the problem."

Terry Nelson, class of 1965, says the food rebellions he witnessed primarily took place in Brown Hall.

"There was a little bit of baked potato throwing," he chuckles. "It was not as much of a riot as you might think."

In fact, Nelson says he had no complaints about the food.

"We had great meals, by the way," he notes. "We probably ate better on campus than off. We had the best balanced meals."

In contrast to earlier years, the opposition was growing more organized. Students in different halls were establishing committees and representatives attended regular meetings of the University Food Service Committee. Not much changed, though, and on March 8, 1967, about 50 Brown Hall residents put on a protest.

Wearing T-shirts that read "Fire Miss Little!" and "Improve Food Service Now!" the students entered the dining room at about 5 p.m. After finishing their meals, they sat in place and played cards. By 6 p.m., the idea had caught on and the dining room was congested. According to the Collegian account, Miss Little was "hissed down" each time she appeared. Most of the demonstrators left by 6:15, with several of them leaving their trays on the dining room tables.

A week later, on March 16, about 350 students marched on the Administration Building with an audience of state newspapers and radio stations — and NBC's "Today Show."

About 20 students initiated the demonstration. One of the organizers, Sondra Ramsell, told the Collegian that students were upset about having their spring semester food service exemptions rejected. The protesters issued a twofold proposal: 1) Abolish the compulsory food service plan; and 2) issue a voluntary system of punch cards.

"In seeking a change in the present system, we feel that as college students we are mature enough to make decisions concerning our health and well-being," the students' statement read. "By instituting a voluntary punch ticket system, we would have the right to decide when, where and what we want to eat."

DeWald says he was not one of the ringleaders, but his involvement and RA status landed him in hot water with Briggs.

"I got called into his office," says DeWald. "He says, 'Look, you're representing me. Are you going to represent me well or poorly?' And, he asked me not to (protest) anymore. ... I think the public attention did help him look closer at the issue. I don't remember any more demonstrations."

Change, however, came slowly. A year later, on March 6, 1968, the Collegian ran a letter to the editor from DeWald. He said the quality of food had improved in the months after the 1967 protest, but was soon back to what it used to be.

"I used to think there was a difference between pork and veal, and pork and beef," DeWald wrote. "But all three of them are generally dry and have the distinct flavor and texture of wet corrugated cardboard, and the only difference is their physical appearance. Chicken should also be mentioned. It looks like a tasty tidbit while still on the plate, but after a bite, it's debatable whether it's chicken, rabbit, or squirrel; and how long it lay around dead before they 'prepared' it to feed the hungry masses is undeterminable."

It would take another two years before the Board of Regents approved a plan to relinquish food service at South Dakota State to a private company.

Tschetter says that decision was monumental.

"It was huge from the standpoint of change in public policy," he notes. "We were the first institution of higher education in South Dakota to have private food service."

The decision also put food service decisions back in the hands of students, a move that brought the system back nearly full circle to what it once was.

Sherwood Berg, class of 1947, says one of the women's dorms housed a cafeteria during his years on campus. But, in those days, it also was customary for local residents to offer dining facilities in their homes.

"They were boarding clubs," Berg explains. "They'd usually have a large room or a couple of rooms and they'd take on up to 50 students. The students organized into clubs (with) a set of officers — president, secretary, treasurer — and they paid the person that ran it. ...

"I was a member of a club two and a half blocks off campus. Mrs. Swanson's. On Eighth Street. It was very reasonable — $2.50, $3 a week. It was convenient and there weren't the lines that there were at the other place. And good food, too."

Chapter 20

Stadium for State

South Dakota State was about 30 years old and its student body 500 strong when construction began on State Field.

Construction on the modest facility, which was located at what today is known as Sexauer Track, began in 1916 and was completed in 1920. Boasting wooden stands, State Field served the campus well. Another three decades later, though, the size of the college, as well as its football program, had outgrown the stadium.

"It was really getting run down, to the point of being dangerous," says Harry Forsyth, athletic department business manager from 1955-65. (Forsyth went on to become assistant athletic director from 1965-80 and athletic director from 1980-90.) "In its time, it was a nice stadium. But, the stands just wore out. The wood deteriorated."

The dilemma, Forsyth explains, was whether to sink money into the old

Pictured above, Charles Coughlin in his 1908 football uniform.

or build new.

"A lot of people at the time thought that we didn't need a new stadium," acknowledges Forsyth. "We were between a rock and a hard place. We would have had to put quite a bit of money into the old one."

Ultimately, the decision was made to go with the new. From a practical standpoint, that made sense. What didn't to many people, however, was the initial plan for a double-sided stadium with both ends filled in — more Ohio State than South Dakota State.

Complicating matters was that the state refused to pitch in with any financial assistance. Nor was there any sentiment at the state level in favor of the project.

"The state fought us all the way," says Forsyth. "They were dead set against us using a cent of state money. It was pretty tough. We had to really scratch and scramble. When we had the first game, we didn't even have fence around it (the new stadium). But, we finally got that. It was a struggle."

More than 40 years later, on any given game day, thousands of people pass through the gates of Coughlin Alumni Stadium, unaware of the vision and the risk taken by a few on behalf of the many. The only lasting sign of the controversy that dogged the project exists in what is not there — no enclosed endzones, no track encircling the field, no submerged locker rooms.

Warren Williamson, class of 1951, returned to coach freshman football at State in 1956. He also coached wrestling for 17 years and headed up intra-

Artist's rendition of the proposed stadium when the fund drive was announced in 1957.

mural sports for 31 years. As a student, Williamson lettered in football and track three times. The strong support for a new stadium from a core group of alumni was natural, he says: "I think, having played in 1947-50, we moved into what many of us call the Golden Era at South Dakota State College."

The success of head coach Ralph Ginn's teams inspired fan loyalty and large crowds, explains Williamson, and, in turn, generated the feeling that the old State Field should be updated.

"We needed something better," says Williamson. "The crowds, particularly at the special ball games — the U games, Hobo Day — the crowds were just impossible to handle. And the wooden bleachers were in bad shape."

And yet, he laughs, the players loved the atmosphere: "It was great. The people were right on top of the field, on both sides and on the ends."

Williamson traces the push for the new stadium to Athletic Director R.B. "Jack" Frost and the Alumni Association. Frost, he says, was patently aware of how important the football program was to State and appreciated the strong feelings of alums, particularly those who had played on Ginn's winning teams after World War II. Ginn coached from 1947 to 1968.

The stadium struggle began in earnest during the fall of 1957. The Oct. 24 Collegian announced the start of a fund drive for a 14,000-seat stadium with the potential seating capacity of 24,000. The plans included locker and shower rooms for coaches, players and referees, a dirt track, restrooms and ticket rooms.

At the time, Frost told the Collegian, "If the drive is extremely successful, it's possible hard court and dormitory facilities could be included in the project."

The target completion date was the first home football game in the fall of 1959. But, Frost was realistic. "Everything depends on the donations," he said. "The big problem is securing enough money."

That certainly proved to be the case. By January 1959, the drive had yet to meet the $500,000 goal. The prospect of falling short was a definite threat. The Collegian reported Jan. 15, 1959, "The Alumni Committee is of the opinion that more interest and support must be forthcoming from the faculty, students, alumni, employees and friends of the college if the goal is to be achieved."

The campus paper quoted an anonymous committee member as saying: "Apparently many of the people interested in State College think that a few rich alumni will build the stadium."

The Feb. 12, 1959, Collegian made the case for a new facility, pointing out that State had the "poorest and most uncomfortable" stadium in the

North Central Conference. What's more, the paper said: "The athletic growth of State College is presently curbed for lack of facilities. A new stadium will enable State to schedule teams like K-State and Montana State regularly. The possibility of scheduling national track meets will be very good. Generally, it will enable State to graduate into a higher class of athletic competition."

The paper also cited enrollment predictions that would fill the old stadium, uncomfortable seating that left ticket sales untapped, and a press box that needed improvements to encourage better media coverage.

For students, an increased fee plan called for a maximum $15 contribution, or quarterly payments of $3. Seniors would be assessed $3 for the spring quarter; juniors, $3 per quarter for their remaining four quarters; and sophomores and freshmen, $3 per quarter for five consecutive quarters. By class, that meant seniors would contribute a total of $2,328; juniors, $8,868; sophomores, $11,925; freshmen, $14,970; and incoming students until 1966, $105,000.

By today's standards, $3 a quarter is pocket change. But, 40 years ago, that was hardly the case. Frank Kurtenbach, class of 1961, pitched in with the fund-raising effort. Still, he says, the student assessment was a lot of money for the times.

"Tuition was $36 a quarter," he remembers. "I lived in Gym dorm (the basement of the Barn) for a dollar a month. Back in those days, life was different. Burgers at Nick's were 10 cents. I worked for a dollar an hour."

Building a new stadium was farfetched enough. But, to enclose both ends?

"In hindsight," Kurtenbach says, "it would have been a good time to enclose it. But that was more than what most people wanted."

Jim Burg, class of 1963 and the father of four State grads, also reflects on the difficulty in getting students — who typically are cash poor and living for the moment — to buy into a long-range plan: "As a student, you don't become nearly as involved, as a general rule, as when you're alumni. Students are all strapped for money and any fee increase is seen as complicating that situation for them. They don't see as strong a connection to the university as they do later on. I'm not so sure you wouldn't have the same votes today."

By Jan. 15, 1959, the drive to raise money for the new stadium had generated $182,054.94. The Alumni Committee hired 1920 grad Charles Dalthorp to organize the fund-raising campaign. In early February, the Students' Association Board of Control voted 15-5 for a student election on the proposed $15 assessment. That fee was expected to raise another $135,000 to $139,000. Only undergrads were allowed to vote and a 60 percent majority was needed for passage.

Stadium for State

Thursday, March 19, 1959, the front page of the Collegian announced in big, block letters: ASSESSMENT FAILS. With a stunning 80 percent turnout, students voted 1,487 to 1,200 against the fee. A Collegian editorial attributed the defeat to two key interest groups — married students and out-of-staters:

"The married students evidently felt, and perhaps rightly so, that they could not afford the assessment. The out-of-staters had even more impetus to vote against the assessment. It isn't enough that the out-of-staters get hit hardest by the raise in tuition, but just before the election they find themselves being asked to purchase South Dakota license plates and pay sales tax on their cars. ...

"The defeat of the assessment isn't the end of the world. We will get a new stadium eventually. The assessment shouldn't have been a necessity to begin with. The alumni started to build the stadium and by all rights should have been able to do the job without a student assessment."

Perhaps, the Collegian surmised, there was a reason alumni didn't respond more favorably. The majority of grads left State and never heard another word, according to the editorial, "until they were asked, not so pleasantly, to contribute toward the Stadium for State."

Disappointed, but not undaunted, stadium supporters forged ahead. At a March 25 meeting in Sioux Falls, the Stadium for State Committee decided to pursue a scaled-back version of the project, building half the structure with a seating capacity of 5,000.

"We'll build just as far as our money will permit," Dalthorp reported as donations hit about $215,000, less than half of the $500,000 needed.

When students returned to campus in the fall of 1959, the Board of Control voted unanimously to put the assessment fee to another vote. Dalthorp told the Collegian that the stadium could not be built without student support. Pledges reportedly reached $262,500. If the assessment passed, the stadium committee would borrow $200,000 toward the half a million dollars needed.

According to an Oct. 8, 1959, account in the Collegian, the pledges broke down into four categories: students, $24,853.74; faculty, $20,011.11; local residents, $35,836.06; and alumni and friends, $181,799.20. The pledge amounts ranged from less than $100 to $25,000.

A week before the second vote, the Collegian reminded the student body in an editorial that State had one of the most outstanding physical education programs in its conference, but the poorest athletic facilities. The campus also had seen many new buildings go up since the end of World War II, but there had been no enhancements made to athletic facilities — not since 1945, nor 20 years prior.

"The stadium project is beyond the buck passing stage," the editorial reasoned. "It does no good for the students to point their fingers at the alumni and say, 'You should build it.' Most of us will be alumni soon. If the stadium is going to be built it must be a joint effort ...

"Progress is easy to oppose. South Dakota is full of small towns, and some that aren't so small, that are dying on the vine because of dyspeptic individuals who are chronic (naysayers). A town or an institution that is standing still is actually going backward. Progress never comes easy. New schools aren't built or streets paved, or water systems installed by merely wishing they were done. Someone has to pay."

Tuesday, Oct. 13, the measure failed a second time, with 60 percent of the student body, or 1,961 students, heading to the polls. This time, the margin was 1,061 against the assessment and 900 in favor.

Two weeks later, the Stadium for State Committee announced a petition drive to get the 60 percent of the signatures needed to assess students. But by Nov. 5, the group had collected only 500 of 1,800 signatures. The Collegian reported that Dalthorp was prepared to resign from the campaign if an interim goal of 1,400 signatures was not met. If the petitions succeeded, officials were planning to let bids for the stadium early in 1960.

Williamson recalls the frustration stadium boosters felt. He also voices the dilemma that gave rise to the opposition.

"I think a core of students felt that there were other needs as well," he says. "There was an awareness that the Barn, as a gymnasium facility for all the other sports, was pretty darn inadequate, too. Basketball was successful, too — they just packed the place."

Part of the frustration stemmed from the fact that the accomplishments of State's teams led to high expectations for performance, but people weren't lining up with fistfuls of dollars to build new facilities.

At the same time, however, Williamson allows that the initial stadium plan with both ends enclosed was too ambitious.

"You have to realize that the college at that time had never undertaken something so grandiose," says Williamson, taking a look at the larger picture. "You can go back to the Campanile, but that was an outright gift. I don't know of anything really that we had ever done of that size and enormity with that amount of gifted dollars."

The entire athletic staff was involved in the fund raising — Williamson, Forsyth, Stan Marshall. They were both expected to and excited to carry the ball. And, they soon discovered how difficult the task was. The concept of donating money, whether for a building project or scholarships, was new.

In fact, says Williamson, "the scholarship program hardly existed. We started IPTAM — I Pay Ten A Month. It was an appeal for a hundred and twenty buck donation. We even had a dollar a month. It was a struggle, but it was an introductory way to get alums and friends involved. ...

"People didn't quite understand what was going on in the world of athletics. You had a part-time job here, a part-time job there. The veterans had the GI Bill — that was the best scholarship going. But, it took a long bit of selling to generate giving, not just for scholarships but also for building purposes."

On the one hand, Williamson adds, the fight over the new stadium can be viewed solely as a battle over funding priorities. In a broader sense, though, he says, the issue signaled a significant shift toward private dollars paying for programs and activities on public college campuses.

After the failure of the second vote and the push for petition signatures, the stadium debate raged on without the benefit of the hindsight that history eventually would provide.

"Do we have a democracy here at State College?" asked Ronald M. Duehr, a junior ag student, in a letter to the editor in the Nov. 5, 1959, Collegian. "I don't think we do! Didn't we vote down the Stadium for State issue twice? That was a democratic way to find out if we wanted to assess ourselves for a stadium. Now we have a petition in circulation. Is this democratic? How many times is this issue going to be forced on us?"

Duehr pointed out that many students already paid $150 per quarter, and he was working 60 hours a week to put himself through school: "We don't have time to go to football games. Do we have to work harder to pay for a stadium?"

In the Nov. 12 edition, the Collegian reported that the petition drive had gathered about 1,400 signatures. The drive also fueled questions about campaign tactics. A watchdog committee was set up to investigate procedures. By December, the petition was about 250 signatures shy of the 1,800 goal.

Still, on Monday, Dec. 7, the Students' Association Board of Control approved a motion for a third election on whether students wanted to assess themselves to help fund the new stadium. The vote was set for Jan. 4, during registration, when students would be issued secret ballots, asking if they would pay $2.50 for six successive quarters.

For the third time, the measure failed — 1,401 to 928. The Stadium for State Committee decided that there would be no more votes on the matter for the remainder of the 1959-60 school year.

"Several different types of construction which might provide more for the money invested will be investigated," Frost told the Collegian. "We will probably proceed with preliminary work such as grading and seeding the field, possibly constructing the track, and other plans which would not seriously alter plans for a desirable stadium. ... Efforts will be made to continue securing funds from alumni and other friends of the college."

Ten months later, at a meeting on Tuesday, Nov. 15, 1960, the stadium steering committee opted to scale back the project and authorized the architects to draw up specifications accordingly. Bids would be let March 1, 1961. Pledges collected to that point covered the costs of building one side of the stadium without lights or a track and seating for about 4,000. If all the pledges were paid up, seating could increase to as much as 7,000.

Ultimately, in April 1961, the Board of Regents approved the bids for a new football stadium. The facility would seat 6,384 people and be completed in time for the 50th Hobo Day celebration Oct. 21. The winning bid came in at $179,859.

However, that figure did not include a dressing room. And once again, debate simmered over whether students should contribute. The Students' Association decided not to offer any of its funds because of earlier criticism by the state comptroller when $20,000 was shifted from student bookstore revenue to the stadium project. Also, given the three failed votes, the Board of Control figured the decision to contribute should be left up to individual students.

Amid this final wrangling over financial details, distinguished alumnus Charles Coughlin stepped up to the plate as he would do so often. Having already donated $50,000 to the stadium project, Coughlin gave a "substantial gift," which along with other contributions, foot the bill for the 4,000-square-foot dressing room. The concrete block building included space for both home and visiting teams, officials, coaches and equipment storage for baseball and intramural athletics.

Coughlin, whose name graces the stadium, graduated from State in 1909. The new facility, which initially was going to be called The Students Memorial Stadium, opened for the first home game of the 1962 season — a full three years after the original target date for completion.

A festive mood graced the campus and the celebration kicked off with a special luncheon. Guests included Gov. Archie Gubbrud, Coughlin, members of the Board of Regents, the stadium steering committee and presidents of other South Dakota colleges. Also on hand for the ceremonies were members

Stadium for State

Ozzie Schock, chair of the stadium fund drive, smiles during a break from a football game with the University of Manitoba in 1946.

of the 1922 football squad, the first to play before fans on the old State field after its dedication Oct. 28, 1922.

Al Schock, class of 1942, says the stadium's completion carried a lot of meaning, particularly for his brother Ozzie, class of 1947, who died in 2003. A member of the infamous '44 Kings, the younger Schock played football for State after World War II and led the steering committee in the Stadium for State fund drive.

There were critics, says Schock, and money certainly was a limiting factor. But, he is quick to add, supporters didn't let that damper their enthusiasm.

"When you believe in a project, you go all out," Schock says. "The school needed the facility. We just thought all along that it would work out."

He suspects that every student, alumnus and Jacks fan who goes to a game today is glad it did.

Although the stadium was not built to meet the original specifications and controversy dogged the project, the new facility left the Schock brothers with a sense of pride and continued loyalty for their alma mater. Schock notes: "There's always a lot of satisfaction when you're done. A lot of people never get to have that feeling."

Chapter 21

1971 Engineering Crisis

South Dakota State University has weathered its share of controversy throughout the years. Yet, few episodes rival the factional and all-consuming Engineering Crisis of 1971.

The melee began in secret, with a preliminary report by an 11-member advisory committee charged with reviewing the academic programs and roles of the state's institutions of higher learning. After 12 months of closed-door meetings and hearings, the panel recommended that the South Dakota School of Mines and Technology absorb the SDSU College of Engineering for projected cost savings of $200,000.

Oddly enough, but entirely characteristic of this bizarre story, Education

This monument, approximately 100 yards due west of the entrance of the Stanley J. Marshall Physical Education Center, commemorates the loyalty of students rallying to the aid of their alma mater. (Photo courtesy of Eric Landwehr)

Commissioner Richard Gibb rejected the recommendation when he first submitted the master plan to the state Board of Regents. Instead, Gibb said he thought SDSU ought to take in the School of Mines' program. It was at the regent level that the committee plan was resurrected and approved.

That move ignited a free-for-all that raged across the state and created one of the most contentious issues ever to face South Dakota's college and university system. It also touched off a troubled decade that threatened the viability of the state's campuses and resulted in the 10-year rule for college presidents, which many believe was aimed solely at getting rid of the late SDSU President Hilton Briggs.

"Gibb developed the master plan," recalls then-Rep. John Bibby, R-Brookings and SDSU class of 1942. "In his plan, he suggested that the school of engineering at Mines be closed. I think he did this knowing full well it would never happen. Then, at a regents' meeting in Pierre, while the Legislature was in session, the board flip-flopped and voted to close the school at South Dakota State. I attended the meeting as a spectator, but I was not really surprised. We had a little inside information. ...

"It happened in the morning, so I immediately went that afternoon and introduced a bill that would necessitate legislative action because the constitution of South Dakota was — and still is — specific that part of the curriculum at South Dakota State was engineering. It ended up being one of the controversial bills of the session."

It most certainly was.

Detailing the secretive nature of how the plan came to pass, the Associated Press reported: "How and why the committee reached the decision it did is not an easy question. None of the group's meetings were open to the public and its deliberations were held in confidence."

However, based on committee minutes filed in Gibb's office, this much became known: The committee was formed in June 1969 as one of seven study groups created to develop the master plan. The others were designated to study everything from admissions and building needs to retentions and transfers, enrollment, financial aid, faculty salaries and working conditions. The group responsible for studying academic programs and the roles of each institution was known as Committee D. The first meeting was held in July 1969. The committee toured each of the campuses, took testimony from various people, and wrapped up its efforts by December.

The preliminary report from Committee D concluded: "There should be only one college of engineering in South Dakota, which should be located at the South Dakota School of Mines and Technology, with the exception that if a program in agricultural engineering is deemed necessary, it should be located at South Dakota State University."

On Dec. 14, 1969, two of the committee's members — SDSU chemistry professor Leo Spinar and former state legislator John "Matt" Sutton of Agar — proposed to continue both schools of engineering, but the motion was defeated. And, curiously, there was no record of the exact vote. The following May, after a long discussion, the committee voted again to remove SDSU's engineering program.

Spinar, Sutton and a third Committee D member, Dale Hanke, a Dakota State University dean, later filed a minority report in support of keeping the two schools open. That recommendation was reviewed by the 29-member citizen advisory committee on Oct. 30, 1970, and approved by a 12-2 vote.

"Where were the other 15 of the committee members?" asked the AP story. "Gibb said ... that every effort was made to have everyone present, but not all could attend. The committee's minutes do not show who voted against the proposal."

Once the so-called Master Plan for Higher Education broke open into public debate, it unleashed a furor across the state. The projected impact on SDSU was devastating, from dollars lost and enrollment decline to the local economy and industrial development. Even Stephen F. Briggs, who invented the Briggs-Stratton engine while an SDSU student, threatened to yank his annual $40,000 scholarship grant for State students.

"It seemed like our university was under attack in an effort to save money," recalls then-Students' Association President Tom Stanton, who graduated in the summer of 1971. "It looked like they wanted to move everything down to Vermillion and leave us the ag school. A lot of us thought, engineering and nursing today — who knows what it will be tomorrow?"

Keith Jensen, class of 1956, remembers the engineering crisis as his baptism into becoming director of the Alumni Association. As the issue heated up, Jensen, who was working as managing editor of the Watertown Public Opinion, heard from friends who were having difficulty getting their voices heard by South Dakota's newspapers.

"I said I'd take a week off, kind of do publicity, and I went around and talked to editors," Jensen says. "It was pretty contentious. In the Legislature, there are not that many bills that get named and are remembered as long as the Bibby bill. In fact, I lobbied in the Legislature for 25 years, and I can't think of another bill like that."

In his capacity as a journalist and SDSU alumnus, Jensen traversed South Dakota, pushing State's argument:

THE COLLEGE ON THE HILL

A cartoon taken from the 1971 Jackrabbit shows a tractor transporting Crothers Engineering Hall to a western destination.

"We're in the eastern part of the state, with two-thirds of the population. We're an engineering school and the School of Mines was mining and engineering. We had civil and electrical and they were more chemical. We had technology and research. The big argument was South Dakota State and the eastern part of South Dakota needs an engineering program if they were to develop and grow. The opposition was saying we only need one engineering school. That was seen as the precursor to doing away with other programs."

When the week was done, he returned to Watertown, but only until the association director, Art Vandall, died after a battle with cancer. It was February 1971 and Jensen was encouraged to apply for the job, and he got it.

The loss of the engineering college would have dealt a huge blow to SDSU, Brookings, East River, and, in turn, all of South Dakota. When South Dakota State College became a university in 1964, the university concept meant in the traditional sense that the campus was a collection of colleges.

"After having achieved that goal, to take one of the largest colleges out — I believe it was third after ag and arts and science — was thought to be the first step in trying to destroy us," Jensen says.

Perhaps they were looking too deep for motivation, but some saw the move as stemming from the rivalry with the University of South Dakota. Real or not, there was the perception that the engineering fight was a reaction to the so-called cow college becoming not only a university, but a university bigger than the actual U. What had been an athletic rivalry spread into new and more dangerous territory.

Jensen, however, thinks the matter was more one of efficiency and economics: "There was the feeling in the '60s that we had too many schools or too many programs and we had to find ways to cut. It was after the war, the military folks were coming back, school enrollment was increasing, buildings were having to be built. There was this atmosphere that this all cost too much; we had too much duplication."

The opposition organized, including students, alumni, legislators and citizens. President Briggs led the fight, calling the regents' decision "the biggest step backward ever taken in higher education in South Dakota." But that wasn't Briggs' most memorable quote. In testimony before the regents, Briggs said removing the engineering college from SDSU would be the same as a rancher castrating his prize bull.

The point was, as Harold Bailey, then-vice president of academic affairs, explains, "You won't kill him, but you affect his productivity."

Adding to the political nature of the conflict, Board of Regents Chairman Richard Battey charged that the regents met in a hotel room the night before a scheduled meeting and discussed the Master Plan for Higher Education, as well as another controversy involving the membership of the board. Gov. Richard Kneip, a Democrat, had unsuccessfully attempted to withdraw two appointments made by his predecessor, GOP Gov. Frank Farrar.

The regents denied the accusations that a meeting had been held. Instead, they said, they just happened to wander into one room. Said Regent Loren Lewis of Sioux Falls: "They just dropped by to shoot the breeze. There was no meeting. We didn't decide anything."

In Brookings, concern about the college and what losing it could mean to the community led the Chamber of Commerce Governmental Affairs Committee to start the Save our State (SOS) College of Engineering Committee, which was chaired by local resident and businessman Wayne Hawley. More than $2,000 was contributed to the cause.

A former regent stepped forward and claimed that the master plan was created and approved in haste without any serious study. Regardless of how people stood on the issue of closing State's engineering college, Dona Brown of Huron said, "the motion should have been under study by the board for two weeks rather than 20 minutes."

She further charged that Commissioner Gibb had "taken matters into his own hands and many members of the current Board of Regents have heard no arguments but his. ... The most startling of all was the lack of factual information on which the ultimate decision was based."

Bailey says the move to consolidate engineering programs was not a new tactic. "Quite frequently," he says, "the Legislature or Board of Regents have tried to find ways of eliminating duplication of programs. The first effort came in 1954 after a study by a company whose report concluded that the College of Pharmacy should be moved to Vermillion. That created tremendous controversy. ... They never accomplished it. The next one was engineering."

With the Bibby bill in the legislative hopper and the battle raging across the state, SDSU students and alumni continued to mobilize the opposition. How serious was the threat to the engineering school?

"I think it was closed," says Stanton. "Had there not been the political reaction from alumni, it would have been closed.

On March 4, 1971, the Associated Press reported that as much as 80 percent, or 6,000 students, stayed out of class after the House State Affairs Committee postponed a decision on the Bibby bill. Briggs said classes were being held as usual, and the question of absences was a matter between instructors and students.

The walkout came after a rally in the Barn, where an estimated 4,000 students gathered and heard Stanton talk about the effects of losing engineering. According to a Collegian report, Stanton said the walkout was not a protest or demonstration, but was "a constructive exercise in democracy."

Many students headed for home to discuss the issue with their parents, townspeople and legislators. More than 200 State students gathered at the Western Mall in Sioux Falls to organize an informational, door-to-door campaign. Stanton told the Collegian he was surprised by the number of students who participated in the walkout: "I want to stress again that this is not a boycott against SDSU. I hope it is a constructive effort to take our story to the people."

In Pierre, some lawmakers were hesitant to step into the fray. As Bibby sought passage for his legislation that would require keeping the engineering college, a Faith representative offered a resolution that urged the regents to review and clarify their decision between June 1 and Sept. 1. Said the sponsor Rep. Carv Thompson, "I believe the responsibility for the administration of the state's seven institutions of higher education belongs to the regents, not the Legislature." Passing the Bibby bill, he added, would be the same as telling the regents "we know more about this than you do, and we're overruling your decision."

By March 6, the House rounded up the needed one-third support to smoke out the Bibby bill from where it had been languishing in the State

Engineering stays; regents lose battle

The legislature approved a compromise bill last Friday that will leave the engineering school at State University.

The bill, which came out of a joint House-Senate committee after hours of deliberation late Thursday night, specifies that the Board of Regents can take no action to change the present status of engineering in the state unless an independent study is first made.

If the regents initiate the study, the members of the committee will have to be approved by State University, School of Mines and the regents. The committee will have to submit its findings to the regents for their final decision by Nov. 30, 1971. If the regents decide to close either school of engineering, or any part of them, they must first obtain approval by legislative act of the 47th (next years) legislative session.

Commissioner of Higher Education Dr. Richard Gibb said he thinks the board will initiate the study at its April meeting. He estimated that, using the material he and his staff have already gathered, the study would take only two or three months. No comment has been made by the board.

If the study is made and shows that only one engineering school is needed in South Dakota, another hassle similar to the one just ended could possibly take place at Pierre at the initiation of the school that stands to lose its engineering program.

However, for the present, all three Brookings area legislators have said they are happy with the decision that was reached. Rep. John Bibby, Brookings, whose initial bill redefined the role of State University as including engineering, pharmacy, nursing and education, was a member of the joint committee that came up with the compromise bill. Pharmacy, nursing and education were not included in the compromise bill.

President Briggs issued the following statement about the compromise bill: "I have been extremely pleased that the students, staff, alumni and friends across the state have shown interest in maintaining an engineering college and the integrity of State University as a typical land-grant university to serve the people of the state.

"The legislature has now indicated that it does consider the integrity of a college as a justified consideration by the legislative bodies and that the elected representatives of the people will continue to have concern for the programs of higher education. If the regents decide to continue to study the matter of engineering, we will of course cooperate in that study. It is our hope that not only students and faculty, but former students and friends from all over the state will help the regents and the legislature to build the best possible system of higher education in this state."

John Lagerstrom, dean of engineering, said that all programs in engineering will proceed as usual for next year in all five branches of engineering offered at State University – agricultural, civil, mechanical, electrical and engineering physics.

The regents have issued their reasons for supporting a single engineering school at School of Mines to the Associated Press. Some of them are:

Higher education in this state has doubled enrollments while absorbing a net budget loss of 40 per cent due to inflation during the past 10 years. Drastic actions are called for to eliminate unnecessary duplication.

Engineering is very expensive, nearly double the average cost of other disciplines. The state has approximately 2,100 engineering students, which is nearly as many as Nebraska and far more than many surrounding states. The state has twice as many engineering students as some states with double its population and twice as many as the national average. Continuation of two programs will result in detriment to other programs.

–SDSM&T could absorb all students who would

(Continued on page 2)

Unique walkout staged to SAVE engineering

From 3,500-4,500 students canvassed the state last Wednesday through Sunday to draw support for keeping the college of engineering at State University.

The action came after a mass student rally in the Barn Wednesday when members of all colleges and Tom Stanton, SA president, spoke on the effects that the engineering college's removal would have on the entire student body and State University's quality of education.

Following the rally students began to pour from Brookings for the remainder of the week with only 4.4 per cent of the students attending classes by Friday morning in a survey conducted by the Joint Engineers Council and volunteers who manned the state headquarters for this movement in the Student Association offices.

All across the state it was emphasized that the two-day walkout from classes was not a protest or a demonstration but as Stanton said, "a constructive exercise in democracy." Speakers at the rally stated that "the administration has done all it can. It is now up to the students to convince the state and particularly the legislature that transferring engineering is a bad move. Go home!"

The rally came about when the House State Affairs Committee decided to leave House Bill 766 in committee. The bill by John Bibby (R-Brookings) would reverse the board of regents decision and keep engineering at State University.

The attempt to save engineering saw students gaining state-wide television coverage and many students spoke on radio programs up to an hour-long stating their cause. With this unique type of college behavior to an unfavorable "establishment" decision, the students decided that it was best to "try and work through the system of representative democracy." Speaking to the citizens of the state students encourage letters, telegrams, and phone calls to legislators in Pierre in support of retaining engineering in Brookings.

The results of the effort are only half-complete at presstime with the House scheduled to vote on placing the bill on the calendar between this Collegian's deadline Tuesday morning and distribution time today. Friday members of the House "smoked" the bill out of committee on a standing vote. The State Affairs Committee Monday then reported the bill onto the House floor with no recommendation after motions for "do pass" and "do not pass" endorsements failed.

The House was also expected to discuss a resolution by Carveth Thompson R-Faith, which would ask the Regents to review the decision to move the engineering college throughout this summer, delaying their decision until next fall. This resolution was combined with a letter by John Bibby calling for a year's study of the bill and the master plan and a report in the fall of 1972.

If the House voted to put House Bill 766 on the calendar, it would have to be brought before the House for a vote by Wednesday.

For immediate information on the status of the bill, students should contact the Student Association Office on second floor, Pugsley Union, or the Engineering 2-gether Room on first floor of the Union.

The faces of part of the 4,000 students attending the Barn rally show the seriousness of the issue to the State University students. The spontaneous effort by the Joint Engineers and the Student Association saw individual students from cities across the state take charge of their particular area.

Headline (above) from March 24, 1971, SDSU Collegian proclaiming the outcome and another headline (left) from March 10, 1971, heralds the method.

Affairs Committee. The committee approved the Thompson measure. And, the regents passed a resolution, saying that if requested by the Legislature, they would hold further hearings to reconsider their decision to remove the engineering college from SDSU.

The House voted by an overwhelming margin of 64-12 on Tuesday, March 9, to place the Bibby bill on its calendar for a vote the following day. On Wednesday, March 10, the House voted 56-17 to retain the engineering college at SDSU, in effect nullifying the regents' consolidation effort.

On March 12, Gibb released a statement that said: "The members of the board hereby express their willingness to reconsider their decision" to make the School of Mines the state's only college of engineering. However, regents Chairman Battey said he was not consulted about the statement, and that he only learned about it from news reports. The AP quoted Battey's response: "I'm just amazed. I couldn't believe it."

That same Friday, late in the afternoon, the Senate Education Committee voted to recommend passage of the Bibby bill by a 4-3 margin. On Monday, March 15, the full Senate voted 20-15 to amend the bill, substantially changing the measure. The split hardly fell along party or geographical lines. There were Democrats and Republicans on both sides. East and West River area legislators also were divided.

The Senate amendment turned the Bibby bill into a request for an outside study of engineering education in the state, the result of which would be binding on the regents, who, of course, initially had sought to dismantle the college at SDSU. The bitter controversy flared as the House refused 56-17 to go along with the bill's amended version.

A conference committee was formed with three senators and three representatives, but they were unable to craft a compromise. A second committee, however, came up with an acceptable alternative. The final version, which was adopted in both House and Senate, said the independent study of engineering would be advisory to rather than binding on the regents. The measure also required the regents to gain approval of the 1972 Legislature if, after the study, they still intended to close any of the state's engineering schools.

But, the matter was hardly settled.

In a painful twist, Gov. Kneip signed the wrong bill into law. Instead of the amended legislation, he penned his name to a preliminary version of the Bibby bill. Lt. Gov. William Dougherty, presiding officer of the Senate; Rep. Don Oscheim, R-Watertown, speaker of the House; Senate Secretary William Berguin; and House Clerk Paul Inman signed the law as well. Those five officers must sign each bill passed by the Legislature.

However, the legislation that was signed had not been approved by the Legislature. Rather, it was the version of the Bibby bill that carried the initial Senate amendment, calling for an independent study, the results of which would be binding on the regents.

Kneip told the AP he was embarrassed by the mistake and said he was doubtful that the error could have occurred on any other bill. The governor's staff reads through each bill before it is signed. In the case of the Bibby bill, so much study had taken place in the legislative process that the first amended version was assumed to be correct.

Attorney General Gordon Mydland next entered the fray. He said that despite the error, the signed bill was state law: "It is clear what the intent of the Legislature was. But every organization has to have rules, even the Legislature. The rules are made for the majority, and sometimes we don't get what we want."

1971 Engineering Crisis

In the aftermath, Sen. Charles E. Donnelly Jr., a Rapid City Democrat, called for the resignation of Briggs and the entire state Board of Regents. In a letter to the board, Donnelly wrote that Briggs' "gross insubordination" was sufficient cause for his removal.

"If another area of cause is needed," Donnelly added, "I submit that there have been substantial diversions of tax-supported manpower, services and supplies for the express purpose of engaging in lobbying activities on behalf of SDSU during the past session of the Legislature."

Donnelly asked the regents to resign because doing so would be in the best interests of higher education, the general public and the regents themselves. The resignations would allow the governor to appoint a new board and settle any remaining legal questions.

In time, though, Bibby says: "Things went back to where they were before the regents had acted and before the bill was passed and incorrectly signed. In the 1972 Legislature, there was the possibility that it might come up again. They were expected to bring the issue back. At the same time, I went from the House to the Senate.

"The only reason I ran again was to be damned sure I could watch what happened."

Although Gibb threatened to bring back the issue, he never did. Bibby says opponents were prepared to go to court if he had. The regents did, however, draft the policy that university and college presidents in the state system of higher education could not serve in their position for more than 10 years.

"That essentially ended Briggs' career," notes Bibby.

Briggs retired in 1975 after serving as president for 17 years.

Chapter 22

A Decade of Unrest

"OH LOOK! OLD CENTRALS ON FIRE."
"OH NO. ITS ONLY THE REGENTS."

Of all the struggles to play out on the South Dakota State campus, none have been as persistent as funding and few have spawned such epic battles.

The 1970s — a protracted, painful decade in the history of higher education in South Dakota — stand as a classic example.

SDSU ushered in the '70s with the gloomy threat of losing its engineering school. Before the decade was out, SDSU would grapple with the state's other campuses, regents and legislators over faculty salaries and mandates to prioritize programs, all of which were seen as a move to condense schools and create a single university system.

"It was a tumultuous decade," reflects Keith Jensen, class of 1956 and former director of the Alumni Association. "Dick Gibb was hired to be commissioner of higher education — hired under pressure from the Legislature to

Cartoon from the 1912 Jack Rabbit.

come in here with the ax and find a way to cut costs. It changed the whole theory of the regents being advocates for higher education. They became agents of the Legislature."

As a result, Jensen and others formed the group Citizens for Public Higher Education. The engineering crisis had passed, Jensen says, but there was increasing talk about consolidating schools and eliminating duplication. Ultimately, the discussion reached the point of a single university system with satellite schools. The big question was: Which school would be the main campus — State or the University?

It wasn't the first, nor would it be the last, time that debate arose. Some reports of intercampus feuding date the concept back to 1918. Money squabbles, however, have plagued the state's system of higher education since its inception.

At the 1938 annual banquet of the Engineering Society, longtime and beloved engineering professor Halvor Christian Solberg detailed the history of the engineering department. Even as early as his 1887 arrival on campus as a woodworking instructor, funding was meager — if it existed at all.

In 1892, Solberg had sought to provide adequate space for the new and growing department of engineering. But, as he noted in his speech, conditions were less than favorable:

"The state had several poor crops. Politics were boiling. The governing boards were fighting among themselves. The President was fighting to hold his own. Hence I had no support from any quarters whatsoever in getting any new quarters to work in, but I prepared plans for a small building and took them direct to the Legislature in 1893."

Unfortunately, at that moment in time, South Dakota State, the Board of Regents and the Board of Trustees were embroiled in a political upheaval that was under legislative investigation. No new funding would be appropriated until the matter was closed. Several years later, the prospect of receiving any extra money had failed to improve.

"When the Legislature of 1897 met, the conditions were so bad that no other member of the faculty besides myself dared to go to Pierre," Solberg said. "I took the bits in my own hands and went to Pierre. I stayed there for four weeks during that session and secured a small appropriation for what we called an addition to the Mechanical Laboratory. I paid my own expenses while in Pierre."

Despite his small victory, Solberg noted the difficulty in actually obtaining the funds. The original bill introduced was for $15,000. An agreement in committee cut the figure to $10,000. The measure passed the House for

$7,000 and the Senate for $6,000.

"Naturally," Solberg recalled, "I expected a compromise to be effected in the conference committee granting $6,500. But, when the bill came out of that committee, it was passed (with) $5,000. I learned the next day that the Governor had requested the chairman of the conference committee to cut $2,000 out of this appropriation and add that sum to one of the items for the University."

That gesture more than a century ago signaled the trouble that would dog State for decades to come.

In the fall of 1901, Sen. Philo Hall of Brookings County secured $40,000 for a new engineering building. The following spring, State established a department of civil engineering.

"When this building was finished, I thought my troubles were at an end and henceforth I would devote my energy to the upbuilding of engineering in State College," said Solberg. "Candidly, I expected that in a short time we would have the best engineering college on the west side of the Mississippi River, but somebody else had made different arrangements."

At about the same time bids were let for the new building at State, the University was authorized to start an engineering program. That action, however, was kept under wraps.

Solberg noted: "In 1902, like a thunderbolt out of clear sky, advertisements appeared in several newspapers that the University was the only institution in the state authorized to confer degrees in civil engineering and mechanical engineering. At that time, there was not a single member of the faculty of the University that had any engineering education whatsoever. I went directly to a member of the regents and asked him the meaning of this. He laughed and said it was partly a mistake."

The advertisements stopped soon after. But, in the spring of 1903, State's course catalog committee was told by a member of the Board of Regents to substitute the phrase "mechanic arts" wherever the word "engineering" appeared.

"The next move was a request to the attorney general for an opinion concerning the removal of engineering from State College to the University," Solberg said. "The law was plainly in favor of State College; hence the opinion was also in favor of State College. This completely frustrated the plans to remove engineering to the University. However, there was no opposition offered anywhere by the friends of State College against the University going ahead with engineering education. But, because of the bitter feelings engendered by these actions, it became practically impossible to get any financial support for engineering education at either place for a long time."

In January 1931, Collegian headlines trumpeted the news of Regent Guy Harvey's plan to provide South Dakotans with "better schools for less money." Harvey proposed taking the pharmacy program from State and combining it with the medical school at USD "where it properly belongs," and transferring all home economics courses from the U to State. Courses leading to arts degrees were to be cut at the School of Mines, which would get State's engineering courses.

Understandably, the Harvey plan was not well received in Brookings. The Collegian accused Harvey of building up USD and the School of Mines at the expense of South Dakota State:

"Whether the proposal will be considered seriously remains to be seen, but it is obvious that State college gets the knife in the back out of the deal, and would lose about 400 students."

The Harvey plan failed, but State still suffered a disastrous blow. The legislative session of 1933 saw huge cuts handed down. At the committee level, the college faced a proposed 46 percent cut — the largest of any campus in the system. In the end, though, the regents slashed salaries by an average 10 percent. The board also discontinued State's four-year courses in commercial science and music, and curtailed subjects in both departments.

Much to the dismay of the U, the regents also discontinued engineering and home economics in Vermillion. But, there was no joy in Brookings. A number of faculty members, grad assistants, custodians, secretaries and others were let go. All told, State lost $140,000 in appropriations compared with the prior budget year.

Amid the budget carnage, a group of USD alums sued the regents in the state Supreme Court, claiming that they expanded curricula at State and School of Mines without having the authority to do so.

The motive of the May 1933 lawsuit essentially was to gut South Dakota State, or at least to put the threat in writing. The USD group wanted the justices to: eliminate or curtail at South Dakota State civil, electrical, mechanical and chemical engineering; all music courses; journalism; commercial sciences (including economics), all courses in education and teaching, pharmacy and general sciences (including history, political science, sociology, chemistry, mathematics, physics, art, English, foreign languages, and psychology).

The action also sought to eliminate civil, electrical and chemical engineering at Mines while restricting the regents from abolishing engineering and home economics at USD and requiring the board to defend why pharmacy was not included in the U's curriculum. The justices sided with the regents and issued a decision Sept. 8, 1933.

"Now that the University has lost its first encounter of the season, that on the court room floor," editorialized the Collegian, "we can turn our attention toward showing our power on the gridiron. Unless Coyote football men put up a better fight than their attorneys did, we need show no signs of worry. Nor need the University worry about having a grandstand full of spectators if the battle is anything like that which came to an end September 8."

Forty years later, little had changed. Emotions ran at a fevered pitch and passions fueled an endless round of squabbles. One proposal after the next — whether originating in the governor's office, the state House or Senate, or a Board of Regents meeting — sought to cut costs by eliminating and/or condensing programs. The underlying concept of a single university system, although defeated repeatedly, failed to die.

Two bills pushing for a single university system were introduced in the the 1967 Legislature, and both passed out of the Senate State Affairs Committee despite opposition from then-Gov. Nils Boe.

"As far as I'm concerned," Boe said in a February 1967 press conference, "I want a president representing the individual institutions."

Boe even blamed student unrest at the Berkeley campus of the University of California on administrators being out of touch with students, a result he attributed to single university systems isolating their administrators from students.

Proponents argued that the single university system would save money and improve the quality of higher education in South Dakota. One of the bill's sponsors, Robert Hirsch, R-Tripp, said: "With seven institutions, we are spending a fortune on mediocrity."

Hilton Briggs, then president of South Dakota State, countered that the single university system would increase administrative costs. The individual system, he said, actually operated at a lower administrative cost per student than any school with a chancellor. The issue went nowhere.

Then in 1976, with Richard Kneip as governor and Democrats in control of the House, Jensen says a single university bill started moving through the legislative process. By the time the measure passed the Senate, it had been stripped substantially.

Still, says Jensen: "There was a real fear that we were moving to a big knockdown, drag-out fight. Politically, the question was how everything was going to fall out, how was it going to work?"

The single university measure made it to the committee level in the House, where it kept getting put off. Finally, the bill was set for a hearing.

Everybody made a pitch. Then, committee member Menno Tschetter moved to table the bill. Bernie Kopecky seconded the motion.

"Then this student waves his hand, says he's from the School of Mines and he came all this way to testify," Jensen laughs, shaking his head. "The kid gets up and gives the same speech we had just given. Menno Tschetter grabs his books and walks out. Kopecky walks out, but then comes back. Menno won't come back. The committee takes a vote and ties, 3-3. The committee met for three days, but Menno wouldn't come back. Everybody is working on these guys. But the votes kept coming back — tied, tied, tied. Finally, they just ran out of time. They couldn't pass it out and we couldn't kill it."

Next came a succession of resolutions passed by the regents in an effort to control costs. But finances were not the sole motivating factor. Intercampus politics played a significant role.

In 1977, Resolution 20 directed the state's university and college presidents to list the areas in which they could make cuts to fund faculty salary hikes. A year later, the regents handed down Resolution 1-78, dictating that the campuses list their top 25 percent programs to receive special consideration for funding.

In response to that measure, USD President Richard Lien cut allocations to arts and science and shifted the money to the law school and business programs. The USD student body went on strike to protest the loss of seven positions from the College of Arts and Science. SDSU students decided to support their peers at USD, not because of the internal strife, but rather to highlight the problems higher education was facing in South Dakota.

As part of the SDSU Students' Association resolution, the student senators stressed that the non-priority programs were an important part of the university as a whole: "Many of the priority programs rely on those non-priority programs for the basis of their core curriculum, and the uneven distribution of funds, as called for by the resolution, causes a competitive rather than cooperative relationship between programs which should work together."

At the time, State had roughly 60 programs. That meant about 15 programs would make the top 25 percent cut. An additional 50 percent of the programs were deemed "support programs," which would be funded to a lesser degree. That left about 20 programs that did not fit into either the top 25 percent or the support category. Those were informally deemed to be part of the "Limbo" category.

Programs that made the top 25 percent at SDSU were: agribusiness, agriculture, biological sciences, education-secondary, agricultural engineering, civil engineering, electrical engineering, mechanical engineering, home economics, journalism, nursing, pharmacy and sociology.

Some people, such as Regent David Morrill of Sturgis, questioned whether the April 13-14 boycott was actually a protest or a break. But, students rallied around the cause and undertook efforts to inform their peers, legislators, high schools, parents, chambers of commerce and newspapers.

The SDSU student body turnout was overwhelming — more than 4,000 students attended a rally in support of quality education. A similar event at USD drew fewer than 500 students.

Jane Christman, class of 1979, knew she was going to attend law school after SDSU. At State, she pursued a more general course of study, focusing on economics and foreign languages.

"A lot of the people I hung out with were in the same boat," says Christman, who also was a member of the Students' Association. "We weren't ag or engineering."

The resolutions aimed at a single university system, Christman notes, threatened the viability of the nonspecific programs. And yet, she says: "I think there definitely was the sense that we could effect change. ... We were at the tail end of Vietnam, but everyone had the sense that you could do something."

Being young and idealistic probably helped fuel those feelings, she adds, but the rally and the class boycott truly seemed to have an impact.

Jim Tienken, class of 1978, served as vice president of the Students' Association during the 1977-78 school year. Tienken says he and SA President V.J. Smith, along with their leadership group, closely followed higher education issues, attending regent meetings and trying to make the student voice heard. But all too often, the students felt their concerns were dismissed.

The SDSU rally, he says, "seemed like the thing to do. ... It was the right thing to do."

Tienken adds: "It was a sense that we could, by our actions, impact things that went on statewide, or at least focus the attention of the regents. ... It was pretty heady stuff."

The SA worked diligently to publicize the rally and educate the students. At some point, the effort seemed to take on a life of its own.

"The rally itself was electric," Tienken muses in hindsight. "I can recall walking into the Barn. They had set up tons of sound-system equipment. Emerson, Lake & Palmer was playing that song, 'Welcome back my friend to the show that never ends ...' It was perfect. The leadership was up on stage. It was a packed house."

Tienken was the first to speak.

"The atmosphere was so infused with enthusiasm," says Tienken. "Every time I'd say two or three words, the whole crowd would erupt into raucous applause. I think I introduced myself and there was applause."

Twenty-five years later, Tienken says he barely remembers the specifics: "I do recall that I implored people to make a difference — not just to cut class. We all thought our wishes and thoughts and feelings had been ignored. The rally was a means to show that we would not be taken lightly. We wanted them (the regents) to stop and assess. I think they did that. In that sense, we were very successful."

Heading home with petitions asking people to call on the regents to reconsider their position, students responded overwhelmingly with more than 10,000 signatures. The petitions, in turn, were presented to the Board of Regents.

By the time students returned to campus in the fall of 1978, Resolution 21 was awaiting them. The regents had approved the measure in July, dictating that the presidents of SDSU, USD, Northern State, Black Hills State and Dakota State either phase out or shift 15 percent of their school's programs. The School of Mines and USD-Springfield were excluded from the plan because of their specialization and lack of class duplication.

The process was slated to begin in the academic year 1980-81 and end the following year. For SDSU, Resolution 21 amounted to a $2 million cut.

Mike Freeman, class of 1980, was the newly installed SA president. Those times, he says, "were very, very intense. From a Students' Association perspective, it was all-consuming. We had other things to do, like allocating money to the band, but we were spending 98 percent of our time on figuring out how to generate a public information campaign to defeat Resolution 21. ...

"I still remember it to this day, sitting in the lounge at the Staurolite Inn in Brookings, with my cabinet around me; we just sat down and brainstormed this thing, jotting down ideas. We carried out a campaign, letters to the editor, meeting with legislators, going to Pierre."

The activity culminated with a 200- to 250-car caravan down Interstate 29 to a regents meeting in Vermillion. The problem with Resolution 21, explains Freeman, was that it set up a system of specialized satellite schools in the state.

"Instead of a broad, all-purpose institution, South Dakota State University would be an ag school," he says. "Northern State would be another specialty and Black Hills State another. The University of South Dakota would be the one all-purpose institution. Essentially, it was the single university system — that's what it was moving to. The surface reason was financial.

Headline from the Nov. 22, 1978, SDSU Collegian highlighting 250-car caravan down Interstate 29 to a Board of Regents meeting in Vermillion.

There were budget problems and some of the regents really believed this was the way to go. But there was never a rationale put forward."

At the time, Freeman told the Collegian: "The regents are putting the cart before the horse with Resolution 21. They're saying, high school numbers are going to decrease so let's cut programs right now and save money."

The USD student body didn't help matters by endorsing the latest regent resolution. In a Dec. 6, 1978, Collegian column, Freeman wrote, "Last spring, when cuts were made in the Arts and Science budget at USD, the students screamed and urged other schools to join them. ... Although Resolution 21 embodies the same concepts and principles of Resolution 1-78, USD has made a 180-degree turn. ... It is disturbing to remember that when USD was in danger of losing academic programs, they asked other schools to give them assistance. Now, when State University and other institutions are in the same type of danger, the USD students move to have the Federation (the South Dakota Student Federation of Governing Bodies) endorse those cuts."

Chuck Cecil, who served as assistant to the president during former President Sherwood Berg's tenure, describes the 1970s at SDSU as being marked by "chaos and continual efforts to change the way things were established."

"After the engineering crisis," notes Cecil, "administrators pretty much got the word to keep our mouths shut and stay out of Pierre. So, I kept my mouth shut and stayed out of Pierre."

Berg, who arrived in 1975, reflects on the decade as both turbulent and trying: "The students were concerned about the loss of programs. The staff was concerned about losing symmetry. We thought we had a very defensible program, that you could get the required prerequisites and then move into a professional program."

There was tremendous pressure, says Berg, to operate the institutions of higher education on very stringent budgets. Even during good years, he adds, securing funding was difficult. According to Berg, one of the big losses for SDSU in that era was the secretarial program.

"A number of us who worked together at the time, our greatest accomplishment was to maintain the integrity of the institution," says Berg. "We had a strong program, we were putting out kids. The faculty was a strong faculty. When I came here, I read a lot of accreditation reports. And one of the statements said something to the effect that the faculty was a lot, a lot better than they believed they were."

In retrospect, Freeman says: "I think the university could not have had a stronger or better leader than Sherwood Berg. This was a real time of crisis for South Dakota State University. He was able to crystalize the vision of what the university should be, and he fought for the university. He didn't just sit down and take it, and do what he was told. He fought for that school. He was an inspiration for the students."

Both Berg and Freeman to this day have vivid memories of SDSU's tenuous situation — how with every vote, the Board of Regents could have altered drastically the future of the school, and consequently the lives of legions of students.

The regents' votes on these critical matters were consistently — and frighteningly — close: "It was always a 4-3 margin," says Freeman. "There were old regents getting off the board and new regents getting on. The question was which way the 4-3 vote was going to go."

The two men remember one meeting that featured a crucial vote. Berg says the session was taking place in Pierre, but Regent Russell Peterson of Revillo, whose vote SDSU could count on, was not there.

"We called him and said, 'We've got to have you at the meeting,'" Berg says.

SDSU sent a plane to pick up Peterson, but a snowstorm prevented the plane from landing in Pierre. Instead, he was about 45 miles out. Freeman was dispatched to pick him up.

"There was this huge, freak blizzard," says Freeman. "Peterson was the deciding vote on our side. I took a car, someone was with me, but I was driving, scared out of my wits. We had to get Regent Peterson to the meeting. I remember driving back, cars all over the road; we were spinning all over. Regent Celia Minor — she was the most active advocate of Resolution 21 — she thought she had the votes on her side until we walked in covered with snow. ...

"These were the days before cell phones. No one knew if we were going to make it in time. Some of the college presidents were stalling the meeting. I couldn't call to let them know where we were. The whole thing was quite dramatic. It scared the heck out of me."

With the episode nearly 25 years behind him, Freeman says: "Looking back in retrospect, what made me very proud, was that even the students who ostensibly served to gain — the ag students — fought this measure just as hard. They believed, and rightfully so, if they made this an ag school, it would be less of an institution."

Regent Peterson, who was not at the July 1978 meeting when Resolution 21 was adopted by the regents, told the Collegian he was opposed to anything more than a 5 percent cut. Quoted in the Nov. 22, 1978, issue of the student newspaper, he criticized the regents for adopting "too darn many resolutions" in the past year and a half: "I think it's high time we charge the presidents with running their institutions rather than dictating through resolutions."

As Freeman contemplates that period in his life, he notes that despite the controversy, the experience had a lifelong impact.

"There was something very special about that time," says Freeman. "This was actually a student action on behalf of the university. It was very constructive, very meaningful. We really believed in the purpose of South Dakota State University. We believed in its value. ...

"It was also a real eye-opener in terms of realizing the intersection between politics and education; to realize that politics isn't just political science, that politics is trying to move people to do the right thing. ... Everybody was doing what they thought was the right thing."

Although, he says, laughing: "When you're 20, you look at it as good versus evil. Age does give it some perspective. But, I still think we were right."

To this day, Cecil maintains that the USD-SDSU relationship — equally, if not more so, than finances — played a key role in the upheaval of the 1970s.

"My feeling, and I have no proof, is that all of this originated in a town on the river south of Brookings," Cecil says, "I can't prove that, but I think, since the '30s, there have been efforts going on down there to return USD to prominence. ... People in Vermillion, in my opinion, can't stand it that this little old cow college can attract more students."

Cecil reasons: "I think it's prestige-oriented. The U has always felt it should be The University. They felt their prestige slipping and the money pie being divided according to student numbers. ... I think it was always felt that they should be the jewel in the crown.

"That's why people in my era are so paranoid about it. We've lived through the efforts being made through the political system to dumb down the rest of the university system."

Cecil adds that fighting against the tide posed a serious dilemma: "You were putting your career on the line. There were people in political positions who would just as soon shoot you in the knees. They didn't like people stating their opinions."

Berg says the anti-SDSU sentiment clearly was a factor: "There was still an override from the engineering scrap. There was quite an alignment of sides at that point in time. I think SDSU wasn't a particular favorite; the Board of Regents was highly influenced by USD. At the time, we had one or at least two members who were SDSU grads. Today (in 2002) we have none. In the minds of many, that raises a question."

Still, Berg concedes, the regents tried to be rational and resolve the issues. There is, he says, no getting around the fact that "the paucity of resources is a problem in this state."

For Tienken, who left South Dakota after graduation, the funding battles and efforts to bring about change imparted lifelong lessons: "Certainly, there was a kind of euphoria. Look at what we did. But, you also walk away with the underlying understanding that principles are important. ...

"When something is being done or forced upon you that is unjust or unfair in life, there comes a time when you need to take a stand and stand up for what you believe in. That is the lesson."

Chapter 23

Cleve Abbott

Cleveland Leigh Abbott, class of 1916, had the kind of athletic record of which legends are made. He lettered in track, football, basketball and baseball, chalking up accolades as if they were points on the scoreboard.

Yet, Abbott's greatest contributions came after he left South Dakota State and they reverberated far beyond the world of sports.

Known as a coaching legend and inducted into several halls of fame — SDSU's included — Abbott's most notable achievement was his advancement of women's sports, particularly for African-Americans.

Evelyn Lawler Lewis, the mother of Olympic track great Carl Lewis, ran track at Tuskegee and named her second son, Cleveland Abbott, after him. After college, she went on to compete in the 1951 Pan American Games in Argentina. Later, she also turned to coaching.

"I never would have gone to college; I never would have known anything

Pictured above, Cleve Abbott from the 1917 Jack Rabbit.

had it not been for him," says Lewis, a 1949 graduate of Tuskegee University.

One of seven children, Abbott was born on Dec. 9, 1894, in Yankton to Molly Brown and Elbert B. Abbott. Abbott's family moved to Watertown, where he graduated from high school in 1912 having won 16 letters in sports. That fall, he arrived at State for his freshman year.

Abbott was assigned to work in the dairy building for his room and board. When a faculty adviser at registration asked him which course of study he had selected, Abbott replied "dairying."

However, the May 1955 Alumnus noted, "At the time he had never lived or worked on a farm and chose dairying to escape the embarrassment of not having decided what course he should pursue in college."

According to the Alumnus account, Abbott had been on campus only a few months when then-President Ellwood Perisho attended a meeting in New York City on the advancement of African-Americans. After the conference, Perisho met Booker T. Washington, president of Tuskegee Institute, on the train.

"At the time," said the Alumnus, "Washington was considered as the Negro leader of America. As they visited, Washington told Perisho he had been operating Tuskegee since 1881 and that he had nothing but a work and study program for his young people. He said he realized that he must inaugurate a program of sports if he was to hold the interest of the young folks attending his school and attract greater numbers to the institution. He asked President Perisho if he had any young man who might qualify as a sports director."

Perisho told Washington about Abbott, but cautioned that he was only a freshman and had yet to prove himself. Washington reportedly replied: "You go back to tell this young man, if he will be a good boy and study hard, he can be my sports director when he graduates from college."

When Perisho returned to Brookings, he called Abbott to his office and related his conversation with Washington. In response, Abbott committed himself to excellence both on the field and in the classroom.

The 1916 yearbook said Abbott, nicknamed "Fox," held the edge on all opposing centers in football: "He was a wonder on the defense, if not better on the offense. His coolness and headwork made him a most valuable man; in fact one of the best centers State ever had."

The following year, the 1917 Jack Rabbit opined:

"Of all the men who leave this year
We'll miss our center most;

Cleve Abbott and the three other members of the SDSC squad that participated in the Drake Relays in 1915.

*For Cleve outplayed each man he met,
This is no guess, nor a boast."*

In football, the 172-pound Abbott earned All-State honors four consecutive years. One year, Abbott was selected All Northwestern Center. He was a starting center for basketball and captained the team as well. He also anchored the relay team in track.

In April of Abbott's junior year, Washington died. Not knowing what this meant for his future, Abbott continued his studies at State with the goal of being a coach and physical education leader for African-Americans — if not at Tuskegee, somewhere else.

Then, the Alumnus said: "In March of his senior year he received a memorandum from Booker T. Washington's secretary in which she told him she had gone through (Washington's) files and found a memo of agreement for Abbott's employment. She informed him further she had investigated his scholarship and athletic prowess along with his character and general conduct, and found them all satisfactory and was enclosing a contract for him to come to Tuskegee."

The April 4, 1916, edition of the Industrial Collegian reported that Abbott, who had specialized in the dairy husbandry department at State, "has been elected to the position of dairyman at the famous Tuskegee Institute,

Tuskegee, Alabama."

In his new position, Abbott was to have charge of 150 Jersey cows and 25 men. He would teach various phases of the dairy business to agricultural students and serve as an assistant coach. The Collegian stated:

"This sounds as though Mr. Abbott will have plenty of opportunties to continue his diligence after leaving SDSC. Mr. Abbott has made a fine record while at State College, and his many friends are confident that he will make good. He worked his own way through his four years at this institution, kept his work up to a high standard, and was a participant in four branches of athletics. ... Mr. Abbott's election is another illustration of the demand for students who have been trained in the State College dairy department."

Within a few years, Abbott found himself in the same situation as other young men his age — fighting for the United States in World War I. Abbott, a lieutenant, served as a regimental intelligence officer attached to the headquarters company of the 336th Infantry of the 92nd Division.

A Collegian story dated Jan. 7, 1919, printed excerpts from a letter Abbott had sent his father a few weeks earlier. In his letter home, Abbott detailed the efforts of his regiment in France's Vosges Mountains, about five miles from the city of St. Die:

"Here we had our first taste of fire and believe me it scorched a bit, nevertheless everyone stood it in fine shape. We remained in this sector for five weeks and then started for the D'Argonne forest. We reached there about September 25 and we will never forget that day as it was the day on which the great drive that decided the war began. It was an American victory and colored Americans helped to make it so.

"After being taken out of the Argonne drive, we were sent against the great fortress of Metz. During the first day's attack, we gained all along the line and on the morning of November 11 we renewed our attack with new vigor. The armistice taking effect at 11 o'clock that morning cheated us out of new glory."

Abbott also reported that he had enjoyed the good fortune of carrying the message of cease-fire from his colonel to the troops after armistice had been declared.

After the war ended, Abbott joined the faculty of Kansas Vocational School, Topeka, Kan., where he coached and was commandant of cadets. In 1923, Abbott returned to Tuskegee as the school's athletic director and head football coach — positions he kept until he died in 1955.

In 32 seasons of football, Abbott notched a record of 203 wins, 95 losses and 15 ties. Abbott's teams brought home 12 Southern Intercollegiate Athletic

Conference (SIAC) titles and six mythical National Black College championships. In 1954, Abbott was the first coach in African-American college football to rack up 200 victories. To put that in perspective, through July 1, 2002, Tuskegee University held the record for total team victories — 532.

Inducted into the USA Track & Field Hall of Fame in 1996, Abbott is credited with being one of the pioneer coaches of women's track and field for a period that spanned four decades. He is said to have developed the program that opened track and field to women in the United States.

Among the notable female athletes he coached were Alice Coachman, Mildred McDaniel and Nell Jackson. Coachman, the first African-American woman to win a gold medal, took the 1948 Olympic Games high jump title in London. McDaniel repeated that feat in 1956 with a world-record clearance in the Helsinki Olympics.

All told, from 1935 to 1955, Abbott's Golden Tigers won 14 national team outdoor titles in track and field — eight of which were consecutive. His teams won 21 International AAU track and field championships. Individually, Tuskegee athletes brought home 49 indoor and outdoor titles. Six made it onto Olympic track and field teams.

Abbott served on the women's committee of the old National AAU (one of USA Track & Field's predecessors) and twice was on the U.S. Olympic Track and Field Committee. He is also a member of the Alabama Sports Hall of Fame. And, he was one of the founders of the SIAC Basketball Tournament.

Major, as Abbott's athletes called him, was still coaching at Tuskegee when he died on April 14, 1955. At the time, the editor of the Alumnus wrote:

"I doubt if we have ever had newspaper clippings, letters and other information from so many people and from so many places as we have concerning the death of Cleve Abbott. Newspapers and magazines carried notices of his death in all parts of the country."

Evelyn Lewis says she never would have gone to college had it not been for Abbott. Growing up in Gadsden, Ala., she lived on the outskirts of town. Her parents had a first-grade education.

"I didn't know anything about college," Lewis says. "I had no idea of possibly going to college."

In her sophomore year at Carver High School, eight girls were chosen to start up a track team. Lewis was not one of them. But, she was interested enough to watch practice and asked to try the long jump.

"I jumped farther than anyone else on the team," she recalls. "That was my start."

Abbott saw Lewis at a track meet and invited her and another girl to join his college team during the summer. "That was how I met him. I had no idea of who he was, no ideas about Tuskegee. ... It was difficult, though. My mom and dad did not want me to go away, but Major convinced them to let me."

Once she arrived on campus, Lewis laughs: "I thought Tuskegee was New York City. I was a country girl. I had not been exposed to anything. To travel and be away from home was astounding for me. I had never been exposed to anything of that nature."

She soon discovered the many roles Abbott would play in her life — mentor, father figure, coach and confidante. Lewis returned to Tuskegee the following summer, after her junior year in high school.

"At the end of my senior year, when I graduated, that was supposed to be the end of it," says Lewis. "My dad especially did not understand college. ... Coach Abbott came and talked to my parents, but my father wasn't convinced. He said he wasn't going to spend a penny for me to go to college. But, my mom convinced him. Coach Abbott said he had a scholarship to help pay. My mom went to work for the first time and paid my board. It was $7 a week."

It was clear, even in his day, that Abbott was well ahead of his time — from his coaching to teaching and training techniques. What's more, Lewis says, Abbott inspired his athletes.

"He made us believe we could be something," she explains. "His main theme — what he always talked about — was 'you can do it.' You can do what you want. You can be as good as you want. He wasn't a driving type of coach — he was a motivator."

Lewis adds that her late husband, William, played football for Abbott and would have echoed her sentiments. There was no question when Abbott died during Lewis' second pregnancy that the couple would name their unborn child after the beloved coach. Abbott's namesake grew up to play professional soccer.

"Major passed away about three or four months before Cleveland was born," Lewis says. "We were both very much admirers of him. We immediately decided that if the baby was a boy, he would be named for Cleveland Abbott. If it were a girl, we didn't know how we would work it in other than we might use his middle name, Leigh."

For Lewis, Abbott's influence played out on a personal level. She gives him credit for her going to college. And because she pursued higher education, so did her two younger sisters. By the time her children were born, college was an automatic assumption.

Abbott also had an immeasurable impact on the lives of countless individuals with his pioneering role in track and field and his efforts on behalf of women in sports. Other coaches, such as Ed Temple, who coached track great Wilma Rudolph, patterned their programs after Abbott's.

Lewis says, "I think if it were not for him and his dedication to promoting track and field for women, we possibly would not have had an Alice Coachman."

Equally possible is that without Abbott the world may not have enjoyed the achievements of her children.

"I don't think my children would have been the children that they are had it not been for him," Lewis theorizes. "Of course, your parents are there, but my success and my children's successes — Major Abbott is basically responsible."

Chapter 24

The Great Weert Engelmann

Who was the greatest athlete to grace the fields and courts of South Dakota State University? That loaded question could spark endless debate.

One of the contenders, though, has to be Miller native Weert Engelmann Jr., class of 1930.

In fact, there is no talking about Engelmann without prefacing his name by two simple words: "the" and "great." Every breathless reference to the football, basketball and track standout runs it all together — superlative and name — as if mentioning him by name alone does not do him justice. A look at his record backs up that contention.

Engelmann, at 6-foot-2 and 185 pounds, came from German stock. His

Pictured above, Weert Englemann poses for the 1932 Jack Rabbit.

paternal grandparents emigrated to Illinois, where they raised a family of six boys and one girl. His dad, Weert Sr., married Lena Schultz in 1890. They headed for Hand County, settling in Logan Township. Weert Jr. was born in 1908. After an outstanding athletic career in high school, he enrolled at SDSU in 1926.

Lawrence "Lorne" Bartling, class of 1938, was a few years behind Engelmann, but growing up in Brookings, he certainly knew who the legend was.

"He lived a half a block south of where we lived at 816 Fourth Street.," says Bartling. "He used to walk by our house. One day my brother and I were kicking a football around as he came by. We said, 'Bet you can't kick it over the house.'"

Sure enough, the Bartling brothers retrieved the ball from the other side of the house.

Engelmann's record offers a classic example of the early collegiate athlete — a true contender who excelled in not just one, but three seasons of sports. The Great Weert earned prominence as an all-conference selection, leading the SDSU football team to three winning seasons. He also claimed an all-conference title in basketball, as a forward and center.

But, many insist that his ultimate athletic prowess was in track and field. A nine-time letterman (three in each of his sports), "Iron-man" Engelmann notched the greatest record ever achieved in the North Central Conference.

Engelmann, in his first NCC meet, won the discus and low hurdle events and took second in the broad jump and high hurdles. He placed third in the javelin and fourth in shot put. The following year, he won six events, including the 220-yard low hurdles, shot put, broad jump, discus and high jump — a record that remains untouched.

His best marks were: discus, 154-6; shot put, 43-6; javelin, 172-6; 120-yard high hurdles, 15.0; 220-yard low hurdles, 24.7; 100-meter run, 11.1; 400 meter run, 51.0; broad jump, 23-3/4; high jump, 6-0; and pole vault, 11-9.

In three years of competition, Engelmann racked up 45 first places, 12 of which were at NCC meets. He took first place in two different events at the Drake Relays — the first South Dakotan to win an event in 20 years of the Des Moines, Iowa, meet.

The 1934 Jack Rabbit yearbook proclaimed Engelmann "the most outstanding athlete State college has ever produced." As a sophomore, he tried out for the U.S. Olympic team in the decathlon, securing fifth place — just .25 of a point shy of making the four-man squad. Engelmann earned the slot of first alternate. He also tried out in 1929, but again narrowly missed a berth.

The Great Weert Engelmann

April 30, 1929, article from The Industrial Collegian proclaiming Englemann's athletic prowess at the famous Drake Relays.

Eleanor Roscoe, 88, attended state from 1932-33. She remembers Engelmann arriving at her home on Seventh Aveune, between 10th and 11th streets, every Friday night to take her sister dancing: "He was a great big fellow; a Viking type of person — a great big blond, very pleasant, happy-go-lucky person. He was great in football and anything else he decided to do — javelin, shot put. He dated my sister and she loved to dance."

Engelmann graduated with an engineering degree in 1930 and went on to play halfback for Wisconsin's Green Bay Packers for four seasons. The Packers were the National Football League champs in both 1930 and 1931. After the 1933 season, Engelmann left football for the oil business. Then, he worked for 30 years in maintenance at a paper mill before retiring at age 65.

However, his achievements on the field would not be forgotten. Nearly 30 years later, in 1960, he was named to the Howard Wood Dakota Hall of Fame and was honored at the May relays in Sioux Falls. He was inducted into the SDSU Hall of Fame in 1970.

Engelmann's son, Weert "Rusty" Engelmann III, says he grew up knowing his dad was a sports great. Green Bay was a smaller town then, and his dad seemed to know everyone.

"He was a super guy," Rusty Engelmann says of his legendary father, who died in 1979 at age 70. "But, he was also hard and disciplined. If I didn't behave, I got a drive in the butt."

After his years in high school, college and professional sports, the senior

Engelmann treasured his time outdoors.

"He was more of an avid fisherman and hunter," notes Rusty. "We did a lot of trout fishing on the Bay. ... He only had a short retirement. If he could have, he would have stretched that out and he still would be hunting and fishing."

And yet, the past is never too far removed from the present. Rusty muses: "As a matter of fact, we are still sitting in his alumni seat in our multimillion dollar renovated Green Bay Packer stadium."

Chapter 25

A Great Road Trip

On Friday, Dec. 3, 1926, the Jackrabbit football team received a cablegram from the University of Hawaii, inviting the South Dakotans to play a game on the Pacific island.

"We thought someone was crazy," Johnnie Johnson, class of 1926, recalled in a 1985 Collegian story.

The invitation for the all-expense-paid trip to Honolulu was legitimate — thanks to the team's undefeated season — and the Jacks embarked on their trans-pacific trip on Dec. 11. With the length of the round trip estimated at more than 10,000 miles, the jaunt would be the longest ever made by a State College football team.

Head coach C.A. West and his wife led the team trip, which included 18 men. The Jacks first boarded a train for Omaha and then San Francisco, where they set sail on the USS Wilhelmina for the Hawaiian Islands.

Pictured above, artist's sketch taken from the 1908 Jack Rabbit.

Above, team members, coaches and wives pose for a picture shortly after arriving in Honolulu, Hawaii.

"The team left here Saturday evening amid the cheering of a large delegation of State College students and townspeople," reported the Dec. 14, 1926, Collegian. "The State College band and cheering squad helped to make the send-off a noisy one. ... When the squad left here, there was much bantering as to who would be the first of the football warriors to become seasick."

Judging from the 1928 yearbook, it didn't take long to settle the speculation:

"Leo Schweinfurt says that it's bad enough to have rheumatism and St. Vitus Dance (an old mental illness), but still worse to have lockjaw and be seasick. We heard the only reason that George Seeley was able to overcome seasickness was to put glue in his soup. Walter Parmeter said the best cure was to put a piece of paper on your throat — this would keep it stationary.

"But still another remedy that sounds the best and as results were the most satisfying, I think that we should recommend this to the public. Art Eggers and Buck Starbeck each bought a slab of bacon before leaving San Francisco and proceeded to cut it up into small-sized chunks. A piece of string was tied to each slab and then hung in a convenient place. When feeling an attack coming on Buck and Art would each rush over and slide them up and down their throats and in this this way grease things up so that there no longer was any excuse for being sick."

The February 1927 Alumnus reported that only two of the players escaped "an attack of mal de mer."

"Some of the guys got sicker than horses," team member George Frandsen, class of 1929, told V.J. Smith in a 1995 Rabbit Tracks magazine interview.

Also making the boat trip memorable was Knute Rockne. The famous Notre Dame coach officiated the two games State played in Honolulu.

"He sat on a deck chair and drew up plays," Frandsen recalled. "After he finished a play he would hold it up and say, 'What do you think of that one, boys?'"

The Jacks played their first game against the University of Hawaii on Christmas Day. According to Frandsen, coach West issued his team a challenge: "Coach said if we defeated Hawaii, he would take us to Waikiki Beach."

South Dakota State won, 9-3, with all nine points scored by kicker Frank Kelley on three field goals. The points did not come easily. As they had throughout the season, the Jacks battled the elements.

"The Bunnies probably have begun to think by this time that the weather man has a grudge against them," reported the Dec. 30, 1926, Brookings Register. "They played in snow and mud at Grand Forks, N.D., during conference season; they played in deep snow on the home field in the Hobo Day game with South Dakota University; at Omaha, in the Creighton game, the field was a regular quagmire of mud and water; and at Honolulu, a gale of wind was blowing so that punting against the wind was practically an impossible feat."

But the wind, as the Register noted, failed to stop Kelley from making a record number of field goals in one game. Frandsen said that after watching Kelley play, Rockne commented that he could have been an All-American at Notre Dame. Johnson told the Collegian that Kelley was the greatest player, responsible for the Jacks' entire 157 points during the 1926 season.

Coach West kept his word and took the team to Waikiki Beach after the victory. A week later, though, on New Year's Day, the Jacks lost their first game of the season in a close contest.

The Jan. 6, 1927, Register reported: "It was the All-Star town team at Honolulu, Hawaii, which did what all the other teams met by the Jackrabbits the past season failed to do, but they did it only by one point, 13-12. The game was played New Year's Day under a broiling hot sun before a crowd of 12,000 ukulele players, dusky maidens and a sprinkling of Americans. ... The Rabbits were scheduled to start for the homeland yesterday. No doubt they will be given a royal reception when they reach Brookings."

After 34 days on road, rail and sea, the Jacks returned home. Upon the team's departure, one of the Honolulu papers commented:

"This morning there sails away from Honolulu a rare collection of gridiron talent, Knute K. Rockne, greatest and most colorful figure in football today, and ... along with 'Rock' goes Jack West's South Dakota State College football team, as fine a squad as has ever invaded these fair isles. We have known splendid sportsmen who have come here to meet our local grid teams in the past, but we remember none more thoroughly endowed with these qualities than State.

"We say 'Aloha' this morning with regret that their visit has terminated so quickly, before we could become better acquainted, but we entertain high hopes that some day our Deans will invite Jack West and his men to come here for another gridiron test — and that State will accept."

Although the Jacks lost the second game, the local paper continued: "The South Dakota team goes back to the west with a defeat against it, but with keen admiration of thousands of Honolulu fans. No visiting team in recent years has put up a pluckier fight or shown greater determination. And while the South Dakota eleven plays hard and vigorously, it should be recorded to its credit, too, that it plays clean — one of the few visiting teams to contest here without penalties for unnecessary roughness or unfair tactics."

The team arrived in Brookings on Jan. 15, heralded by accolades. The season of 1926 was deemed to be the most thrilling in campus history.

"It was a typical State College student reception that the boys got when they piled off their private coach," reported the Jan. 20, 1927, Register. "The

The famous Notre Dame football coach, Knute Rockne (left, dressed in white with arms raised, signaling a touchdown), refereed both games State played on its trip to Hawaii.

mob met them at the foot of the steps and loud cheers rent the air while everybody tried to shake hands, or slap the boys on the back, or in some way demonstrate to them that they were heartily welcome. The college cheer leaders mounted the passenger coaches and led the bunch in vociferous yells of a triumphant college bunch, while the college military band played 'The Yellow and Blue.' It was a very happy occasion for everyone present."

State President C.W. Pugsley was out of town, so Dean G.L. Brown gave a short welcome-home speech. Coach West and several of the players also spoke.

"Starbeck told of the games and also informed the public that he had learned what the porthole in a ship is for — that he wore one as a lavaliere most of the way over," the Register quipped.

Summing up the thrilling season, the 1928 Jack Rabbit proclaimed, "That team, every man in the pink of condition, loyal to State, and full of all the fight and pep in the world, leaves a great record for future grid teams to aspire to equal."

Johnson, in a more plain-spoken tribute, told the Collegian, "We were quite a bunch of guys."

Chapter 26

Winning Silk Pants

On Sept. 28, 1935, the South Dakota State football team gave the whole town of Brookings something to cheer about — the Jacks beat the University of Wisconsin Badgers 13-6.

For one game in a less than stellar season, the Jacks were golden.

State alum Charles Coughlin walked into the Jacks' locker room after the game and asked SDSC head coach R.H. "Red" Threlfall how much a set of silk football pants for the team would cost.

"Oh, about $500," said Threlfall.

"Well, order 'em and send me the bill," Coughlin reportedly replied. "A team that can beat Wisconsin certainly deserves them. Have them for the team in time for the Hobo Day game."

And, that was how the benefactor of the SDSU Campanile came to furnish the Jacks football team with bright, gold silk pants. "The latest," said the

---

Pictured above, captain of the 1935 football squad, Rollins Emmerich.

Standing: Threlfall, Diehl, Barber, Rouseff, Miller, Mernaugh, Herting, Ringsrud, Rude, Kloster, Pylman, Johnson, Hecker. **Kneeling**: Fenner, Wicks, Halverson, Lassen, Gray, Dragash, Thompson, Kulish, Lathrop, Reeves. **Sitting**: Lienhart, Goldstein, Trapp, Sundet, Leach, Price, Evans, Ware, Stenson.

Register, "in gridiron attire."

Lorne Bartling, class of 1938, recalled: "Boy, they looked fancy. And the pads were right inside."

Coughlin's enthusiasm over the victory was matched by the entire community upon the team's return to town Sunday night. In those days, train was the common mode of team travel.

"When the victorious SDSU team returned to Brookings from Wisconsin, they were met by the entire populace," recalled Dorothy Ringsrud, whose husband, Ron, was a tackle from Elk Point.

Judging from the Register story, that was no exaggeration:

"The North Western station was crowded so thickly with college and town fans the overflow went up on the roof of the station, and cars that could not jam Main Avenue found space in the side streets and alleys as far as two blocks away. The demonstration was the greatest ever seen or heard in Brookings.

"Staid old Brookings on Sunday evening was awakened by the new fire engine siren, the college pep band, cowbells, auto horns, whoops and yells, and any source of noise that happened to be handy at the time."

The squad finally managed to depart from the train and get into waiting cars. A parade formed behind two motorcycles and the new fire engine, complete with horn blasting to clear a path.

"Then followed the band," the Register story stated, "tooting the college song and familiar, stirring military marches. Cars fell behind and those who did not ride, walked.

"With a merry din all the way, the parade ended at the College Campanile where the cheer squad took charge and led Coaches Threlfall, (Fred) Hecker and (Lemme) Herting to the stage with Captain (Dick) Emmerich and members of the football squad. Speeches were demanded ... until the crowd was thoroughly satisfied.

"The demonstration gave vent to the pent-up enthusiasm of college students and citizens who had crowded around radios at home while the team played so gloriously on the gridiron at Madison. It was a fitting tribute to a grand team."

The excitement was understandable. The Big Ten Conference was arguably the best Division I conference in America and the Jacks' win was the first time a North Central Conference team had beaten a Big Ten foe.

The fall of 1935 was Threlfall's second season. The yearbook described Threlfall as "the congenial sort of coach who gets along well with his associates and possesses those qualities which make him popular and efficient." As legend has it, Threlfall arranged games with his old teaching buddies in the Big Ten Conference. Supposedly, the match-ups with the Jacks were considered good practice for the Big Ten teams.

Consequently, according to Dorothy Ringsrud, it was a huge upset when the Jacks won. For the 50-year anniversary of the game, she recollected: "Dick Emmerich, an SDSC player, was heard to say that they could hardly put it in the paper there in Madison, Wis. Another player said that Wisconsin coach Doc Speers could be heard all the way downtown yelling at his team."

Perhaps, the victory was some kind of fluke. The year prior, Wisconsin had won 28-7. The year after the big win, the Jacks suffered a 24-7 defeat. SDSU's record in the fall of 1935 was a mixed bag — from a 33-0 win against Northern Normal to a 38-0 loss vs. Cincinnati U. In-between was a tie with UND, a loss by one point to NDSU, and a 7-2 loss to USD, among others. "Listless playing by the Jackrabbits," said the yearbook, almost cost them a game against Morningside.

The yearbook summed up the season: "Football in the 1935 season rather disappointed the Jackrabbits. Starting with a powerful and promising eleven of championship caliber, they lost important games by only a few points time after time, and wound up their season with four victories and a tie out of nine games, and an average of .250 in the North Central final standings."

It is important to note that football, still a grueling sport today, truly tested an athlete's stamina and ability in those years. Players were in the game for the full 60 minutes unless they suffered a serious enough injury to be taken out. Jesse Robinson, class of 1938, had transferred to SDSC and was playing freshman ball in the fall of 1935.

"It wasn't anything like it is now," Robinson says. "We played both ways. There wasn't offensive or defensive. There was no facemask and you couldn't block with your hands — you blocked with your body."

The Register's preview of the Wisconsin game said the Jacks were in "fine physical trim for the encounter, the game last Saturday against Northern Normal uncovering a few weak spots that have been strengthened this week in practice." The coach placed a special emphasis on passing, which had been the source of Wisconsin's win the year before.

According to the paper's account, a crowd of 18,000 took in the Madison game. At least 50 South Dakota State College alums were in the stands, having "eaten a noon dinner together and been filled full of Cow College spirit."

In the third quarter, with no points for either team on the scoreboard, SDSC's Paul Miller caught a punt on the Jacks' 45 and made it down to the Wisconson 32-yard line. Teammate Wally Diehl caught a pass on the 16-yard line. Ed Lienhart gained 8 more yards. Then, Miller caught a pass and was tackled on the 1-yard line. On the next play, Sid Goldstein snuck the ball over the last yard to score a touchdown.

Early in the fourth quarter, the Badgers returned the ball down to the Jacks' 9-yard line, tying the score with a pass into the end zone. Wisconsin then launched a passing attack that nearly ended the Jacks' ride to victory.

With two minutes left in the game and the score tied at 6-6, Miller intercepted a pass and ran for 75 yards to make the winning touchdown. The Jacks made the conversion and ended the game 13-6. The SDSC Industrial Collegian deemed Miller "State College's gift to the sporting world." Not only did he score the winning touchdown, said the yearbook, Miller also gained "the acclaim of every sports critic in the country."

"Local Lads Upset Dope in Encounter with Big Ten Foe" crowed the headline in the Brookings Register the Tuesday after the big contest. Days later, in the Collegian, starting end Ken Halverson credited Coughlin with getting the team geared up for the game: "You all know the feeling one gets on Memorial Day when a salute is fired over the heroes' graves — well, that's the feeling that came over the players down in that dressing room.

"Being fortunate enough to be one of those eleven fellows who started in that ball game, which stands out in my mind as my biggest thrill, I don't mind confessing that tears came to my eyes while the same thing was happening to those other ten fellows.

"That little talk that Charles Coughlin gave us fellows before the game

Winning Silk Pants

and the faith that he had in his alma mater no doubt played an important part in the Jackrabbit victory. The members of the team not only had State college in their minds when they were out there blocking and tackling but also this man — one of the most successful of State's alumni."

Halvorson did not elaborate on exactly what Coughlin said. But, the silk pants surely underscored just how Coughlin felt about his alma mater's upset over Wisconsin.

Chapter 27

The First National Championship

The story of South Dakota State College's 1953 national track championship team sounds, by today's standards, a little farfetched.

After all, who would think that you could stuff five guys and their gear into the coach's yellow Buick sedan, drive straight south to Abilene, Texas, and run away with the first national title in State's sports history?

Who, indeed, but the infamous coach Jim Emmerich?

Hurdler John Popowski, a junior that spring, remembers: "It was the NAIA small-college championships. Jim Emmerich piled the five of us in a car and the six of us drove down there. It was the end of May, and we hadn't had any decent weather. All these Southern schools had been running since January."

Pictured above, Jackrabbit great Pete Retzlaff follows through after throwing the discus.

The car ride "was pretty much the way you went to any meet," according to Pete Retzlaff, a senior who competed in shot put, discus, high jump, javelin and hurdles.

"You either chartered a bus or went by automobile," Retzlaff explains. "Because there were only five of us, we went in Coach Emmerich's car. It took us a while to get there."

Rounding out the group were milers Arlin Patrick, Russ Nash and Jack Pearson. Nash said he ran a 4:21 mile and a 9:45 — "or something like that" — two-mile.

"Back in those days," he says, "we hadn't broken the four-minute mile."

Still, South Dakota State consistently fielded teams of fast-paced runners in the 1950s. Says Nash: "We always had a pretty big bunch of milers. We used to sweep (the competitions). The distance runners — it seemed like that was always the team's strong point."

Giving Emmerich credit for the runners' success, Pearson points out: "Coach Emmerich was wonderful. As a man, he was super, too. He took interest in you off and on the field. He was always interested in how you were doing. Kind of a father figure."

He also "worked us pretty hard," says Nash.

Popowski adds: "He was a kind of guy that got out there in front of you — gave you your calisthenics. He was a calisthenics instructor during World War II. If he expected you to do it, he'd do it right along with you."

As an athlete, Emmerich, class of 1940, was co-captain of the State football team that won the North Central Conference title in 1939. He was an all-conference and all-American selection in football and lettered in track and field.

Emmerich's coaching fame in track and cross country spanned 15 years at SDSU, from 1946 to 1960. During that period, Emmerich fielded a team for 13 NCC meets, winning 10 and finishing second in three. Six years after the 1953 team took home the National Association of Intercollegiate Athletics title, his 1959 squad won the National Collegiate Athletic Association College Division title.

In addition to his work at State, Emmerich was a trainer for the U.S. Olympic team for the 1956 games in Melbourne, Australia. He served as head trainer for the U.S. Pan America team in Chicago in 1959, the 1964 Summer Olympics in Japan and the U.S. hockey team. Emmerich was inducted into the SDSU Hall of Fame in 1972.

None of the five team members can recall having any great expectations for the national meet in Abilene that spring of 1953.

The First National Championship

Russ Nash, Jack Pearson, John Popowski, Coach Jim Emmerich, Pete Retzlaff, and Arlin Patrick are all smiles after winning the national title.

"We knew Pete Retzlaff would be up there someplace," says Popowski. "And our distance men were really good. They were our bread and butter. Everybody went and scored some points. I got fifth in the 400-meter hurdles and I had never run them before. In fact, we had never set up a full flight of hurdles in practice — three or four — and I got my spacing between 'em.

"I don't know that we expected anything. Jim Emmerich had a better idea than we did. He was keeping track of who was throwing shot and discus around the country, and what other milers and two-milers were doing."

Pearson remembers the sense that the team might put on a solid performance. "We had some pretty good times that compared well with the competition. I don't know if we had it in mind that we would win. But, the chips all fell in place and we had a lot of fun."

In retrospect, Retzlaff allows, it's amazing to think a team of five individuals topped the competition. "Abilene Christian was noted for its prowess in track and field. And, they being the host team, they probably had quite a few people."

Retzlaff also says the caliber of athletes was of national stature. "For five people to win a national meet," he added, "the only way you can explain it is that all five of us happened to compete in events where we were dominant."

With no idea of what they might achieve, Patrick notes, "Pete won shot and discus and broke records in both. I got fifth in the mile and Russ and Jack got first and second."

In the mile, Pearson says he was leading at the start of the last lap: "Two guys from other schools pulled up, but I held them off until we came right into the finish. I strayed away a little bit from the pole and Russ came through on the inside and won it."

According to Nash, the point spread was so close — maybe a point or two — that the meet was over before anyone knew who had won. The SDSU team was so elated that everyone wanted to head straight home to Brookings and celebrate. Except, Patrick says, for the coach: "Jim Emmerich wanted to stop and eat."

Pearson recalls, "We had dinner about midnight, then we jumped in the car and headed for home. Jim was notorious for getting lost. We all sacked out, of course, and he was driving. A couple of hours later, we got back to about where we were."

Popowski remembers: "When we left down there, it was 86 degrees — the warmest weather we had had since the fall. Then, we came home. It was great to win. I don't think it sinks in until after."

As it turned out, in the case of the SDSU track champs, there would be ample opportunity to ponder their victory.

"I guess it was rather euphoric," Retzlaff reflects. "I don't think we thought we were going to win. But, we all scored very well. Coming back, we felt pretty good about it — until we hit campus and no one was around. ... School was out. When we got back to campus, it was deserted. No one was there. We checked our gear at the athletic department and went home."

Chapter 28

Tragedy and Triumph

When people talk about State's NCAA college division basketball championship team of 1963, the conversation typically turns to the infamous one-handed, midcourt jump shot by Sid Bostic.

It was, as assistant coach Jim Marking says, the shot heard 'round the world — or, at least, the world of basketball.

And yet, as spectacular as Bostic's game-winning basket was, that shot was just one part of a much larger story: a tale of tragedy and triumph, and the irrepressible and prairie-hardened South Dakota spirit.

"It was something that took place in our lifetime that we'll never forget," says Wayne Rasmussen, class of 1964. "What made that possible is that you had a group of young men at the time that pulled together. We were a team that was not without some hardships."

The year before the championship season was as emotionally draining as

---

Pictured above, Sid Bostic is carried off the basketball court after making the game-winning shot.

First row: Nick Brod, Mick Anderson, Tom Black, Dave Fischer, Wayne Rasmussen. **Row two**: Freshman and Assistant Varsity Coach Jim Marking, Doug Peterson, LaMoine Torgerson, Denny Busch, Coach Jim Iverson. **Row three:** Jerry Buri, Bob Glasrud, Dick Cronberg, Sid Bostic, Dave Tjaden.

they get. Marking had gone hunting north of town with sophomore Bob Sheldon, a Brookings boy.

"That was preseason and we were practicing," Marking says. "We were hunting, and he says, 'Coach, I can't walk anymore.' He went to the doctor the next day and was diagnosed with acute leukemia. That was Oct. 30 or something. He died the following April."

Sheldon, who played guard for the Jacks, was a great competitor, says Marking. Marking and his wife, Carola, named a son after Sheldon. The ball field in Brookings also carries Sheldon's name.

The team pulled together, overcame Sheldon's death, says Rasmussen, and returned in the fall of 1962 to an ambitious schedule of preseason games.

"I think we knew that we were pretty good," he says. "But, back in those days we got humbled. One of the things we were able to do was 'play up.' Before the season started, we could play teams such as Kansas, Iowa, Iowa State, Brigham Young. I think you could go back and look at those scores and

Tragedy and Triumph

find that we'd get clipped pretty good. But it was an experience that made us better."

Tom Black grew up in La Crosse, Wis., and went to the University of Wisconsin his freshman year. "That's where I met Nick Brod, and he said, 'We're going to have a greater opportunity in South Dakota, under Jim Iverson.'"

So Black and Brod came to South Dakota State that same fall of 1962.

"I think you had a great balance of seasoned veterans with a lot of experience, and a great coach and assistant coach with a knowledge of the game," says Black, class of 1964. "Everybody sort of felt like it was all coming together — the coaching experience, the understanding of what the other teams were capable of. As the season advanced, the win column showed a lot more excitement than normal. Everybody was talking about it. ...

"I would not say we were cavalier in our thinking, but then again, as the season presented itself, we felt we could beat everybody in our conference. And then, we were starting to say, 'What about the next level?'"

The prevailing thought became that there was no reason the Jacks should lose to anyone. The team was just as good as any other. The Jacks stuck to their approach of one game at a time.

The success of that mindset played out in the team's win-loss record. At the season's start, State was 4-4. The Jacks moved on to the national tournament after winning the NCAA Midwest Regional Tournament and posting a 21-5 record.

Still, State headed into the quarterfinals at Evansville as the underdog, expected to lose to Fresno State. Instead, the Jacks emerged victorious 84-71. At the same time, Evansville was matched up with Southern Illinois.

"Jerry Sloan was playing for Evansville," recalls Marking, referring to the player who would go on to Washington Bullets and Chicago Bulls fame, and to coach the Utah Jazz. "He was an outstanding player. The other guy was Walt Frazier (of New York Knicks lore). He was playing for Southern Illinois. It was dog-eat-dog. They set up extra benches for all the pro scouts as they knocked each other around. Southern Illinois won and played South Dakota State the next night."

That was a good break for the Jacks. Southern Illinois had to turn around and play after a tough, emotional game. Still, Southern Illinois led for much of the match-up. State was behind at halftime and remained that way until the last few minutes.

"Then," laughs Marking, "one of the Southern Illinois kids lost a contact. They looked for a contact lens for six or seven minutes, and lost their momentum. We went on and beat 'em. We couldn't have beat them once out of 10 times."

Head coach Jim Iverson, who coached State from 1956-64, led teams to the national tournament in 1959, 1961 and 1963. In 1961, the Jacks took third place and Don Jacobson earned MVP honors. Wayne Rasmussen was named MVP when the Jacks won the championship title in 1963. Those were considerable achievements for a South Dakota school, says Iverson, particularly in those days of the college and university divisions. The competition was fierce.

Iverson credits the Jacks' success to the mostly homebred nature of the players. "They were almost all South Dakota kids. I think that helped a little bit."

With all those seasoned veteran players and coaches and big-name schools, the Jacks knew what they were up against. Yet, the South Dakotans stayed grounded.

"We looked at each other with respect," Black remembers. "We knew we were not just there for fun and games. We had come a long way to represent South Dakota in a very prestigious NCAA format. We were able to keep a degree of decorum and never let it get too high in our minds. But, we never thought why we should lose and we never got manic or thought we were in over our heads. We just went out and played."

The team members also bought themselves big 10-gallon cowboy hats. Rasmussen says the idea was simply someone's suggestion and "everybody was, 'sure, let's do it.'"

"To see them walk down the streets in Evansville," chuckles Marking, "they looked like a bunch of giants. They looked like they were 10 feet tall. Psychologically, that helped us."

In the final game, South Dakota State was pitted against the Wittenburg College Tigers. It was a slow game as the Jacks tested the Tigers' match-up zone defense.

State led throughout the first half, at one point leading 20-11. By halftime, Wittenburg cut the Jacks lead to two points, 25-23. Then followed a 13 and a half minute drought, where State managed only three points. Rasmussen fouled out with 2:56 left in the game and the Jacks down 38-34. Bostic nailed two field goals and the score narrowed to 40-38. Wittenburg responded with a free throw to make the score 41-38 with 1:08 remaining.

The Jacks' Bob Glasrud joined the fray and, according to Collegian accounts, pumped in a shot, cutting the Tigers' lead to one point. Wittenburg was fouled and sunk the first shot, but not the second. With 19 seconds left,

Glasrud tied the game.

"Those are the key plays," Marking says. "Today, they would be three-point shots. Glasrud was just as much a hero as Bostic."

Bostic says the Tigers' style was difficult for the Jacks to play. "Wittenburg was a very deliberate team. They'd walk the ball up the court. They did not shoot very often, and when they did, they tried to take high-percentage shots. We liked to move the ball up the court in a hurry. We liked the fast break."

Says Iverson: "They slowed the game way down. But, they were not as big as we were. I told the guys we're not going to try to speed up and waste energy — we have to beat them in a low-scoring game. That helped. We went into the game knowing that we were not going to kick this team up to 80s and 90s. We were going to play their tempo."

In the waning seconds, the Tigers had possession of the ball, but missed the shot.

"Ironically," notes Bostic, "for a team that was so patient, one of their players took a shot he never should have."

Brod grabbed the rebound for the Jacks and set up Bostic, who had one foot on the midcourt stripe when he made the game-winning basket.

"I just knew I had to shoot fast," says Bostic, class of 1964. "You don't have time to really think. A lot of it is instinctive. You just do the same sort of thing for the last 16 to 18 years you've been playing basketball. And, obviously, when a ball goes into the basket from somewhere around midcourt, you're very lucky. ... When you're running, you just shoot from whatever foot you're on. There isn't any skill involved."

What was going through his mind?

"To play as hard as I could," says Bostic. "When you get toward the end of a season, you've played 25, 26, 27 games, you're just physically worn out. I wasn't very heavy — just skin and bones by end of season. You just say to yourself, 'one more game.' You've got to keep playing hard. You've come this far, you've got to take advantage of the situation."

Says Black: "The last shot was like everything else. It's not as if you focus on one element throughout a close game. You keep the whole thing in context. You have to be seeing where the outlet pass is, if you're in a position to get it, if it's right-handed. It's all happening at the same time. You see Sid Bostic, three seconds, two seconds, the ball is coming, he's off the wrong foot and almost off the wrong hand."

From the sidelines, coach Iverson says he saw the ball passed to Bostic, who "took two or three dribbles and shot the ball. It was maybe a 38- to 40-foot shot. I was right in line with the shot. I could see he had it lined up real well. The score was tied, so we still would have had overtime if he didn't make it. It happened so fast. Everybody was running around on the floor. I looked down the line and saw (Wittenburg coach) Eldon Miller lying on the floor."

The implication of the basket took time to sink in.

"When the basket was made," Black muses, "it took five seconds for me to remember to jump up and be elated. We worked hard the whole game."

Marking says he wasn't thinking too much at that moment. "I saw the other coach. I saw him fall flat on his face. The ball went in and he just collapsed on the floor. They've got the last shot. They miss it. We throw a three-quarter length shot and make it. It was a great moment for South Dakota."

Rasmussen watched the final moments play out from the bench. He doesn't remember what thoughts were going through his mind.

"It went so fast," he says, noting that Bostic thought the Jacks were behind instead of tied when he tossed the ball. "It was quite a classic. I can still see it happening 40 years later."

Bostic says it still feels good to know that the game was actually tied, because had they gone into overtime, the Jacks would have had a good chance of winning. And, if he had known the score was tied, would he still have made the shot?

"Time was running out," Bostic says. "I had nothing to lose."

Of Bostic's toss, Rasmussen laughs: "It gets longer every year. When you look at it on video, it's just beyond half-court."

Rasmussen was the tournament's top individual scorer with 56 points,

Per the 1963 Jack Rabbit, "Nick Brod, 6-5 forward, struggles under the weight of the huge trophy while his amused teammates look on."

averaging 18.7 per game. The sports media covering the event also named him the Most Valuable Player. Both Rasmussen and Black also were named to the all-tourney five.

Doug Peterson, class of 1964, had played in Watertown for coach Marking and then came to State with him. The thrill of the championship season and the journey to Evansville remain treasured memories after four decades.

"We just played game to game," says Peterson, echoing the simple philosophy the players and coaches of the 1963 team espouse. "We went out with the idea that we could win any game if we played our game."

Yet, they could not help but marvel at how far that idea had brought them.

"At the national tournament in Evansville," Peterson muses, "we were sitting in the lobby of the hotel, saying about ourselves, 'What's this bunch of country hicks doing here?'"

As for his memory of the final moments of the game, Peterson says: "We were tied at the time, and then, just bingo. It was a sudden shock to us and the other team as well. The minute Sid made the shot, we were as high as you could be and then there was the other team, their heads are down and they're crying."

Brod, credited by both the Collegian account and Bostic with making the pass for the infamous half-court shot, laughs at the moment of glory and claims he can't say for certain where he was — or, even if he was on the court.

"All I can remember is this wonderful bunch of guys and having the greatest coach," insists Brod. "They're just the neatest people you'd ever want to meet."

After the tournament, as the team headed back to South Dakota, Brod went his separate way. He and his high school sweetheart, who had been dating since high school in Huron, got married and went on their honeymoon.

"We started dating when we were 14," explains Brod. "Here we were, eight years later, 22 years old, and she's asking me, 'When are we getting married?' I said, 'When we win the national championships this spring, we'll get married.' So (the Jacks) won the game and we went to the justice of the peace."

Prodded to conjure up his memories of Bostic's winning basket, Brod says: "Yeah, it was a shot from midcourt. It was beautiful."

What was he thinking?

"I was thinking I was getting married tomorrow; I was in a haze," he laughs, noting that 40 years later he is still married to the "most beautiful girl in the world."

The Jacks, sporting their western headwear, returned to Brookings shortly after midnight and were greeted by fans at Ward's Cafe with a steak feed. A voice singing "SDSC, hurrah for the Yellow and Blue. SDSC, all honor and glory to you" blared from a loudspeaker and the cafe's window bore the message, "Welcome home national champs."

In retrospect, Bostic attributes the team's success to its attitude.

"It would be easy to say we were pointing toward a national championship," he says. "But you never do that. You just sort of play one game at a time, hoping to win. Then, when we began to get toward the end of the season, there was a sense among the players on the team that we would have a chance. We never talked about it, though. We always talked about the next game."

For a team to make it to the national tournament is an impressive feat in and of itself.

"There are several hundred teams in Division II," reasons Bostic. "To have the audacity to think you could be one of the eight teams to get into a national tournament — that's pretty presumptuous."

The South Dakotans were rooted firmly in the ground. They were a close-knit group with diverse personalities and respect for each other. After the championship season, they finished school and went on to make their mark on the world. They carved out successful, enriching careers, and many have turned around and made significant contributions of time, effort and money to State.

Iverson notes: "We were fortunate. They were a bunch of real good kids. They all graduated and have done very well in life. That's what really counts."

In an interesting side note, Black was invited to join the Olympic basketball team as an alternate. He traveled through Europe on a 30-country tour. He was drafted in the fourth round by the Baltimore Bullets, but opted instead to join what was called the Industrial League. In those days, he says, there were only 10 NBA teams. As a Phillips 66 Oiler, Black played basketball six months out of the year and then worked in the company's management program for the other six.

In 1969, he tried out for the Seattle Sonics and made the team, earning his place in contemporary history as a question in the Trivial Pursuit board game: Who was the oldest rookie to make the NBA?

Black still remembers his third NBA game, when he started against Wilt Chamberlain: "There he was, all 7-foot-2 of him, and he says, 'Welcome to the NBA, Mr. Black.' ... It's been a marvelous career, the honors, the tremendous people and coaching. It's a neat thing to be able to say, 'I went to South Dakota State.'"

Bostic attributes the team's success on the court and in life to the good fortune of being raised South Dakotans.

"We were mostly Midwestern kids, from smaller communities, with a very strong work ethic," Bostic says. "We were the kind of kids who were willing to dedicate themselves to a cause and then work hard to achieve it."

The Evansville experience as a whole — beyond the tournament — struck the group as a once in a lifetime event. One of the local service clubs took care of the Jacks with what seemed like royal treatment. Jokes Bostic: "We were common, ordinary Midwestern kids, who nobody had paid a whole lot of attention to."

In the big picture, Bostic says, the championship was a fun time and a great experience. But, the long-lasting impact comes from the meaning behind it:

"It helped to solidify that when you made a commitment and were willing to work hard, and be diligent and honest, you could achieve anything you set your mind to. What it teaches you is how to be committed, not just to athletic things, but the more important things in life."

Looking back, Black savors the moment.

"A memory," he says philosophically, "is only as good as the substance that goes into it. When you take a championship tournament and a championship contest — and you win it — and you've got 10 people on the team that you have a lot of respect for, and two coaches, and all the students, you can't get any better than that."

Chapter 29

Détente with a Round Ball

April 17, 1961, an armed force of about 1,500 Cuban exiles landed in the Bahia de Cochinos — the Bay of Pigs — on the south coast of Cuba.

Trained and given arms by the United States, the rebels intended to fuel an insurrection and overthrow Fidel Castro's communist regime. The effort failed, and it destroyed the little that was left of American-Cuban relations.

Sixteen years later, SDSU men's basketball coach Gene Zulk and his USD counterpart led a joint team of Jackrabbits and Coyotes to play a series of exhibition games in Cuba. The South Dakotans were among the first Americans to visit Cuba since the Bay of Pigs.

Pictured above, SDSU basketball player Bob Ashley holds the team's interpreter while standing on a Cuban beach. Bob Sundvold (11) and Larry Nickelson (14) enjoy the moment, too.

"They picked us up on a plane in Sioux Falls, maybe 30 of us," recalls SDSU athletic trainer Jim Booher. "We flew to Washington, D.C., and another 100 people — congressmen, press — got on. It was wild. Then we flew to Miami, and then Cuba. ...

"We didn't have much to do with the press. They weren't there to cover the games. They were there to get into Havana."

The visit, organized by George McGovern and Jim Abourezk, both Democratic senators from South Dakota, brought together a team comprised of five SDSU players, five USD players, coaching staff from both campuses, the SDSU and USD sports information directors, and Booher, as the trainer.

McGovern says he had been to Cuba to meet with Castro as a member of the Senate Foreign Relations Committee: "After a five- or six-hour meeting, I asked if he had any suggestions on what might improve relations between Cuba and the United States. He said, 'Send the New York Yankees to play us in baseball.' He was serious."

McGovern put in a call to baseball Commissioner Bowie Kuhn, who said he would check with the owners.

"Two, three days later, Bowie calls me back and says, 'George, the owners say they can't play unless every team has a player,'" says McGovern. "I said, 'OK, let me call the Cubans.' They said fine. So, I go back to Bowie. He says, 'I'll get back to you.' Then he gets back to me and says, 'Now the owners say they can't go unless they can recruit down there.' I said, 'Bowie, there's no way the Cubans will agree to that.'

"So I went back, this time to Castro, and he says, 'No, they'll take everybody we've got.' So it fell through."

Abourezk says Castro also liked basketball. The two senators offered Castro a game with the South Dakotans and the Cuban leader agreed.

"I remember Red Auerbach — he was coaching the Boston Celtics — and he says, 'That's the most stupid thing, taking a South Dakota team down there,'" laughs Abourezk. "Well, I said, 'I don't represent Boston.'"

Of the many unforgettable memories, Abourezk adds: "We were welcomed by the minister of sports. He gave a speech. And then, I gave a speech and said this was the most Americans in Cuba since the Bay of Pigs. They loved it."

The game was supposed to feature a Cuban team of equal ability. But, once in Cuba, as coach Zulk remembers: "we came to the arena to practice and we learned that we would be playing their Olympic team. Obviously, there was quite a difference in ages."

And ability, too.

"They were very good," says Zulk.

Détente with a Round Ball

SDSU basketball player Larry Nickelson tries to save the ball from going out of bounds under the watchful eye of Cuban national hero, Che Guevara.

Of the two games played, Cuba won both — 91-72 and 88-69.

Booher still has vivid recollections: "To get to the game, they put us on a bus, with a police car in front and behind, red lights and sirens. We just flew. ... Then, it was really something to walk out into the arena.

"Of all the things I've done in athletics, it was probably the neatest experience, walking out of this tunnel into the arena and the people really went nuts."

Zulk adds: "Their fans were great. They loved basketball. The place was packed."

The experience truly was something to behold for the South Dakotans, many of whom had come from small towns and never had dreamed of being part of such an adventure. The fact that the group mixed two in-state rivals — archrivals — also left an indelible mark.

"You battle the U every year, your whole life as a South Dakota State coach," says Zulk. "You always like those guys, but here you are, not only going to Cuba together, but we practiced together, we lived together, we traveled together. It really was a unique opportunity."

Steve Brown, a junior from Bryant, says the mood of the players was a combination of excitement and nervousness. It was one thing to play USD.

Quite another to go to a communist country and compete against its best players.

"Stepping onto the court," says Brown, now living in Madison, Wis., "that was something a little different. ... Of all the great sports teams of the country, there we were — USD and SDSU."

More than 20 years later, Brown remembers one play in particular. "I can't remember how I did it, but I went up to block a shot and I accidentally hit this guy. All of the sudden, the crowd was doing this hissing thing. It wasn't booing, but it was a hissing thing. Fifteen thousand people."

But, he laughs, "we got out of there OK."

Bob Sundvold, a political science major and Canton native, says the players had some idea of the trip's significance, but the full realization of what it implied did not come until later.

"One of the funny quotes at the time," he says, "was that it was a big deal all of us were going to Cuba, but it was a bigger deal that SDSU and USD were dressed in the same uniform and played on the same team."

For Abourezk, the most thrilling moment occurred at the start of the first game. "The Cubans played the American national anthem. I was just overwhelmed with emotion. And, everybody stood up. It was a vast diplomatic

Steve Brown gets tangled with a Cuban player while Bob Ashley (No. 16) and Bob Sundvold (No. 11) look on.

opening, although it didn't bear much fruit."

All the men all remember the royal treatment they received, from the resort accommodations on the beach and the banquets replete with entertainment to tours of the country's schools and a baseball manufacturing plant. They met dignitaries, including Castro's brother, Raúl, and a few of Cuba's Olympic athletes.

Ron Lenz, SDSU sports information director, was sports information director for USD at the time. He says the visit completely altered the playing field. As Americans in a communist country that had strained relations with the United States, he explains, "For the most part, you didn't know what you could do and what you couldn't. You didn't know who was watching."

And yet, Lenz adds, "it was a great experience, a great opportunity."

He still remembers standing next to Dave Martin, his SDSU counterpart on the trip, during the pregame pomp and circumstance. Martin noticed right away that the United States flag was one-sided.

"The wall flags have the blue background, but no stars on the backside," says Lenz. "The photographer from The Associated Press got the photo (of the flag) and it showed up in so many places."

John Gross of Madison, class of 1954, was among the South Dakotans who traveled with the team: "It was just one of the most fantastic trips I've ever been on. A lot of press was there, NBC, ABC, CBS. George McGovern. The owner of the Miami Dolphins (Joe Robbie)."

One of the more lasting memories from the game, adds Gross, was the crowd: "They never clapped — they whistled."

More than 30 years later, Gross says he still has a few trinkets from the trip — a baseball signed by Juan Torino and a few Cuban cigars.

Beyond the basketball, visiting the communist country gave the South Dakotans a greater insight into the people who lived there. McGovern says any feelings of Cold War hostilities dissipated.

"The players from both sides loved it," he says. "They admired their skills and enjoyed the exchange of ideas. They got to know each other somewhat."

Zulk says tours of schools, sports facilities and factories gave a new-found appreciation for American freedoms.

"It was decided for you whether you were going to a sports school or you were going to be a farmer or factory worker," says Zulk. "Your dye was cast. We went to a factory where they made baseballs. Those people, if they were a factory worker making baseballs, they did the same thing their whole lives."

From a player perspective, adds Zulk, the trip posed greater meaning than the typical game schedule — particularly for the Midwestern youngsters.

"You recruit area kids who may not have had such exposure, flying to wherever," he says. "It wasn't something we did every year. You couldn't compare going to Cuba with going to Nebraska or Texas. This had to be about as unique a college experience as you can have."

The following November, the Cubans visited South Dakota and played games both at USD and SDSU.

McGovern quips, "I thought we ought to show them that they can't just roll over the American players and we asked if they'd come to the U.S."

In addition to playing the South Dakota team, the Cubans also competed against the University of Minnesota, Holy Cross in Massachusetts, and several other teams. And, according to McGovern, they experienced some losses.

"I thought that was good," he says, smiling.

Harry Forsyth, who at the time was SDSU assistant athletic director under Stan Marshall, had an inside view of all the plans and preparations for the visitors.

"It was our first experience with a lot of security," Forsyth says. "Boy, we had Secret Service people all over our building for about two to three days before they got here. Bomb-sniffing dogs went through the locker room. ...

"The CIA was talking to the airplane since they left Minneapolis. It was pretty tense. We met 'em in Sioux Falls and brought 'em up on a bus. There were about three or four highway patrolmen ahead and behind us."

Lenz laughs at one incident in particular: "KELO-TV got on the bus and rode part way with the Cuban team. It just so happened that they pulled off by the Crooks Gun Club and all of the sudden shots are being fired. (KELO) just wanted to get some film and they happened to pull over at that spot. It got a little hectic."

Once in Brookings, as the Cubans had done for the Americans, the South Dakota hosts offered gifts.

"Our exchange was jeans," says Booher. "They were really interested in our jeans."

Adds Forsyth: "The thing they wanted and liked more than anything else, we gave them all a pair of jeans. They thought it was the greatest thing since sliced bread."

Chapter 30

Oh, How it Hurt(s)

Some seasons, you have a great run and win every game. Other times, the losses overwhelm the wins, but the kids are good and you still love the season.

And then, there are the times when everything comes together and life just doesn't get any better. Such was the case with the 1984-85 men's basketball team,

"We not only had a team that was disciplined and balanced, and fun to be around," says then-head coach Gene Zulk, "but we also won."

The inkling of what the year might bring started with a preseason game against Division I Kansas, which SDSU lost 85-72.

"Danny Manning, one of the top college players in the country, was playing at Kansas," Zulk recalls. "And Larry Brown, (now) an NBA coach, was the coach at Kansas. We played a great game. It was close, very competitive. We

---

Pictured above, SDSU cheerleader Renee Schimkat reflects on the heartbreaking outcome of the NCAA Division II finals loss to Jacksonville State.

were clearly the underdogs. Larry Brown, after the game, was talking to various players and saying how impressed he was."

With All-American Mark Tetzlaff, among others, on the Jacks' team, the Kansas game "let us know kind of early on what an extraordinary run we were going to have," Zulk says.

SDSU won the North Central Conference with a 14-4 league record and wound up hosting the regional tournament and quarterfinals in Brookings — all won by the Jacks in front of the home crowd.

"It was the year where nothing went wrong," Zulk fondly recalls. "In coaching, either somebody gets hurt or something goes wrong. But, we just flowed from game to game, from beginning to end."

In the regional game, SDSU played California-Hayward. The Brookings crowd lined up early and long — from Frost Arena south to Young and Binnewies halls — for a then-record Frost Arena attendance of 9,339.

"We let 'em in early," Zulk says. "The crowd could always entertain themselves. It was a big party. The Hayward players were just awed. They went out early with cameras, went into the stands and had their pictures taken with the fans. I can remember after the game they said they hated to lose, but this experience was so unbelievable, they didn't mind as much."

SDSU won the quarterfinal game 62-58, earning a berth in the Final Four opening round. The Jacks had won the national championship in 1963, but this was the first time SDSU had reached the Division II semifinals since the college division of the NCAA was split into Division II and III in 1975. About 300 loyal Jacks fans followed the team to the tournament.

The Final Four was held in Springfield, Mass., where the festivities kicked off with a banquet. All the coaches introduced their teams and made comments about their season.

"I jokingly said that it was fun to be on the East Coast and have ESPN cover the tournament because in South Dakota we're not able to get ESPN," Zulk laughs. "They honest to gosh thought I was serious."

In the first game, SDSU clearly was the underdog with Mount St. Mary's heavily favored to win. With an impressive 28-4 record, the Mountaineers boasted an average score of 80 points per game while holding opponents to a 67-point average. But, the Jacks emerged victorious, 78-71. Tetzlaff, named the tournament's Most Outstanding Player, was credited with a nearly flawless game and a career-high 32 points. He had 14 rebounds, 13 of 18 from the field, six of nine at the line, two assists, two blocks and one steal.

The next night, in the contest for the national title, the Jacks were again the underdogs, this time to Jacksonville State of Alabama. The 'Rabbits trailed the Gamecocks most of the first period and were down 40-35 at halftime. SDSU outscored Jacksonville 14-6 in the first seven and a half minutes of the second period. The Jacks built the lead to seven, 71-64, with 2:14 left in the game. Fourteen seconds later, a Gamecock field goal closed the gap to 71-66.

Athletic trainer Jim Booher recalls: "All of the sudden, we find ourselves in the championship game against Jacksonville State. We were leading by seven with two minutes to go in the game. ... The last two minutes, we couldn't get the ball inbound. ...

"You don't find yourself in that position very often — to win a national title."

Former Brookings Register sports editor Terry Borns recounted in his game story how Tetzlaff drew his fifth personal foul — "one of many controversial calls and non-calls by referees Eric Harmon and London Bradley."

It was a tough moment. Until that point, Tetzlaff had led both teams with 21 points and 13 rebounds. With less than two minutes to go, he was condemned to sit on the sidelines and watch the Jacks' lead slip away. Jacksonville sank both free shots off Tetzlaff's foul. SDSU called a timeout. A half-court inbound pass barely avoided interception. Tom McDonald flew off the court and the Gamecocks were awarded the ball.

Borns wrote: "The play brought an enraged reaction from the SDSU bench and Jackrabbit fans, who felt McDonald was fouled. Instead of McDonald, a 91.1 percent free throw shooter going to the line, Jacksonville was awarded the ball and McDonald fouled Earl Warren, who calmly sank both ends of the bonus with 1:37 left to bring the Gamecocks within one, 71-70.

"Jacksonville's pressure forced another SDSU turnover seconds later when Mark Schultz was stripped after hauling in the inbound pass. That led to a Melvin Allen layup with 50 seconds left and a one point Gamecock lead."

The remaining seconds were painful. An SDSU timeout was followed by a loss of the ball and then a foul. Jacksonville made both free throws. SDSU's Mark Schultz slam-dunked for two points and time ran out. The final score: Gamecocks, 74; SDSU, 73.

Tetzlaff, the 6-7 center from Hayti, says the championship run in his senior year at SDSU had a tremendous impact on him and he often relives that moment of his life.

"We jelled real well," he recalls. "Coach Zulk seemed to be able to pull the best out of all of us. The guy was not only concerned about coaching. He made you feel important as a person. Those two aspects, you put them together, and people are willing to work hard for you."

From the Cal-State Hayward game in Brookings — where Tetzlaff still remembers walking into the HPER and feeling the noise vibrations pulse through the building — to the finals in Springfield, the players knew they had it in them to win despite their underdog status.

Seventeen years later, those last minutes of the championship game, with color commentary by the infamous Dick Vitale, still hold amazing clarity.

"Two minutes to go, Mark Tetzlaff fouled out," says Zulk. "He never fouled out of a college game. It was the first kind of damning event."

For Tetzlaff: "That was the toughest minute and 56 seconds I've ever played in a game on the bench. It's one of those things. You can disagree with the ref ..." His voice trails off.

Then, the game was down to under a minute.

"It appeared as though Tom McDonald had been fouled on the sidelines," Zulk says, "but for whatever reason, it wasn't called. Tom was the leading foul shooter in the country. They get the ball back and go ahead to win the game.

"It was one of those things — it took me about 10 years to forget how close it was. Since then, I've moved on. I remember it for the experience and what a great team it was."

McDonald, a junior point guard, says the team's greatness stemmed from how well the team played together: "We were not the most talented. ... But, there was such good chemistry. Somehow, we clicked."

Coach Zulk played a big role, too.

"I played for my dad in high school," says McDonald, "so I can't say Zulk's the best coach I ever played for. But, he was such a player's coach. He was easy to play for."

Whatever "it" was, Zulk and his players found themselves on top of their game, in the game of the year — until those final two minutes.

"Tetzlaff fouled out and the roof caved in on us," recalls McDonald, who now coaches basketball and teaches high school in Ely, Minn. "They tried to get an inbound play to me, but a guy came over my back and pushed me. ... Coach wanted me to get the ball because I was shooting 90 percent from the free-throw line."

Former athletic director Harry Forsyth credits part of the officiating problems to the fact that Division I had gone to three refs per game instead of two. But, Division II had not: "In the infinite wisdom of the Division II basketball, they felt they should have Division I officials work the final game. But, the game they worked was the first game they worked all year as two officials instead of three."

In fairness, Forsyth says, the official "didn't see McDonald get creamed. It was right at midcourt. The guy tried to take the ball away and knocked McDonald right under the scoring table. We all saw it. He was laying under the table."

And the rest, as the saying goes, is history. Even though the Jacks were not expected to win, the fact that the team had the national title in its grasp and then lost it remains a sore memory.

"It's still hard to handle," McDonald says. "I have it on tape and can't watch the whole game. It's too painful, and it's how many years later? I like watching it — we played so well. But, I usually turn it off."

In fact, he concedes, he doesn't remember ever watching the final two minutes of the tape.

"The ref didn't call it like we saw it," says Tetzlaff. "Anytime you have the game in your grips and there are some very questionable calls, it's like somebody stole something from you. ... But, life goes on."

Says Booher, "It was really a bitter pill to swallow."

John Gross of Madison, a 1954 State grad, had a press pass and watched the game courtside at the press table. To this day, he has no doubt about what happened: "The referees choked."

Oddly enough, the referee who failed to make the call when McDonald was sent sprawling into the scorer's table was also at the receiving end of the infamous chair-throwing incident with Indiana coach Bobby Knight.

"It was the same official," Gross says. "I understood why Knight threw the chair. I wanted to throw the table."

A State fan who was an Indiana grad wrote to Knight and told him about the game. Knight, in turn, sent Zulk a congratulatory letter, one of his signature red ties and a

Coach Gene Zulk shortly after the loss to Jacksonville State.

Mark Shultz (No. 40) starts to celebrate and Mike Round helps Arvis Young off the floor after SDSU beat Augustana in a wild finish that has been dubbed, "The Miracle at Frost Arena."

picture of Knight coaching a game. Zulk has the items framed and hanging in his office in Mound, Minn., today.

As he reflects on the 1984-85 team and its 26-7 season record, Zulk remembers a midseason game against Augustana — dubbed "The Miracle at Frost Arena" — that typified that group of young men he coached:

"We were down three to five points with under a minute left. Mark (Tetzlaff) got fouled. He missed the second shot. We scored, they pressed, we stole the ball and scored again at the horn to beat them by one.

"Everything just went right. We always found a way win."

Until that final game in Springfield, Mass.

Chapter 31

A Run for Glory

Barely two weeks had passed since South Dakota State women's basketball team blazed its way into the history books on March 29, 2003, with a 65-50 win over Northern Kentucky.

Yet, there the players sat with their coaches, reviewing weekend weightlifting and workout schedules, making plans to referee a children's basketball tournament and taking mental notes on the dress code for a steak dinner.

"Khakis and a nice blouse," instructs head coach Aaron Johnston. "No jeans or T-shirts."

With the thrill of State's first-ever women's national basketball championship title slowly sinking into reality, life quickly returned to the mundane details.

What a glorious run, though, the 2002-03 season had been.

Pictured above, national tournament most valuable player, Melissa Pater, reacts to the crowd after cutting down the basketball net in St. Joseph, Mo. (Photo courtesy of Eric Landwehr)

"I don't know if I ever felt we were actually going to do it," reflects Johnston about six weeks after the title game. "Early on, I knew we could be one of the best teams in the conference. Our goal was to win the conference championship. History has shown that the best team in this league ... could carry on."

Laurie Melum, assistant coach, adds: "You always feel deep down inside what you can accomplish. But, to get out of the region is really difficult. ... We were playing well and the teams we faced were some of the best teams in the nation."

The season showed promise early. The Jacks dropped their two exhibition games — Drake University and the University of Minnesota — but went on to chalk up a streak of 17 wins. Then came the first disappointment — a loss to the University of North Dakota in Grand Forks. Two wins followed, then a bitter blow. The Jacks lost to the University of South Dakota in Vermillion.

For Melissa Pater, tournament MVP, the loss to the U was in a sense the most memorable game of the regular season. "Just because of how we felt," she says.

Just playing the Coyotes was an experience for freshman post player Christina Gilbert from Stillwater, Minn.

"The USD game here," says Gilbert, her voice trailing off in awe. "At my high school games, your parents were there, if that. Maybe five high school kids. We were in the training room before the game and someone asked me if I was excited. I had no idea what it's like. Then, we come out and people run to their seats — adults, running, carrying kids; parents, grandma following. It's just something you don't expect."

After the loss in Vermillion, the team turned around and pulled off four more wins, thereby winning the first conference title in the school's history. SDSU hosted the NCC Wells Fargo Tournament, which the Jacks lost in the title game to the University of North Dakota.

"I probably felt the most comfortable with us after the region tournament," says Johnston. "Those were better basketball games we played and a good home crowd."

Melum says, "By winning the region, we knew we had a really good shot."

Backed by a force that would be dubbed by the media "Jackrabbit Nation," the team headed for St. Joseph, Mo. First up was Cal State Bakersfield. What had been expected to be a tough battle turned into a decisive win, 83-62. Next came Bentley College in a completely different game.

A Run for Glory

The Jacks fell behind 15-5 in the first half. Bentley built its lead to 13. The Jacks fought their way back. Then, in the second half, the spread widened again. With little more than 10 minutes left in the game, SDSU was behind 49-39. The momentum shifted like a seesaw and soon the Jacks were within one point, 55-54, with one minute left.

Bentley sunk two free throws to command a three-point lead, 57-54. The Jacks had 5.4 seconds on the clock to decide their destiny.

First, Shannon Schlagel had the ball: "I was running down to rebound and I almost threw it out of bounds. But, I thought, 'no way am I going to lose this.' I passed it to (Heather) Sieler."

"We basically called out a play," Johnston explains. "The ball wasn't specifically supposed to go to Stacie (Cizek). Heather gets the ball, penetrates, and she's supposed to kick it to Brenda (Davis) or Stacie. We were confident. All three had a lot of big shots this year."

Stacie Cizek's last-second shot ties the semifinal game against Bentley College. (Photo courtesy of Eric Landwehr)

Cizek recalls: "I was about two feet away from the three-point line. I knew there was a girl standing right in my face. I faked, dribbled and took the shot. She partially blocked it and tipped the ball in my hand. ... I never really thought about it. It happened so fast. It just went in. I was, like, whoa. Just shock."

Brooke Dickmeyer notes, "We were all just holding hands."

Adds Stephanie Bolden, "And our breath."

From the coaches' standpoint, Melum says: "The shot was right in front of the bench. (Cizek) took it. But, it's not like it was a wide-open shot. ...

235

2002-03 South Dakota State University Women's Basketball Team. **Front Row:** Student trainer Delynda Brink, Christina Gilbert, Karly Hegge, Brenda Davis, Melissa Pater, Shannon Schlagel, Sarita DeBoer, student trainer Namiko Kato. **Back Row:** Trainer Matt Raml, student assistant Jamie Nelson, student assistant Chris Marquardt, Heather Sieler, Megan Otte, Stacie Cizek, Brooke Dickmeyer, Dianna Pavek, Stephanie Bolden, head coach Aaron Johnston, graduate assistant Sheila Roux, assistant coach Laurie Melum. (Photo courtesy of Eric Landwehr)

Everybody was sitting there. Watching it, watching it, watching it. You could tell it had just the right angle to bank in and you just lost it right there."

Announcing the play-by-play for Depot Radio 910-AM, Scott Kwasniewski says: "It was classic. To be in a place you've never been with a shot like that. ... You're down by three, you need three to tie. It was only five seconds left. They inbounded, boom, ran it up the floor, hit the shot and it banked in. It was as freak a shot as you could get.

"The first thing, I was looking at the fans. I remember seeing Stacie's dad just trying to contain himself. I honestly don't remember what I said. ...

"In five, 10 years, a lot of people won't remember the championship game. That was the game they'll remember. It was probably the toughest match-up. Bentley had been there (to the nationals) more than any other team in the nation. ... It was the hardest fought game."

Surreal is the only word Johnston can find to describe the feeling of watching Cizek's shot head toward the hoop: "You can read the lettering on the ball as it travels through the air."

Johnston and Melum, both having wrapped up their third season coaching at SDSU, say they have watched that shot on videotape several times.

Smiling, Johnston says, "It still makes me feel like I was there. I get goose bumps."

With the score tied, the game headed into overtime. But that posed no problem for SDSU.

Davis says, "Right after that, Coach said, 'Now we know the game is ours.'"

It certainly was. The momentum of Cizek's shot carried the Jacks to a 69-62 win. Pater walked off the court with a career high of 31 points. The only trouble now would be getting to sleep.

"There was no way we were going to get to bed," laughs Bolden.

Davis says: "We came back to the hotel and got pizza. How many times do you think we replayed that shot, to see who jumped the highest?"

On Saturday, March 29, the Jacks returned to St. Joseph Civic Arena. Nearly 2,000 SDSU fans filled the metal bleachers, making it seem like a home game. The cameras and commentators of ESPN2 were on hand to broadcast the game nationwide. The Jacks, however, handled the hype.

Karly Hegge explains: "You don't get all that keyed up. You stay focused. It was a dream of ours. But, you put aside the media, the expectations. You play it just like another game."

Says Dickmeyer: "As a whole, the team was really confident. We always felt that the whole year. ... We were just thinking it's another game, just another game."

Davis adds: "I think how we acted in overtime (against Bentley) carried into Saturday night. Everybody probably thought about Stacie's shot. It had a lot to do with the confidence."

The lights, though, were literally shining in their faces.

Laughs Sieler: "Before the game, a camera guy was right in Pater's face. I passed the ball to her for 10 minutes so he could get footage."

Schlagel recalls, "There were cords everywhere."

The championship game was the moment these young women had dreamed about — not just all season, but throughout their lives leading up to that point. This was the moment they thought about during summers in the gym. This was where all the hard work would pay off.

SDSU got off to a fast start against Northern Kentucky, first leading 6-0 and then opening up the advantage 21-10. The Jacks dominated the entire game. They forced UNK into 21 turnovers and out-rebounded the Norse 47-35. After Cizek's amazing, game-saving shot during Thursday night's battle, the championship game — with the Jacks' dominance — seemed almost anticlimactic.

The final buzzer rang. The score: South Dakota State, 65; Northern Kentucky, 50.

Instead of celebrating alone on the court, though, the Jacks headed for their fans.

"I was never prouder of them than at the moment of absolute glory and admiration, when they had every right to be totally in their own world," sighs SDSU President Peggy Gordon Miller. "They were given the (championship) sign and they ran straight to the students and held up the sign in front of them. It was a quintessential moment. Even in this moment of frenzied glory, they were thinking of someone else. Nobody told them to do that. They just spontaneously ran over to where the people who supported them sat."

For Miller, that display of gratitude and appreciation speaks volumes about the team. The experience moved her enough to write the NCAA and offer up the Jacks as a poster team of everything that is good about collegiate athletics.

"They're responsible, caring and even thoughtful at the time of victory," Miller says.

For the team and the coaches, the championship was the end of a long, hard and tiring road.

"The last six games are do or die," says Melum. "Basically, it's a lot of pressure and stress. You have to be really focused. You're not just going out and putting your time in. It's something you're constantly thinking about. You go to bed thinking about the next game."

To the spectators, Johnston was a picture of calm and cool. More than anything else, though, he was tired.

"The whole process is exciting," he says, "but it's the most exhausting thing I've ever been through."

Johnston also says he was trying to make sense of the situation: "I was just trying to figure how I got to where I was, how I got to South Dakota State, why I was given this chance. I was looking down at the other coach, from Northern Kentucky, thinking she's put in more time than me, she's probably more deserving. Why me? Why not somebody else?"

It was a much more introspective reaction than the jumping-in-the-air, raw emotion of the Bentley game two nights earlier.

Kwasniewski, who spends the season following the team, says there was a hint early on of the Jacks' potential:

"This year, obviously, there were a lot of expectations. They did so well last year. ... When they came in the first couple of games and you saw how well they played against Drake, Minnesota — Division I teams — you knew there was something special about this team. You could tell they had worked hard.

"Also, the maturity level of this team ... their demeanor. They're level-headed, no cockiness, no bravado. Everybody is willing to play a role. There's a cohesiveness. ... One of the biggest jokers was Dianna Pavek, who sits on the bench because of a knee injury. But, she's every bit a part of the team. That's not something you can coach or teach."

That assessment strikes at the core of what coach Johnston sees as the key to his team's success.

"To win a national championship," says Johnston, "you really have to be driven."

The 2002-03 season started with practice in October and the first game took place in early November. By the time the final buzzer rang in St. Joseph five months later, the Jacks had played 35 games. Throughout the season, team members played basketball two hours every day. Add another half-hour before and after to get ready and then cleaned up, and that's three hours a day. Several days a week, they also watched films or lifted weights. Rehab also played a significant role and added more time to the day.

"It's a huge commitment," says Johnston. "Of the 12 who finished the season, five had surgery at some point, either last summer, or through the end of the year. There was a broken nose, a stress fracture, sprained ankles — a lot of physical wear and tear."

Johnston is equally proud of his team's academic achievement, which he calls amazing. The average GPA is 3.3.

"Student-athlete is a (phrase) I don't think everyone knows what it means," Johnston says. "It's a commitment."

Johnston also talks about the unselfish nature of his players. All too often, sports today are about "me." The Jacks, however, proved what can be accomplished when the focus is "us." When it comes to playing time, these young women know they are competing against their friends.

"You have to have a certain level of respect for other people," Johnston says. "You have to root for somebody when they do take your spot. We talk about that. It has to go back to the players. They have to be willing to accept and believe in the idea. It won't work unless they want to buy into it."

The 28-year-old coach grins and adds: "It's a mature team. Talk about wisdom beyond years."

In retrospect, there are many special memories for the team and the coaches. During their time in St. Joseph, each squad was paired with a local school. The Jacks were sent to a school for at-risk kids.

"It was awesome," recalls Cizek.

Bolden says: "We just went and introduced ourselves and talked about different stuff. We did a shooting demonstration."

True to character for the Jacks, the experience also left them laughing.

Davis explains: "(Coach) A.J. split us up, 12 people into three groups of four. He gave each group something to talk about. The freshmen, they talked about SDSU and Brookings, how they got here. The next group talked about staying in school. A.J. gives us (the upperclassmen) drugs and alcohol, how to surround yourself with positive friends. Then, Stacie gets up and tells the kids to eat healthy and to take their vitamins."

Still, the players managed to keep their college basketball career in perspective — particularly as the United States was at war with Iraq during the playoff season.

Says Cizek: "I was watching Sports Center (on ESPN) and one of my friends who plays basketball for Creighton, he had a really good quote. He said, 'One of my good friends is overseas. If he screws up tomorrow, he'll die. If I screw up, it's just a game.'"

The hometown fans also hold a special place in each player's heart. They revel in the support of the community.

"You don't realize it until you're out of the game," says Dickmeyer. "You just look up into the stands and it's never-ending just how packed it is."

Megan Otte notes, "At USD games, you can't even hear yourself."

Says Sarita DeBoer: "What really brought it to our attention was the slide show (at a tournament banquet in St. Joseph). At all their gyms, there's like 200 people. Ours comes on, and they bring the USD game tape, and you just hear the whispers, 'How many does your gym hold?'"

Sieler adds, "They're all pretty down to earth. The little kids look up to us — they're always hanging around outside for autographs."

Schlagel finds it amazing that people don't go South for the winter because of Jackrabbit basketball. "Even my 87-year-old uncle. It's his horses and SDSU basketball that keep him alive. It's just awesome. You can come and see everybody at a game or they're listening to it on the radio. So many people want to see you do well. Brookings just seems different."

Pater says: "You get to know our fans on more of a personal basis. You know them by name, know something about 'em. They take time for you. They're interested in your life."

"Well," Cizek points out, "there's not a lot to do in Brookings."

Sieler quips, "She's from Omaha."

A Run for Glory

March 30, 2003, headline in the sports section of the St. Joseph News-Press heralding the news of a Jackrabbit national championship.

Thinking about why Jackrabbit basketball means so much to people, Davis theorizes: "It's something bigger than themselves. ... A lot of times, people are devoted to something that is bigger than they can imagine."

Johnston points out that basketball is unique in its intimacy with the crowd. Fans sit close to the court and can see the players.

"You can see the players' emotions," he says. "It's just the right kind of game. And, Brookings is a small town. All those things came together and just made for a great season. If you took South Dakota State and put it in downtown Minneapolis, I don't know if it'd be the same."

Certainly, there are few other places in the world where a pair of eager fans would pull off the interstate and jump up and down, holding up a sign reading "Jacks are No. 1" as the bus carrying the champions home drives by. That is exactly what happened as the Jacks returned home on Sunday, March 30.

"As long as I live," Johnston told the welcoming crowd at Frost Arena later that day, "Interstate 29, mile marker 109, will be in my memories."

The reality of what the Jacks accomplished in the 2002-03 season took hold as they turned their attention to final exams. In the immediate aftermath, Gov. Mike Rounds, class of 1977, joyously announced the cancellation of classes on Monday, March 31. A few weeks later, he and his wife, Jean, class of 1975, hosted the team at the governor's mansion in Pierre. At another team gathering, the Jacks also took permanent markers in hand and penned their names on piles of T-shirts and a stack of basketballs.

The players began to understand what the championship trophy meant, not just to them, but to their many supporters. When Johnston returned home from St. Joseph, he had 150 e-mails waiting. Only about 50 were from people he knew. The team also received many cards and letters expressing congratulations.

"I think, yeah, we're starting to realize how it affects everybody, how long everybody will be talking about it," Johnston says. "I don't think you get that at many jobs — a place in history."

What began as the preseason goal for a group of young women and their coaches ultimately consumed campus, community and Jacks fans across the country. Then as the players prepared for summer break, their coaches handed out their workout regimens.

Melum says each player has her own program to follow, including weightlifting and skill development. "Things they need and should work on."

Explains Johnston: "The next season starts now. That's what we're preparing for, that's what we're training for. You keep the national championship in mind — it's a motivator and you want to get back there again. But that doesn't guarantee that you will. I wish it was that easy. You have to be driven. You have to realize the sacrifices."

Chapter 32

Tossing Critters

*"I really remember not the wins and losses,
but the atmosphere at Frost Arena."*
Bob Sundvold, former SDSU basketball player

When State played the U on Feb. 7, 1976, it was no different than any other time the two in-state rivals met. Frost Arena was packed. Excitement pulsed through the crowd. A few dead rabbits were tossed onto the court.

Then, with a little time left on the clock, something happened that would bestow legendary status on the night.

"I was standing on the floor, looking at the game," recalls former Jacks cheerleader Margie Fiedler, class of 1977. "A flying, frozen, dead coyote came out of the stands above me and hit me on the back of the head."

Pictured above, a referee discards a rabbit while a player shoots a free throw during an SDSU vs. Augustana game in 1980.

SDSU cheerleader Margie Fiedler is helped off the basketball court after being hit in the head with a frozen coyote.

Fiedler fell and was taken to the training room.

"I was so hyped from the game, all I wanted to do was get back in the game and see what was happening," she says. "I actually saw the end of the game. I think we won, but I can't remember for sure.

"Then, a guy came down from the stands and I knew him. He asked if I was OK. He was just devastated, just horrified. Obviously, he didn't mean to hit me. I said, 'Oh yeah, I'm fine.' Then, I started throwing up blood."

That night's game was the only one Fiedler's parents had attended that season, and they ended up taking her to the Brookings Hospital emergency room. Fiedler laughs, recalling how her mother explained to medical personnel what had happened. Out of context, getting hit on the back of the head with a 55-pound frozen coyote sounded a little bizarre.

"Thank God we weren't playing the Bison," Fiedler quips.

Jacks player Steve Brown remembers being "sort of stunned," although it wasn't unusual in those years to see dead critters being tossed onto the court.

"We didn't realize the severity of it," Brown says. "The game went on. A few days later, we found out she was really severely hurt."

Teammate Bob Sundvold echoes Brown's recollection: "State was a small enough school that you knew everybody. And here, she's hurt and we won. We didn't really know how bad until the next week."

From the players' perspective, the dead animals and rowdy crowds were part of the experience, particularly when the contest was between SDSU and USD.

"When you go to play that game, you know it's going to be standing room only," says Brown.

Sundvold remembers the beginning of one game in Vermillion, when the USD fans tossed a dead jackrabbit — complete with slit throat and noose around the neck — onto the court for every SDSU player who was announced.

"It was typical USD mentality," Sundvold says dryly.

Athletic trainer Jim Booher was on sabbatical when the frozen coyote hit Fiedler, but he heard about the event.

"There were always a lot of stories," he says. "Rabbits and coyotes ... kickin' the chicken to death. Someone (from USD) drop-kicked it up into the stands. You wouldn't think of seeing that today."

Harry Forsyth, assistant athletic director from 1965-80 and athletic director from 1980-90, also remembers the chickens being drop-kicked into the stands, their wings painted blue and gold.

"I saw a little bunny rabbit kicked to death right on the floor," Forsyth says. "Of course, we weren't completely innocent. We found a frozen coyote hanging in the rafters of the Barn. They were going to lower it and play 'Taps' after the game. We put a couple of big football tackles on the pulley to make sure nothing happened."

Former men's head basketball coach Gene Zulk says: "When I look back on my years as coach, the rivalries were great; the fans raucous and rowdy. There were always jackrabbits thrown on the floor, carrots on your chair. I'd like to say the University crowd threw more stuff and we were more well-behaved."

Jim Marking, who coached men's basketball from 1960-74, notes, "They threw everything." A folded newspaper, tin cans. At one game in Vermillion, a fan tossed a dead rabbit on the floor.

"Vern Schoolmeester, class of 1968, dribbled around it, made the basket and then beat the ref to the rabbit," recalls Marking. "He picked it up, carried it to the U student section, and threw it in the section. You could see the blood fly."

Augustana was no different.

"They threw everything out there," Marking says. "One of our best players, they stole his jacket and had it on a mop, and used it to clean up the floor before the ball game."

At another Augie game, the fans threw live chickens onto the floor. Johnny Johnson, the legendary SDSU equipment manager, started grabbing the birds and stuffing them into a ball bag.

"He took home five live chickens," laughs Marking.

Once, during a game in Vermillion, a U fan threw a whiskey bottle and it hit Jackrabbit Paul McDonald, class of 1985, in the head.

"It was a very, very crazy atmosphere," McDonald recalls. "It was a game with a lot riding on it for both sides. We were both at the top of the league, so there was a little more spice added to the rivalry. And, being that it was the first State-U game in the new DakotaDome, it was pretty intense."

The tossing of animals and vegetables onto the court was not a new experience. McDonald says the late 1970s and early 1980s were as crazy as the in-state rivalries got.

"I think back and just say, 'Wow,'" McDonald says with a laugh. "Whether we were at the U or Augie, we'd come out on the court and there'd be a few carrots thrown at you, a jackrabbit here or there. Actually, in that game (when he got hit), they threw a couple of live rabbits that they had shaved and painted — one blue and one gold.

"It was the typical State-U game. It was very, very close. I remember throwing a pass to Steve Lingenfelter and he made a basket. That sort of iced the game with roughly a minute to go. There was a little lull in play — I don't know if they were retrieving the ball or what — but this bottle came out of the crowd. When I think back, I could sense something coming. It glanced off my head and hit the floor. That was the part I really remember."

As the bottle shattered across the court, McDonald says, it sounded as if a grenade had exploded. Officials called the game. McDonald's sequence of emotions ran the gamut: first, a sense of shock; next, worry about whether his eyesight was damaged; and then a wave of relief knowing that he was not injured.

"The crazy thing was that I ended up knowing the guy who threw it," says McDonald. "He didn't aim it at me."

A few weeks later, State hosted the U. When McDonald's name was announced for the starting lineup, a few pranksters put a hard hat on his head and then tossed an inflatable whiskey bottle from the stands.

Fred Oien, class of 1972 and SDSU athletic director since 1990, has seen it all — vegetables, rabbits, bottles of hard liquor: "Obviously, there are the carrots. In a game against Augustana in the Sioux Falls Arena, along with the carrots, there was cabbage, lettuce — the teams were just pelted as they left the court."

It wasn't until the 1980s that the conference schools started enforcing technical fouls when fans threw items from the stands. Although, such severe consequences don't always make a difference.

Forsyth says: "Augustana, in the last five years, has lost four (home) games because of technicals for throwing rabbits on the floor. I feel sorry for the players and the coaches."

Of course, SDSU students are not without their lapses in good judgment and sportsmanlike conduct.

The Rabbit mascot, in a firsthand account in the Collegian, said a February 1968 game against USD would go down as the most interesting event of his junior year: "The highlight of the game came when a brave Stater snuck a dead coyote in. As I dragged it onto the floor, the students went wild with joy. What would a SDSU-USD game be without a dead coyote?"

Fiedler laughs today, but the concussion she suffered was serious. She endured many tests, hospitalization in Minneapolis and three weeks out of school. She experienced intense headaches and dizziness and couldn't touch her fingers together. The doctors, she says, told her the impact of the frozen coyote literally moved her brain to the front of her head.

The incident also drew widespread — if not national — attention.

"I ended up getting so many visitors in the hospital, they had to restrict them," she says. "I got flowers and cards from people around the country. People told me they heard it on Paul Harvey."

One time, Fiedler was in Pocatello, Idaho, talking to someone who had been at the University of North Dakota when she got hit: "And, he remembered when it happened. It's so weird."

Although she never could confirm the publicity on Harvey's popular radio show, Fiedler says she remains amazed at how far the story traveled. Long after she left SDSU, she was skiing in northern Idaho, riding up a lift and talking to a stranger in the seat next to her.

"I said I was from South Dakota and he said, 'South Dakota? That's where cheerleaders get hit with frozen animals,'" Fiedler recounts. "I said, 'No, frozen coyotes.'"

Chapter 33

The Best

Kristie Thorstenson barely remembers life before rodeo.

"I've probably been rodeoing ever since I could get on a horse," laughs the class of 1995 grad, known to most people by her maiden name, Price. "I can remember competing when I was five, running around the barrels, calf riding."

A rodeo standout since she first stepped into the ring, Thorstenson ranks as one of the best in South Dakota State rodeo history. That is no small feat, considering that State will hold its 50th annual Jackrabbit Stampede Rodeo in spring 2004.

Rodeo enjoys a rich tradition at State, and the campus typically fields a solid team and strong individual finishers. But, as with other sports on campus, national titles are cause for celebration.

During her years on the State rodeo team, Thorstenson took home the

---

Kristie Price Thorstenson competes in a barrel racing event at a college rodeo in Lincoln, Neb.

national goat tying championship in 1994 and, from 1993 to 1995, racked up eight Great Plains Region titles.

She also was a team captain at State and a member of the squad that took fourth place at the College National Finals Rodeo in 1994. The women's team also earned the regional championship title for three consecutive years, beginning in 1993.

Tom Richter, who coached the State team from 1988-98, says: "Kristie will go down in history as one of the best — if not the best — female rodeo athlete at State. She's just one of the greatest all-around athletes at SDSU."

That lofty status was not handed to Thorstenson, Richter adds. "A lot of people who have the talent don't have the work ethic. Kristie had the talent and she worked very hard at what she did."

Like farming and ranching, and the endless prairie that stretches as far as the eye can see, rodeo is part and parcel of South Dakota life. The sport grew out of everyday ranch work, making a competition out of common chores.

Thorstenson was reared on rodeo. Horses were a permanent fixture on the family's 10-acre ranch on the edge of Buffalo. Her parents, Connie and Jay Price, competed in rodeo, and Connie qualified for the National Finals Rodeo twice.

"My mom trained barrel horses," she says. "We'd run horses all the time. I guess I didn't know any better. I was just having fun. ... Once I got into about seventh or eighth grade, I started working really hard on goat tying. I'd never done much roping before."

How much time did she spend on the new skill?

"Oh, goll," sighs Thorstenson. "Pretty much the whole day. During the summer, I spent all day doing something with horses, whether it was working barrel horses with my mom or tying goats. During the school year, my basketball team always made fun of me 'cause I'd have my goat tying rope around my neck. I carried it around a lot, practiced, tied my foot or something. My coach was, like, 'You don't need to bring that to basketball.'"

Thorstenson competed with her high school rodeo team, but the athletes were scored individually. All four years, she accumulated enough points to make the annual trip to nationals. As she neared college, the recruiting battle began. Thorstenson says Montana State University won out largely because it was her father's alma mater. But after her freshman year, she decided to transfer.

Richter, well aware of Thorstenson's talent, took advantage of the opportunity.

"I drove from Brookings to talk with Kristie and her family," he recalls. "I got there midafternoon and sat at the kitchen table with her mom and dad and two brothers."

During the visit, Thorstenson fielded phone calls from Southwestern Oklahoma State University.

Finally, Richter says, "I left shortly after midnight that night, after she had signed the letter of intent."

Thorstenson explains: "My family and I, we had all decided it would be best if I went to South Dakota State. I would be close to home for changing horses if something happened. And Tom, he was so intent — calling all the time. And then, he shows up."

Both coach and athlete agreed it would be best to redshirt the first year because of rules that govern participation for transfer students.

"I would have had to sit out so many rodeos, and then the team suffers because I wouldn't be able to get enough points," says Thorstenson. "It made more sense to sit out and then compete a full year."

Although rodeo was what brought Thorstenson to South Dakota State, her move to the Brookings campus evolved into a life-changing experience. She met her husband, Jeff, overcame her dread of public speaking and, with Richter's guidance, changed her outlook.

"Tom helped me with a lot of things," Thorstenson says. "I didn't always see things so positively. Tom was always real positive. He'd say, 'Here, read this book,' or 'Read this article.' Jeff, he's very positive, too. Between the two of them, I started to change. It was a nice change."

Richter likes to relate the story about Thorstenson and rodeo announcer Jim Thompson: "He interviewed her after she won one of her state high school titles. In the arena, Kristie was a very gifted, talented athlete. She was very confident. But outside the arena, she was a very shy person. Jim told this story about interviewing her — he would ask her a question and she kept backing away, looking at her feet. So he just started walking with her. He backed her up about 40 feet and ran her into a barrier fence."

Thorstenson laughs at the memory: "Yeah, Jim says he backed me up until I had no place to go. I've always been the kind of person who likes to conquer her fears. My big problem was public speaking. At State, I started making myself go to communications classes and I ended up with a mass comm degree. I had to get up and do a lot of speaking. By the end of it, I was starting to get comfortable with it."

So comfortable, jokes Richter, that during a press conference before a rodeo Thorstenson's senior year, when the team captains took turns talking about their year, "I finally had to take the mike out of her hand."

In 1994, Thorstenson took home the national title in goat tying.

"I had won the national title in high school, so I kind of knew what it feels like," says Thorstenson, who now trains horses with her husband. "But the college title, it was awesome."

Richter no longer coaches rodeo, but he remains in awe of Thorstenson's talent.

"Rory Lemmel, who competed for another college, once told me, 'Put a rope in her hand and she can beat anybody,'" Richter muses. "But then he said, 'Just don't ever let her buy a bull rope.'"

Chapter 34

1904 St. Louis World's Fair

In 1904, the world gathered in St. Louis to celebrate the centennial of the Louisiana Purchase. The occasion marked an event in American history considered secondary in importance only to the Declaration of Independence.

And, as it would be at other significant events throughout time, the South Dakota State band was on hand to participate in the festivities.

Acquiring the territory from France extended the nation's boundaries westward to the Pacific Ocean, embracing all the land between the Mississippi River and the crest of the Rocky Mountains. The purchase fulfilled President Thomas Jefferson's vision of a continental United States.

The World's Fair in St. Louis, which also honored the westward journey

Pictured above, members of the SDSC Military Band pause for a moment just prior to a performance during the 1904 World's Fair. (Courtesy of SDSU Archives and Special Collections)

The band and ROTC contingent on the fairgrounds. All structures seen in the background were removed after the fair as they were made of a hard, reinforced plaster. (Courtesy of SDSU Archives and Special Collections)

of Lewis and Clark, enjoyed a seven-month run as people from dozens of nations turned out for what would become the greatest and grandest turn-of-the-century fair. A huge array of palaces and glittering attractions drew 20 million visitors and exhibits from 43 countries. The fair introduced ice cream cones and the novelty of the South's iced tea.

The October 1904 Industrial Collegian credited "our commandant," Capt. J.C. McArthur of the 28th Infantry, with making the trip possible after many months of hard work. Each cadet in what was then State's military band had to pay $25 to cover expenses, including railroad fare, sleeping car fare, a place to stay in St. Louis and one admission ticket to the fairgrounds. The fair association provided quarters in barracks and passes to the fair. In exchange, the band gave one guard mount and one hour's drill each day at hours specified by the fair.

"The battalion formed on the college campus at 7 p.m., June 16," reported the Collegian, "and marched to the depot, where their special train, consisting of a baggage car, three tourist and one standard Pullman coaches, awaited them. ... The special left about 7:30 amid the cheers of several hundred students and friends of the battalion, who had gathered to see its departure. As soon as the train was well under way and the number of passengers had been checked up, guards were posted at the car doors, and no one allowed to pass between cars without a written pass or being accompanied by an officer or a non-commissioned officer of the guard."

The group traveled with the band in the first car, Company A in the second, Company B in the third, and those who were either not in uniform or could not stand the extra expense were in the rear, or standard Pullman car.

The first stop was for breakfast in Winona, Minn., followed by a lunch stop in Madison, Wis., and then the Chicago & North Western station in Chicago at 5 p.m., where the battalion ate supper.

Before leaving Chicago, McArthur picked up "very fine battalion colors of heavy blue silk decorated with the state seal and 'South Dakota Agricultural College,' which had been purchased by the regents a short time before." The train left Chicago at about 9 p.m. and arrived in St. Louis at 6:30 in the morning on June 18.

Once at the fairgrounds, the Staters were assigned to barracks and issued orders: 1st call, 5:45 a.m.; reveille, 6 a.m.; breakfast, 7 p.m.; dinner, 12 p.m.; supper, 6 p.m.; and taps, 11 p.m. The men, however, "were given liberty, and put upon their honor, to conduct themselves as gentlemen, which they did in a very creditable way."

Participating in the fair, undoubtedly, was a thrill for the South Dakotans. For most, it probably was the farthest they had traveled, and the international crowd was unlike anything they had experienced back home. They had 10 days to take in the sights. The Collegian reported:

"To those who had never seen a large exposition, it was indeed a revelation. One was fairly dazed by the multitude of things of interest, and educational value to be seen, and by the magnitude of the whole affair."

There were fountains and rushing waters, buildings illuminated at night, gondoliers singing and bands playing. If someone "watched the great tide of humanity ever passing, he might well think himself in dreamland, and rub his eyes, and pinch himself to make sure it was not all a mere hallucination."

The cadets rode home with some regret, having not seen everything there was at the fair. The trip was uneventful with only a few exceptions — a "poor" meal in Chicago and "crowded hotels and a scarcity of eatables" in Mankato, where the Ringling Bros. Circus had stopped as well.

"The battalion reached Brookings about 7:30 p.m., June 29," said the Collegian account. "There was a large crowd and the remnant of the city band out to welcome us home. On account of the absence of a number of men who obtained stopovers in Chicago, the battalion was formed into one company. It was then marched up main street three blocks and halted and the final orders read. In these the Commandant thanked the men for their good conduct during the trip and as he was soon to leave Brookings, he bid the battalion goodbye. Nine rousing cheers were then give for 'McArthur' and the battalion marched to the college and dismissed."

During their journey home, the cadets had voted to spend $75 of the battalion fund to buy a cup that the companies could compete over. And, as a token of appreciation for McArthur's leadership, they also had voted to give their commandant $50 so that he could buy something to remind him of SDAC.

That was the end of the band's trip. "It was," said the Collegian writer, "thoroughly enjoyed by all."

Chapter 35

A Brush with Royalty

South Dakota State University sits in a small, quiet Midwestern community, isolated from much of the world. Yet, throughout the decades, the marvelous sounds of its marching bands have gained international attention.

In the 1980s and 1990s, 2000 and beyond, the renowned Pride of the Dakotas played for two presidential inaugural celebrations — one Republican, one Democrat — and marched in the Rose Bowl Parade, just to single out a few stellar performances.

Given the history of State's bands, however, such achievements, although noteworthy, are hardly out of the ordinary. Few other college and university bands can lay claim to having played for presidents, not to mention full-fledged royalty.

In May 1939, South Dakota State's then-Military Band earned what has proven to be a once in a lifetime invitation to play for the king and queen of England. The Monarchs — King George and Queen Elizabeth — were visiting Winnipeg on May 22-27, and the Winnipeg Royal Welcome Week organizers asked professor Carl Christensen to bring his band north.

Pictured above, a young boy listens to the SDSC Marching Band as it plays a concert for a Winnipeg, Canada, orphanage.

"It was pretty thrilling," says John Bibby, who played slide trombone with the 1939 band in his freshman year. "At that time, the band was over 100 pieces. It was pretty big, and it was all men. We wore our Army cadet uniforms."

Palmer Dragston, class of 1939, was the president of the band that year. In addition to being a fun trip, the Winnipeg journey was a long one. The band traveled in three buses from the Jackrabbit line.

"It was kind of a grueling trip," Dragston says. "The assistant director (Edward Schroepfer) played the clarinet almost the whole way up and back — anything to break the monotony of the long ride."

The trip took more than just an invitation from Winnipeg, though. The band had to raise a considerable sum for those days — $1,000. By May 15, campus organizations had pitched in $850. Wednesday, May 17, was set as Band Tag Day in an effort to round up the remaining funds from the community.

"It's up to residents of the city to finance the rest of the trip, I think," S.H. Johnson, secretary of the Brookings Chamber of Commerce, declared in a Brookings Register story. "When you are approached, dig as deep in your pocket as you dare."

Johnson said the trip was a reward for the band members, who had been working hard all year. More than that, however, he said the publicity would be a boon for both college and community: "Such a trip should give music-minded high school students some idea of the band's prominence and fill them with a real desire to play in so fine a musical organization as that directed by Prof. Carl Christensen."

The Brookings community characteristically responded to the call for donations. The Band Tag Day netted another $225 from various groups and individuals to finance the remainder of the trip. A benefit dance also was held to help raise additional funds.

With three buses of 103 band members, two passenger cars and a truck bearing instruments, the caravan left for Winnipeg on Tuesday, May 23, at 4 a.m. That night at 7, the band competed in a marching contest.

The next day, the Collegian reported: "The South Dakota State Military Band earned its breakfast last night when it walked off with first prize in the marching contest in the International Band Festival — the only contest it entered while here to welcome King George and Queen Elizabeth."

Along with the first-place honors, State took the cash prize of $50, which the band turned over to the building fund for the new student union. Christy, reportedly, was the last to know about the prize-winning performance.

According to the Register, Christy "couldn't understand why all the whooping and hollering Wednesday morning until he was told about winning the prize of $50.

"'The h--l we did,' was all he could say."

State also thrilled the crowds gathered along the parade route. Nearly 65 years later, those who marched through the streets of Winnipeg share two main memories.

"It was a tremendously long parade," says Bibby. "The other thing I can remember is that the people were so responsive. As we went down the parade route, which was really crowded, they applauded. The drum major decided we had to play a lot. I can remember my lips were so sore."

Dragston echoes Bibby's recollection: "It was a long hike. We walked and walked and walked. We were one of the first units. ... It seemed like an awful long walk, and playing an instrument the whole way."

Roger Young, class of 1942, played the trombone, and like Dragston and Bibby, laughs at the memory: "The thing I remember the most is the length of the parade. The people just went nuts about the band. They followed along behind us, clapping. It was several miles long. We had to march in the parade and then we had to march back to the buses."

The route was every bit as long as it seemed — eight miles, according to the Register account. And, it was as grueling, if not more so, than the bus trip Dragston remembered. The State musicians had been on the buses since 4 a.m., arriving in Winnipeg 5 p.m. They marched and played, then slept at St. Joseph's Orphanage, and awoke at 7 a.m. Wednesday, May 24.

That day, the Staters and 18 other bands were assigned to special places along the route, each group playing "bright, short numbers" while awaiting the royal procession. In the afternoon, the State band stood in one of the parks along the trail of the royal march. When King George VI and Queen Elizabeth passed, each band played the British national anthem, "God Save the Queen."

As glamorous as the event sounded, the Register said the full day of activity on May 24 "would have caused any ordinary individual to have a nervous breakdown. For two hours and 45 minutes the band stood in the rain waiting for things to start and then had an opportunity to see the King and Queen three different times before the day was over. The first time was during the parade and the royal car passed within five to six feet of the unit and the couple waved a greeting to the members.

"That afternoon they were bundled into street cars and taken out into the snooty residential district where they played another concert attended by the

The SDSC Marching Band plays as the car carrying the king and queen of England passes by its location.

royal couple. ... Following the afternoon concert, the band went back to St. Joseph's Orphanage and played another concert for the inmates and royal couple."

A week later, quoting from the Winnipeg Free Press, the Collegian gave greater detail to the event:

"Sixty beautiful floats, symbolizing authentic or historical episodes of the past, and ideals of the present highlighted the Royal Welcome Week parade. Spaced at regular intervals through the spectacle, 19 spirited bands sent the bookish dust flying from the history and infused it with gaiety, color and music ...

"Bands were judged for appearance as they marched past the city hall. First prize, $50, went to the State college Military Band of Brookings, S.D., whose flawless unison in marching and trim khaki uniforms, left little doubt in the judges' minds as to the winner."

For the band members, the brush with royalty passed quickly and uneventfully. Dragston says: "The car the king and queen rode in was an open sedan, not a convertible. He was in British uniform and Queen Elizabeth, I imagine she wore her usual hat."

The Brookings Register reported: "Queen Elizabeth's smile won the hearts of all who saw her, the bandsmen were agreed, while the king was decidedly the more serious type. During the morning parade George was dressed in his uniform while Elizabeth appeared in a pink dress. During the afternoon the King changed his uniform for an afternoon suit with a silk hat, and the queen favored a sky-blue gown."

The band members did more than just march and play their instruments. They also, as Young says, "did a little roaming around." Sousaphone player Roy Masson, class of 1940, quips, "The beer was sure good up there."

Wherever they went, the State bandsmen were treated as if they were royalty themselves — wined and dined, feted and honored. Four band members were asked for autographs by Winnipeg residents. Street cars reportedly stopped in the middle of the block if it looked as though the band members wanted to go somewhere. Many of the men were taken to lunch, the theater or dance hall.

Understandably, the band members were tired upon their return to campus.

"We got back late one evening," Dragston recalls. "We had to get our uniform all polished up. Some of us had applied to get into the Army Air Corps. We went to the armory, where they were going to check us out. The first thing they did was put up an eye chart. My eyes are good, but after two nights like that, I couldn't see the wall."

Chapter 36

Playing for the Gipper

The election of a Republican president meant many things when Ronald Reagan swept into office in 1980. But for Darwin Walker, director of the SDSU marching band, one idea in particular came to mind.

Perhaps, he thought, given South Dakota's conservative voting record, the Pride of the Dakotas might have a good shot at winning a slot in Reagan's inaugural parade.

"The Pride was well-known in the state and the region because of our indoor shows around South Dakota and a few televised National Football League performances," Walker says, reflecting on his rationale.

Little did he know that not only would his band be a part of the celebration, but the South Dakotans also would be in the nation's capital to witness

---

Pictured above, Ronald Reagan smiles to the crowd during his inaugural parade on Jan. 20, 1981.

history beyond the presidential inauguration.

As Reagan's formal induction into office got under way Jan. 20, 1981, news arrived of the imminent and long-awaited release of hostages who had been held in Iran for 444 days.

"Tremendously interesting stuff," Walker says.

Intent on his goal for the Pride, Walker contacted arts and science Dean Allen Barnes, who in turn sought permission from SDSU President Sherwood Berg. Two days after the election, Walker contacted members of the South Dakota delegation (Sen. Larry Pressler, Rep. Tom Daschle, Sen.-elect Jim Abnor and Congressman-elect Clint Roberts), asking if they would put in a good word with the Inaugural Parade Committee.

Detailed application forms arrived in mid-November. Walker supplied the necessary information, submitted the forms and waited. The formal invitation came in early December.

"We had until the first week of January to raise $104,000," Walker says.

He called on Walt Conahan, a 1952 State grad and then executive director of the SDSU Foundation. The pair hit the fund-raising trail, making personal calls on businesspeople throughout the state and airing public service announcements on television.

"I will never forget calling on Jeanette Lusk at the Huron Daily Plainsman," laughs Walker. "She was a strong financial backer of SDSU projects. I walked into her office in Huron, and before I could even sit down, she took a drag on her cigarette, and said, 'Young man, you're busy and I'm busy — here's something for you now, and if you need more, come back to see me.'

"I looked at the check and it was for $5,000. I said, 'Mrs. Lusk, do you mind if I come behind your desk and give you a hug?' She said something like, 'I think that would be quite appropriate.' I was dumbfounded. That $5,000 gave us a benchmark with which to approach other donors."

Walker also devised a plan whereby each band member — and there were 180 members — had to buy or sell 50 raffle tickets at $5 apiece. The prize was cash or a free trip to Washington, D.C., with the band. Bill and Gladys McCracken won the drawing and joined the band on the trip. With the raffle, donations and other funding from the student and alumni associations, Walker says, "we met our goal in under 30 days."

Conahan notes: "I think we were pretty confident we could accomplish it. I think we were so delighted with the opportunity and the chance to participate, that we thought we'd have a favorable response. It probably never occurred to us that we might not do it."

As the fund-raising effort neared completion, the Pride worked on marching — one rank at a time in the old Barn: "We mostly worked on corners," says Walker, "the nemesis of all marching bands. After Christmas break we went back at it again and even had two days in January when we could go outside and march. All this time, we also were preparing the Symphonic Band for an early February concert performance for the South Dakota Music Educators Association — a very important event for us."

Tim Peters, class of 1981, played the trumpet for the Pride. "Everyone was pretty happy that we were selected to go. I remember practicing outside. Fortunately, that winter wasn't that terribly cold. One evening, we marched to Frost Arena and filled up one end of the lower bleachers. I don't know if the whole band had played for a game. It was a U game, and we won. That was kind of a neat experience."

Two planes carrying the 180 band members, their equipment and boosters flew out of the Sioux Falls airport Jan. 17, 1981. It was the Friday prior to the Tuesday inaugural. The Pride was one of 20 bands selected to perform in the inauguration parade and one of eight at the college level. Four hundred college and university bands had applied for the honors.

The group arrived in D.C. late at night, greeted by cold temperatures and red double-decker buses, with little or no means of heat.

"We rehearsed Saturday, Sunday and Monday," says Walker, "and we did the normal sightseeing, got our photo taken with the congressional delegation. ... We went to a U.S. Army Band rehearsal and had lunch in their mess hall, we went to most of the Smithsonian museums, the Mint, and every monument. Lincoln (Memorial) at night was the most memorable for me."

Walker also points out that with the country in the midst of the Iranian hostage crisis, everyone and everything was patriotic. "It was a very stirring and uplifting time."

On Inauguration Day, Walker says: "We had a strict schedule to observe. The best I can recall is that we had to be at Andrews Air Force Base by 11 a.m. to put all the marching units in staging order for the parade. The parade was scheduled for 1 p.m."

However, he adds, "shortly after arriving, word came to us that the Iranian hostages were to be released at any moment, and the parade would not begin until the release was completed."

The band waited, listened to the radio news and received briefings about every 15 minutes.

"It was a classic case of all dressed up and no place to go," says Walker.

By 3 p.m., news arrived of the hostages' release and the parade began, flowing onto Pennsylvania Avenue.

"I get goose bumps telling this," says Walker. "It's so hard to describe the feeling of beginning to parade down Pennsylvania Avenue. Many, many thousands of people, many with flags, all cheering the 180 musicians in our group — quite a large band for 20 years ago. There were people sitting in trees and on lamp posts along the way."

For Conahan, it wasn't enough to stand and watch: "It was great. I followed the band along Pennsylvania Avenue, going along the back of the sidewalks. I watched them go by several times. It was really exciting to see the SDSU band coming along — a tremendous thrill."

The route was long, says Peters, "but I don't know how many miles. We walked right by the reviewing stand (where the new president watched). We weren't supposed to look to the side, but I'm sure we all tried to steal a look."

After returning to campus, band member and Collegian staff writer Todd Murphy recounted the glory of the experience:

"After we waited for what seemed like an eternity, Fred Ellwein, drum major, blew his whistle for us to get in line again. He blew his whistle again and we started to march toward the street.

"This was it! As we got to the street we had to wait for a float and some horses to get in ahead of us. The horses must have been as nervous as we were, at least that's what the obstacles they left behind suggested.

"As we marched down the street, I kept drilling myself on what to do. Look straight ahead. Keep the line straight.

"The crowd roared. I had never seen this many people at a parade before. I had never seen this many people at a football game before.

"It seemed that my fingers were playing the music by themselves, without me even thinking about it. All that work the week before was worth it. Anything was worth this."

Murphy was far from alone. Many of the band members had never traveled so far from their home state, nor had they flown on a plane before.

"It's the only time I've been to Washington, D.C.," Peters says.

According to Walker, the Pride of the Dakotas performed "March Grandioso" and the "South Dakota State College" march. All the bands were supposed to march at 120 beats per minute, with 30-inch steps, which, Walker notes, "was quite a large step for the shorter young ladies in our group."

He explains: "This was all designed by the Presidential Inaugural Committee to complete the parade in one hour and 20 minutes so that the president did not have to stand in the reviewing stand so long. Military personnel were assigned to each band to ensure that goal was met. And, it was!"

Playing for the Gipper

Members of the Pride of the Dakotas Marching Band gather for a photo on the steps of the United States Capitol.

Twenty years later, Walker still remembers passing by the reviewing stand with the president and first lady, who was wearing a bright red dress. There were television cameras stationed at the stand as well.

"Our goal was to really pay attention to our alignment," says Walker. "To do that, we asked the students not to look at the reviewing stand as we passed. On the videotape of our group, we could see that we did quite well, but it was obvious which ranks had a few lookers. But, who can blame them?"

Peters says his memories of the 1981 trip remain strong.

"I've thought about it a lot," he says. "And, it means more and more as time goes by. It still gives me chills when I hear the SDSU band march. Those memories just don't go away."

Walker echoes Peters' sentiments: "This trip — including the planning leading up to it, the fund raising, and the response we received for our efforts — is likely the highlight of my 39-year teaching career."

And, he adds, much of the credit goes to Conahan.

"Of all the people who made all of this work out for us," Walker says, "Walt Conahan heads the list."

Conahan laughs and graciously accepts the kudos, granting, "That's very flattering. It's very nice of Darwin to say this. But, I'd have to say Darwin Walker was the one prime mover and shaker. It was his enthusiasm, his direction on the whole thing that made it pay off. And, of course, there was great support from Dr. Berg and Dean Barnes."

Chapter 37

The Smell of Roses

P residents and a king, inaugurations and millennium celebrations, parades and athletic events — State's marching bands have played in countless venues for audiences of every kind.

Each performance, of course, carries its own special meaning and creates lasting memories.

But, in terms of sheer numbers and showmanship, no experience in 100 years of existence — from the early all-male military corps to today's foot-stomping, heart-pumping Pride of the Dakotas — can match the 2003 Tournament of Roses Parade.

"I think it's the most prestigious parade a band can be involved with," says James McKinney, SDSU director of bands. "It's the oldest, for one thing. And, because of the national exposure, more than a million people see it live on the parade route. It's beamed to 90 countries. They claim, when it's all said and done, the band is seen by 400 million people."

With both happenstance and hard work, about 350 band members, 30 staff members and chaperones, parents and friends of the band headed for

Pictured above, the Rose Parade pin specially designed for the Pride of the Dakotas Marching Band.

California on Friday, Dec. 27. Together, the SDSU contingent numbered nearly 700 people. Starting at 1 in the morning, they boarded buses at the Stanley J. Marshall Physical Education Center bound for the Minneapolis and Omaha airports.

McKinney, who in 1968 had marched in the parade with his high school band, explains: "I've always had it in the back of my mind, taking the band to the Rose Bowl, but basically they don't take college bands (outside of California) whose teams are not playing in the Rose Bowl — less than 10, I think, in the 114-year history."

About eight years ago, McKinney was in Chicago and met a former band director who had become a travel agent and had taken bands to the Tournament of Roses Parade. Several years later, during the summer of 2000, McKinney was touring Europe with a band and ran into the same travel agent in Rottenburg, Germany. Again, McKinney raised the idea of the Rose Bowl parade.

"He said he'd call me when I got back to the States," McKinney recalls. "He put me in touch with the right people and I got the application. It's quite complex. It takes a year just to put the application together. You need certain pictures of the band — an overhead shot of a band in a parade, a picture of the flags, a non-playing picture, a picture of the drum major, support letters. The big thing is to videotape the band."

It happened that the Pride had performed at the 2000 Millennium Parade in Washington, D.C., and in the 1997 inaugural parade.

Consequently, says McKinney, "we had all the footage they require. We were actually able to put the application package together in about 30 days instead of a year. That was the fall of 2001."

As difficult as it was to get accepted, the work truly began once the SDSU application was approved. From figuring out travel accommodations and itineraries to how many musicians would march abreast, the details were mind-boggling.

"Say you have a 40-pound sousaphone over your shoulder and you're marching seven miles with it," explains McKinney. "But, you're not just marching. You're standing around for two hours before, then moving up a little bit in line, then stopping and then moving, stopping and moving. Just the physical demands were enormous. Even if you're carrying a flute — your arms are up in the air, parallel to the ground. Or, the big bass drums. Those were the kids I was really worried about. ...

"Then, there's the music. You have to get that prepared. You try and tie in with the theme of the parade, patriotic or whatever, and submit your music to a committee and they approve it. ... We wound up playing just one piece, a special piece written by Jim Coull (assistant director of bands). There was the memorization and lack of practice time. We put it together in the winter in Brookings, S.D., and everybody is trying to do final exams and wrap up the season. It's not exactly an ideal situation.

"Then, in addition to marching formation and the music, we did a complete halftime show at Pasadena City College. That was a great experience. ... But, we found out just about two weeks before we left that we were to follow the University of Oklahoma band. And they had been performing football halftime shows all through the playoffs. We hadn't performed since Nov. 1. I hadn't even seen all the kids since November and December. ... When we found out about Oklahoma, I was scared."

But, true to Pride style, the SDSU band took the best of its season, performed a spectacular show and garnered a standing ovation.

There also was the dilemma of transporting all the band equipment and the matter of raising enough money to pay for the trip. These were the nuts and bolts of McKinney's grand idea that kept him and his wife, Mary, awake nights.

"It just consumed us," says Jim.

Mary adds, "It was 24 hours of ringing of the phone."

The price of the package came in at about $1,300 per student. Multiply that by 400 members of the Pride, and the financial prospects grew daunting. McKinney approached SDSU President Peggy Gordon Miller:

"She didn't hesitate. She said, 'I will pay half of every student's trip. All of the sudden, students are looking at $650 instead of $1,300. That, in and of itself, allowed hundreds more students to go. If I had told kids they'd have to come up with $1,300, I doubt we'd have taken 150. Once it was $650, that made it a lot more affordable."

Miller says the invitation to play in the parade reaffirmed the high caliber of the Pride. In her mind, not going was not an option.

"I wanted to be sure everybody could go," says Miller. "I said, 'Nobody stays behind because of money.' This event gave them the best kind of educational experience. It allowed them to practice what they had learned, to be judged externally and to do it in a context that gave them a different view of the world. And, it was an opportunity to broaden their own perspective."

Erin Carsrud, class of 2004, plays the piccolo. Before the Pride trip to California, she had flown only once in her life.

"The first time we heard about the trip, Mr. McKinney had a meeting in the Christy Ballroom," Carsrud says. "None of us knew what it was about.

There was a cake on the table and roses. We were kind of looking at each other, thinking 'what's going on?' Then, they told us. I was really excited."

Mary McKinney came up with the idea to buy two Volkswagen Beatles, one yellow and one blue for the SDSU colors, and sell raffle tickets. Each of the 350 students was issued 65 tickets to sell at $10 each.

Jim McKinney credits the university's Alumni Association, particularly former staffer Andy Clayton, with taking care of all the details to make the trip a success. Clayton essentially served as the travel office for the hundreds of parents, friends and boosters who made the trip with the Pride.

"I couldn't have done it without them," McKinney says.

As the fund-raising effort got under way, the McKinneys and their daughter, Jamie, and Mike Reger, vice president for administration, and his wife, Pat, traveled to California to watch the Tournament of Roses Parade in 2002 to understand how it operated. It was a surreal experience, says McKinney, to sit and watch, knowing that a year later, the Pride would be part of the festivities.

The actual parade route posed yet another problem. There are only two turns in the parade, and one is an infamous corner with 86 television cameras trained on it.

"You couldn't design a parade with a worse nightmare," McKinney says. "The hardest part of the parade is turning that corner. It's where all the bands look their worst. It's hard to keep the lines straight and hard to keep playing along."

Once back in Brookings, practicing at the Swiftel Center, the band director discovered just how difficult that corner would be. Typically, the Pride marches seven across. But the 2002-03 crew was so large that seven across meant the marching formation would stretch for one and a half blocks. McKinney and his staff used tape on the

The grand marshals for the 2003 Rose Parade were Art Linkletter, Bill Cosby and Mr. Fred Rogers. (Photo courtesy of Eric Landwehr)

The Smell of Roses

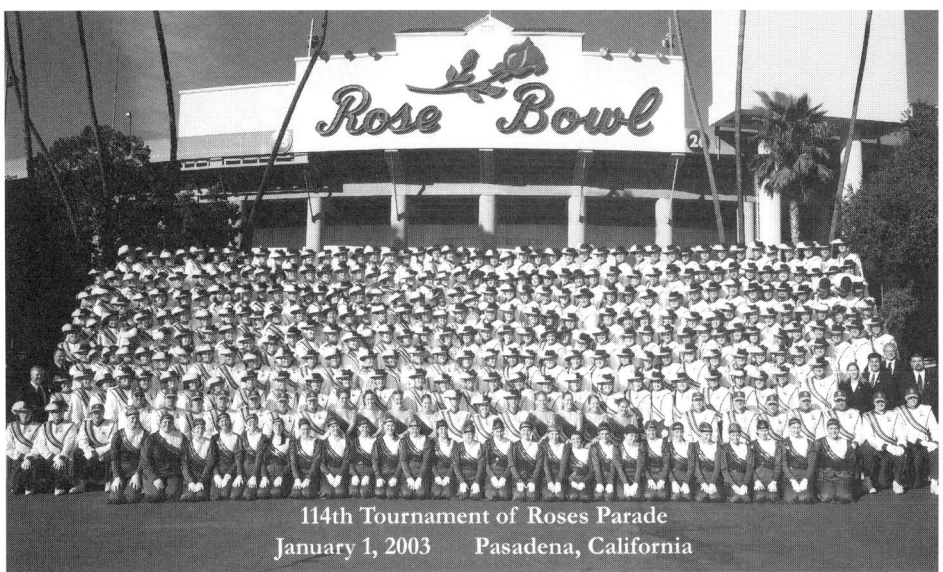

114th Tournament of Roses Parade
January 1, 2003   Pasadena, California

Pictured above, the 2003 Pride of the Dakotas Marching Band.

floor to simulate the feared corner.

"The first time," McKinney says, able to laugh about it now, "we imploded. It just didn't work. I'm thinking 'we're just not going to make it.' I called some of my band director friends across the country (for advice). We decided we had to go 11 across."

Carsrud says the musicians found the corner ordeal equally frustrating.

"We don't do corners," she explains. "When we march in the Hobo Day Parade, it's free-form. We practiced the corner for three hours. Then, we got there and it was over, like, in a second."

McKinney says he felt better once the band had a chance to practice in California. But, finding a place to practice was another complication. It had taken months to locate a school that would permit the Pride to practice at its facility. McKinney had to send "all kinds of documents" and proof of $1 million in liability insurance.

Then, the rains came and that school's fields were underwater. The travel agent and found another practice field.

Sophomore Peter Rice, who plays the snare drum, says all the scrambling was stressful.

"It was a little intense getting ready for the parade," he says, "but it was definitely worth it. It was my first time in California. I couldn't believe how warm it was. It was hard to believe that it was the same time of year in South Dakota."

For the parade, McKinney says, the Pride earned a spot of distinction — the first nonmilitary band, and right behind the president of the Tournament of Roses.

"He goes to every hometown of every band," McKinney says. "Then, he can decide who he wants where. I think he was impressed (with the Pride). When he came to Brookings in September, he said, 'I want a big, loud band right behind me. That's going to be you guys.'"

The Pride's No. 6 position in the parade lineup saved the band members many hours of standing around, according to McKinney.

Lynn Darnall, a nontraditional student who graduated in 1995, her husband, Brian, and the couple's two daughters, Sam and Sarah, were among those who joined the Pride for the Rose Bowl journey. In the days leading up to the parade, they watched the band perform at various locations, including the Santa Monica Pier and Disneyland.

Wherever the group went, laughs Darnall, "there was a sea of blue." Pride members and supporters alike wore souvenir blue fleece pullovers designed specially for the occasion. It was no different on the day of the big event.

Darnall, sitting with the South Dakota contingent, remembers: "Standing on the street, looking up at the bleachers, it was like looking at an SDSU game in the fall at Coughlin stadium. It was solid blue and gold. Everybody was visiting. It was a beautiful California morning."

Director of Bands James McKinney smiles to the crowd as the Pride of the Dakotas Marching Band marches through Main Street USA at Disneyland. (Photo courtesy of Eric Landwehr)

Down on the street, marching with the Pride, Carsrud says: "It was just amazing to see all the people, on all sides of the street — more than the number of people in South Dakota. All these people see your band, see you march."

McKinney knew the State section was about three miles into the route. He says: "I went ahead of the band and was waiting to give the signal to play. I wanted to start our music so the band would be playing when we passed our people."

As the Pride approached, the South Dakotans went nuts.

Says Darnall: "We could see them almost a block away. The bleachers erupted. We stood up and screamed and yelled. We never heard them play in the Rose Bowl parade because the entourage was too loud."

McKinney says he saw the sea of blue jackets and was flooded with emotions.

"Everything just culminated at that point," he recalls. "Seeing and realizing what all those people had sacrificed to come along — the emotions were totally unexpected."

Later, everyone gathered for a barbecue.

Laughing, Darnall notes: "The Pride kids said we were exactly what they needed. They could hear us a block away — all these maniacs screaming and yelling. That afternoon, we went back to the hotel and got dressed up. We went to the Queen Mary for a celebration dinner. That was just extraordinarily cool. It was kind of a relief to have the parade done. The pressure was off. The kids were on vacation. It was the best day of the whole trip."

John Bibby, class of 1942, and his wife, Mary, were among the SDSU celebrants. Sixty-four years earlier, Bibby was a member of the State band that had played in Winnipeg for the king and queen of England.

"They were two completely different scenarios," he says. "I suppose I was 18 years old when I went up to Canada, as opposed to 82. And, we had a 100-piece band compared to a 300-piece band. The logistics of this trip weren't even comparable to the Winnipeg trip."

Despite such differences and the passage of time, McKinney says, the Tournament of Roses trip continued the legacy of State's legendary band director Carl "Christy" Christensen.

More than a century ago, Christy laid the foundation for the Pride of the Dakotas with his military band. Throughout the years, with the support of dedicated directors and passing administrations and the willingness of band members to work hard, SDSU's musicians have repeatedly demonstrated that they can compete with the best.

The band's performance in California only enhanced its reputation, according to Jerry Jorgensen, class of 1978 and dean of the College of Arts and Science.

"The quality of their playing and the manner in which they behaved reflected well on everyone," says Jorgensen. "They made everyone so proud."

Along with his memories, Jorgensen has on his office wall a picture of the band marching in what he calls "the granddaddy of them all."

He says: "The thing to remember about the Tournament of Roses Parade is that there is something along the line of a million people watching. That's the whole state of South Dakota and add 250,000 more. To see the band marching down Orange Grove Boulevard, it brings tears to your eyes. I'll never forget it."

Months after the trip, McKinney reflects: "In some ways, it seems like it was just a dream, like we never really did it. We spent so many hours planning, and so many people worked so hard to make it happen."

Rice echoes McKinney's sentiments: "It was a lot of hard work, but it was a lot of fun. It was the trip of a lifetime."

Chapter 38

Peace Pacts Meant to be Broken

These days, collegiate rivalries are limited to athletic contests between school teams and the bragging rights that come with victory in the field or on the court.

But throughout the late 1940s and '50s, the timeworn tradition of besting one's opponent transcended scheduled games and evolved into the high art of playing pranks.

"We would have forays," laughs Bob Karolevitz, class of 1947. "One of the guys would get their folks' car and we went down in the still of the night to steal a cannon or something."

John Gross, class of 1954, chuckles: "Everything we did was in the middle

---

Pictured above, former student body presidents Jack Marshman and John Gross, celebrate the return of the Rooter King with college president, Dr. John Headley.

of the night."

Sure enough, Collegian articles dating back to the era detail an ongoing series of back-and-forth intercampus capers, from midnight paint raids — painting college symbols or letters on campus property — to the theft of mascots and signs and the sawing down of football goal posts.

"Mysteriously appearing on the campus Tuesday morning, after an enforced absence of 18 months, State's giant Rooter King Cowbell became the rallying point for Hobo Day preparations," reported the Collegian on Oct. 15, 1947.

Staters earned sweet revenge with a victory against Augustana that Hobo Day. After the game, the Augie goal posts came down and pieces were put on display in downtown Sioux Falls. The motive, stated the Oct. 22, 1947, Collegian was "to clear up any doubts as to who won the game."

Walt Conahan, class of 1952, recalls another plot to steal the Rooter King when he was student body president his senior year:

"We went down to the Augie game, Ted Tabor and I. I put the Rooter King in the trunk of the car, took it down to the game and rang it. I thought that was the job of the student body president. After the game, we went out and put the Rooter King in the trunk of the car. I had a pair of handcuffs and there was supposed to be a rod. I handcuffed it to what I thought was the rod."

The trunk wouldn't lock, but thinking that the mighty bell was safely secured, Conahan and Tabor went off. Little did they know that (a) they had been followed to the parking lot by a few Augie students, and (b) Conahan had handcuffed the Rooter King to the jack. Needless to say, the Rooter King was gone when Conahan returned.

Once back in Brookings, Conahan continues, "we got a call from the bus depot. There was a package for us. They sent the jack back. They took the Rooter King and paraded it in a student assembly the next day or so. Then, we played the U down at Vermillion. ... From where I was seated on the corner of the basketball court, at halftime, all of the sudden, I see a couple of guys come running out with what looked like the Rooter King. I chased 'em, but it was fake. ...

"Not long after that, the war of attrition started. Pretty soon, Augustana was missing one of the four corner signs that were on each corner of campus. It just disappeared and it was hanging from the top of the student union building here, at Pugsley. How it got there, I don't know."

The Oct. 9, 1952, Collegian reported the theft of the Rooter King. Student representatives had agreed to give back the cowbell, but word spread of the pending return. Three Augustana students intervened and took the cow-

Peace Pacts Meant to be Broken

bell from the Minnehaha County Jail, where it had been held since the original theft.

Ultimately, the Rooter King was returned to State and safely handcuffed to a radiator. Augie got its sign back. But as the Collegian headlines indicate, this was not the first, nor the last time the Rooter King would be missing in action.

"It's back!" crowed the Thursday, March 18, 1954, Collegian, which ran a picture of the Rooter King with Gross, student body president; Jack Marshman, incoming president; and South Dakota State President John Headley.

Throughout the years, various student body presidents tried to form a truce. Both Gross and Marshman remember repeated efforts, but any success was short-lived. Time and again, student leaders met, signed pacts and agreed to various financial penalties to discourage raids only to wake up one morning and find their work undone by some mischievous deed.

"I think it came from professor Walder, who said the student associations ought to get together and discuss things," says Gross, referring to Orlin Walder, dean of men, and the so-called peace pacts. "I remember having a meeting in Brookings with the student body presidents from Augustana and the U. We were trying to keep everything on a friendly basis."

In 1951, for example, an agreement spelled out details for property damage fines (up to $500) and arbitration of incidents (neutral campuses would assess the damage).

Under Marshman's reign, delegates from State, Morningside, Augustana and the University met on the Augustana campus in October 1954 to revise the North Central Conference peace pact.

In February, 1952, students Harlan Olson and Walt Conahan remove the Augustana College sign from the top of Pugsley Union.

"As I recall," says Marshman, "our main competitor, or enemy, at that time prank-wise was Augustana. I remember they came up to State and did some damage, sprayed some paint around. Then, some State students retaliated and shaved some heads of Augustana students. Then, I remember at least one raid on a girls' dorm at Augustana and they got a cheerleader's megaphone."

The peace pacts managed to calm things down for certain periods of time, notes Marshman, but not for long.

"We used to have a bonfire on Hobo Day," he says. "They'd come up and start the bonfire before we were ready. We were so dominant over Augustana athletically. And their Viking Day parade was pretty abysmal at the time. That just made them kind of mad, so they stole the cowbell. The other big deal was the Bummobile and keeping track of that."

On Oct. 13, 1955, the Collegian reported that the ink was barely dry on the 1955-56 school year pact when Augie students violated the measure by painting big A's on the State campus. At a meeting of student representatives to determine how to handle the matter, the Augustana delegation returned a plaque that had been taken from State during the raid. In exchange, State students gave back an Augie sign.

In 1957, a group of North Dakota State students made a futile attempt to steal the Rooter King during halftime of a basketball game. The Collegian surmised that the thwarted effort was in retaliation for the alleged theft of a torch used in homecoming events at NDSC.

The repeated failures of the peace pacts did not keep the student bodies from trying to instill good relations between campuses. In September 1957, the four colleges — South Dakota State, Augustana, the University and Morningside — signed yet another document aimed at keeping campus destruction at bay.

Weeks later, on Oct. 10, 1957, the Collegian reported that the students who had hacksawed the goal posts at Howard Wood Field in Sioux Falls after State's 16-0 win over Augustana were facing possible disciplinary action.

Early in the spring semester, on Feb. 13, 1958, the Collegian noted that Augustana's Viking head was returned to the Sioux Falls campus after a monthlong hiatus in Brookings.

"The Viking head was originally stolen from Augustana during halftime of the Augie-State basketball game in Sioux Falls, Jan. 7," the Collegian story said. "Its next public appearance was at the basketball game between the two colleges in Brookings, Feb. 7. It had been hung from the ceiling directly over the State band."

During halftime, officials took the head down and locked it in one of the

On February 7, 1958, students hoisted the stolen Augie head up to the rafters of the 'Barn.' It was removed at halftime.

athletic offices. However, sometime during the second half, State students retrieved the head and their Augie counterparts saw them leave the building. A chase ensued and the Ole head was ditched along a country road.

"Only minor damages were inflicted on the head and State's Students' Association will pay for them," reported the Collegian.

On Oct. 3, 1959, a group of State students made a valiant halftime effort to steal Augustana's infamous Ole Horn. The plot not only failed, but it also succeeded in breaking the treasured horn and landing the State student body with a $180 bill.

What's more, to this day, more than 40 years later, the debate still rages on over who was at the center of the melee, and, perhaps more importantly, over whose head the horn was broken.

The horn wasn't necessarily special or valuable other than the fact that it belonged to Augie. It was a long Viking horn, says Jim Woster, class of 1962, and it made an "ooh ahhh" sound. "It sounds like one of those horns you hear in a Scandinavian country, like a cowbell ... like a cowbell with class."

Woster says his memory has been marred by the passage of time. But, he is clear about this: "The bottom line was, there was a group of people," Woster recalls. "I don't know if there was ever a meeting about it. I just remember everybody talking about it."

Chuck Cecil graduated in the spring of 1959 and was working in Pierre that fall.

"My wife and I decided to go to see the Augie game. We drove down, got a seat way up in the top of the stadium," Cecil says. "I was hoping to see Ralph Nachtigal. At halftime, I just happened to look down and there was a scuffle with an Augie cheerleader. I said to my wife, 'One of those people looks like

Ralph Nachtigal.' So, I rushed down the steps and got down under the stadium just as the police were escorting Ralph out of the stadium. I ran up to Ralph. I hadn't seen him for a while. I just ran up and shook his hand. The police misunderstood and kicked us both out. My wife was still up in the stadium."

Nachtigal, however, says he had limited involvement in the Ole Horn fracas.

"I was an innocent bystander in the whole deal," he says . "Really. I was a spectator up in the stands, watching the game. ... Everybody thinks I was the one hit over the head. It makes a great story. But, in all honesty, I was on the periphery of the whole incident."

Nachtigal concedes that he was thrown out of the game as Cecil remembers.

"And," he notes, "I cleverly came behind the stands, climbed on a cart and jumped over the fence into the waiting arms of policemen. That time, they hauled me to jail. ... I'm sure I'm the only one who ended up in the Minnehaha County Jail."

So, he wasn't in on the plan to toss the horn into the stands and have it handed off to a waiting car?

"If there was a plot," Nachtigal insists, "I was an innocent bystander who got involved. When all this happened, the police converged. When they got to the edge, I happened to be on the edge."

Derald Schoon, class of 1961, doesn't know Cecil, Woster or Nachtigal, but he remembers the horn incident as "the one that almost got us kicked out of school."

According to Schoon, the motive to steal Augie's horn was simple.

"Everybody always thought it was the most ugly sound they ever heard," he says.

It seemed like an easy enough stunt — grab the horn and run. But, others got involved and the ensuing racket alerted Augie students to what was happening.

"I ended up with one piece," says Schoon, "and a big bump on my head."

Schoon also was summoned to speak with Walder.

"He informed me about how serious an incident it was," Schoon recalls. "I thought for sure I was going to get kicked out. Also, at some point, we were informed that Augustana wanted compensation."

And yet, Schoon adds, during the lecture from Walder, "I felt he had a grin behind his stern face, as if he realized it was sort of funny. But, he certainly couldn't say that. In those days, we took the rules seriously. We knew the consequences. I know that after the horn incident we laid very low."

A few weeks later, the Oct. 22, 1959, Collegian reported that the matter continued to plague State.

A meeting of the two student body presidents, which was mediated by a representative from the University of South Dakota, determined that the SDSC Students' Association would be held fully responsible for damages to the Ole Horn. A sum of no more than $180 and no less than $150 would be assessed, depending on the extent of the damage. Augustana initially insisted that State students also be held responsible for obtaining a new horn, but that request was tossed out.

By spring, the Augie horn was still making news in the Collegian columns. The May 12, 1960, issue reported that profits from the Alpha Phi Omega booth at the chapter's carnival went to Augustana to help cover the bill for the Ole Horn.

The paper noted: "The voluntary action was to show the Vikings that there were no hard feelings over the battle last fall which produced a broken Ole Horn, which State College students were forced to pay for."

Looking back on the simpler times, Marshman says the era of pranks likely stemmed from the fact that in those days students had fewer opportunities to pursue in their free time. Most students lived on campus — and they stayed there on weekends because few had cars.

Still, students thought they were taking big risks when they set out for mischief at other campuses.

"We thought the pranks were serious at the time," he sighs. "By today's standards, they wouldn't even draw print."

Chapter 39

In Quest of Lingerie

For a few decades, from the early 1940s through the early 1970s, South Dakota State students occasionally found fun and diversion in the quaint campus trend of panty raids.

"Actually," laughs Mary Zulk, class of 1967, "girls threw their panties out the window more than actual raids. It was innocent fun. It really was."

Bob Karolevitz, who attended State from 1940-43 and then graduated after the war in 1947, remembers there being "some panty raids, but I wasn't involved. I was in the library or something."

Carola Marking, class of 1952, says the raids were fairly common in her days on campus. "The guys would break in and try to steal panties. It was almost an annual thing."

Walt Conahan, also class of 1952, remarks: "There'd be a big ruckus and quite a crowd. The girls would be hollering and waving things from the window."

"Oh, yeah," grins Chuck Cecil, class of 1959. "Panty raids. They were pretty innocent stuff. We'd just stand down on the ground, yelling up and enticing the girls to throw something to us."

Pictured above, headline from the South Dakota Collegian on May 22, 1952.

The only problem was that most administrations didn't look on the episodes as innocent. These incidents typically were quashed by campus and local authorities. And in a few instances, the perpetrators found themselves facing serious consequences.

The front page of the May 22, 1952, Collegian led with this story: Girls Rebuff 150 Eager Men in 'Panty Raid' Tuesday Eve.

"The raid, part of a national craze for raiding women's dorms, broke out at 11:20 and was soon quelled by dormitory managers and Brookings police," Bill Blankenburg reported. "Most of their insurgents were back in their rooms by midnight.

"The only known casualty of the evening was Mel Henrichsen, manager of East Men's hall, who was splashed with water thrown by one of the girls from a Wecota window, as Henrichsen was trying to quiet the raiders.

"None of the self-styled invaders got inside of the girls' dorms, and few ventured as far as the front door where the housemothers were waiting with a hostile welcome."

According to Blankenburg, the raid failed to retrieve any undergarments: "The only trophy of the incident was one brassiere, which the rioters had enough forethought to bring along before the raid had started. Early reports showed no deficit in any of the girls' wardrobes, as a direct result of the raid."

Adding to the evening's excitement, the fire alarm sounded in Scobey Hall and sent students from their rooms. No disciplinary action was taken, and dorm officials would not say if future efforts might be viewed in a harsher light. Still, the raid apparently was tame by campus standards.

"The raiders were not quite so brazen as undergrads in other colleges that perpetrated similar aggressions," wrote Blankenburg. "Some of the local invaders attempted to preserve anonymity by wearing masks fashioned out of handkerchiefs.

"Probably the only persons who really enjoyed the affair were the girls in the dorm, who took in the whole show from their rooms. When the rioters began to break up, the Wecota and Wenona residents taunted the boys as they made their retreat.

"The final box score: 1. No invaded boudoirs; 2. One slightly watersoaked dorm manager; 3.One brassiere, lost in the scuffle; and 4. Approximately 150 red faces."

In 1959, college officials were taking panty raids more seriously. That spring, on June 9 and 11, large crowds of more than 200 students gathered in front of Wenona and Wecota for panty raids.

The Oct. 8, 1959, Collegian reported that the incidents resulted in the

In Quest of Lingerie

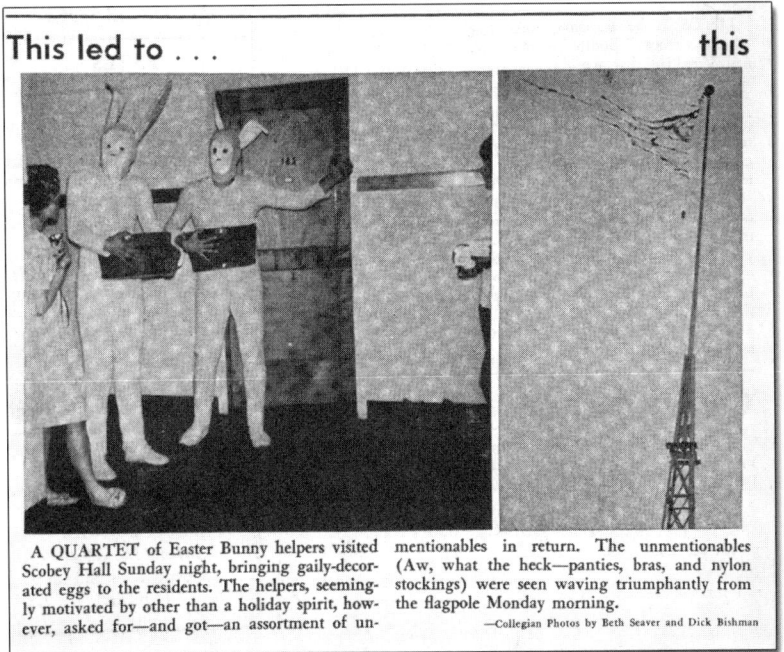

A QUARTET of Easter Bunny helpers visited Scobey Hall Sunday night, bringing gaily-decorated eggs to the residents. The helpers, seemingly motivated by other than a holiday spirit, however, asked for—and got—an assortment of unmentionables in return. The unmentionables (Aw, what the heck—panties, bras, and nylon stockings) were seen waving triumphantly from the flagpole Monday morning.
—Collegian Photos by Beth Seaver and Dick Bishman

Article on the front page of the South Dakota Collegian on May 26, 1964.

suspended classification of 29 students pending a hearing by the Student Conduct Committee. Eleven of those 29 did not return to school in the fall and remained on suspended status. Charges were dropped against three individuals. Fifteen students — 13 men and two women — were placed on probation. Of that group, 13 remained on probation through the spring quarter and two through the winter quarter.

"To our knowledge no one actually entered any of the dormitories," Guilford C. Gross, chairman of the conduct committee, told the Collegian. "However, any person who was on the dormitory grounds was actually violating college regulations."

A few students in 1964 took a new approach to panty raids. They succeeded not only in getting inside a women's dormitory, but they also hoisted up the flagpole the spoils of their victory.

Beth Seaver, class of 1966, was one of two photographers to capture the sequence of events. It was March, so two appropriately dressed Easter bunnies arrived at Scobey Hall one Sunday night bearing baskets filled with holiday treats.

"We were studying," says Seaver. "Most of us were running around in housecoats. The word spread that they wanted to bring Easter treats."

Escorted from room to room by the housemother, the furry duo carried the treats in baskets, which had holes underneath, says Seaver.

"The word also spread that they were collecting panties, but not to tell the housemother," she explains. "When girls went to get a piece of candy, some would stick panties in the basket. I heard what was going on so I grabbed my camera."

Sure enough, the March 26, 1964, Collegian ran Seaver's picture of two bunnies, baskets in hand, chatting with a coed in housecoat and slippers. A second picture, taken by Dick Bishman, showed the flagpole with strings of lingerie attached.

Underneath the pictures, the caption noted, the "Easter Bunny helpers visited Scobey Hall Sunday night, bringing gaily decorated eggs to the residents. The helpers, seemingly motivated by other than a holiday spirit, however, asked for — and got — an assortment of unmentionables in return. The unmentionables (Aw, what the heck — panties, bras, and nylon stockings) were seen waving triumphantly from the flagpole Monday morning."

Terry G. Nelson, class of 1965, says he remembers walking across campus that morning and seeing the bounty from the covert panty raid. But like everyone else, Nelson says the identities of the bunnies remain a mystery to this day.

Says Seaver: "We always suspected it was somebody from the sports teams, but no one ever knew for sure. Maybe some fellows knew, but they weren't about to squeal and get anyone in trouble. I don't remember anyone ever knowing for sure."

Nearly 40 years later, Nelson laughs at the innocence of the times: "We were really backward. It was really such a straight-laced place."

Chapter 40

The Fictitious Candidate

> "Mjork's the guy
> For You and for I
> So join his support
> And never say die."

Student body elections routinely come and go at South Dakota State without much excitement or intrigue.

In February 1941, however, a few students managed to stoke the political fires, as well as student body interest.

"The three candidates for student president were all Ags," recalls George L. Brown Jr., whose father, George L. Brown Sr., served in various administrative and faculty capacities on campus, "and many people felt we should have someone from General Science, so I was asked to run. We gathered enough signatures by petition."

But, Brown Sr. threw a wrench into the plans when he told his son that he would finish school before the next fall term with summer classes.

"We had all these good petitions and could not see wasting them, so we wrote in the name of Gordon Mjork," says Brown Jr. "I can't remember all of the conspirators, but I believe most of it was planned at the Collegian offices."

Pictured above, campaign song sung by supporters of an unknown candidate in the 1941 race for student body president.

Headline from the Feb. 27, 1941, South Dakota Collegian announcing the candidates for the upcoming student election.

The way Brown Jr. remembers it, he was managing editor and Marion Billings was editor. Someone delivered the petitions to the registrar's office, says Brown Jr., "and we phoned five minutes later to get the news story — not allowing enough time to check."

Decades before technology brought the world virtual reality, the Collegian pranksters photographed the back of a head for Mjork's "mug shot." The other candidates were Orville Bentley, John Bibby and John Billington.

The Feb. 27, 1941, edition of the campus paper trumpeted the headline New Candidates Enter Political Campaign underneath photos of the three smiling candidates and Mjork's back. Amid the great enthusiasm from ag college students, the Collegian bemoaned the failure of other students to get involved.

"The unusual laxity of interest in this year's election was shown by the unorganized general science students' failure to nominate enough candidates, and by the fact that ten minutes before the doors were closed on petitions the dean of one division didn't know the nominations were due," the Collegian reported.

A sidebar story by Jack Hagerty appeared below a series of headlines that read:

Majority's For Mjork
Campaign Manager Gives Candidate's Credentials
Backers Warn Against Unscrupulous Trials to Discredit Candidate

If anything, the Mjork candidacy spiced up the annual process of student body elections. Calling Mjork a "dark horse" candidate, but quoting no one by

The Fictitious Candidate

name, Hagerty wrote, "Heading the Mjork boom was a completely organized Mjork for President club, which announced plans to carry on a vigorous campaign.

"Until last week few students had even heard of the 'mystery nominee' but at week's end an ardent group of supporters had gathered to the Mjork standard to put him in the running."

Somehow, the students managed to get Mjork certified — or, at least, they said he was. To help dispel the mystery surrounding the candidate, the anonymous chairman of the Mjork for President club issued this statement:

"The Mjork for President club feels that no man whose last initial is 'B' could make a suitable president for the Students' Association. Therefore, we surveyed the field of possible nominees and chose a man whose brilliance has been missed in the myriad of activities in which he is engaged.

"Gordon Mjork, who comes from Commutes, is a junior in the general science partition. Everyone knows him — he's the fellow with the heine. Last fall he was third in the purple beard contest, and on February 11 he was the shadow beside 'Abe Lincoln in Illinois.'"

The chairman told the Collegian he anticipated trouble throughout the campaign, charging that there were "certain unscrupulous interests" that would work to keep Mjork's name off the ballot. Mjork's supporters, however, would persevere, the chairman said, and virtue would triumph: "We will carry on the campaign until Mjork is declared officially elected. The majority's for Mjork."

Billington had started classes at State in 1937, but financial hardship and then World War II kept him from graduating until 1947. More than 60 years after the Mjork candidacy, Billington, who ultimately won the election, laughs as he recalls what transpired.

"I really believe it was the Collegian," he says. "But, I don't know who. It has always been a mystery as to whom on the campus Mjork's supporters were. We were always under the impression that it was the guys on the Collegian."

For a nonexistent candidate, Mjork managed to make it through much of the campaign. Of course, there was the picture of the back of his alleged head. When the candidates had to give speeches, Mjork, understandably, fell ill.

Brown says: "My cousin, Gordon Carlson, assembled a German band to march into the assembly at which the candidates were to speak, and a campaign song was written — 'Mjork's the guy / For You and for I / So join his support / And never say die.'

"The candidates who appeared on stage were very rattled by all of this, and one demanded that Mjork appear immediately. He did not."

By the March 6, 1941, edition of the Collegian, Mjork had pulled out of the race in what the campus paper deemed a "dramatic withdrawal."

"Mjork's managers announced that he was dropping out of the race for student president to accept another position," the Collegian reported, "and refused to give more information."

If the Mjork candidacy accomplished anything, it was to drum up interest in the student elections.

Calling him a "mere nobody," the 1941 Jack Rabbit said Mjork became the most talked about candidate. Students demonstrated in support of Mjork, complete with banners and band music. As a result, the yearbook said, "Student voters snapped out of pre-election political lethargy to elect a vice president, 12 board of control members and four Union directors. Close returns left presidency, one board of control seat and one Union board position for a runoff election the following week."

Bentley was eliminated in the first round, leaving Billington and Bibby for the runoff.

Billington muses: "History has shown both Orville (Bentley) and John Bibby had very respectful positions in life. They were probably better administrators than I was. It was a pretty close election, really."

Billington says his edge was that he lived in the residence halls on campus, whereas Bibby, a Brookings resident, lived at home. That factor, along with Billington's running mate John Haynes being a pharmacy student, swayed the race.

"I know we had the complete block of pharmacy students," says Billington.

The three "known" candidates for student body president, Orville Bentley, John Bibby and John Billington share a lighthearted moment.

The Fictitious Candidate

That was the end of Gordon Mjork. For most students who were on campus at the time, the fictitious candidate is just a fading memory.

But, 56 years after he disappeared into the nothingness from which he was created, Mjork returned, if only for a brief moment.

In June 1997, the SDSU Alumni Association held a reunion titled "The Fabulous Forties." The event was attended by more than 200 alumni who were students during the 1940s.

Part of the festivities included the alumni organization's annual meeting, when the reigning president of the association proposes a slate of officers for the ensuing year. This is typically a routine event. Nominations are prepared in advance and none are offered from the floor. The June 1997 session, however, broke out of that mold.

Alumni Association President Darwin Britzman offered a slate of candidates. Someone in the audience made a motion to approve the slate. Another voice sounded the call to second the motion.

Following procedural rules, Britzman asked if there were any nominations from the floor. After a brief moment of silence passed, Ozzie Schock, class of 1947, rose to his feet.

"I nominate Gordon Mjork," he said.

A few chuckles rippled through the audience and soon everyone was laughing.

Britzman was visibly stunned. No such motion had ever been offered from the floor. Nor did he know what was so funny.

The laughter subsided, and Schock stood again.

"I withdraw my motion," he said.

The audience broke out in laughter once more.

For a few minutes, warm smiles graced the faces of the audience members. Though in reality a nobody, Gordon Mjork had revived the memories of earlier days and the innocent fun of a college prank.

Chapter 41

Whipping to White

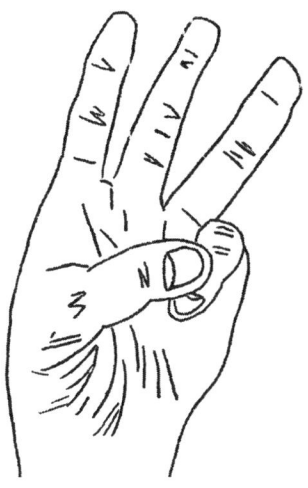

In the spring of 1968, roommates Dennis Ludwig, class of 1969, and Jeff Chicoine, class of 1968, and a few other SDSU students decided to stir up some fun in White, S.D.

Thirty-five years later, they can't remember exactly what led them to the small town eight miles north of Brookings on state Highway 77 and eight miles east on state Highway 30. But somehow, they ended up shooting pool and drinking a few beers.

"I don't know quite how we decided to go to White," muses Chicoine, "but we did. We went to the pool hall and were just kind of your typical obnoxious college students."

Little did the students — or the community — realize that their little road trip would be the impetus a year later for a massive party, called Whip to White, an orchestrated effort to literally "drink the town dry."

Pictured above, a drawing of a hand forms the "Whip to White" symbol, which students used on posters to promote the event.

Headline in the May 15, 1969, Collegian questioning whether the upcoming trip to White, S.D., would cause some of the same types of problems experienced when North Dakota students invaded the town of Zap, N.D.

"It was kind of the original Whip to White," Chicoine says of the 1968 visit. "We were just looking for something to do. That was the genesis of the whole thing. ... Dennis had this great idea. ..."

Reluctant to take full credit, Ludwig laughs: "It wasn't any one person. That thing got legs of its own. ... People were putting up posters on library bulletin boards. They'd stay up about an hour before a professor would spot it and tear it down."

Still, word passed around campus. Helping to fuel the grapevine was an event, billed as Zip to Zap, the week earlier in North Dakota. Those festivities had turned too rambunctious and set South Dakota authorities on edge. However, Ludwig maintains, Whip to White had been in the planning stages long before Zip to Zap.

Concerned that Whip to White might get out of control, the governor put the National Guard on alert.

The invitation to the Saturday, May 17, 1969, event was nothing fancy. The artwork consisted of a hand showing three fingers — a 'W' for White. "Wear something white," the notice urged. All SDSU students were invited to meet at the White Cafe at noon.

The Thursday prior, on May 15, the Collegian editorial urged a calm celebration. "If there's trouble," the editorial stated, "those causing the trouble will find out how fast a certain Guard unit can drive from Brookings to White."

Bob Quinn, class of 1970, cautioned in his Students' Association president's column that Whip to White was not sponsored by any organized group, and particularly not the student government: "Yet, if students do go to White, it becomes their responsibility to maintain sanity ... and people are being presumptuous if they think students won't. One of the best parties of the year was held last Saturday night with somewhere between 500 and 800 people there. There weren't any police — and there wasn't any trouble.

"The same thing is feasible with White, South Dakota. There's nothing there any of us should want to destroy. It's just a quiet little town."

In a front-page story, the Collegian reported on the planned "drink-in." An anonymous organizer said the plans were to "drink beer, have a bonfire, roast weiners, eat watermelons, play a few games and leave."

Residents of White were not completely opposed to the idea. Art Graslie, then president of the town's Community Club, told the Collegian: "We want the kids to come over and have fun, but we don't want any trouble. We have not extended an invitation, but we're not going to object to their coming, as long as they act like ladies and gentlemen."

Townspeople were preparing for the onslaught by hauling in firewood for the bonfire and working to secure a band to play in a park. Graslie also encouraged students to bring their own food because White had only one small cafe.

The morning of the Whip to White, Ludwig says he went to Nick's "for a delicious breakfast. The rumor was that there was a busload of students from Missouri that just went through town on the way to White. I don't think that ever happened."

However, there was a parade.

Recalls Ludwig: "A guy from Lemmon wore all white — white pants, white socks, white shoes, white T-shirt, a white Arabian style hat with a white towel hanging out the back. He rode on the front of a car, flashing the (three-fingered) Whip to White sign. Then, there were people walking behind the car. That was the official parade. Somebody wanted to put a white sheet up on the flagpole at the Post Office, but people thought it would be disrespectful. But, they were just going to put the white flag underneath the American flag."

Aside from the drinking, the students behaved themselves. Activities included a whiffleball game on the town's main street, climbing the flagpole and a performance by the Talisman band.

"As owner and leader of the R&R band, The Talisman," says Dennis Gerald, class of 1965, "I received a semi-urgent call — I don't remember where I was or who called — from someone wanting to know if I could get my band together quick and head for White. ...

"When we arrived in White, they headed us down Main Street to let the kids know we were there and lead them to an area away from downtown.

Many of them jumped on the front end of my station wagon and up on the Talisman trailer as we drove to the park."

Gerald says he doesn't remember how long the band played, "but we had a great time. The only thing bad that happened, as far as I was concerned, was that I got a flat tire from driving on broken glass."

Chicoine's sister, Marcia, who attended SDSU from 1966-68, returned for the festivities.

"It was really fun," she says. "Did we drink? Yes. There were hundreds of people. I truly remember walking down the street. You could barely get through, there were so many kids there. It was like New York City."

With Whip to White more than three decades in the distance, Chicoine says she can't imagine the same kind of event taking place. "Not in today's world," she says. "I don't remember anything being destructive. I guess we were pretty mellow."

In the aftermath, Collegian managing editor Dan Simpson reported that the twofold objective was half accomplished. It was successful in that it was peaceful, but the effort to drink the town dry failed despite the best efforts of an estimated 1,000 students:

"Just in case White had not had enough to quench their thirst, they brought their own. Happiness wasn't a dry martini, but usually a six-pack of beer commonly attached and carried on their belts. The local pub, called Sing's Place, had stored up 900 cases and that supply was trimmed down to 350 cases by around 6:30 p.m."

A large but unknown quantity of hard liquor also was consumed at Sing's Place, Simpson wrote. In describing the event, he observed, "It was a merry Saturday afternoon for most with the peak of students and other interested alcoholics numbering at approximately 1,000." Most of the group hailed from State, but others made the trek from the University of Minnesota, Southwest State College, Augustana, Northern Iowa, Dakota Weslyan and the School of Mines.

"But students weren't the only ones that numbered," Simpson wrote. "There were an impressive number of highway patrolmen strolling around the perimeter of White, fortifying the shattered nerves of some of the citizens."

Guardsman Pat Lyons, class of 1969, remembers spending the weekend at the National Guard armory: "While my classmates were drinking the town dry, I was practicing riot control formations. ... There was no riot."

The media was in attendance as well. The Collegian ran a picture of cameramen atop a building, identifying them as being from the Chicago bureaus of ABC, CBS and NBC.

Headline from the May 22, 1969, Collegian.

Despite concerns to the contrary, the day passed peacefully. Two windows were broken — one at the L&M Tractor Co., which was paid for immediately, and the other at the White Leader, the local paper. There also was an effort to get a bonfire going.

"Somebody was going to start a fire, to cook hot dogs, in the middle of Main Street," Ludwig says. "Then, in comes this State Police patrol cruiser, real slow. The officer gets out and says, 'You guys got to put this fire out.' And he stomps it out with his boot. Nobody says anything. He gets back in his car, flashes the Whip to White sign and drives off. He was pretty cool."

The Collegian reported varied responses from White citizens: "Some were disgusted at the drinking and drunkenness while others invited students into their homes for meals, etc. One student claimed he had eaten both dinner and supper at different homes."

At the same time, however, the town did not want an annual event. The next year, plans for a second Whip to White were canceled after residents and

SDSU student government discouraged the celebration. All but two or three residents signed a petition in opposition to another Whip to White.

Speaking at an S.A. Board of Control meeting, representing the citizens of White, Chuck Woodard explained the resistance: "A college beer bust, an outlet for spring fever, isn't compatible with a small, rural community."

Chapter 42

Streaking

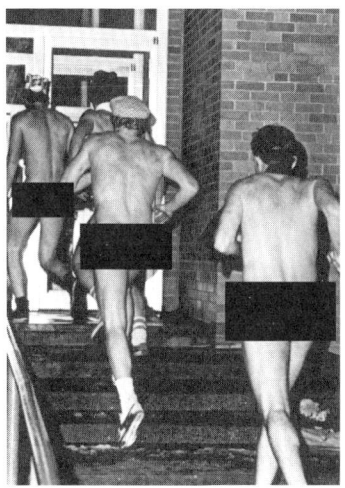

It was March 1974 and spring temperatures weren't the only thing heating up South Dakota State University. That was the moment when the streaking fad — in all its glory — hit the Brookings campus.

"I don't remember how streaking really got started," reflects Paulette Tobin, class of 1977. "I do remember there was a guy who streaked at the Academy Awards. Maybe that was it. It was one of those trends that probably involved way too much liquor."

From the administrative standpoint, Chuck Cecil, then assistant to SDSU President Hilton Briggs, notes: "It really was a new thing for all of us. Of course, no one understood the rationale — Hilton especially. I don't recall spending a lot of time on the issue. Everybody just shook their heads and rolled their eyes, wondering what the younger generation was coming to."

Briggs did not take the streaking matter lightly.

Pictured above, streakers make a local appearance as the nationwide fad hit the SDSU campus in March 1974.

The March 20, 1974, Collegian chronicles what it deemed the start of the streaking fad. The so-called action started on Sunday, March 10, when students returned from spring break. At 10 p.m., four streakers ran from the Campanile to Pierson Hall in "the first reported streak on campus." The next day, four men wearing only ski masks and shoes disrobed in an elevator near the west edge of the student center cafeteria and ran along the south corridor of the cafeteria, shouting and waving their hands.

In an attempt at equal opportunity streaking late Monday night, a female, wearing "a pillowcase down to her eyes, an orange and brown scarf around her neck, dark brown knee socks and saddle shoes," made a dash through the KBRK radio station.

"The announcer at the station remarked that there had been no female streakers reported yet, so I decided I wanted to be the first," the unnamed streaker revealed in a Collegian interview.

Tuesday night, the fad took a serious turn when four students were arrested by campus security officers — two for riding nude on top of a car and two for running nude on campus. All four pleaded innocent in court to misdemeanor charges of indecency. The next afternoon, two male students streaked through Dr. Robert Burke's psychology class. Wednesday night, an estimated 500 students lined Medary Avenue to watch a chain of "mooners."

The Collegian reported: "The display stopped as soon as onlookers began pelting the mooners' derrières with snowballs. Attention then shifted to Pierson, Matthews and Brown halls where numerous streaking incidents were reportedly in progress.

"The Dance for Dystrophy was streaked Saturday evening by an unidentified male student who, after running through the crowd of dancers, ran to the stage and presented the master of ceremonies with a $2 donation to the dystrophy fund."

But, just as the streaking fad seemed to be catching on, Briggs announced a zero-tolerance policy: "We have always followed the rule that when students are involved in abuse of the law, then normal court procedures are followed." The fact that streaking was a fad held no sway with Briggs.

"It comes as a shocking surprise that SDSU students are getting involved in this sort of thing," Briggs told the Collegian. "I am surprised and disappointed that we have students who attempt to attract attention in such an immature manner. It's a type of exhibitionism."

City officials, however, were a little less zealous. Brookings Police Chief Doug Filholm commented to the campus paper: "I'm not telling my men to go out and get streakers. They are instructed to pick them up if they see them.

Headline in the March 20, 1974, SDSU Collegian.

If the officer happens to see a streaker, the officer can arrest the streaker at his own discretion. I'd hate to see anybody get a record."

On campus, head of security Hugh Kirsh said Briggs reinforced the lawless nature of streaking: "We will arrest and prosecute streakers. If we did any less than that, we'd be breaking our oath. But, it would be ridiculous to run into a crowd of 300 students just to arrest a couple of streakers."

Terry Sanderson arrived on campus in the fall of 1974, moving into Brown Hall. There had been several episodes of streaking, he recalls, mostly involving people running through Grove Commons and "the occasional bounding through the basketball game."

One particular night, Sanderson says, "somehow word got through that we were going to have a mass streak. A whole bunch of us guys all gathered together ... naked, standing in the hall of the west wing. We were going to bound out through the lobby and make a loop through the Student Union parking lot. No one was in charge; no one knew when we were supposed to go.

"I got kind of restless. We were all standing there in the hallway and nobody was taking off. So, I ran out the back door and jumped on my bicycle and drove past the front door of the lobby, between the lobby and (Grove) Commons."

At about the same time, a group of the guys inside mustered the courage to head out the door. The only problem was, explains Sanderson, "campus police had heard about it and were hiding around the corner. They turned their lights on 'em when they went out of the lobby and they nabbed a bunch. I turned around on my bicycle so they couldn't catch me, but someone took a picture of my backside on a bicycle."

Briggs admitted to the Collegian that he was baffled by the streaking. If students were trying to get a point across, he said, there were other ways. If they were trying to protest, he welcomed the students to come talk. "Communication is based on language, understanding, or interpretation of actions and I can't understand the language of exhibitionism."

But, perhaps because of the time-tested gap between generations, Briggs had missed the point. Why were students disrobing and running nude across campus?

"Oh," sighs Sanderson, "it was just kind of a way to blow off steam, to do something just totally off the wall, to have some fun."

Michelle Howard, an SDSU student from 1972-76, says she doesn't know who participated in the first streak, but claims fourth-floor Binnewies must have held an unofficial record for the most and longest streaks.

One of the streaks by the fourth-floor Binniwies boys involved Waneta Hall, Howard recalls: "Several ski-masked young men piled into a 1971 Torino and made their plans on the way. They were to be dropped off about a block away, then run to Waneta, down the first-floor hall, emerge at the fire escape, and run a short distance where the getaway driver would pick them up and drive them back to Binniwies."

Instead, panicked and facing a hall full of camera-bearing girls, the streakers ecountered more difficulty than expected in negotiating the crowd. Then, they arrived at the rendevous point with no car in sight. They had no choice but to start sprinting for home.

"Eventually," says Howard, "the driver found them, and not a moment too soon, because they were not, by nature, 'long-distance streakers,' and what started out as a race had already turned into a slow-speed jog."

That night might have marked the end of the fourth-floor boys' streaking efforts — except that the girls down the hall felt left out. The girls pleaded their case and the boys agreed to oblige.

"Since it wasn't a surprise streak, we all waited with cameras in hand at the doors to our room," Howard says, setting the scene. "This was to be a 'formal streak' with ties and belts to accompany the ski masks. ... Finally, the door opened, and the first streaker tore down the hallway. It soon became apparent that there was a problem. Someone had chickened out and closed the door. When he realized that he was alone, he stopped, turned around, and started jumping up and down and waving, trying to get the others to follow."

The girls, of course, found opportunity in such a photographic moment. The rest of the boys finally relented and completed the streak.

Cecil compares streaking to the fads that had existed a couple of decades earlier. "When I was in school, panty raids were all the rage," he says. "There just seemed to be a trend toward individualism as we progressed."

Tobin, a native of small-town Eureka, laughs now as she remembers the thrill of the moment. In her freshman and sophomore years, she lived on the fourth floor of Pierson Hall, in the north wing.

"We always knew when it was going to happen," she says. "People would be sitting in windows, waiting for guys to go streaking. It was just the idea. People would be yelling and screaming. ... We were 19 and 20 years old. We thought it was really hilarious. Things were very different in the '70s than now. People were not so open about sexual things. (Streaking) made us feel so brave, so free, so cool. ... I don't know if there was streaking today, if anybody would notice."

Tobin doesn't remember any women streaking. "I can't imagine any of us would be that brave."

It's easy to joke today about the short-lived fad, but Tobin says that the streaking ceased being humorous for the four young men who were arrested.

"It was one of those things," she says, "that was really funny, until they were arrested. They were totally humiliated. One, he was an RA. His parents were horrified."

Mark Thomas, 1973-74 Students' Association president, remembers the jail house call he received from one of the arrested streakers, who was seeking legal assistance.

"Hilton Briggs ran a pretty tight ship," notes Thomas. "He tried to make sure the school had the best reputation and image, and he didn't tolerate a lot of shenanigans. There were a couple nights of streakers, between Mathews, Pierson and Brown halls, and some poor clod happened to step out into the arms of campus police."

Thomas approached Briggs, looking for some leniency. But Briggs, of course, insisted on pursuing the matter to the full extent of the law. Not wanting others to get arrested, Thomas, in a Collegian column, urged students to think before stripping: "The president and the campus security have no mercy in their hearts for this nationwide craze that exists in our country. If you are caught, you may have a permanent indecent exposure conviction on your presently clean criminal record.

"I hope that you will weigh the situation and know its affects before you streak. The students that you streak probably won't sign a complaint against you, but the ... campus police will, so please exercise the utmost caution if there are 'bare' plans in the making."

The Collegian, in an editorial, pointed out that while Briggs was concerned with the moral decay of the student body, an estimated 380 people had danced their way to exhaustion in raising $23,500 for the Dance for

Dystrophy. The opinion piece also wondered about the status of priorities:

"With the education at State University in the poor condition it is in, the sad situation of some people such as the classified employees, the ecological implications of the Oahe Project, why the alarmist attitude over some harmless nudity?"

The editorial noted that "nature has provided us with some beautiful things," including body parts. "But, it's too bad that we all weren't blessed with one more beautiful thing: a sense of priorities. Roll on big river, roll on."

Ultimately, the four arrested streakers pleaded guilty to charges of disturbing the peace in exchange for the initial misdemeanor charges of indecency. They were sentenced to $75 in fines and given two-day suspended sentences. The students could work off $50 of the fine by putting in 25 hours with the university's physical plant.

Ron Aho, assistant city attorney for Brookings at the time, recalls that there were some jokes about having a lineup of perpetrators. At the same time, however, authorities recognized that streaking violated local ordinances and had to be dealt with as such.

"It seemed to be a passing fad," Aho says. "I don't think that in terms of alcohol abuse and driving while intoxicated that streaking was as great a concern. But, it couldn't totally be ignored. There was a little bit of concern, mixed with humor. In district court, you don't get much to laugh about."

Taking the stand in court, the students told the judge of the embarrassment and hardship they had suffered in the wake of their actions. One lost his RA position as well as a part-time job. Another, who was an honor student, talked about how he had embarrassed his parents and hadn't been home since his arrest.

Nearly 30 years later, Thomas finds this chapter in State history symbolic of a simpler era.

"It was a release of tension, to have some fun," he says. "There wasn't anybody hurt, or abused, or anything in that order. It was just a bunch of guys who decided to get wild and crazy. ... It was a fun, innocent time."

Chapter 43

1990 Hobo Day Incident

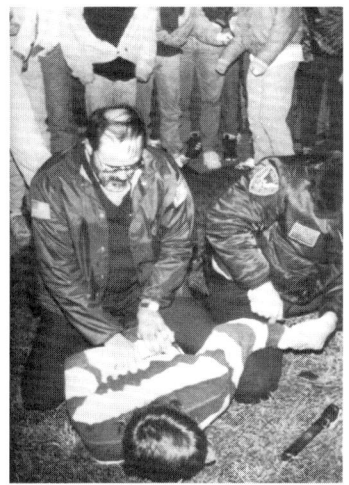

Hobo Day 1990. Then-sophomore Jon Lauck, class of 1993, remembers it well. So does Mike Reger, who was serving as dean of student affairs at the time, and former Brookings Police Chief Dennis Falken.

In fact, most people who were anywhere in the state at the time — and many who weren't — can recall the infamous homecoming celebration.

"I was doing interviews for a week," recalls Reger, now vice president for administration. "The front of my house was a backdrop. The story made USA Today. We had alums calling from Korea, Europe. It went out on AP, UPI. Everyone wanted to know what was going on."

Lauck, working in 2002 as a lawyer in Sioux Falls, says the events of the

---

Pictured above, campus security officers make an arrest during the Hobo Day fracas.

weekend unfolded in front of the house he was renting with six other guys:

"We lived in a big blue house on Ninth Avenue, in the center of the student ghetto. We had a house party (Friday night) — just about everybody on the block did. Lots of people were milling around; there were lots of people in the street. Then, the house parties started to merge into one another and a bunch of people started congregating in the street. Somehow, a bonfire started. There was a couch ... it had been in the garage; there was a bunch of junk from previous renters. A picnic table got tossed into the fire. People were sort of rummaging through the neighborhood for kindling. Once that started, more and more people showed up and it got to be a block party. There were two nights of this."

Reger remembers the 1:30 a.m. Saturday phone call from Chief Falken:

"Dennis called me and said, 'There's a bonfire at Ninth and Seventh.' The fire department had gone and tried to put it out, but the students wouldn't let them through. Someone threw a rock or beer bottle. ... We went down there, and there was a group of students. None of us were really worried about this. Dennis and about six officers and I walked up to the students and said it was time to go. They left. There was no riot. Just a group of students out in the street. That's all there was."

Unfortunately, the situation was sensationalized on the 6 o'clock news Saturday evening.

"They were describing it as a riot, which made it far worse," says Reger. "They started talking about the bonfire. The press was all over it. It was a possible news story and they came up (from Sioux Falls) to cover it."

Twelve years later, Lauck correctly remembers that the weather was rainy. Reger says that one element was a huge contributing factor.

"It was cold and rainy all Friday night," he says. "It broke about 11 o'clock. Everybody had been cooped up all day. The same thing Saturday. It was cold and rainy all day, from the parade all the way through the end of the game. Attendance was down at the parade and the game. I'm convinced that a lot of students just stayed home and drank. So, by around 6 or 7 o'clock at night, there were a lot of very primed people. ...

"The other thing is, students always start drinking with the parade. Then they go to the game. That gives you about three hours to sober up."

But, the weather gave no respite from the alcohol consumption that day.

Reger continues: "I don't think any one of us expected the same problem or any problems to occur Saturday night, until we saw the media coverage. About all we had was another bonfire, around 8:45 p.m. At that point ... things were starting to get out of control. Students were taking furniture, throwing it on the bonfire. We started getting calls from residents in the neighborhood — people were taking a fence apart and throwing it in the bonfire. At that point, we decided we needed to move 'em — get 'em out of the area and get the fire put out. It was a conscious decision on our part to move them toward campus.

"We had officers come up Ninth from the south and come in from the west. ... We moved everybody away from Ninth and Seventh, the whole crowd ... at least 1,000 people. They moved up to the corner of Eighth and Twelfth. Another bonfire started there. We just kept walking 'em. There were no confrontations. We kept moving along Eighth and up to campus. Some turned right to Binnewies and Young (residence halls) — that's when most of the damage on campus took place."

Guided by mob psychology and fueled by alcohol, the group broke light poles and other items in the way. And yet, the campus was where officials wanted the group to be. There was a lot more open space, which would be helpful in dispersing people. And, as Reger points out, better to have them on state rather than private property. Eventually, the crowd split up by the field south of Binnewies Hall, with some heading downtown via Sixth Street.

"In-between 11:30 and 12:30," Reger says, "the third bonfire started. We had a good hour and a half gap in there. And that crowd was far more mellow than earlier."

Falken had called in additional law enforcement help. Officers from sheriff departments, highway patrol and Game, Fish and Parks responded. By the third bonfire, all the law enforcement officials had been pulled back in.

"We decided to let that one be until there were enough officers on hand," says Reger. "Again, all they seemed to be doing was mostly burning up their own furniture. I was wandering through that crowd and so was Dennis. It was not an angry crowd. Mostly, it was kids with beers in hand and a lot of spectators."

The media firestorm, however, continued. Reger wrote down one quote used by KSFY-TV to describe the scene: "An angry mob of a thousand attacked and destroyed nearly everything in their path, including the Eyewitness News Team."

But, Reger says, what he saw unfold differed: "KSFY came down Eighth Street and turned south on Ninth Avenue. They drove right into the crowd, literally pushing people out of the way. They got out and turned on their lights, on the last bonfire, and turned on the cameras right in the middle of the crowd. We just stood there watching.

"A bunch of students got on the car and started rocking it. Pretty soon,

This picture from the 1991 Jackrabbit shows a television cameraman in the midst of the crowd during the infamous Hobo Day incident.

they had it up on its side. Somebody came back and said, 'We need to get that on film.' So, they put it down and rolled it over again. The car went over twice. I was just shaking my head. It wasn't the press' fault, but they played into it. At that point, we brought all the officers up that we had, walked into the crowd and said it was time to go home. And they did."

Lauck remembers a television news crew filming the events from the upstairs of his house.

"I don't know," he says. "Maybe it was to get a good angle. Or maybe it was also to avoid getting attacked."

Nontraditional student Dave Fossum, class of 1994, had just started working with the Brookings ambulance service the summer of 1990 and was doing ride time Hobo Day night.

"We got called for an overturned vehicle, unknown injury," Fossum says. "The police didn't know what they had, yet. We drove up and were just mobbed by people. There was a bonfire in the middle of the street. They threw a couple of items at us — beer cans — and the police told us it was not what they thought. The mob had just overturned a vehicle. We got back in the ambulance and backed away a couple of blocks. We were kept on standby for about an hour or two and then the police told us to just get out of there. ...

"I thought it was just crazy. I couldn't believe it was going on. I had fun party times in the Army, but nothing even came close to that night."

Then a student in the College of Nursing, Fossum also got a taste of the incident as a student senator. The aftermath was amazing, he says.

"They trampled yards, took everything that wasn't bolted down and used it as fuel for the fire or mischief, or whatever," Fossum remembers. "One area south of campus, the trees were just decimated. It was like a little army marching through. They ripped down light posts, street signs. Trash cans and dumpsters were strewn about."

Lauck also recalls the police presence, noting that officers were dressed in "riot gear, like what you see on TV in the West Bank." Like Reger, Lauck credits alcohol with helping push Hobo Day 1990 beyond comfortable boundaries. The media attention, although not the cause, certainly helped fan the flames — in both a literal and figurative sense.

"There was a lot of beer mixed in," he says. "People just got carried away. As soon as the press came in, everyone wanted to get on TV. It was a way of making the situation a lot worse. We know it made CNN — they showed footage of it."

Falken, Brookings police chief for 17 years starting in 1985, says the department always had planned extra staffing. The only difference, he adds, was prior to 1990, the emphasis of law enforcement had been on the parade. Additionally, before the the drinking age was raised to 21, Hobo Day celebrations typically took place downtown rather than in residential neighborhoods.

Echoing Reger's thoughts, Falken remembers thinking that the situation would not evolve into what it did.

"It was a bunch of kids partying, until they started busting things," says

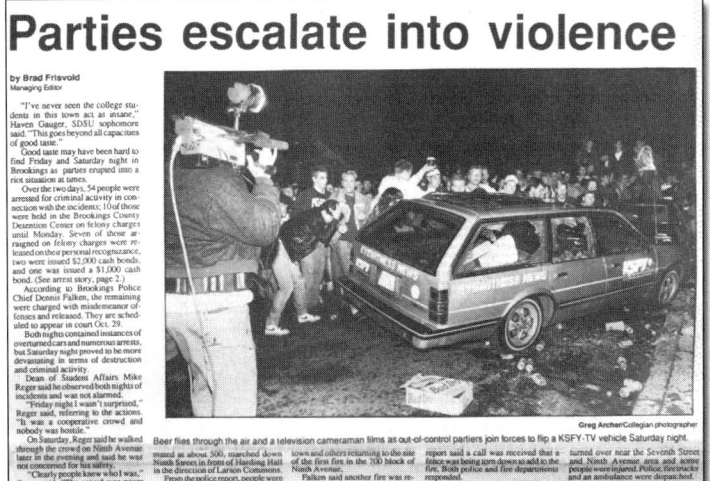

Headline from the Oct. 24, 1990, Collegian showing the crowd rocking the KSFY-TV news vehicle.

> **Students apologize**
> **Students' Association sends its regrets to local residents**
>
> by Matt Schwarz
> Collegian Staff Writer
>
> Following the Hobo Day weekend riots, Students' Association Monday unanimously adopted an apology letter to the Brookings community.
> The letter said SA does not condone the actions of a few students and apologized for their behavior. The letter said it is unfair to blame a few students' actions on a 78-year tradition (Hobo Day). The letter went on to say SA is interested in working with community and university officials to rectify the situation and prevent future incidents.
> John Weber, arts and sciences senator, moved to accept the apology letter, and SA Vice President John
>
> senators agreed the riots did not stem from the Hobo Day activities.
> "This had nothing to do with Hobo Day. This could have happened on any weekend," said Canham, one of approximately 50 audience members.
> Beth Thibodeau, University Program Council president, said, "On behalf of UPC, we're ashamed, and
>
> "You guys don't realize what this community does for this school. We need to be real careful when we start blaming the community for not giving us stuff to do, because they bend over backwards for us."
> -Mike Oster
> Students' Association president
>
> Mike Reger, dean of student affairs, said the blame could not be placed on other people or on strict alcohol policies.
> "I think we kid ourselves if we blame the alcohol laws," he said. "There was in no way, in my mind, a protest going on Friday or Saturday

After the dust settled, reality set in as noted by this Oct. 24, 1990, Collegian article.

Falken. "Then, the media came and started filming the kids. The kids started showing off and it became a big deal. That certainly caused it to get more out of hand. Then, the kids decided to turn on the filming crew. ... With that, we knew we had to do something."

By the end of the weekend's festivities, damages were estimated at $30,000 on campus and $10,000 off campus.

Ten people were arrested and charged with felony offenses: four for intentional damage to property, one for fleeing from an officer and aggravated assault, three for aggravated assault, one for instigating a riot and one for interfering with a law enforcement officer. More than 50 others were arrested on misdemeanor offenses. Four students came up with a T-shirt to sell — Hobo Days 1990 with a raging crowd and overturned car on the front and the phrase "What a Riot!" on the back.

The regents, however, were not laughing. They requested a report on the weekend and planned to consider appropriate actions at their Nov. 1-2 meeting in Rapid City. Regents President Max Gruenwald said at the time that permanently or temporarily canceling Hobo Day was a possibility. He told the Sioux Falls Argus Leader: "We will not tolerate events such as the past weekend, even if it means that we can no longer celebrate Hobo Days."

Gov. George Mickelson objected to calling off the annual festivities: "That's a double whammy to the community."

In a final report to the regents, the SDSU administration detailed the many factors that had contributed to the mess: (1) Hobo Day draws a lot of people, many of whom are not associated with SDSU; (2) the celebration leads to greater alcohol consumption than normal weekend levels; (3) most of the problems took place in the campus neighborhood, where many student rentals are located; (4) there are no scheduled activities after the football game; (5) mob psychology fueled much of the melee; and (6) the rainy weather cleared, encouraging students to cruise the streets, looking for house parties.

The campus, as well as the city, responded to those factors that could be controlled. A new ordinance limited the purchase of kegs to one at a time per location with no more than three total. New zoning controls limited to three the number of non-related individuals who could live in a house. Alcohol education efforts and responsible drinking programs developed.

From the student government perspective, Fossum says: "Our biggest goal was to prevent it from happening again in the future. We had quite extensive meetings with the University Program Council to come up with other things for kids to do — ways to keep them entertained. We figured we couldn't address the influx of people. The biggest problem we saw was not having anything to do."

One idea was to sponsor a big concert, but in the next few years, despite acts like 38 Special, partying remained the big Hobo Day draw.

"Students were not looking for formal campus activities, although we made the attempt," says Reger. "The police chief and I, the following year, did drop in that Tuesday afternoon of Hobo Week ... (at) every house where there had been a complaint prior to Hobo Day. Our basic message was, 'The whole world is going to be looking at us. Keep your heads about you.' They were very receptive. That continues today."

Chapter 44

The War to End All Wars

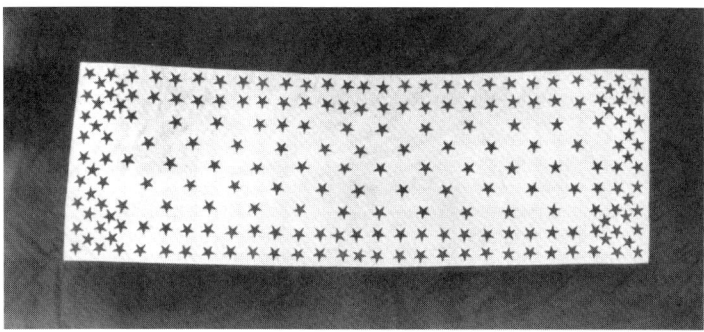

Home Again

Now our soldiers and our sailors back from France, with flag unfurled,
Shout with joy as they behold the grandest sight in all the world,
The glorious gift of France that in our New York Harbor stands,
Proclaiming liberty and love to the people of all lands.
The blazing torch of Truth, held high for emperors and kings,
Henceforth and forever telling that the world a new song sings.
The hungry nations that we feed will never forget our name,
That America helped save the world and won immortal fame.
The Beacon light of Freedom the stately goddess holds on high
Will light the reconstruction work, we will gladly do or die.
We will free the world from slavery in all its many forms.
We will navigate our ship of state through sunshine and the storms
Into the distant harbor of a glorious destiny,
Where children play the live-long day, singing songs to you and me.

Pictured above, a service flag bearing 210 stars was placed above the main doors to the Administration Building in 1917.

*And the beauty of the lilies and the roses red and gold
Will make this world a Paradise, as by prophets oft foretold.*
— N.E. Hansen, 1920

As would happen time and again throughout its history, South Dakota State heeded the call of war in the spring of 1917.

"We, the undersigned, members of the faculty of the South Dakota State College, wish to express our concurrence in the avowed aim of the administration 'to vindicate the principles of peace and justice in the life of the world,' and pledge our support of any measures taken in defense of American rights or liberties."

That resolution was signed by professors and instructors at State and sent by telegram to Washington after war was declared April 6, 1917. And, according to the April 10, 1917, Collegian, "This sentiment ... represents without a doubt the practically unanimous stand of the student body."

In those years, as was the practice for many decades to follow, male students were required to fulfill two years of military training as freshmen and sophomores. Their training led to commissioned officer status. Those not called to duty found their services needed on South Dakota farms, and faculty excused them from classes for a two- to three-week period to help out.

"At the present time farm help is scarce," reported the April 17, 1917, Collegian, "and many of the students are badly needed at home ... In doing this, each student is just as loyal to his country as he would be if serving in the Army. We cannot all be agriculturists, but each can and should do that which he can do best, for now is the time that our country needs the best we can give her."

Those who were trained in the agricultural field became food emergency specialists or county agents, or entered into other lines of Extension work, according to the 1919 yearbook, "appreciating the federal slogan, 'Food Will Win the War.'"

It wasn't the first time State had answered the call of duty. Nor would it be the last. A year earlier, on June 19, 1916, thinking that a crisis was about to erupt at the Mexican border, President Woodrow Wilson had ordered mobilization of all National Guard units.

The 4th South Dakota Infantry, including SDSC troops, spent four days on a train to reach San Benito, Texas. The men saw no combat, but they patrolled the border and trained for warfare for seven months. Some of those who stayed behind admitted envy, thinking the episode offered an adventur-

ROTC drills used to be commonplace on the Campus Green. Note the half-completed Administration Building.

ous break from the campus routine of classes and study, according to the 1918 Jack Rabbit.

"But," yearbook editors wrote, "second thot (sic) brought other aspects into the foreground: the rigid routine of discipline; the grueling training that led to no picturesque climax; the deadly sameness of program; the absence of diversion, except what was furnished by tarantulas, centipedes, dust storms, and tropic suns; and not least, the loss of nearly a year of college. Yes, if envy lingered in our minds it came to be based not upon our notions of military romance but upon the very fact that the boys at the Border were serving, not merely talking and feeling, but 'doing their bit,' sacrificing time, money, ease for the country that bore them.

"So may we all be quick to sacrifice for alma mater and for country in this portentous hour, when sacrifice of some sort is sure to be demanded — nay, is already being demanded. As long as such spirit exists, idealism is not dead in our colleges, nor is the nation wholly sunk into fatty degeneration. Hats off to the Border boys!"

When Company C headed out for training and war on Sept. 28, 1917, classes were canceled so that the whole community — both college and city — could join together for the occasion.

In a mix of celebration and sadness, pride in service and farewell to arms, the emotional departure mirrored wartime throughout the years as Brookings has watched men and women of passing generations called to war. World War

I, World War II, Korea, Vietnam, the Gulf War and Iraq — the pomp and circumstances change, but the underlying currents of patriotism, conflict over purpose and fear of what may come to pass run deep.

"The students and faculty met at the auditorium at noon where plans were discussed as to the form which the parade should take," the yearbook recounted. "On leaving the auditorium two files were started, one headed by Professor Mathews, the other by Dean Brown. The entire procession first marched to the fairgrounds, where the guard camp had been stationed for several weeks, and then eastward toward Main Street.

"On reaching Main Street the two lines separated, one file going on each side of the street. After a long line of civilians had passed in parade, the flower girls strewed a carpet of flowers for the Guard Boys to walk upon as they marched between the two files of spectators. At the station the boys entered the sleepers which had been prepared for their transportation. Another troop train was expected at any time to come and carry the Guards to some training camp in the East. While waiting for this train to arrive, many people were engaged in what they thought might be the last conversations with their friends and loved ones who sat in the open car windows.

"To add a little enthusiasm to the occasion, a group of college boys gave several yells for the Guards. Among them was a very appropriate locomotive yell which ran like this:

'Rah-rah-rah-rah
Get-the-Kai-ser.'

"As the train moved away from the station the band played the 'Star Spangled Banner' amid the multitude of waiving hats and handkerchiefs."

Those who stayed behind remained enthusiastically devoted. State President Ellwood Perisho issued a memorandum outlining the three ways the campus had thrown its support behind the country and servicemen: training and education, food production and food conservation.

"Thus by instruction, experiment and statewide Extension service;" Perisho wrote, "by furnishing officers and privates, Christian workers and Red Cross leaders, by teaching of patriotism that is effective and loyalty that expresses itself in service, State College is meeting the emergency of this War."

To conserve food, the days of the week received special designation. Monday was wheatless; Tuesday, meatless; Wednesday, wheatless; and Saturday, porkless. Wheatless meant no food items containing wheat. Wheat flour could be used in small amounts for cooking. Meatless meant no cattle, hog or sheep product. Porkless meant substituting fish, poultry or eggs. Breakfast was meatless; supper, wheatless; and people were urged to save fats and sugar.

The 1919 yearbook included a special war section to pay tribute to the more than 200 students who served in World War I, either as commissioned officers or enlisted men. Throughout the duration of the war, a white service flag, bordered in red, hung above the entrance of the Administration Building, commemorating each of the soldiers with a single blue star. By the war's end, the flag had 210 stars stitched on it.

In 1920, the college established Liberty Grove as a permanent tribute to the 27 State students who lost their lives in World War I. A large boulder was placed on the front lawn of the old library — which is now Lincoln Music Hall — among trees planted by graduating classes.

The 1923 Jack Rabbit explained: "State College holds dear the memory of her students who left the classroom for the battlefield in France, never to return. To them is dedicated Liberty Grove, the small group of trees — white birch and mountain ash — one of the most picturesque of all the campus spots.

"For the students of the future, strangers perhaps but with unfailing understanding, the grove is marked by a large stone bearing the names of those who fell from among State's members, and an inscription to her heroes."

In 2000, the boulder was moved to the Medal of Honor Park directly north of DePuy Military Hall. A formal dedication was held on Sept. 22. In addition to the boulder, the Medal of Honor Park displays two monuments — one for Bill Bianchi, who was awarded a congressional Medal of Honor in World War II, and one for Leo Thorsness, who was awarded a congressional Medal of Honor in the Vietnam War. There also are tablets honoring other veterans of war.

Each year, campus memorial services included the laying of a wreath on the Liberty Grove boulder.

Chapter 45

Omar Bradley

In war and peace, at home and overseas, South Dakota State students repeatedly have demonstrated a devoted willingness to serve their country. Such a deep-rooted sense of duty early on earned the campus battalion the nickname: West Point of the Plains.

It is only fitting, then, that the strong and storied military history of the State campus would include a teaching stint by distinguished five-star Gen. Omar Nelson Bradley.

Born in Clark, Mo., on Feb. 12, 1893, Bradley graduated from the U.S. Military Academy at West Point in 1915. He was commissioned a second lieutenant and assigned to the 14th Infantry, which was stationed in Yuma, Ariz.

In the summer of 1919, less than a year after World War I ended, Bradley (by then a major) was appointed as the temporary replacement for L.C.

Pictured above, Major Omar Bradley as seen in the 1921 Jack Rabbit.

Williams, the commandant of cadets and professor of military science and tactics at State.

In his memoirs, "A General's Life," Bradley explained his transition:

"I had applied, through routine War Department channels, for a position as a military instructor at a college with an ROTC unit. In a box on the application designation location preferred, I typed in 'Northwest,' assuming that to mean the states of Washington and Oregon. My request for ROTC duty was granted, but unknown to me, in those days the states of Washington and Oregon were designated 'Pacific Northwest.' My choice, 'Northwest,' denoted the area of North and South Dakota. As a result of this misunderstanding, on August 25, I was assigned to be assistant professor of military science and tactics at the South Dakota State College in Brookings, a small city in the eastern part of the state."

Despite the error, Bradley dove into his duties and quickly earned the admiration of the cadets and others. As with many who have endured a South Dakota winter, the yearlong stint at State made an impression on Bradley and his first wife, Mary.

Bradley recalled: "Our year at Brookings was a bitterly cold one, but the work turned out to be interesting and challenging. ... After ROTC summer encampment in Michigan and a lovely three-week leave camping and fishing on lakes in Minnesota, Mary and I returned to Brookings in late August prepared for another school year. I was astonished to receive a telegram ordering me to duty at West Point 'without delay,' as an instructor in the math department. ... On Sept. 11, 1920, we loaded the Dodge and drove to West Point. Our dog Birdie had again wandered off and had to be left behind. We never saw her again."

In addition to his dog, Bradley left a lasting legacy. The November 1920 Alumnus stated that no military instructor had a greater impact on the lives of young men at State than Bradley. The 1921 Jack Rabbit deemed Bradley's short tenure one of the most successful in years for the military department.

"Not only has he organized the battalion and brought the drill to cover a larger scope of military tactics than ever before, but he has spent much time and energy in promoting the physical welfare of the students," the yearbook noted. "This he has done by organizing classes in boxing and wrestling. He has also taken an active part in coaching athletics and has won a place in the esteem of every State student."

More than half a century later, Jeff Nerison, class of 1976, revived the legend of Omar Bradley for a new generation of State students. The house Nerison shared with four other guys at 207 Fourth St. became known as the

House of Omar, the legend being that that was where Bradley lived during his year of teaching at South Dakota State.

One of Nerison's roommates, Bill Stewart, class of 1976, recalls: "It came up in conversation one time that Bradley had lived in Brookings. Nerison said he lived in the house."

Nerison laughs: "Yeah, I made it up and it took. It took big time."

Why?

"God only knows," muses Nerison. "This was the one famous guy we had and we lived in this dump. So, I came up with that."

Stewart concedes, "Fairly early on, we were reasonably certain that (Bradley) didn't live there. But, that didn't mean we couldn't tell people. ... We weren't going to apply for national historic status."

Brookings historian George Norby says Bradley actually lived at 706 11th Ave.

Jeff Bloomberg, class of 1976, did not discover the hoax until shortly before graduation, when he was talking to his roommates, Nerison and Stewart, about the house's connection to Omar Bradley.

"The two of them were laughing," says Bloomberg. "I was asking, 'What's the deal?' Finally, Stewart says, 'You actually believed that?'"

He did. And so did a lot of other Staters for years to come.

To say that the House of Omar did not live up to its namesake would be a substantial understatement.

Bloomberg describes the rental: "It cost $100 a month for five of us. There were four bedrooms, a kitchen, dining room area, living room, and a basement that everyone was afraid of going into. ... It was in pretty bad shape. When my mother came to visit — I was in an upstairs room — she demanded that I get a rope and tie it around my bed so I could get out without burning alive. It was a death trap."

Still, it was, as one later tenant described it to The Brookings Register, the geographic center of the universe. The gravitational pull drew in many officers of the Hobo Day Committee along with scores of students looking for a good time.

"We'd have parties," explains Bloomberg, "and several of us played in a band, so we'd have live music. There'd be so many people dancing, the floor would be bouncing like a trampoline."

By 1980, the House of Omar was slated for demolition. Residents of the house talked about mobilizing some kind of resistance. But, the House of Omar finally came down and the East Central Mental Health & Chemical Dependency Center was built in its place.

Bradley died at age 88 on April 8, 1981, having risen through all the military ranks. His leadership in Europe during World War II landed such accolades as a soldier's general and master tactician. War correspondent Ernie Pyle wrote of Bradley:

"The outstanding figure on this western front is Lt. Gen. Omar Bradley. He is so honest and sincere that he will probably not get his proper credits ... but he has proved himself a great general in every sense of the word. And as a human being, he is just as great. Having him in command has been a blessed good fortune for America."

On Aug. 15, 1945, President Harry S. Truman appointed Bradley to direct the Veterans Administration. In 1948, Bradley succeeded Dwight Eisenhower as Army Chief of Staff. The following year, he was selected as the first chairman of the Joint Chiefs of Staff, which is the highest military position open to a U.S. officer.

On Sept. 22, 1980, Congress officially promoted Bradley to General of the Army. He was the last officer in the American military establishment promoted to that rank, and the only one since World War II.

Such a distinguished rank was a long way from the log cabin in poor, rural Missouri, where Bradley had been born and raised. Yet, it was hardly surprising for the man who said, "We need to learn to set our course by the stars, not by the light of every passing ship."

Chapter 46

December 7, 1941

Throughout the late 1930s, much of the world was at war. The Nazis were taking on Europe and Africa, and Japan was invading countries in the South Pacific.

The United States, however, was formally at peace — until, of course, Sunday, Dec. 7, 1941, when the Japanese attacked Pearl Harbor, dragging a reluctant America into the international theater of conflict. True enough, as President Franklin Delano Roosevelt declared, this was the day that would live in infamy.

It was on that day, The Brookings Register reported, that the war in the far-off Pacific came home: "As hostilities spread and reports came in of ships sunk and army fields and bases hit, Brookings people wondered about many young men who are serving in the nation's various forces in Hawaii and the Philippines."

On campus, Dec. 7, 1941, would become one of those events where people — even 60 years later — can recall exactly where they were, what they were doing and the thoughts that were running through their minds.

Pictured above, headline from the Dec. 11, 1941, South Dakota Collegian recapping the all-campus meeting held in the armory on Dec. 8, 1941.

Picture taken on Dec. 8, 1941, of students, faculty and staff gathered in the armory to hear President Franklin Roosevelt's request for a declaration of war against Japan.

Robert Vessey, class of 1943, says he remembers specifically when life as everyone knew it began to unravel. "We were in the Barn," he recalls, "and we listened to FDR's address — 'This day shall live in infamy.' When we left the building, there was almost total silence. Most of us knew where we were going to go."

Les Clarke, also class of 1943, was headed to the library when news of the Pearl Harbor attack first arrived.

"Even though the war in Europe had been going on for some time, as individuals we were somewhat naive," says Clarke, who had come to SDSC from Wessington. "There were a lot of preconceived ideas about how quickly we would defeat the Japanese. I don't think any of us comprehended at the time what the impact would be on us."

Bob Karolevitz, a 1947 graduate on campus from 1940-43, still remembers six decades later how students listened to the radio broadcast of Roosevelt's speech in the all-school assembly in the Barn, and the tumultuous feelings that followed. "We were really confused about our status. I was in basic ROTC."

Bernard "B.J." Gottsleben, also class of 1947, was supposed to graduate in 1944. But, the war interrupted. He was off campus when the news hit.

"I was in my hometown, visiting some relatives," Gottsleben says. "As far as our thoughts ... we were just dumb, green kids at that age. Pearl Harbor shocked everybody. We just knew that sometime soon we were going to go. I had an older brother in the Navy.

December 7, 1941

"Our parents accepted it. A terrible thing happened. I think all would agree that there were two times when all Americans saw things the same way — the Revolutionary War and World War II. We just put our nose to the grindstone and did what we had to do."

Sherwood Berg, also a sophomore in 1941, was working on the books for the boarding club he belonged to, figuring out who owed what: "I had the radio on, and (news of the attack) came through. ... Immediately, I thought of advanced ROTC."

At the time, all male students had to fulfill a compulsory two-year stint in ROTC their freshman and sophomore years. After that, some elected to apply for advanced ROTC, which offered a fast track to officer status upon graduation.

The day after the attack — Monday, Dec. 8 — the student body, faculty and staff gathered to hear the historic address President Roosevelt delivered to the U.S. Senate and House of Representatives.

"Fifteen hundred persons massed in the college armory Monday morning at 11 a.m. in a hastily planned convocation to hear President Franklin Delano Roosevelt ask Congress for a declaration of war against Japan," the Collegian reported on Dec. 11. "The group, composed of students, faculty, townspeople and bankers here for a credit convention, filed into the armory quietly, and portrayed all seriousness in the historic event which came to them via radio and public address system."

Berg recalls: "I was sitting near the top row, and down below they set up a pair of loudspeakers. The president spoke, and made the official speech, 'This day will live in infamy.'"

Former student Ron Peterson adds: "It was really somber."

Lee Engen, also class of 1944, was home on Sunday, the day of the attack: "We were having one of my mother's favorite chicken dinners. Then, all of the sudden, we heard about the attack. We thought, 'Omygosh.' My father had been in World War I and I had two younger brothers. I came back here and went over to the Barn, and got the word."

Another member of the class of 1947, Ed Williamson says he didn't hear the news for a day or two: "I had a job at the college stables. I was working for my board and room there. I think I missed it when everybody was at the Barn — I think we were out milking. I found out later on."

State College President Lyman E. Jackson presided over the assembly, with the public address system flanked by the American flag on the right and the yellow and blue colors of State's ROTC on the left. The military band also was in formation.

John Billington, student body president, read a telegram to President Roosevelt, saying, "The students and faculty of South Dakota State College, Brookings, South Dakota, desire to express their complete support of your efforts in directing the forces of our country in this war which has come upon us."

President Jackson issued a statement, urging calm and completion of the quarter.

"Each of us is filled with a great desire to do something to win the war," Jackson said. "There is tremendous urge to translate our feelings into action. Let us not, however, contribute to the confusion through inconsiderate action.

"Let there be no mistake in the meaning of our intentions. The students and faculty are agreed that our college energies must be directed for the promotion of the war effort.

"It seems advisable to suggest that students and faculty do everything in their power to complete the autumn quarter college work in a satisfactory manner. Next quarter no doubt will bring a number of adjustments."

Led by Carl P. Christensen, the military band played before Roosevelt spoke. The Collegian reported a silent crowd, listening to the radio announcer describe Roosevelt's entrance to the applause of congressmen. After the address, "The Star-Spangled Banner" played.

"As the last note faded away," the Collegian wrote, "the crowd stood in deathly silence, reminiscent, old-timers said, of the end of a similar program held in the college auditorium in April 1917, when news came that Congress had voted a state of war against Germany in World War I.

"After the moment of spontaneous silence, the crowd dispersed slowly, for dinner. The declaration of war had come to South Dakota State College."

John Bibby, class of 1942, says: "It was pretty obvious we were going to

> **TEXT OF TELEGRAM SENT FDR**
>
> BROOKINGS. SOUTH DAKOTA
> DECEMBER 8, 1941, 1 P. M.
>
> FRANKLIN DELANO ROOSEVELT
> PRESIDENT OF THE UNITED STATES
> WASHINGTON, D. C.
>
> BY ACTION IN CONVOCATION: THE STUDENTS AND FACULTY OF SOUTH DAKOTA STATE COLLEGE, BROOKINGS, SOUTH DAKOTA, DESIRE TO EXPRESS THEIR COMPLETE SUPPORT OF YOUR EFFORTS IN DIRECTING THE FORCES OF OUR COUNTRY IN THIS WAR WHICH HAS COME UPON US.
>
> JOHN BILLINGTON,
> PRESIDENT OF STUDENT BODY
> LYMAN E. JACKSON,
> PRESIDENT OF SOUTH DAKOTA STATE
> COLLEGE

The Dec. 11, 1941, South Dakota Collegian reports the text of the telegram sent to President Franklin Roosevelt.

get involved, even before it happened. ... Those of us in advanced ROTC were wondering if we were going to be called up before the end of the school year. We did finish."

Still, Bibby notes, the atmosphere of war was filtering into the campus consciousness prior to Pearl Harbor. Members of the National Guard, many of whom were athletes, had been pulled into active duty and sent to North Africa.

"We knew something was up," says Bibby. "There were a lot of rumblings about what was happening in Europe, Poland had been overrun. People I knew and associated with expected (the declaration of war) and weren't scared."

Two days after graduation in the spring of 1942, Bibby found himself at Fort Snelling, Minn.: "I got my diploma, my commission and my order to report all at once."

There was no question about duty.

"And so today, we are at 'War in our time,'" the Collegian editors wrote in a passionately patriotic editorial in the Dec. 11, 1941, issue. "Let us say here and now that the United States was sincere in the first World War — let us say here and now that the heritage of America for which we fought is again the stake in this battle. And let us make no mistake — what was worth fighting for in 1917-18 is worth fighting for today.

"The American people are united this week, as they always have been united in a time of peril. The American people of 1941 are going to prosecute this war — wherever it leads, no matter how long it takes."

Chapter 47

Hobo Day Lost

In the weeks leading up to Hobo Day 1942, the State student body was as enthusiastic as in years past about the annual homecoming celebration.

"Discounting reports that you have football team. Must be war propaganda. Looking for team made of army misfits. Your trousers against mine that we win the game. Will be exchanged on the field after the game."

That was the "telegram" printed in the Oct. 7, 1942, Collegian, sent by Morningside student body president Wilson Reynolds to SDSC student body president Paul Hanson. Hanson, of course, wired back an acceptance to the challenge for the football contest that would precede State's homecoming week festivities.

Also in the Collegian, Hanson, in an effort to further boost student spirit for Hobo Day, "revealed plans for the cleverest parade that ever moved down Medary Avenue."

Looking to bring back the original theme of Hobo Day, Hanson declared to the student body: "It's out with the new and back to the old. We're substituting rags for crepe paper and jalopies for limousines."

Pictured above, cartoon drawn for the 1943 Jack Rabbit depicting two rabbits doing farm work in support of the war effort.

Board of Control members had voted earlier in the week to forbid the use of cars less than 10 years old in the Hobo Day parade. Plans were intact for a pre-Hobo Day dance on Oct. 17 and the beard judging on Oct. 21. There would also be the Blue Key Smoker, the Torchlight Parade and, finally, the Friday night pep rally and Hobo Day dance — all aimed at setting the stage for homecoming.

But, as world events hit close to home, for only the second time in Hobo Day history, State homecoming festivities were canceled — and, for the second time, because of war.

"It was kind of a letdown," concedes Robert Vessey, class of 1943. "But, we simply accepted it. That's the way things were."

SDSC President Lyman E. Jackson made a last-minute announcement Oct. 13, canceling classes for two weeks after receiving approval from the Board of Regents. With the dismissal, reported the Collegian, "went the hopes of the most enthusiastic student body in years who, since school opened September 28, had been preparing for what could have been one of State's greatest Hobo Days."

In the hours leading up to the announcement, Northern State Teachers College at Aberdeen closed for two weeks. The week prior, the University of North Dakota at Grand Forks, the North Dakota Agricultural College at Fargo and the teachers' college at Jamestown all had opted for similar measures.

At an all-campus convocation, Jackson reminded the students that nearly a year prior — Dec. 8, 1941 — they had gathered in the armory to hear President Roosevelt's request for a declaration of war: "We realized that we would have to try to carry on as usual, expecting changes from time to time. This morning we have been jarred into the unusual, and it is in our pledge to do everything possible in the service of our country that we take this action.

"Dismissal at this inopportune time constitutes a sacrifice on our part in the forwarding of the war effort. We are forced to accept it and its many ramifications as 'one of those things.'"

A representative of the State Employment Service was on hand to detail the urgent need for laborers in the northern harvest fields and for certain defense projects that had to be completed before Nov. 1.

For the two-week work detail, Les Clarke, class of 1943, stayed on campus and continued at his jobs there. He was a "houseboy" at the women's dorm and worked in the swine department. For $25 to $30 a month, he peeled potatoes and washed dishes.

"It was very reasonable," Clarke says.

As for the cancellation of Hobo Day, he adds: "It was kind of the times. I

Picture taken from the 1943 Jack Rabbit showing students immediately after the announcement was made to cancel Hobo Day activities. The caption from the yearbook reads, "More sour faces than an old maid's convention here as State students file out of the auditorium after hearing that Hobo Day had been cancelled and that the two-week work vacation had been proclaimed."

don't think we felt badly or robbed. We were pretty glum, though. Certainly, it caught us unaware. People just started disappearing. We were in a state where we were subject to call-up anytime. You didn't know from one day to the next if you'd be on campus or in the service."

Despite the sudden change of events, the two football games would go on as scheduled — first the game at Grand Forks on Oct. 17 and then the Hobo Day contest Oct. 24 against the University of South Dakota. Members of the football squad remained on campus for the two-week recess, working during the day until late afternoon practices were held.

Administration officials also adjusted the fall quarter, shifting the end date from Dec. 18 to Dec. 23. All the changes were handed down with full support from the student body.

"World War II hit State College students on the chin this week," editorialized the Collegian on the day of Jackson's announcement. Ticking through a list of repercussions, the paper noted that the calendar had been revised so students could graduate and enter vital military positions two weeks early. Senior military men voted to expand their class schedules and summer school was extended from a six-week to twelve-week term.

"These changes came," the Collegian said, "and students became accustomed to them without too much disturbance in their routine of college life.

They accepted them as necessary changes in the pursuance of war. Now students are faced with a live, real challenge. They are being released from classes to cope with a problem more vivid, more concrete than those they have been faced with in the past.

"The labor shortage in this northwest of ours is not the product of fanciful imagination. It is critical. ... We were told our duty in the convocation this morning: To find our cog in the wheel of this labor crisis, whether it be in the fields or in the war programs, and for the next two weeks do our part to keep the home-front war machine humming."

Student body president Hanson agreed: "State College is called upon to do its part, and State College will come through to the last man. ... We're going out now for a big job. The country comes first; we're glad to be able to help. Just as we leave, however, we'll be back. Let's take this thing in stride, prove beyond a doubt what State College can do, and then come back ready to start all over again."

Initially, students were angry with the two-week cancellation of classes and Hobo Day, but they didn't rebel, says Bob Karolevitz, on campus from 1940-43 and a member of the graduating class of 1947. Ultimately, he says, everyone pitched in. Karolevitz got farm duty. "I shocked grain," he says.

Sherwood Berg, class of 1947 and SDSU president from 1975 to 1984, says he was among a group of 50 to 60 students recruited to put in a new runway at the Pierre airfield.

"They gave us a pick and shovel," says Berg. "We were digging dirt, putting in the sub-layer for the runway. It was hard labor."

It was also, he adds, "pretty good pay."

There wasn't much in the way of social activities, Berg notes, because Pierre "was really a small town." But that didn't matter. After a long day of manual labor, the young men were tired. They ate dinner, went to sleep, woke up the next morning and hit the dirt again. Many students were housed at local homes, four or five to a room. Berg stayed in an attic.

"You stayed in a home?" laughs Ron Peterson, one of Berg's classmates. "I was in an abandoned building downtown."

"That was a hotel," jokes Ed Williamson, also class of 1947. "I was at a dairy here in town. In the evening, we'd go out and shock grain for farmers. There'd be eight or 10 of us. We'd take a whole field and shock 'em up all night."

These were the days before combines, and grain had to be shocked, or grouped together in bundles, and readied for pickup by the bundle wagon.

Other students headed home to the family farm. Bernard "B.J."

Gottsleben, another member of the class of 1947, recalls, "I took Lee (Engen) to Clark and we loaded potatoes."

"Yeah," adds Engen, "Bernard and his family would take off for the weekend to visit his brother in Minneapolis and here I am picking potatoes in Clark."

Putting the prevailing sentiment of the times to verse, Karolevitz wrote in the Collegian's Oct. 28 edition of the "The Poet Scorner" column:

>Futility
>
>*We fussed and strained to grow our beards*
>*— Like hermits without caves.*
>*We looked like heck, but still we pledged*
>*'Tis death to him who shaves.*
>
>*The facial hair grew thicker then —*
>*The "day of days" grew nigh.*
>*What matter how we looked or felt*
>*As spirit soared sky-high.*
>
>*Two weeks to go — all plans were made.*
>*We knew the "outs 'n' ins."*
>*Still whiskers grew and covered up*
>*"A multitude of skins."*
>
>*Then came the proclamation which*
>*Would bare our face again.*
>*The shock was kinda rugged, but*
>*We cut 'em off like men.*
>
>*It seemed to us quite futile,*
>*Though no person shed a tear.*
>*We settled back, and vowed to wait*
>*Till Hobo Day next year!*

The poem was sandwiched in-between an editorial offering information about the reserve programs and Camp Notes, which gave updates from alums in the service.

After the 1942-43 basketball season, Karolevitz recalls: "A number of us hitchhiked to Minneapolis to try to get into the Marines. We were going to go to Quantico (the Marine Corps Base in Virginia). I flunked the damn physical. ... I wasn't wearing glasses then. I came back to Brookings, went to the eye doctor, got eye glasses and got into Army reserves."

Karolevitz laughs at the memory of one buddy: "He tried to get into the Navy Air Corps. He went to Minneapolis and they told him he was too light, so he bought bananas, a big sack. The Minneapolis Star Tribune took a picture of him sitting on the curb, eating all those bananas. He ate enough to get his weight up — passed the physical and became a Navy flier."

World War II was having a profound impact on the college as well as the students. Writing in the 1943 Alumnus, President Jackson spoke proudly of the "Staters," both civilian and service, who were working to "turn the tide of this great struggle."

"The supreme sacrifice has been made by many," Jackson said, "but I know that the spirit of their efforts is the very foundation of what it will take to make freedom a world reality."

At the same time, State faced the same dilemma that many other educational institutions, from elementary to college level, found themselves in — maintaining a curriculum and teaching staff during a war emergency.

State College found itself engaged in a three-pronged venture. The college continued to offer its programs for civilian students as well as services provided by the Agricultural Experiment Station and Agricultural Extension Service. State also was conducting war service training of soldiers, a program that had started in December 1942. As civilian enrollment decreased, the number of soldiers — 1,500 — on campus rose.

Ada May Yeager, class of 1943, remembers when the soldiers arrived on campus: "We had to move out of our dorm rooms to make room for them. I moved into the attic of a house. I got the attic room for $6 a month." To help offset the cost, she worked in the library, with a starting wage of 24 cents an hour.

Jackson wrote: "The fact that these men are being cared for at State College is very important both from the standpoint of having the institution make an outstanding contribution to the war program and because the contracts make it possible to preserve the institution as a functioning concern. We are hoping that when it comes time for the soldiers to leave it will be possible for civilian students to return."

That issue led to the third area of planning — the postwar period.

Said Jackson: "It is obvious that our postwar program cannot be a mere revision to prewar procedures. It is expected that there will be a large increase in the number of students attending State College as compared to prewar enrollments. We are also expecting a wide variety of students as to ages and experiences."

Within three years, World War II ended, the soldiers returned home and SDSC embarked on the postwar era. The years that followed saw a steady rise in enrollment, which, in turn, posed a multifaceted challenge. There were more students to house and teach, new demands for a broader curriculum and a need for new and updated buildings to carry out the mission of higher education.

Chapter 48

The '44 Kings

You don't have to be a student of South Dakota State history to have heard about the '44 Kings. Although six decades have passed, the legend lives on, told and retold throughout the years.

In their junior year, in-between basic training and the front line, they found themselves at State for a few months. They knew the ropes and a bit about the real world beyond. All were bound for unknown danger. Thus was born the legend of the Kings, the young men of the class of 1944.

But, this is more than a romantic tale about a group of guys who went off to war, returned to school to get their degrees, and somewhere along the way immortalized a bottle of whiskey to be drunk by the last man alive. Rather, the story of the '44 Kings is about the hopes and dreams of young men, the sacrifice of putting country above self, and the incredible lasting bond forged by the common experience of combat.

Pictured above, the bottle of whiskey to be opened by the last remaining member of the '44 Kings. (Photo courtesy of Eric Landwehr)

THE COLLEGE ON THE HILL

The story of the '44 Kings began with the Japanese attack on Pearl Harbor on Dec. 7, 1941.

Lee Engen, then a sophomore, says the immediate reaction to the declaration of war was: "How can we go? Let's do it the best way we can. My dad always said, 'If you go into the service, go first class. Get that officer's commission.'"

Reminiscing with Engen and several other '44 Kings, Sherwood Berg explains: "The decision was made to apply to advanced ROTC. The plan presented to us was: Enroll in ROTC, which simultaneously enlisted you in the Reserve Corps, and you will graduate; and, you will be commissioned upon graduation."

Ed Williamson adds: "You also had to enroll in summer school. We thought we would graduate."

So, 52 sophomores signed up for advanced ROTC and jumped into an accelerated program, starting their junior year in the summer of 1942. Everything was going according to plan until early the following spring.

"In March, we got our orders to report to basic training," says Berg.

Authorized on Jan. 27, 1943, the orders sent from Omaha on March 18 called up the 52 privates in the SDSC infantry unit. Several of the men still have the original orders, now yellowed with age:

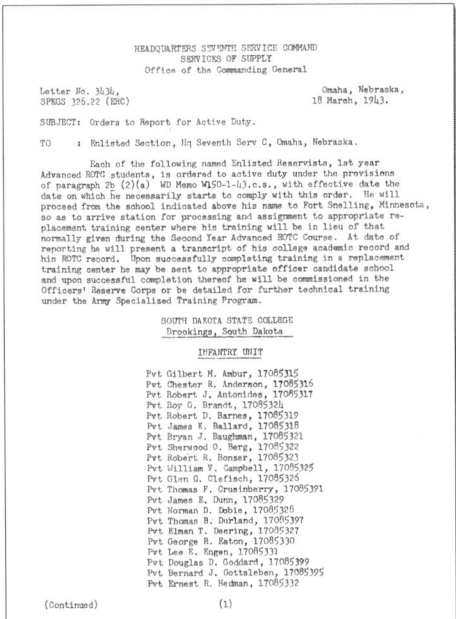

A copy of the military orders issued on March 18, 1943.

"Each of the following named Enlisted Reservists, 1st year Advanced ROTC students, is ordered to active duty ... with effective date the date on which he necessarily starts to comply with this order. He will proceed from the school indicated above his name to Fort Snelling, Minnesota, so as to arrive at station for processing and assignment to appropriate replacement training center where his training will be in lieu of that normally given during the Second Year Advanced ROTC Course. At date of reporting he will present a transcript of his college academic record and his ROTC record. Upon successfully completing training in a replacement training center he may be sent to appropriate officer candidate school and upon successful completion thereof he will be commissioned in the Officers' Reserve Corps or be detailed for further technical training under the Army Specialized Training Program."

In those few terse sentences, 52 lives took a dramatic detour — particularly, the first name on the alphabetized list. Gilbert M. Ambur, solely because of his last name, got bumped up into the class ahead that was short one man. What seemed like an innocuous detail at the time ended up costing Ambur his life. He graduated from basic training a week ahead of the others, on April 12, 1944. The rest of the group graduated on April 18.

Ambur was sent to the European theater of operations, where he was assigned to the 10th Infantry of the 5th Division. Those troops, says Berg, were heavily committed in France, around Caen and St. Lo. Five months after he was commissioned, on Sept. 15, 1944, Ambur was killed.

"He was the only person from our group not in our company," Berg notes.

With plans and promises derailed, the men headed for Fort Snelling, Minn., to be screened and issued equipment. Those who didn't leave on the train from Brookings were given the reservist travel allowance of 5 cents per mile.

"They changed our orders," Engen says plainly, with no hint of bitterness, just a matter-of-fact acceptance of the turns life takes. "We were going to basic training and then wait for a spot in officer training. Here we thought we'd get a commission after we graduated."

Instead, they were bound for Camp Wolters, Texas.

"We had another name for it," jokes Engen, "but we don't talk about it."

Tom Lyons, another '44 King, interjects, "It was one of those hurry-up camps they built."

Still, the men made the best of the situation. Retelling their story, they kindle fond memories.

"I can remember all of us getting on the train," says Ed Williamson. "The whole college was down there to see us off."

"Yeah," laughs B.J. Gottsleben. "We were kissing all the girls."

Lyons says he left his belongings in the basement of East Hall.

Engen adds, "All we had in those days was toiletry articles and clothes."

Once at Fort Snelling, near the Minneapolis airport, Gottsleben says: "We had a lot of time to ourselves. I went on KP (kitchen police) at 4 o'clock in the morning until 9 o'clock the next day. It was the worst day of my life, that KP."

But, the first stop along the way to basic training wasn't all work. Gottsleben chuckles, "We did run around Minneapolis and St. Paul a bit."

Williamson adds: "There was a big show downtown. We got up on stage and sang. We were great singers."

The next stop was Camp Wolters. Berg says the Staters did not receive the ordinary basic training the draftees were getting: "We had heavy weaponry training — water-cooled .30 caliber machine guns and 81-millimeter mortars. ... We were also somewhat of an oddity. We knew how to march."

After 17 weeks in Texas, the training was over. But, moving men in the Army was not so simple as sticking them on a train and sending them back home. Like many other college campuses, State was housing servicemen, so there wasn't a ready place. The men were sent to Grinnell College in Iowa for a week to 10 days, housed in the basement of a dormitory.

"There were double bunks," recalls Berg, "and a long table down the whole length of the room."

One end of the table was reserved for the poker games with small wagers, the other end for the big stakes.

The men arrived back in Brookings in October, and they were dubbed the Kings.

"When we got back, we were very important people on campus," says Gottsleben.

The nickname, intended in fun, had a serious essence to it. These young college men had undergone a change and, clearly, more change was in store.

"When we came back, we had to spend the summer training — rigorous training," says Berg. "We had the same ROTC staff when we got back, so they were going to really pour it on us. The second or third day, they organized a forced march to Volga and back. ... It was no problem for us, but the ROTC staff that went with us, they went down. ... Captain Randall had blisters all over his feet."

But Gottsleben reminds Berg: "We were pretty stiff the next day."

Not expecting to ship out before spring, the men returned to the school routine. Then, in yet another swift change of plans, the orders came in for OCS, or Officer Candidate School. They left the day after Thanksgiving. For

Members of the war-bound '44 Kings gather at the 7-0 Club on the evening of Oct. 8, 1943.

many of the men, it was their first time on a Pullman train — a passenger train with berths for sleeping.

It also the first time the men were split up. Engen and Williamson were assigned to the 103rd Infantry Division; Berg, the 78th; Peterson, the 23rd; and Lyons, the 76th. Gottsleben headed to the 1st Armored Division: "I was in the tank division. We lived underground — we slept underground, we ate underground."

And yet, even on the other side of the world, in the midst of a war, South Dakotans managed to cross paths.

"The 78th Infantry Division was the first across the Remegan Bridge, the last bridge across the Rhine River," says Berg. "The 9th Armored captured it that morning. We were about 12 miles away. The whole place was smoked. The Germans were coming in, trying to bomb it. We made it across the bridge, turned to the left, and went down about 800 yards. Right on the bank of the Rhine, there were three fellows — the company commander, the lieutenant commander and the full commander.

"I asked where the front line was. The battalion commander pointed and said, 'See that tank down there?' There were two dead GIs. 'That's the front line.' Eight years later I was at an SDSC alumni chapter meeting in Aberdeen, and here is this fellow, the commander. He was the county agent for Potter County."

Near the end of the war, at Innsbruck at the Brenner Pass in Austria, Berg saw both Engen and classmate Walt McCarty. Peterson, in a hospital in England, met fellow Stater Howard Wood. All of the men were in Europe in May 1945, when World War II came to a close.

Lyons says German soldiers just dropped their weapons: "They wanted to quit and make it to a prison camp. They knew what the Russians were going to do. The Russians didn't take any prisoners."

"We finished up in the Ruhr pocket, in the middle of Germany," says Berg. "The British and American troops came in from the north. ... You knew the war was ending. About the 26th or 27th of April, the battalion commander said, 'You've been on the front lines since Dec. 6, take some time off. You can go back to London for 10 days.'

"V-E Day occurred while I was in London. Tens of thousands of people were pouring out in the street in front of Buckingham Palace. Every 20 minutes, the king, queen, two princesses and Winston Churchill would come out on the balcony, stand there and wave. People were celebrating. It was tremendous."

The vast majority of State soldiers made their way back to Brookings. They knew if they didn't finish their education then, they probably never would. Several married and moved off campus. Others lived in the married student housing barracks placed on campus for the returning GIs.

"A number of us lived in Scobey Hall," says Williamson, who was single at the time. "Professor (Orlin) Walder, he decided that with the veterans coming back, we ought to be in one wing of the building. He knew what he was doing. Someone might leave a whiskey bottle on the desk. Our wing was off limits to freshmen and sophomores."

Engen adds: "You had to take your hat off to the administration. They were very tolerant of all these veterans. We'd done things that if you had even thought about 'em before, you'd have been kicked out. We set a bar up for dances, we had drinks. But nobody got out of line. There weren't any fights, there wasn't anybody who got all boozed up. ... They let us do things we were used to doing."

Gottsleben recalls: "We used to have our whiskey in the car. You'd go out of the dance, pour out some of your Coke and top it off with whiskey."

Williamson laughs and describes one memorable event: "There used to be ag barn dances. I remember, the year we come back, we spiked the cider. The dean of agriculture, Dean Larson, and his wife were chaperoning. Somebody happened to give a glass of the cider to the dean, and he liked it. He went back several times. At cleanup time, he patted his wife on the shoulder and says, 'You go on home. I'm going to help the boys.' And he did."

The '44 Kings

The '44 Kings suffered two casualties among the 52 men sent to fight in the war — in addition to Gilbert Ambur, T. Reed Smith of Madison. Engen remarks, "I think we all felt pretty proud that we lost only two."

In the decades that have followed, as death has exacted its toll, the numbers of the '44 Kings dwindled. For the last man, there awaits a bottle of whiskey — a half-pint of Seagram's V.O. Canadian. Marian Davis DeKraai, the honorary cadet colonel for the Kings, was the keeper of the bottle until her death. Now, it sits inside a plastic box, with a picture of Marian and a brief statement that reads "'44 Kings Last Man Award."

Reminiscing about the bottle's origin, the men say Bryan Baughman, the group's unofficial historian, picked it up on his way back to campus from Fort Benning.

Berg says, "I think he stopped in Chicago and got it there."

Williamson quips, "He couldn't take it home. That's for sure."

Notes Berg, "So, he dedicated it to the cause."

"He didn't figure there'd be this many left," laughs Engen. "The last man won't be able to drink all that."

Berg interrupts, "Don't be too sure."

Chapter 49

A University Honors a Hero

As the days of teaching turn into months and then years, the passage of time often blurs the line from one class to the next. But former sociology professor Howard Sauer remembers one particular afternoon early in his career at South Dakota State College.

"We had a class, but the people in there (the room) before us, didn't come out," says Sauer, who started teaching on campus in 1939. "We waited for a little while. Then Bill Bianchi said, 'Let's go in and throw 'em out.'"

More than 60 years later, the 95-year-old Sauer chuckles at the memory.

"I can say honestly that he's the only one I remember in that class because of what he said," Sauer muses.

Pictured above, Willibald C. Bianchi, class of 1940.

Only a couple of years later, Bianchi's take-charge attitude would earn him the third congressional Medal of Honor awarded in World War II. Bianchi, class of 1940, would be the only graduate of South Dakota State to achieve such distinction in the military.

Yet, if it hadn't been for a Brookings woman's chance purchase of the March 16, 1942, issue of Life magazine some 40 years later, the heroic actions of Willibald C. Bianchi likely would have gone unnoticed by his alma mater.

Pat Beattie, whose husband, Tom, taught in the nutrition and food science department from 1973-88, bought the wartime Life issue in about 1983 at the Yellow Pages used bookstore in downtown Brookings.

"She bought this magazine because I was in World War II," explains Tom. "She often buys magazines that date back to relatives' birthdays."

Congressional Medal of Honor, the nation's highest citation awarded to a member of the military.

Nearly five years passed before Tom picked up the magazine and decided to read it cover to cover: "There were 10 men on the Roll of Honor, some of the earliest medals of honor in World War II. The war was only about 100 days old. I started reading. The first one was Willibald C. Bianchi. He was the only one on the page who got the congressional Medal of Honor. So, I went over to the the Alumni Center. They weren't computerized, yet. There was a 3-by-5 card for Willibald Bianchi. It said he died in the Bataan Death March."

Tom continued to pursue Bianchi's story, talking to people who had known him and those who didn't. A professor of military science at the time, Flash Gordon Helm, was skeptical that a State grad had earned the congressional Medal of Honor. (Flash Gordon was Helm's real name. His parents let an older sibling name him.) Helm tracked down the information, found out it was true and decided that Bianchi ought to be recognized Dec. 13, 1990, at the annual ROTC banquet.

The citation recounts how Bianchi earned the Medal of Honor:

"For conspicuous gallantry and intrepidity above and beyond the call of duty in action with the enemy on February 3, 1942, near Bagac, Province of Bataan, Philippine Islands. When the rifle platoon of another company was ordered to wipe out two strong enemy machine gun nests, Lieutenant Bianchi voluntarily and of his own initiative, advanced with the platoon leading part of the men. When wounded early in the action by two bullets through the left hand, he did not stop for first aid but discarded his rifle and began firing a pistol. He located a machine gun nest and personally silenced it with grenades. When wounded a second time by two machine-gun bullets through the chest muscles, Lieutenant Bianchi climbed to the top of an American tank, manned its anti-aircraft machine gun, and fired into strongly held enemy positions until knocked completely off the tank by a third severe wound."

Jim Daly of St. Paul, Minn., summed up the events in a March 6, 1942, letter to his mother: "Lt. Bianchi did an outstanding piece of work. ... His action was the bravest and the most singularly outstanding of the present action."

Bianchi was the only boy and the second oldest of five children born in New Ulm, Minn., to Carrie and Joseph Bianchi. Several members of Bianchi's family attended the 1990 ROTC banquet, and Tom learned a lot more about the hero's life and death.

"I found out he didn't die in the Bataan Death March," Tom says. "He was killed toward the end of the war when one of our planes dropped a bomb on a ship that had POWs (prisoners of war). When I talked to his relatives, they began to give me stuff — letters, telegrams. I went over to New Ulm and spent a day in the Brown County museum."

The new information gave much greater insight into the man Bianchi had become. The Medal of Honor citation paid tribute to the hero. Humorous and detailed letters home and correspondence from those who fought alongside Bianchi fleshed out the person.

"Hope you received the money order OK," Bianchi wrote to his sister, Jerry, whom he was helping with the expenses of nurses' training school. "Don't spend it all at once now — stuff like that doesn't grow on trees."

Bianchi requested duty overseas after being commissioned as a second lieutenant. He shipped out for the Philippine Islands in the early months of 1941. In the letter to his sister from sea, Bianchi, the farm boy, could not believe his luxury accommodations:

"Making 500-600 miles a day, traveling 22 knots per hour or about 30 mph to you land lubbers. This trip really is grand. I'm traveling 1st Class aboard the best liner in Pacific waters. (It) has a passenger load of 3,000 human souls and a weight of 25,000 tons. Jerry, this thing is immense, has swimming pools, theater, dance floors, lounge rooms, game rooms, courts for handball, volleyball and deck tennis. It has immense dining rooms, smoking rooms and card rooms. I never dreamed I'd ever enjoy such luxury as this. My room is perfect. Inner spring mattresses, closets, thick rugs, tile bathroom, buzzers for steward and stewardess service, portholes where you can throw empty Coke bottles out of without being afraid of hitting anybody in the head. If I were in civilian life, a 7,000 mile trip like this would cost $1,000, and here I am getting it all free, plus travel pay from Omaha to Frisco. ... Jerry, you haven't any idea the luxury I'm in, why, I don't know what to do I'm so amazed at times."

Enclosing copies of the menu, Bianchi told his sister: "We can order the best for every meal, and we really do. It's all on Uncle Sam, the good old scout. Maybe he's giving us one last grand farewell party."

On Tuesday, May 4, still at sea, Bianchi wrote to his sister again, saying everyone was getting homesick: "I suppose I should, too, but I just can't. I regret being so far away from Mom, but I have a chance to either make or break over here, so I might as well take a chance."

By July, Bianchi was in the Philippines. There were rumors floating around, he said, that he and other officers would be sent to the Philippine army to train its recruits. In the meantime, Bianchi carried on with his regular duty:

"I just came off of two weeks guard, 24 hours on duty and 24 hours off. During my tour, I, myself, caught four sentries asleep on post. This is a court-martial offense only, now in peace time. In war, death. They all got six months' hard labor. I felt sorry for them, but you can't afford to stick your neck out for anybody."

A letter in October gave yet another glimpse of Bianchi:

"I had a detail of 40 men cutting a trail through 6 miles of jungle to one of my outposts so we can reach it by truck. Previously, we always relieved the guard by boat. Well, in order to do it I had to get special permission from the Col. He said it would be impossible to do it in a week. All I asked for was three days. Well, he didn't know I had an ace up my sleeve. I've been over every inch of the ground while he and some of the rest of the officers that laughed at me said it would be impossible. There used to be an old (railroad bed) that the timber companies had used 20 years ago when they cut timber in the vicinity. Well, this R.R. bed was so covered with small vines, brush and fallen trees that you could be two foot away and not know it was there. The R.R. reached from the road to within 1 mile of camp. The bed was in perfect shape, hard and smooth. ... The night of the second day, I radioed him that the road was complete. He didn't believe me, I guess, for the next day he and his staff was out. I personally took him down the trail and when we reached the end, he said, 'Bianchi, I'm proud of you.' Boy, that made me feel good. I'll never have to worry about a good efficiency report from him."

The tropical jungles of the Philippine Islands were about as far from Bianchi's Midwestern upbringing as he could have imagined. He wrote to his sister after a two-week mission to select possible gun positions. It was, he said, an experience he would never forget. What was supposed to be a 200-mile truck route along the shores of the China Sea soon turned into a daily trek of 20 to 30 miles.

"In some places, we had to fjord streams 4-5 feet deep. We hacked our way through steaming tropical jungles of bamboo and vines. Well, we found our positions OK after sending nearly 1/3 of our company and one officer back with malaria fever. On our first day back, the rains started. It rained for 5 days straight. Everything was soaked and ruined. I tore my new raincoat, lost a pair of leggings, tore my shirts, but I made it. I guess that's the main reason the command officer sent me along anyway."

Still, Bianchi saw humor in many situations. An invitation to a reception at a palace specified that the men bring a companion, who had to be female and white. "I don't know where there's 40 white gals unless they are Spanish or Russians," he told his sister, "but then I guess we can't draw the line too close."

As war drew closer, Bianchi also managed to keep his sense of wonder at new experiences, from visiting the famous Moro headhunters to wearing the same clothes — all wet — five days in a row:

"All the natives wore in the provinces are loincloths. The women are continually nursing their young, so it seems. All the gals are married and pregnant by the time they're 15. (They) have a baby in their arms and are ready to have another one by the time they're 16. It seems to be a disgrace not to have 5 children before you're 20. The kids don't wear a stitch of clothes ... until they're at least ten. All of them have potbellies like Milwaukee beer barons. Your name for it is malnutrition."

In yet another letter, Bianchi described the complex culture of the Philippines and summed up his philosophical observations. The Chinese and Japanese controlled business and industry. The Spanish owned the land, the church and the banks.

"In fact," Bianchi said, "the average Filipino has absolutely nothing. They are, in a sense of the word, ashamed of their past, bewildered by their present, uncertain of their future."

Within months, war came. The Japanese bombed Pearl Harbor on Dec. 7, 1941. At about the same time, they invaded the Philippines. The American and Philippine armies were outmanned and overrun.

In his letter to his mother, Daly, the soldier from St. Paul, wrote about Bianchi's heroic efforts on Feb. 3, 1942:

"He advanced with B Co., commanded by Lt. R.K. Roberts. When a machine gun located behind a large tree stopped the advance, Roberts and Bianchi crawled up and threw grenades into the position. Lt. Bianchi was hit by fragments of a grenade, but continued to help direct the advance. He was hit in the right arm by two machine-gun bullets. He dropped his rifle and used his pistol. He then crawled behind a tank and climbed to the top of it, manning the anti-aircraft machine gun. He gave (them) hell until he was knocked off by a mortar or grenade."

The wounded Bianchi was hospitalized, and given the Medal of Honor. The other two men to receive the medal had been killed in action. Then, on April 9, 1942, the Americans surrendered. Numbering more than 70,000 American and Filipino soldiers, it was the largest American army in history to surrender. The Japanese forced their prisoners on what would become the notorious Bataan Death March — more than 60 miles in intense heat with almost no food or water. An estimated 5,000 to 10,000 men never made it from the tip of the Bataan peninsula inland to the prison camp, Camp O'Donnell.

But, even before the surrender, the soldiers' lives in Bataan had grown increasingly difficult. Without enough food, the men were put on half-rations. The men who survived say they were starving, eating everything from cats and dogs to monkeys and horses.

On the death march to Camp O'Donnell, men were shot and killed for any sign of weakness — breaking rank to sip water from a ditch, stopping to rest because they could not go on. True to character, Bianchi tried to keep men going, boost morale and assist the weakened.

"After the war was over," says Tom, "Bianchi's mother got hundreds of cards and letters from men who were there and who Bianchi helped in one way or another."

Life for the POWs did not improve any once they reached their destination. There are no exact figures, but two out of every three soldiers alive at the time of the surrender did not live to see the end of the war. It is estimated that about half of the 24,000 Americans and nearly three-quarters of the Filipino troops died during the Japanese occupation.

A University Honors a Hero

Bianchi, of course, rose to the occasion. Then-Capt. Theodore I. Spaulding wrote to Bianchi's mother on June 8, 1951, recounting her son's stellar character even in the worst of situations:

"I wonder if anyone has told you of what I consider Bill's most difficult assignment. Much to our dismay, we discovered in prison camp that few could be trusted to honestly divide the rather short rations that were issued by our captors. All too often, we found that those put in charge of food distribution were using their position to better the lot of themselves and friends at the expense of the overall group. This human weakness showed itself in all ranks and in people from all walks of life. Bill was one of those chosen who proved to be absolutely honest and fair in the performance of his assignment, and it was considered a lucky break to get to eat in his kitchen.

"To you or to any other American who has not had the experience of being hungry for months and years on end, the above story may seem of no importance. One must be starving to understand the mental processes of a hungry man. To a hungry man, everyone else is always better off than he is and everyone else always has more to eat. You can well imagine the position of the mess officer when each of the hundreds he feeds each day feels that his own portion is short. It took a man of great character and determination to, first, see that all men received a fair share and, second, to convince them that they were actually being fairly treated. Your son Bill was such a man."

As the war neared its end, and the U.S. victory was imminent, Japan loaded hundreds of POWs onto unmarked ships — nicknamed "Hell Ships" by the captives. The men in the hold had to contend with temperatures into the triple digits and little, if any, food. Whatever rations they did receive were covered with black flies.

The first boat Bianchi was on, the Oryoku Maru, headed up the west coast of Bataan on Dec. 14 as U.S. planes flew overhead. In his book "Ghost Soldiers," author Hampton Sides recounts how the Oryoku Maru first took a bomb hit above the water line and then ran aground in Subic Bay. The next day, the prisoners were told to prepare to leave the ship and swim ashore. Navy dive bombers, writes Sides, "dropped a string of bombs and scored a direct hit on the aft hold of the ship."

The survivors, Bianchi among them, were put on another ship, the Enoura Maru, on Dec. 28. The conditions of this ship were so bad, according to Sides, that prisoners died at a rate of four or five a day. On Jan. 1, 1945, the Enoura Maru anchored in a harbor off Formosa. On Jan. 9, Bianchi was tending to sick prisoners in the ship's hold when another round of dive bombers struck — unaware that prisoners of war were on board. The friendly fire attack killed 295 men.

This time, Bianchi, at age 29, was among the dead. Wounded three times and survivor of the Bataan Death March, three Japanese POW camps and one incident of friendly fire, he had almost made it out alive. Instead, as fate would have it, Bianchi put himself in mortal danger to help others. If he hadn't, chances are he would not have been killed.

Spaulding told Bianchi's mother in his letter: "I knew Bill quite well in the islands and was with him at the time of his death in Formosa aboard a Japanese ship. As you no doubt know, he was killed by a bomb from an American plane during an attack on the Japanese (ships) in the harbor at the time. His death was instant."

As he was delving into Bianchi's story, Tom happened to attend a reunion at Texas A&M. The student union had a display of memorabilia from the different wars in which students had fought.

"On the wall were seven bronze plaques for seven fellows that got congressional medals during World War II," says Tom. "I was pretty impressed with that. So, I got involved with this. I felt we should do something for Bianchi. He was forgotten by the university. The information was totally wrong. There wasn't any more than a line that said he had been killed in the Bataan Death March."

Tom approached the Alumni Council and asked if there wasn't something that could be done for Bianchi. "I got pretty emotional about it. I felt quite bad. This was the only graduate from South Dakota State who got a congressional Medal of Honor and he was forgotten. I never even knew he existed."

A committee was formed with Sauer as chairman and Beattie and several others as members. The cost for the bronze relief, or sculpted plaque, was estimated at $14,000.

On April 30, 1998 — 56 years after Bianchi earned his medal — South Dakota State University dedicated the relief in remembrance of its only graduate to receive such a distinguished honor. The bronze artwork, which bears an image of Bianchi in uniform, is displayed in the west staircase of the University Student Union.

Red, white and blue flowers and ribbons decorated tables in the Volstorff Ballroom. About 160 guests attended the ceremony, sharing a noon meal and listening to speakers who recounted their thoughts on why Bianchi should be remembered.

SDSU President Peggy Gordon (Elliott) Miller remarked: "A university defines itself not only by what it does, but by what it honors. By honoring

A University Honors a Hero

Bronze relief of Bianchi dedicated on April 30, 1998, is on display in the west staircase of the University Student Union.

Captain Bianchi's courage and character, we even better define South Dakota State."

On Sept. 22, 2000, SDSU formally dedicated the Medal of Honor Park, located directly north of DePuy Military Hall. The site, which honors veterans of war, displays a monument in honor of Bianchi.

For Beattie, the unveiling of the bronze relief marked not so much closure as a sense of satisfaction.

"I guess the thing I felt best about was that the university did what it should have done many years before. I got this letter from one sister and she said, 'My family tells me that you know more about my brother Bill than we do.' That felt good."

The process also left Beattie with a lasting impression of the men who have earned a congressional Medal of Honor:

"I read through all the citations for medals of honor, from World War I through Vietnam — there's over 400 — because the Alumni Association wanted to make sure that nobody else was missed. The only way I could be sure was to read them all. The common thing was how can these guys be so brave that they forget about their own life and do things that are superhuman? As I've thought about it, what it is, it's not so much that they're doing it for their country. They're doing it for the men they're with. Of course, they were motivated to begin with because of their country. But, case after case, they're doing their damnedest because of others. ...

"We've traveled some ... and in Europe, every town has a square that has some hero. If you go to New Ulm, there's a big statue of a German hero back around 1400. They don't forget their heroes. We do. That was the big thing with me. That's why I wanted Bianchi's plaque in the union — so every kid would see what a hero was."

Chapter 50

The Heartache of Vietnam

F riday, May 15, 1970. Governor's Day at South Dakota State University. Just weeks earlier, on April 30, President Richard Nixon had announced an offensive in Cambodia. Then, on May 4, four students were killed and nine were injured during Vietnam War protests at Kent State.

Brookings wasn't Berkeley or New York. But, northeastern Ohio was the Midwest — a little too close for comfort.

"It was a rough time all right," says Harold Bailey, dean of academic affairs under President Hilton Briggs. "We were all on edge. Buildings were being burned on other campuses. There was a difference of feelings about the war among faculty and students. It made us nervous."

In those years, ROTC remained mandatory for all freshman and sophomore male students at South Dakota State. And, as his predecessors had done in years past, South Dakota Gov. Frank Farrar was coming to review cadets at Coughlin Alumni Stadium.

The Pride of the Dakotas Marching Band forms a peace symbol during its Hobo Day performance in 1971.

War protestors walk in front of the Air Force and Army ROTC cadets during Governor's Day activities held at Coughlin Alumni Stadium in 1970. (Courtesy of Stephen DeLay, class of 1969, MA 1970)

The Brookings campus had been relatively quiet, particularly in light of heightened tensions across the country.

Still, says Bailey: "We didn't know what to expect. We policed the area under the stadium and removed all metal fragments and bolts so they wouldn't be available to throw."

Chuck Cecil, also a part of the Briggs administration, recalls the explosive atmosphere. "Every male was in ROTC. ... Up until that point, we were all naive about it. You served your country if it needed you."

The antiwar movement was barreling headfirst into a confrontation. Even at SDSU.

The week of Governor's Day 1970, the student Board of Control voted 16-10 for a resolution condemning U.S. involvement in Southeast Asia. The resolution stated: "BOC condemns the involvement of U.S. forces in South Vietnam, the invasion of Cambodia without the consent of the Cambodian people, and the renewed bombing of North Vietnam and Laos."

As the vote implied, the resolution was not arrived at easily. And, as Bailey indicated, sentiment was split on the war. In that case, the student board argued, should it take a stance and speak for everyone?

For Governor's Day, an estimated 400 students from State, USD, BHSU, NSU and Augustana converged on the Brookings campus for a fairly peaceful demonstration.

During the military display on the campus green, 18 placard-carrying protesters picketed the ceremony, taking up positions behind the cadet honor guard before moving to the north end of the green. After the national anthem, they circled the formation and spectators several times. Some of the signs stated: "SDSU manufactures targets," "ROTC builds bigots," "Conscience is a casualty in Vietnam," and "They may be Viet Cong, but they live there."

From the campus green, the marchers headed for the stadium. Tom Stanton, then SDSU Students' Association president, led the protesters into the stands, where they sang, "All we are saying, is give peace a chance."

Then, in a startling show of dissent, a group of 12 cadets broke rank during the governor's review.

Gordon Jackson, class of 1971, was covering the event for the Collegian.

"Stanton led the march into the stadium," Jackson remembers. "For South Dakota State, it was big. They marched right down in front. ... Some of the marchers hollered out at the ROTC people, who were in review formation, 'Join us.' "

SDSU Athletic Director Fred Oien, class of 1972, was a sophomore.

"They walked off the field with their uniforms on," says Oien. "These were people who were probably no different than myself or my roommate. It was probably the first time for a lot of us to see people that age being so passionate."

Remembering her thoughts and feelings as she witnessed the events unfold, Barb Fishback, class of 1972, says: "It was a pretty scary thing to do, but also pretty gutsy. To watch it, I felt proud, but also afraid, like, now what's going to happen?"

Such mixed feelings were widespread, according to Jackson, who as a reporter couldn't help but feel that he was observing a great news story. At the same time, as a farm kid from the Egan-Flandreau area attending a conservative university in a conservative state, Jackson found himself in the same emotional place as many of his peers.

"I was in my formative years; I just turned 18," he says. "Like everybody else, the day I stepped on campus, I wasn't totally anti-Vietnam. But as time went on, we didn't seem to be going anywhere. ... The goals were never that clearly stated. Guys were dying over there."

In fact, Jackson says his resident assistant from third-floor Mathews — Rich Larson — was killed in Vietnam. A high school buddy was wounded.

"As far as kids coming off the field, the fact that they broke ranks," Jackson says, "I understood what they were doing."

The draft only intensified the internal conflict and turmoil.

Says Jackson: "The draft tended to be people who weren't in college. ... The poor, the blacks, the guy working down at the gas station. College students, in most cases, could get a deferment."

And then, Jackson notes, there was Kent State.

"People were in disbelief ... that the National Guard would use live ammunition," he says. "There was fear — horror — that this could happen on an American campus."

Taking a stand, though, was not a clear-cut option.

Dennis Everson, class of 1973, says there had been talk among the cadets about breaking rank, but for most the consequences were too great.

"We knew what the repercussion would be," he says. "You'd get expelled from school and lose your 2s (the college deferment status). I'm thinking, 'I'm a sophomore, I've got a couple of years left, I have to go out and serve my country.' Day to day, you'd forget about it. But, standing there in uniform, with guys breaking rank, brought it close to home. It was a big reminder."

Events would escalate that spring day in Brookings, but not to the degree they did on other college campuses. However, for SDSU, it was a defining moment. If nothing else, May 17 signaled the complicated and contradictory emotions of the times.

"You thought, what is this country coming to?" Cecil says. "In the morning, we got through it all right, but it was a mess. We had the traditional Governor's Day luncheon in the old union. Briggs was there with the governor. I went to the luncheon and came back early. People were milling around. ... I went into the president's office, the secretary pointed to Briggs' office, I opened the door and there were about 30 kids in there. Some of 'em I knew, some of 'em I didn't. They were yelling and screaming, and there was vile language. In those days, you didn't swear in front of women. I heard women swear — worse than in the Navy.

"They were sitting on tables. ... I called security or I had the secretary call security. We called the president. The governor, for the better part of valor, decided to leave."

One man, John Crangle, was sitting in Briggs' chair. Crangle was teaching at National College in Rapid City after having been fired from State.

Cecil continues: "Crangle was sitting in the president's chair with his feet up on the desk. Hilton came back and told the kid to get out of the chair. All these other people are screaming and yelling. They wanted the flag to be lowered to half-staff (in mourning for two young African Americans shot to death by police at Jackson State College in Mississippi). That's why they were wait-

President Hilton Briggs moments before he 'removed' John Crangle from the president's chair. (Courtesy of Stephen DeLay, class of 1969, MA 1970)

ing for Briggs. Before they could talk about the grievance, Briggs told Crangle to get out of the chair. He didn't. I was looking in the door. The president pulled the chair back, Crangle slipped and went right on his keester. That made him mad. He took a swing at the president and another, before the kids could hold him back.

"The president was slightly injured — hit in the cheek or something. They hauled Crangle away. The other students said they would like to have the flag lowered, but Briggs said he had no authority. It was a big argument. Then, they left to lower it themselves."

Charges were filed against Crangle. Based on the recommendation of the ROTC instructors, the Academic Affairs Committee voted 6-6 to continue action against 11 of the so-called SDSU 12 who broke ranks. The 12th student had not been identified. Bailey broke the tie.

"It was determined that we would follow the necessary regulations and requirements for various things, normal participation in classes, that sort of thing," explains Bailey. "They broke ranks when ROTC was required. They were not fulfilling that requirement."

But as the administration pursued that set course, Bailey reflects on the tremendous inner conflict: "We were betrayed in those days by our government. We wouldn't have said it then, but it was kind of like pulling the rug out from under us. We were told, 'Follow the rules, be patriotic, do the right thing, tell the students they were wrong.' Then, here we are, finding out there was a betrayal."

Bob Burns, SDSU distinguished professor, director of the Honors College and head of the political science and philosophy departments, arrived on campus as a student in the fall of 1960 and graduated the spring of 1964.

"When I was a student, the war in Vietnam had not really heated up yet," Burns says. "It was more of a limited involvement, special forces. Although, through ROTC, we were becoming increasingly aware. The rest of the student body, for the most part, was unfamiliar with or even ignorant of what was going on. The war had not reached its point of maximum exposure."

Despite the oft-repeated characterization of SDSU as a conservative campus, Burns notes, "We did have our teach-ins and some demonstrations. ... South Dakota is not known for its political radicalism. We have a more politically subdued student body, largely because of its background. It's more rural."

The generation of students on campus in the early 1960s, says Burns, straddled a huge societal divide.

"It was pre-radicalism," he explains. "We were probably stuck more in the Elvis Presley, Buddy Holly clique than the Beatles. For those of us who entered college in the early 1960s, our parents had been through the Depression. They were very, very dedicated to making sure it didn't happen in this country again, that their children didn't have to experience it. The emphasis was on staying focused, following the straight line, graduate from high school, go to college, graduate, get married, have kids, be thrifty and put away for a rainy day."

It wasn't until the presidential election of 1964 and the subsequent escalation of events that Vietnam generated widespread interest. The Gulf of Tonkin Resolution gave President Johnson the authority to order additional ground troops to Vietnam, although, Burns says, the measure was based on what many believed to be a fabricated incident. On the pretense of protecting the troops already in Vietnam, Johnson ordered up another 540,000.

As casualties and questions mounted in 1968, 1969 and 1970, the SDSU student body grew increasingly opposed to the war. Burns served as an active duty commissioned officer in the Army in Vietnam from September 1969 to August 1970.

Oien says he has vivid memories of sitting in the day room in Brown Hall, watching draft numbers get pulled on KELO-TV.

"Every state in the union had to produce so many numbers," he says, explaining that the numbers were matched with birthdays. "It was just like going to bingo. There were 365 days a year. If April 1 was picked, then anybody with an April 1 birthday — that was your number. You're sitting there with your friends, people you're going to school with, and then all of the sudden, they're drafted early. And you're thinking, 'Here's reality.' If you were an early number, you knew you were going to get drafted."

Everson, too, remembers students watching the draft numbers get drawn.

"Every time someone got picked," he says, "they peeled out of that room."

When Stanton led the Governor's Day protest, he had already had firsthand experience with the war. After spending the 1965-66 school year on campus, Stanton headed for Vietnam. He lost an eye while on active duty and returned to SDSU in the fall of 1968. He graduated in 1971.

"It was really weird," allows Stanton. "One day, people are shooting at you. You're shooting at people. And the next day, you're with a bunch of college kids."

Stanton says he never thought the war was a moral dilemma. Looking for adventure, he was willing to serve. His experience didn't change his attitude.

"However," he notes, "once I was out of the service, I didn't think we had any business being over there."

Burns says his views changed, too.

"The strange thing about me was that I was not a dove before I went to Vietnam," he says. "I was not a dove while I was in Vietnam. But I became a dove when I got home. I sensed the futility of it. We really were not in a winning situation — not because we couldn't win military battles, but simply because of the incredible staying power of the North Vietnamese and the Viet Cong. They were willing to incur unmentionable suffering."

Recounting the difficulty and the division of the Vietnam years, Oien remembers one Harding Lecture in particular.

In an effort to be provocative, the lecture committee brought in controversial attorney William Kuntsler. He represented the Chicago 7 (Abbie Hoffman, Jerry Rubin, David Dellinger, Tom Hayden, Rennie Davis, John Froines and Lee Weiner) — the seven radical activists brought to trial in 1969-70 on charges of conspiring to incite a riot at the 1968 Democratic National Convention in Chicago.

"There was a letter sent to David Pearson, vice president for administration," recalls Oien. "This lady had written it entirely in her own blood."

The woman objected to the choice of speakers — a choice the Harding Lecture Committee expected to be controversial.

"We knew it wouldn't be popular," says Oien, "but, the university felt it was important to hear all sides. Nobody was advocating any positions. That's what was happening at that time."

James Pedersen, who was designated dean of student affairs in 1969, says the late 1960s and early 1970s saw both campus and community at a major crossroads.

He remembers the Kent State incident and the struggle of administrators to meet expectations and maintain control. Understandably, they were concerned about the integrity of the university as well as its reputation. They also were from a generation when you did what you were told.

Still, he says wistfully, "you had to join students in the feelings that this can't be happening in America. It just defied your understanding of what this country was about. ... As an administrator, you couldn't help but have empathy for what the students were trying to accomplish."

Today, says Pedersen, it is much easier to look back and put the issues into perspective. He now can see how truly momentous the experience was in the context of history. And, he credits Briggs with steering the campus through such trying years.

"Our institution was extremely blessed that he was president at the time," Pedersen reflects. "He kept a sense of institutional direction and stability because of the strong person that he was. He was trusted by essentially everyone — even the students who were in dissent and not happy.

"He was strong enough that he wasn't going to be pushed off the path of validity and honesty, and all of the central values that the institution stands for. And the amazing thing about him was that it never seemed that he had to stop and think about whether he was doing the right thing. He just seemed to know. At the time, we didn't fully understand how important that sense of confidence and direction was."

Chapter 51

'They Were All So Young'

It is too easy to say the Easter Sunday 1965 death of Lt. Josef L. "Joe" Thorne — one of South Dakota's first Vietnam casualties — brought the war home to the State campus.

He was, after all, one man — one of how many thousands of lives lost. The Vietnam War, however, was an incredibly complicated, divisive issue that exacted a huge toll on Americans, both individually and collectively.

And yet, distilling the war into personal terms and putting it into human context was exactly what Thorne's death accomplished.

"It was really devastating," remarks Harry Forsyth, who was assistant athletic director at the time. "Joe was the first of seven we had in the athletic

---

Pictured above, Joe Thorne (48), teammate Mike Sterner (64) and coach Ralph Ginn poses for a picture in the 1962 Jack Rabbit.

department who died in Vietnam. We lost a lot of fine young men. Whenever you lose someone like that, it brings it really close to home. I don't know what more to say — that is exactly what happened."

Joe Thorne, class of 1963, was born in 1940, in International Falls, Minn., the namesake of his maternal grandfather.

"J-o-s-e-f," spells Mary Jane, Thorne's mother. "That's the way my mom spelled my dad's name on their marriage certificate."

Young Joe Thorne grew up in Gettysburg before the family moved to Beresford.

"It broke his heart," Mary Jane says. "He was a junior or senior in high school. He had all his friends; he played football."

But, once in Beresford, as was Joe's nature, he settled in just fine, making new friends and playing football. With a sister at the University of South Dakota, Joe signed on to continue his gridiron career in Vermillion. That is, until Stan Marshall — who would become athletic director at State — came along.

"He knocked on the door and said, 'Do you know where Joe is?'" Mary Jane recalls. "And I said, 'What do you want?' He said, 'I'm looking for him to come to State.' I said, 'He's already signed up with the University.'

"He looked at me and said, 'Oh, we'll see about that.' Then next thing you know, Joe is signed up with State. It kind of bugged me at the time. You know, when you're connected to the University, you're not that crazy about State. And, my daughter was at Vermillion."

Indeed, says Warren Williamson, head freshman football coach at the time, "there was quite a recruiting battle for Joe. At that time, he lived in Beresford, which was the back yard of Vermillion." Williamson, better known as varsity wrestling coach, concedes that he can't say for sure what swung Joe over to the SDSU camp, but he certainly helped sweeten the deal.

"Joe really wanted engineering as a curriculum choice," Williamson explains. "With that in mind, I had an uncle who owned a bridge-building company and he was building bridges on the interstate south of Sioux Falls. I was able to get Joe placed with my uncle's company. I like to think that was part of his decision."

Once the good-looking, athletic Thorne arrived in Brookings, he quickly carved out a place for himself on the football team as well as around campus.

"My first impression of Joe," says Williamson, "was how intense he was about his plans and his interest in athletics. ... He was very, very talented, very intense, competitive, and he was a sharp guy. He knew what he wanted, where he was going. He was a very mature senior in high school.

"Joe was not a real vocal sort of guy, but his attention and intensity was so obvious, it rubbed off on everybody around him."

Thorne played fullback. Weighing in at nearly 200 pounds, he wasn't that big as football players go. But, he was tough and he cooperated. According to Mary Jane, Thorne's coach "just loved him." So did everyone else. In Thorne's senior year, when the football team voted for captains, Thorne got all the votes but one — his own, which he cast for the co-captain.

Wayne Rasmussen, class of 1964, was a freshman the year Thorne captained the football squad. Rasmussen had received a basketball scholarship to State, but opted to pursue football and track during the off-season of his first year. That spring, Rasmussen decided to concentrate soley on basketball. Thorne, however, had other ideas.

"He sat down with me and just sort of convinced me that the right thing to do would be to go out for football," says Rasmussen. "It's been so long, though, I can't remember exactly what he said that convinced me."

Whatever Thorne said, his words certainly made a difference. Rasmussen went on to play football for the Detroit Lions. He was in Michigan, having just completed his first season with the Lions, when he got word of Thorne's death.

Characterizing Thorne as an individual and an athlete, Rasmussen says, "He was a quiet leader. He was tough. Tough on himself, as far as getting in shape. He led by example."

Thorne's coach, Ralph Ginn, called him the best fullback he ever coached. Ginn told the Collegian: "He was one of the greatest young men I have ever worked with. His football records speak for themselves, but as a young man he was first team all the way. In your years of coaching, you work with a lot of boys and it seems like some of them become a part of you. That's the way it was with Joe. ... We've never had a football player that commanded as great respect of his teammates and coaches as Joe did."

Bob Burns of Brookings, SDSU distinguished professor, director of the Honors College and head of the political science and philosophy departments, had just started his mandatory two-year stint in ROTC as a freshman in 1960. Thorne was in his senior year and served as Burns' ROTC cadet company commander.

"Joe was not a spit and polish cadet," recalls Burns. "He was not a great believer in the rigors of close-ordered drill, but he was a true patriot. ... I think it was in part because of who he was. He did not have to bark at us or get on our case. He was more of a laid-back commander. He got a good response from us because we respected him so much, respected who he was."

Thorne was a legend. In his time at SDSU, he set three records (which have since been broken): most carries in one game, 30; most carries in one season, 174; and most net yards gained in one game, 200. He was twice All-NCC fullback in 1960 and 1961 and Jackrabbit co-captain in 1961. In his greatest year — 1961 — Thorne tied with Dan Boals of State College of Iowa for the Most Valuable Player in the North Central Conference. He finished second in league scoring with 50 points and had 75 for the season. He gained 964 yards for a 5.5 yard per carry average.

Thorne was drafted by the Green Bay Packers, but his mother says he opted to fulfill his obligation to the service. "He figured he'd get that out of the way. When he left, I asked him, 'Where are you going? What for?' And he said, 'I'm going over to protect the rice fields.' I didn't know what that meant. Vietnam didn't mean anything."

In August 1963, Thorne was commissioned a second lieutenant in the Army Reserve Officers Training Corps at State. At the same time, he received his degree in civil engineering. On Sept. 18, Thorne was assigned to active duty, attending school in Fort Sill, Okla., and then flight training at Fort Wolters, Texas, and Fort Rucker, Ala. In early November, 1964, Thorne headed for a year long tour of duty in Vietnam.

Initially, Mary Jane says, Thorne hauled mail and other assorted items; nothing as dangerous as people thought. "He said he felt like a cheerleader at a football game. He wanted to be in the middle of it."

On Easter Sunday, April 18, 1965, Thorne was the aircraft commander of a UH-1B helicopter assigned to a combat assault mission. Hostile small arms groundfire hit the helicopter, which then crashed and exploded on impact. Nearly 40 years later, the incident, as well as the war, fails to make any sense to Mary Jane.

"It was so stupid," she says. "I just couldn't understand why we were there. I never did figure out why he had to get killed there."

For many, the death of Joe Thorne inked one of those indelible moments; it marked an instant in time when you remembered exactly what you were doing when you heard the news. Such was the case for Don Barnett, class of 1964. A sophomore during Thorne's senior year, Barnett was in graduate school when the news hit.

"It really shook us up," Barnett says. "He was absolutely a wonderful guy. He married a beautiful lady. He was a good student, a good ROTC cadet ... really a nice fellow."

At age 24, Thorne left behind his wife, Diane, and 3-year-old son, Travis. In addition to his mother, he was survived by his father, Mel, three brothers

Mary Jane Thorne touches her son's name, which is etched into the dark granite of the Vietnam Veterans Memorial in January 1997.

and two sisters. Just a few days after his death, Diane, who was enrolled at State and commuting to campus from the couple's home in Clear Lake, told the Collegian that Joe had died doing something he loved.

"He was fighting for a cause and never once did he complain or regret what he was doing," she told the student newspaper. "He wasn't afraid and it was his choice to go into assault training. ... I'm sure Joe had no regrets. He could never sit on the sidelines."

Chuck Cecil, who at the time worked in SDSU President Hilton Briggs's administration, echoes the sense of shock as well as the accolades: "Everyone knew Joe. He was a wonderful person, a perfect kind of guy, friendly, smart, handsome. He was built like a Greek god. He was a wonderful football player. It really was a shock."

Joe Thorne was, as Williamson says, the type of individual people enjoyed being around. People identified with his success.

"You're talking 40 years ago," Williamson says. "There weren't as many students on campus. To wear a letter sweater ... that kind of caught people's attention."

Combine Thorne's athletic record, his personality, brains and good looks, Williamson adds, "and I almost think that as you watched him through his college years, you thought nothing could damage him."

Thirty-two years after the death of her son, Mary Jane Thorne traveled to Washington, D.C., with the Pride of the Dakotas Marching Band, which was

Pencil etching taken from the Vietnam Veterans Memorial bearing the name of Josef L. Thorne.

performing in the January 1997 presidential inauguration celebration. Mary Jane made the pilgrimage to see her son's name etched in the black wall of the Vietnam Veterans Memorial.

In years past, others who had visited the wall had brought back pencil etchings of Joe Thorne's name to his mother. She knew his name was there. In fact, she knew exactly where it was — in the corner with the other early victims of war, where the wall branches off in two directions.

Still, she says, "seeing his name just kind of took my breath away. It's hard to describe. It's just a black wall, kind of low, kind of dignified."

The wall is etched with the names of more than 58,000 young men and women who lost their lives in the Vietnam War.

Gazing at the names, Mary Jane remarked to Collegian reporter Aaron Myers: "It's such a waste of life here. What a waste, they were all so young and innocent. These were really good boys."

Six years later, as the unfolding news of war in Iraq drones on in the background, Mary Jane finds herself flooded with emotions.

"Even right now," she says, "with the Blackhawk helicopters going down. It's been a long time, but it still comes back."

Chapter 52

The Little Engine That Did

Steve B. is fond of recreation;
He's up to all things in creation;
He thinks he'll win renown
By building an engine, the best in town.
His Sunday clothes he wears each day,
Can you guess how much he has to pay?
He's both an Elk and loves Milwaukee
Poor boy, he fears so to look gawky.
— 1908 Jack Rabbit yearbook

Pictured above, Stephen Briggs as seen in the 1907 Jack Rabbit.

> *"Stephen Briggs, '07, writes that the gas engine of which he is the inventor will soon be on the market."*
> — January 1908 Industrial Collegian

> *"We are the world's largest producer of air-cooled gasoline engines for outdoor power equipment."*
> — 2003 Briggs & Stratton Corp. Web page

Since the first graduating class, legions of South Dakota State students have gone on to make their mark in the world. Large or small, in any number of fields, their varied contributions to society run the gamut.

Stephen Foster Briggs is no exception to the rule. In fact, the 1907 grad offers one of the earliest examples of State alumni who not only went on to achieve great success, but also turned around and gave back to the institution many times over.

Born in Watertown on Dec. 4, 1885, Briggs followed the typical public school path. He came to South Dakota State to pursue his field of interest — engineering.

According to Collegian accounts, Briggs developed his interest in gasoline engines during his college days, building an experimental model as a class project. Briggs & Stratton Corp. history says Briggs was eager to produce his six-cylinder, two-cycle engine and enter the emerging automobile industry after graduating in 1907.

"Bill Juneau, a coach at South Dakota State, knew of Briggs' ambition and the entrepreneurial interests of Harold Mead Stratton, a successful grain merchant who had a farm next to Juneau's," the company history reads. "Steve Briggs and Harry Stratton were introduced, and with that introduction, Briggs & Stratton was born."

As it turned out, Briggs' first engine was too expensive to mass-produce. After developing two touring cars and one roadster, the partners were out of money — and the automobile business. But, on Feb. 22, 1910, Briggs received a patent for a gas-engine igniter.

Within another 10 years, Briggs & Stratton, headquartered in Milwaukee, Wis., was a major producer of electrical specialty items. Other motors followed. Soon, the company's engines could be found in everything from lawnmowers and garden tractors, washing machines and refrigerators to concrete mixers, milking machines, small compressors, paint-spraying equipment, portable saws and electrical generators.

Living in Wisconsin, Briggs kept his alma mater close to his heart. In the August 1925 Alumnus, he wrote to his former classmates:

"You have promised time and again to come to Milwaukee to see us — why don't you make good? We should be most happy to see you and I know you would enjoy the visit. Business is quite good with us and we have about recovered from the after-the-war slump. We went through some pretty rough times but now that is all past and we have every reason to be happy and content. It has been a great help to have Charley Coughlin, '09, back with us and I feel that a great deal of the credit for our complete comeback is due him. I can hardly believe it has been eighteen years since I left Brookings — in fact, I don't believe it. The figures must lie."

In 1954, Briggs & Stratton once again forged into new territory with the introduction of the aluminum alloy engine. Briggs also founded the Outboard Motor Corp., producer of the Evinrude engines, and served as the company's chairman of the board. Outboard Motor later merged with the Johnson Motor Co. to form Outboard Marine Manufacturing Co.

But, there was more to Briggs than engines.

After moving to Florida in 1935, he raised beef cattle, hogs and roses. He also turned his attention to wildlife photography, focusing on native birds in particular. Briggs' photography talent earned him the rare honor of being named a fellow of the British Royal Society of Arts.

Two major movie companies — Walt Disney and Warner Brothers — bought some of his flamingo footage for use in films. Briggs also made several movies of native life in Hawaii, Guatemala and the South Seas, and of customs in southern Europe.

He told the Milwaukee Journal in a 1962 story: "I had a devil of a time finding a village where they still pressed grapes with their feet. But, I finally found one in southern France and got what I wanted."

The Journal story described Briggs as "a man who forcefully encourages colleagues to greater efforts ... (and) as a man not afraid to take a chance when he believes he is right — on a new product, a new process, a new plant."

Asked about the biggest factor in his success with outboard motors, Briggs explained: "I'd have to say luck. There's an element of luck in any successful business and it's been especially important to me."

In turn, Briggs and his wife, Beatrice, shared their good fortune with generations of South Dakota State students. The couple started the Briggs Scholarship Program in 1958 with the goal of helping young men and women who demonstrated potential for success in college, leadership and creative thinking.

That first year, 10 Briggs scholars were selected to receive $500 a year. By 1966, 10 incoming freshmen were selected for the annual grant, joining an estimated 30 upperclassmen who already were part of the program. Of the 10 freshmen, half had to be enrolled in the College of Engineering. The academic criteria was maintaining a 3.0 grade point average.

The scholarship program was one of three main projects funded by the Briggs Family Foundation. The Foundation was dissolved in 1993 and sufficient assets were given to the SDSU Foundation to endow the scholarships on a permanent basis. A 2002 bequest from the charitable trust of Eleanor Sweet, Briggs' secretary for many years, will help to expand the scholarship program.

SDSU Foundation statistics indicate that in 45 years the Briggs Scholarship Program has awarded more than $3 million to more than 600 South Dakota State students. From its initial $500 a year for 10 incoming freshmen, the Briggs scholarship by 2003 was providing 12 new students each year with a $6,500, four-year renewable scholarship.

Bob Burns, class of 1964, director of the SDSU Honors College, distinguished professor and head of the political science and philosophy departments, says the Briggs scholarship program made it possible for him to attend State.

"Our generation probably had fewer choices," he says. "We didn't anguish over decision-making. You have to remember, too, that we considered the opportunity to go to college a really big thing. There was no federal loan program. You couldn't just go to the bank. If I hadn't been given a Briggs Scholarship, I wouldn't have gone to SDSU."

Nearly a century ago, Stephen Briggs was tinkering with an experimental gasoline engine in a Solberg Hall lab. That single discovery led not only to the world's largest manufacturer of air-cooled gas engines, but also to the opportunity today for 48 students every year to pursue their dream of higher education at SDSU.

State awarded Briggs an honorary doctorate in engineering in 1956. In 1961, he was honored as an SDSU Distinguished Alumnus. Briggs died on Hobo Day, Oct. 16, 1976. He was 91 years old.

Chapter 53

President Coolidge Visits

South Dakota State University has a lot to brag about in its rich and colorful 118-year history, including a campus visit by a sitting president.

Seventy-five years ago, before the United States slid into the Great Depression, the South Dakota Board of Regents invited President Calvin Coolidge to formally dedicate the Lincoln Memorial Library. The presidential bid wasn't as much of a long shot as it might have seemed.

Prior to becoming president of South Dakota State, Charles Pugsley had worked for the U.S. Department of Agriculture from 1918 to 1923. The Harding administration was in office and Coolidge, of course, served as vice president until Harding's death. Coolidge and Pugsley enjoyed a professional relationship, but also grew to be friends. Some said Pugsley's departure from the USDA to head up State played a role in Coolidge's decision to spend his summer vacations in South Dakota.

Announcement of the invitation came on July 7, 1927. About a month

Pictured above, Grace and Calvin Coolidge stand at the foot of the Coolidge Sylvan Theatre on Sept. 10, 1927.

later, Coolidge, summering in the Black Hills, told visiting newspaper editors that he planned to drop by Brookings on his return to Washington to dedicate the new building on campus. The president also was invited to visit Aberdeen, but The Brookings Register reported that he could make only the Brookings stop.

With the date of the visit set for Sept. 10, the campus and the city had four weeks to prepare. According to newspaper accounts, special committees were established to handle the countless details involved, from the president's arrival to his route through town, traffic and parking, seating, a dedication tablet for Sylvan Theatre, and the dedication ceremony itself. The excitement generated by the prospect of a presidential visit was evident in the extensive and detailed preparations.

"Oh, yes," exclaims Mary Louise DeLong, class of 1929. "People were really excited. And for years afterward, we heard about it. It was really special to have the president here."

The Brookings County Press reported that the streets would be "gaily decorated." Large United States flags were planned for each intersection and alternating red, white and blue pennants would hang midway of each city block along the procession route. A large portrait of Coolidge was to be placed in each store window, with "the usual small decorative flag placed in front of each store as is the custom on special days."

The program was scheduled to start at 9 a.m., with music played by visiting bands from across the state. The Rev. F.E. Morrison, president of the Ministerial Association of Brookings, would give the invocation; presentation of the library would follow. Plans included having the president speak from the north end of the library, on a high platform, so people could see and hear him.

In a history paper on the event, SDSU student Tim Eighmy, class of 1988, theorized that there was more to

Advertisement in the Brookings Register notes the presidential visit and tries to take advantage of the opportunity.

Coolidge Day than all the fanfare generated by a visit from the leader of the free world. Putting the event into a greater context, Eighmy wrote: "Coolidge Day can probably be best understood as being an event which took place in the midst of national controversies, as a distinguished event which helped bring a sense of prestige to a small land-grant college, and as an exciting community affair in which a small rural town got the chance to host the president of the United States."

As Eighmy set the scene, Coolidge Day in Brookings took place the year before a presidential election and in the same year as Charles Lindbergh's crossing of the Atlantic Ocean. And agriculture, of course, was hit hard by the Depression. The same summer of Coolidge's visit, Lindbergh was in all the headlines, crossing the country in a nationwide tour. In fact, two weeks before Coolidge arrived, Sioux Falls had hosted "Lindbergh Day." A week after the Sioux Falls event, Lindbergh landed in Omaha, Neb.

As the nation trained its spotlight on the Midwest, Coolidge added to the commotion with an Aug. 2 announcement. Sitting at his desk for a press conference, he handed each member of the press an envelope that contained the simple comment, "I do not choose to run for president in 1928." The early statement was unexpected and touched off frenzied speculation. Did he truly not want to be a candidate or was it that he preferred not to be? Would he accept the position if nominated by his party?

Coolidge arrived in Brookings not only amid this swirling mix of excitement and uncertainty, but also carrying the weight of a political controversy that had occurred earlier in the year, when he vetoed the McNary-Haugen bill. The measure would have given the government power to fix farm prices and Coolidge believed that would hurt consumers. Although Coolidge's intention was to keep government out of private business, the veto did not play well with the agricultural constituency.

Still, Coolidge Day was huge. An estimated 12,000 to 15,000 people crowded into the city that day, starting at 7 a.m. — more than two hours before Coolidge's train was to arrive. The train pulled into the depot downtown at 9:35 a.m., greeted by the sounds of the college military band. Coolidge, wife Grace and son John, were driven to campus in a Packard open-air car. It was the same seven-passenger car used days earlier in Omaha to transport Lindbergh in a celebration there.

Eighteen cars carrying the presidential party and the reception committee, Secret Service men and others, drove north on Main Avenue to Eighth Street, then east to Medary Avenue. The planned route then changed, with the motorcade heading north on Medary to the north end of campus and then swinging back by the armory, past the Administration Building to the east door on the south side of the new library. The last-minute switch in routes was done to give Coolidge a view of the campus and the crowd a chance to see the presidential family.

Once delivered to the library, the Coolidges walked to the speaker's platform as the band played "Hail to the Chief" and the crowd cheered.

Brookings resident Lawrence "Lorne" Bartling, class of 1938, was 12 years old that day.

"I remember him standing out on the steps of the old library," Bartling says. "It was a big crowd."

In introducing the president, Pugsley said it was only fitting to have Coolidge dedicate the new library, named after Abraham Lincoln. Sixty-five years earlier, congressman Justin S. Morrill of Vermont had brought forth the bill — signed by Lincoln — that established the land-grant college system. In 1925, a bill signed by Coolidge earmarked government funding for research work. The Lincoln Library was the first building erected on a land-grant college campus in Lincoln's memory.

Contracts for the library were let March 31, 1926, and ground was broken about three weeks later. Construction costs were estimated at $200,000, which was provided by the tax levied on cigarettes in South Dakota. According to The Brookings Register, this was the first educational building in the United States to be funded in such a manner.

The new library was spectacular, particularly for its time, boasting green and brown marble in the main entrance and woodwork finished in silver grey and brown. A small alcove in the entryway displayed a statue of Lincoln, which was done by Baltic native and State art grad Gilbert Riswold. In lavishing accolades, The Brookings Register wrote: "It will rank with the finest college libraries in the country and is planned to meet the needs of the college for many years to come."

The building faced north toward the main campus and other buildings. To the south of the library was a small grove of trees dedicated to the memory of State's World War heroes. To the east was a wide boulevard that was designated as the main campus gateway. To the west, was the new Sylvan Coolidge Theatre.

With thousands attending the event in person, even more residents throughout eastern South Dakota tuned in on the radio to hear Coolidge speak. Rather than deal with the controversial issues of the day, Coolidge praised South Dakota's achievements in less than 40 years of statehood. He also spoke of Abraham Lincoln's pioneering contribution to land-grant col-

President Coolidge Visits

Autographed pictures of President Coolidge and Grace Coolidge. The photographs are now a part of the collection of the SDSU Archives and Special Collections.

leges and stressed the moral importance of education.

"No progressive community can afford to neglect the education of its people," Coolidge told the crowd. "It is impossible for any community to hold its place in modern society unless it is fully equipped in the educational field of arts and sciences and research."

An institution of higher learning also shouldered the responsibility, the president said, to inspire its students with an understanding of subject matters both broad and deep:

"There is something more in learning and something more in life than a mere knowledge of science, a mere acquisition of wealth, a mere striving for place and power. ... Unless our graduates are inspired with the right ideals, our colleges will have failed in their most important function and our people will be lacking in true culture."

Coolidge said people could measure the desire and appreciation for life's advantages by the sacrifices individuals were willing to make. It was evident, he said, that such determination had a hold on South Dakotans. The state's people were pioneers, who had arrived with the hunger to improve their lives. It was nothing short of spectacular to think that in less than 75 years of settlement, South Dakota had built thriving cities, transportation systems, schools, a body of laws, state and local governments, and "a vast agricultural empire."

"Perhaps there is no better example of this wonderful development than your own State College," Coolidge remarked. "It was opened 43 years ago today as a preparatory school with 35 students. Since that time it has reached the proportions of a college of agriculture and mechanic arts, with an enrollment of about 1,400 students. ... It is a mighty inspiration to realize that American communities have a capacity which is demonstrated by their record of the accomplishments of such wonderful works."

Coolidge went on to praise Lincoln, saying it was fitting to honor him with the name of the new library. Lincoln had a profound interest not only in education, but also in agricultural education, which was particularly visionary for someone who lived in a time when the methods of tilling soil had not advanced for 2,000 years.

According to Coolidge, the land-grant system realized "the vision of Abraham Lincoln, which may have come to him as he rode the circuit over the prairies of Illinois, or as he went up and down the state in conduct of political campaigns." However the vision came to pass, Coolidge added, "Its material and spiritual effect upon the well-being of our country is beyond estimation."

After the speech, Pugsley conferred an honorary degree of doctor of science upon Coolidge. Then, the Coolidges headed to Sylvan Theatre to lay a memorial stone in commemoration of the event. Both the president and his wife were given silver trowels to mortar the stone in the theater. The press reported that Coolidge spilled two trowel-fuls of mortar while his wife skillfully applied her portion.

Robert Burris, class of 1936, grew up about a half a block from campus in a house at 915 Ninth St. He was a Boy Scout when the Coolidges visited.

"A lot of us Boy Scouts were ushers for the ceremony," recalls Burris. "We saw the whole operation. It was a big occasion to have a president come. There were a lot of people. Everybody talked about how much better Mrs. Coolidge was with setting the mortar."

The granite stone, measuring 9 feet by 2 feet, bore the inscription, "Coolidge Sylvan Theatre; this stone laid by Pres. and Mrs. Calvin Coolidge September 10, 1927." Donated by Dakota Granite Works of Milbank, the stone was polished to a dark mahogany color to blend with the stone wall. The plans were donated by the Sioux Falls architecture firm of Perkins & McWayne, which had designed the new Lincoln Library.

President Coolidge Visits

Built on a natural slope, Coolidge Sylvan Theatre forms an amphitheater that can seat an estimated 5,000 people. The front stage wall and stage steps are a ruble stone design, and the gateways and entrances are made from red brick and imitation stone. The intent was to match the brick and Bedford stone of the library and main campus gateway.

After the stone was laid, 5-year-old Betty Jean Peterson offered Mrs. Coolidge a bouquet of flowers grown by the Faculty Women's Club.

Brookings' big day passed. The Coolidges took the train back to Washington, the crowds departed and the excitement faded. The nation turned its attention back to more pressing matters.

Still, both campus and community basked in the afterglow. Pugsley thanked the citizens for making the visit "the splendid occasion that it was."

Chapter 54

Campus Life

To look at South Dakota State throughout the generations is to catch a glimpse of who we once were and what we have become. All the social intricacies — what we do for fun, how we look at life, the manner in which we conduct ourselves — play out on the college campus in a microcosm of the world at large.

In 1907, the rules were simple, according to the Jack Rabbit yearbook. These were the "Commandments":

1. Thou shalt have none other college before thine own.
2. Thou shalt not bow thyself down to Sophomore nor serve them.
3. Thou shalt not take the names of the Faculty in vain.
4. Six days shalt thou labor and do all thy work, but the night time is for thy recreation; in it thou shalt not do any work, thou nor thy roommate, nor thy pony; lest thou shatter thy constitution with arduous toil.
5. Honor the president of your college that thy days may be long in the land to which thy father has sent thee.
6. Thou shalt not bum.

Pictured above, illustration taken from the 1920 Jack Rabbit.

7. Thou shalt not make eyes at the co-eds.
8. Thou shalt not steal thy neighbor's umbrella nor text-book.
9. Thou shalt not bear false witness against thy boarding house.
10. Thou shalt not covet thy neighbor's foxy clothes, nor his social position, nor his meerschaum pipe, nor anything that is his, for if thou art a wise guy thou wilt, in due season, have all these and more.

Ten years later, in the Oct. 2, 1917, edition of the Collegian, walking on the grass rather than the sidewalks was an affront serious enough to warrant editorial comment:

"The custodian of the campus is putting in his annual complaint over the 'hick.' The 'hick' is any person inconsiderate enough to use the campus lawn instead of the concrete sidewalk when walking to and from the college. While we hold no mandate in the matter, we feel it imperative to ask all the students, as well as the faculty members and other officials, who either do not know or have forgotten the good custom of keeping the campus free from untidy paths, to keep on the cement walks and keep off the campus."

According to the February 1926 Alumnus, "hicking across campus" was just one of many infractions that would bring on a paddling over the old boiler. The term "boiler," the Alumnus said, referred either to "an old steam engine boiler, splashed with 'green blood' of hundreds of unlucky freshmen," or the "drastic act of stretching some tradition-breaking student over the official campus boiler and applying the paddle with zest."

"One thing I remember quite vividly is the old boiler on campus over by the military building," says Martin Taylor, class of 1932. "If an upperclassman would catch a freshman breaking a rule, he'd put him over the boiler and paddle his rear."

The 1921 Jack Rabbit ode to the boiler offered a picture with the caption "freshman instructor." In an account titled "An Episode in the Life of the Boiler," the yearbook recounted an effort by the class of 1923 to end the tradition. The "green-cropped boys" stole the boiler and left in its place a grave and tombstone bearing the inscription "Gone, never to return, your memory still remains. — Freshmen."

Upon finding the grave, the upperclassmen discovered about 40 pallbearers and a hearse heading off campus:

"A desperate attempt was made to rescue the beloved friend who was so irreverently and carelessly being carried away in disgrace — intervention was of no avail, the deed was done and the college community was shrouded in woe and sadness.

"But, alas! Upon appearing for classes the following morning, the

Campus Life

Two freshmen are laid out over the dreaded boiler and getting paddled by upperclassmen. The boiler was often referred to as the 'Freshman Instructor.'

Freshmen were greeted by a new boiler firmly cemented in the ground. Besides, at every corner of the campus, a group of concerned Seniors stood with stern faces and long paddles, determined to paddle every Freshman until the burial place of the veteran of a former day was exposed."

The plan succeeded. The following week, the upperclassmen saw that the same hearse and pallbearers brought back the old boiler while singing, "Bring back my boiler to me" and "Cheer, cheer, we've got it here."

According to the yearbook, "The respected veteran was not reburied, but through the efforts of the upperclassmen it was reinvigorated and reborn, and today, as always before, it stands as a fitting and exemplary landmark to all disobedient yearlings as well as others."

The 1924 Jack Rabbit devoted an entire page of text and photographs and described one of the oldest campus traditions:

"What the cry of 'Water' is to the drowning man, and the sight of castor oil to the small boy, the shout of 'Boiler' is to the college man. When the echo of that shout rings across the campus, the student's mind quickly surveys the events of the past week to recall anything he might have done to bring doom upon his head. If he is not a Freshman or has been guilty of no offense, he will grab his trusty paddle and rush to the scene of action, ready to do his share in the forceful education of the victim. However, if he is in doubt as to the probability of the cry being meant for someone other than himself, even a ray of light would have a hard time keeping up with him in his flight. The boiler proves to be the most efficient and effective method of keeping students in the

A birds-eye view shows the State campus at the turn of the 20th century. (Courtesy of SDSU Archives and Special Collections)

straight and narrow and also in preventing the disease known as the 'big head.' LONG LIVE THE BOILER."

The tradition led to such expressions as "give him the boiler," "boiler him," "boiler for you," "boiler party" and "rushing the boiler." In addition to cutting across the grass, other boiler offenses included smoking on campus, failure to wear the freshman green beanie and walking in the company of a coed during a freshman's first few months on campus.

Decades later, the boiler was long gone, but the green beanie continued to play a key role in the freshman experience. Christy Osborne, class of 1982, vividly remembers the fear of getting caught without the beanie.

"You'd have to wear it, or they'd chase after you with a green marker and write a 'V' (for vigilante) on your face," Osborne says. "It put the fear of God in you. I still remember somebody chasing us down Rotunda Hill with a marker."

Mary Stangohr, who roomed with Osborne their freshman year and attended SDSU from 1978-80, adds: "It was just sheer fun, a clue to anyone that you were a freshman. It was definitely not a badge of honor. Of course, I don't think we ever got caught."

Dorm life also involved an ongoing series of practical jokes.

"Oh," laughs Stangohr, "you'd get pennied in — they'd jam pennies in your door so you couldn't get out. Then, they'd call your room. If you picked up the phone, they wouldn't hang up, so you couldn't call anybody for help. I got locked in my room on the day of my world religion test. I tied my sheets together and went out the second floor window. A kid happened to come by, so he helped me get down. They knew I had a test and they did the thing with the phone."

Another big prank to pull was removing the contents of someone's room. Explains Stangohr: "You'd go to your room and it would be gone. We'd put the mattress on top of the bathroom stall and put everything on top of it. Of course, if you took a shower, they'd take your towel, too."

Some years, Hobo Day called for special initiation rites. Stangohr remembers as a freshman being forced to wear the green beanie along with other members of her class. Their hands tied together, they had to walk as a group to the Campanile and eat bum stew.

"You had to eat as your hand was tied to the next person," says Stangohr. "We got everybody to eat with the right hand, but food was everywhere."

Collegian editors in the Jan. 12, 1926, edition contemplated the problem of bringing dates to basketball games. They cited the fact that many of the leading colleges in the country had passed an edict "absolutely prohibiting" male students from taking a date to an athletic contest.

"Whether or not dates interfere with the vocal effort of the couples is a mooted question," the editorial noted. "Certain it is however that the yelling is getting to be of so refined a nature that there certainly must be some feminine influence at the bottom of it.

"Perhaps it would be wise to adopt the policy of some of the other colleges, and set aside one section of the bleachers for male rooters, and the other section for the feminine fans, and thus create a little rivalry between the vocal efforts of the two sexes."

In the spring of 1933, golf course (yes, there was a course on campus) etiquette was waning. Apparently, students were golfing in groups of four or more with four or fewer clubs to share. This slowed down play considerably and angered some of the golfers.

"We realize of course that there is a so-called depression facing students and this may somewhat account for the action of students who have been the cause of enragement," the Collegian editors wrote in the April 26, 1933, edition. "We believe in being 'depression-minded' but wouldn't it be possible to confine 'four-somes,' 'six-somes' and 'eight-somes' of this type to days when the course is not being used by the majority of golfers?"

At issue in 1963 was the dress code in the Men's Dining Hall — a minimum standard of slacks and sport shirts throughout the week except for Sunday, when students were required to wear trousers, white shirt and tie. Shorts were prohibited in the Waneta lobby, and Scobey coeds were forbidden to sunbathe in bathing suits behind their dorm. Shorts, however, were permitted.

When John Bibby, class of 1942, attended South Dakota State, the student body numbered about 1,400.

"Ballroom dancing was the biggest social activity," Bibby says. "There was a college dance every weekend. Most of 'em were in the Barn. ... I think you could count on one hand the number of students who had an automobile. Students didn't take off every weekend. That's why social activities were so successful.

"We could drink beer at 18. There weren't any big house parties. There weren't any liquor stores, but there were bootleggers and a liquor store in Aurora. ... I remember having Saturday morning classes."

Bob Thoreson, class of 1940, was on the football team and pursued a civil engineering degree.

"The dorm wasn't very nice," Thoreson says. "It was just a bunch of guys living together — six to a room. A boar's nest. That's just about what it was like. ... I worked at the Brookings Cafe, a couple of other jobs, worked on campus. I started in the fall of 1933 and after seven years of diligent work, I finally graduated.

"I remember the poker games and betting money. None of us had any. That's about what the games consisted of. Everybody was broke."

Jesse Robinson was a freshman in 1935. He, too, was a football player and lived with the athletes in the basement of the men's dorm.

"A room cost $3 a quarter," Robinson says. "There were six of us in a room, with three double-deck bunks and one closet. ... There was only one study table, so if you wanted to study, you went to the library. There was a study room down at the end of the hall, but that usually turned into a bull session."

Robinson says he and his roommate moved upstairs for the spring quar-

ter of their senior year. Those rooms, he says, ran each roommate about $15 per quarter. Tuition and fees cost about $30 a quarter.

"It was fun," Robinson says of his school days. "We played poker. It was small stakes. Nobody had any money."

Another football player, Ron Ringsrud, class of 1937, recalls that Vivian Volstorff, dean of women, once barred the entire football team from even walking by the girls' dorm.

"In 1935," Ringsrud adds, "money was so scarce that one night the team stole the prize pig from the ag department and roasted it down by the river. The agriculture students never knew who took that pig."

Former SDSU President Sherwood Berg, class of 1944, muses: "The thing that struck me was the democratic nature of this institution. There were no fraternities or sororities. You knew that the social barriers weren't great. We were all conscious of the fact that most students were relatively poor. There was only one car on campus that belonged to two sons of a doctor over in Dell Rapids. Look at that campus today. ...

"Kids were working. I remember Ozzie Schock was working on a dairy farm. He'd get up at 4 o'clock in the morning to milk cows. Others were working for 18 cents to 25 cents an hour in departments, helping instructors prepare for class, typing off tests, grading."

Today's students follow myriad rules in preparing their residence hall rooms for a year on campus. For example, no items may be attached to the ceiling, window screens are to remain in place, sharing cable TV services between rooms is forbidden, approved lofts must meet certain criteria.

Panoramic photograph taken of students on the Campus Green in 1913. Note the work on the Administration Building. (Courtesy of SDSU Archives and Special Collections)

Students arrive in the fall with trailer loads of belongings — furniture, stereos, fans, televisions, VCRs, DVD players, video games, computers, refrigerators, and a whole assortment of kitchen appliances.

Warren Williamson, class of 1951, remarks that in his day, dorm life "was pretty austere. If you had a radio in the room, you had something. There weren't many amenities."

Life, indeed, was much simpler.

"I didn't really have too much free time," says Jack Pearson, class of 1955, who ran the mile and two-mile in track. "We were traveling to meets during the season and then working out after classes. I'd go home and study. The big event was probably at 9:30 or 10 o'clock at night we'd jump in the car and go to Dairy Queen."

Yvonne Fetzer, class of 1973, says, "Only one girl had a TV. Everyone would go to her room and watch soap operas. Then she ended up flunking out and we didn't have a TV the second semester. ...

"There were no refrigerators in the room. I'd put milk outside my window, in-between the screen and the storm, so I could have cereal in the morning. We had a phone, though."

Television made its formal debut on campus in the fall of 1953. A committee sought bids from Brookings dealers. Different models were tested each night for a week and a half to determine which one would be purchased. The class of 1953 donated the funds for the television.

"Monday evening television was tried for the first time in the main lounge of the union," the Collegian reported on Sept. 24, 1953. "A number of students were on hand as the first picture flashed on the 27-inch screen to bring State College one of America's favorite indoor sports — watching TV."

However, the extent of what students watched was limited. Poor reception meant that Sioux Falls was the only channel available to viewers. Cable television did not arrive until 1978.

Chuck Cecil, class of 1959, remembers: "We used to have teas, proper little parties in the afternoon, where us guys from the country would try to drink tea out of a cup. It was part of Vivian's (Volstorff) civilization attempt."

Cecil also gets a chuckle out of the fashion trend of the time: "White corduroys, white bucks (a style of shoes), which had to be dirty. I wore those even after we were married until my wife took 'em out and burned 'em."

Harold Bailey moved to Brookings in 1951 and worked at State in administration for 33 years. When he and his wife first arrived, they lived in old Army barracks that had been brought to campus for married student housing. The barracks were located about where the student union sits today.

"Each of the barracks was comprised of three single-story apartments," explains Bailey. "They were comfortable and cheap. ... The walls, though, were very thin. We all were very careful about how we carried on our conversations. They were so thin that when a child next door hit the wall with a bicycle, the wheel went right through.

"There were two bedrooms. You walked into the living room and straight ahead was the kitchen area. To the left was the bathroom and two bedrooms. It cost $24.50 per month and included electricity. I earned about $400 per month. ... There were wonderful friendships that developed. Only a few of us faculty lived there. They called it Fertile Acres, the reason being the large number of children in the area."

Bailey also talks about the telephone system. Every phone number had three digits and one letter and there were multiple party lines. The population of Brookings was about 5,000 at the time, he says, and it cost 5 cents to ride the bus.

LaVerne Kortan, class of 1942, pauses to think about the evolution of campus life and all that is different: "The thing that is probably the most different is that we knew just about everybody on campus. You were here for three or four years. And, of course, everybody was looking for work. I came in and started working at a filling station. Then, I had a job waiting tables. I worked as a janitor. My last job was washing floors in the heat tunnel."

Kortan also was responsible for picking up the towels from football players after practice. The washing facilities were located underneath the power plant.

"We had a couple of washing machines down there and then we'd hang the towels on a line and then they'd dry overnight," says Kortan. "It was warm in there. We didn't have many problems with drying, as I recall."

Without a car, Kortan adds: "I got home once during the year, or twice. I'd go home at Christmas. Hitchhiking was my standard way of getting back and forth. People would pick you up; they knew you were a South Dakota State student."

Chapter 55

Those Nasty Blizzards

As sure as Hobo Day arrives every October and the crowds jam into Frost Arena for State-U games, winter on the South Dakota State University campus packs bitter winds that blow down from Canada with blinding snow and brutally cold temperatures.

"The lowest temperature was between ag hall and the library, right in front of Admin," insists Don Barnett, class of 1964. "The cold north wind would blow right through there. There was never a temperature recorded lower than in that spot."

An exaggeration? Perhaps. But, only slightly.

What's more, as cranky as Old Man Winter can get, today's students cannot fully appreciate today's protective cocoon formed by campus buildings and such modern-day comforts as the automobile.

The time was when there was little — if anything — standing between

---

Pictured above, a photograph from the 1908 Jack Rabbit titled "After the Storm."

the Brookings campus and the Canadian border as students and faculty alike trudged through the snow, heads bent against the gusting frigid air.

When Dorothy Ayers Mears, class of 1924, arrived in Brookings in 1920, pants had yet to cross the gender boundary.

"We wore dresses, of course," she says. "Nobody wore slacks. Most of us wore boots, laced up. We had to wade across the campus. We had heavy coats and sweaters, and we wore something on our head — we had scarves, mittens, all those good things."

In those days, Mears says, there were few automobiles on campus. One happened to be parked by the armory when a "real blizzard" carpeted the town and buried the car.

"I have a picture with one of the students laying on the top of the car," she remembers.

Constance Mark Goodwillie, class of 1938, says when snowstorms canceled classes, students still managed to gather at the dorms and play records and dance.

"There also was a place, the Campus Cafe, on Medary Avenue," she says. "Everybody went there. When I was in school, we didn't have a union. We went to the cafe for Cokes, to gather and socialize. It was very popular."

Born in 1915 in Pipestone, Minn., Lawrence "Lorne" Bartling grew up in Brookings and graduated from SDSU in 1938. He says the entire winter of 1935 was one big blizzard.

"We got coal from out East," Bartling recalls. "They couldn't get past Lake Benton — the railroad tracks were blocked. They ran out of coal at the college and closed school for two weeks. The plows couldn't handle all the snow."

How did he pass the time?

"I developed my pool game," he answers, laughing. "The North Dakota State University men's basketball team got to Brookings before we got socked in. They couldn't play at the college, so they played at the old high school. They played in the pit, which was well-named. It wasn't very big. ...

"North Dakota was the conference champion that year. They had a great ball team and just swamped us. We played two games. I think they were probably stuck here three or four days."

On Feb. 26, 1936, the Industrial Collegian reported that classes were back in session after two weeks of forced vacation due to extreme cold and lack of fuel. The episode wreaked havoc with the college calendar, canceling extracurricular activities, final exams, assemblies and a variety of other activities. The winter term was extended by eight days to help compensate.

Those Nasty Blizzards

A few years later, John Bibby, class of 1942, was a member of the student union board of managers. He went to Minneapolis with a few other students for a meeting and the group drove back to Brookings on Nov. 11 in the so-called Armistice Blizzard of 1940.

"It was a terrible blizzard," Bibby says. "Several people died. I remember I had my dad's car. There was lots of snow, lots of blowing. One young guy with us played the drums in the Varsity Club and he was supposed to play at (a club), at the intersection of 212 and 77, straight north of Clear Lake. We came in and the wind was blowing. We came home on 77 and could hardly see the road. I had to drive between the fence lines. We had one gal, she lived in a dorm — we got her home at 11 o'clock, an hour past curfew."

Whether it was 1947 or 1953, 1966 or 1975, 1982 or 1985, the story was the same: The wind blew, the snow flew, temperatures dropped, cars were buried and classes were canceled. Yearbook pictures from 1953 show students making the best of the situation, dancing, playing cards, shooting pool and studying.

Harold Bailey arrived on campus in 1951, working in administration at SDSU for 33 years. His most vivid memories of the weather center around his tenure as vice president of academic affairs under President Hilton Briggs:

"The morning of every blizzard, Dave Pearson, the other vice president, and I would get phone calls from Hilton Briggs and he'd ask how we saw it. He had been out walking around the campus and thought things were pretty good and maybe we should hold class."

Pearson lived on 16th Avenue between Olwien and Elmwood streets. Bailey, who lived on Eastern Avenue, remembers looking outside and seeing drifts practically covering the window. "There was no way a lot of the people could get to campus," he says.

Then, there was the three-day blizzard of 1975 during the November Board of Regents meeting. The formal ceremony for installing Briggs' successor, Sherwood "Woody" Berg, as SDSU president was to take place then.

Ten inches of snow canceled classes and paralyzed the city, according to the Nov. 26, 1975, Collegian. Winds were clocked at 54 mph gusts, making efforts to clear roads futile.

"There was the usual drizzle, then it froze, and then the storm," says Bailey. "Woody lived over here (near Bailey) and Briggs still had the president's house. We were picked up by a truck with a plow and taken to the Holiday Inn. It was so bad that the Holiday Inn couldn't receive food and the housekeepers couldn't get in to do the housekeeping. So, the Board of Regents' wives were making the beds. Some of the regents were staying across

Headline from the Nov. 25, 1975, SDSU Collegian.

the street at the Staurolite and they couldn't get back across the street. The wind was so strong and the snowflakes so big. ...

"A snowmobile had to come after us at the end of the regents meeting, about 5 o'clock. We left the Holiday Inn and went up by the big sign. We got stuck up to our chests in the snow. ... I followed Woody, but lost him, and there I was, all alone. I headed to where I thought the snowmobiles were. Then, I decided I'd better stop and listen. The snowmobiles were in the other direction and I was headed out to the interstate."

Ten months earlier, at the start of 1975, a Collegian story on the "worst blizzard to hit the Midwest since 1888" counted eight people dead in South Dakota and at least 46 more throughout the region.

Berg echoes Bailey's memories of his postponed inaugural: "It was one of the most severe snowstorms in the years I've been here. It snowed and snowed and snowed. People were trapped at the Holiday Inn. There was no way that anything could be held. But, some of the students made it from their dorm down to the liquor store."

That was typical. The winds would drive falling snow into a blinding storm so bad that classes were called, but students still found their way to the municipal liquor store.

John Awald, director of the South Dakota Agricultural Heritage Museum since 1980, remembers a blizzard so incapacitating that the campus was shut down. Undaunted, a group of students ripped the hood off an old car and used it as a sled to haul kegs of beer to campus.

Tom Yseth, owner of the infamous Horatio's bar in downtown Brookings, says blizzards meant a brisk off-sale business.

"We'd have to get down there," he laughs. "We knew they'd be coming."

Chapter 56

A Family Affair

When Adam Wirt, class of 2000, won the showmanship title at Little International his freshman year, the honor meant more than bringing home a trophy to put on the shelf.

The event was the crowning achievement of a multigenerational family tradition of South Dakota State, agriculture and livestock showing — and, of course, participation in Little I.

"I've probably been to Little I every year since I was 5 or 6 years old," says Wirt, now 23. "I thought it was pretty neat."

Wirt's dad, Randy, class of 1978, says he has missed only one or two Little I's himself: "My dad used talk about Little I all the time. I remember when they used to televise the Saturday night session on Channel 2. I remember watching him judge one year on TV. That was in the Barn."

The senior Wirt, Russell, class of 1951, was involved with Little I during his years on campus and has been awarding the showmanship trophy for nearly 35 years. The family farms in the Parker area.

"I decided if I couldn't win it, I'm going to give that thing away," quips

---

Pictured above, the well-known red barn façade serves as a backdrop for the students participating in the 73rd Little International.

Russell, who did everything from showing livestock to helping manage the event.

Patterned after the great Chicago Little International Livestock Exposition, Little I is the largest student-run agricultural exposition in the country.

Plans for the first agricultural exposition at State, which was held on Jan. 26, 1921, began in the fall of 1920. The Dec. 14, 1920, Collegian detailed a meeting, where members of the "Shur-nuff" Agricultural Society explored the possibilities for a Little International. The prevailing sentiment was that South Dakota State had "a very good flock of sheep, an excellent herd of hogs and a goodly number of cattle and horses that would look good in the show ring."

As the event neared, the Collegian reported that competition would be "keen" and was expected to showcase the hard work and skill of agricultural students. Totaling more than 100 entries, animals shown included beef cattle, dairy cattle, hogs, sheep and horses. The first Little I also featured several of the college's Holstein cows — including College Belle Wayne and her daughter, College Belle Wayne II, who was the first cow in the state to produce more than 1,000 pounds of butter in one year.

In addition to the showcase of animals, the first Little I included a performance of the band led by Director Carl Christensen. The college creamery offered tours and free tastes of buttermilk.

According to Collegian accounts, State students pulled off a successful show, filling the stock pavilion to capacity. The creamery open house and free buttermilk also drew a large crowd. In retrospect, the college paper reported on May 31, 1921, that the first Little I livestock show held in the Dakotas compared favorably with similar events at other Midwestern colleges.

The following year, the Little International Livestock and Grain Show arrived a little later — on Feb. 16 — but much bigger than its predecessor. The Collegian noted, "Although the show is put on especially for the students of agriculture, all students of State college should be sure to attend, as it is without a doubt, a rare chance to see something really worthwhile."

Little I continued to flourish throughout the decades, the main purpose of the show being to give students practical experience and demonstrate the high caliber of their work. Home economics became part of Little I in 1949, adding a style show and several exhibits from the College of Home Economics.

Since its start in 1921, Little I has been held every year except for three: It was canceled in 1926 because of a scarlet fever epidemic, in 1943 because of the war effort, and in 1945 because of World War II.

At first, Little I was held in the stock pavilion, which now houses the South Dakota Agricultural Heritage Museum. Little I moved to the Barn in 1952, and then the Animal Science Arena in 1977. Dates for the annual show ranged from November to March, and many years saw the event hosted in February. More recent history finds Little I being held in early March. The work, however, starts when students arrive on campus in the fall.

"There's a lot of planning," explains Russell. "There's a whole bunch of committees, a manager, assistant manager — well over 200 people. It's a big thing. You have to keep it running and running fast."

In his days, Russell says, the exposition was more than hard work, livestock and grain: "We had the faculty involved, chasing greased pigs. It was a little bit of comedy."

As has been tradition since the start, students can get involved either through showing animals or helping pull off the event. Randy showed his first two years on campus and then switched to management.

"The managers have to rope in the troops," says Randy. "You have to make sure people are doing their job. That's the biggest headache."

When Little I was held in the Barn, he adds, there was the added stress of returning the building back to its athletic status: "We'd have tar paper, then plywood, then tar paper, and finally a tarp to protect the floor. We used to go to Spearfish to get wood chips — two truckloads of sawdust. Then, we'd dye 'em green. As soon as the dance was done Saturday night, it took all night to clean it out. We weren't allowed to bring in tractors for cleanup. We had till noon on Sunday."

Randy laughs as he remembers the dying process for the wood chips and how the move to the Animal Science Arena his senior year added an unexpected twist.

"Two weeks before the show, we were dying wood chips," he says. "Well, you can't just add the powder. You put it in a bucket, add water, mix it and pour it in the chips. We were in the Animal Science Arena and I grabbed the water trigger, which had 50 pounds of pressure. All the powder and dye came back out of the bucket and went all over me. They were going to have a green manager."

Like his father, Adam showed livestock his first two years and then made the move to management. But first, in his freshman year, Adam earned the honor of overall winner.

"You have to be first in showmanship in your species," he explains. "Then, first and second of each species come back at the end of the night. Every species is shown, and the one with the highest score wins."

To get to that level is no easy feat. Depending on what species of animal a student draws, one or two weeks of intense work takes place prior to showing.

"You don't get a whole lot of training," Adam says, "so that is what makes it tough. It's like when you're training a dog. You can only train them so much in a week. I work on certain things. You can lead a sheep and set it up so it stands in certain positions. That's all I had time for, basically. Any spare time you have, between classes and homework, you're training. I was sleeping maybe only four, five hours a night."

Randy says he had shown market lambs all his life, but Little I features breeding sheep. "You have to shape the wool, bring out its high points and hide the flaws. I had never done that. I spent a lot of hours trying to learn and do it. ... I remember my sophomore year, one kid was out for the fitting award. He had already won showmanship. There was another kid who was bound and determined to stop him. Every night, I'd see what little things they would do to make their sheep look better. That's how I learned."

Proud to see his son win the showmanship award, Randy says he knows how difficult that level of achievement is.

"I actually told him to be feed manager," says Randy, "because showmanship is too much work."

For Adam, the family connection to Little I hit home the fall of his senior year, when he was manager: "Within a month, I started seeing articles from when my dad was manager. Then, I find out how my grandfather was involved and I started thinking about it. It's something special. You just think about how your family has been such a major part of Little I and how Little I has been such a major part of your family."

Randy says maintaining SDSU's agricultural roots remains an important aspect of the livestock and grain show, and the high quality of the event is a reflection on the university.

"Over the years," he notes, "since I've been manager, I've run into some of the judges we had there. They are still impressed at how well-run the show is and how good the participants are."

Little I, adds Randy, broadens the opportunities for students: "It's a different type of extracurricular activity. The kids out there are the ones who excelled in 4-H and FFA (Future Farmers of America), showing livestock, and Little I brings it to the college level. Then, there are a lot of kids who have never shown animals, but they've gotten involved."

As the Wirt family demonstrates, involvement in Little I can be lifelong. Beyond the family ties, Randy notes that the friendships he made during

Little I have withstood the passage of time. "I have friends in Iowa, Minnesota, all over the country just because of Little I. It's a common link."

Echoing his father's sentiments, Adam says the annual show remains as meaningful today as it was for students generations ago.

"It's the largest student-run ag exposition in the country," he says. "You stop and think about that — the number of students and participants, the effort that goes into it, the amount of people who come here and travel through, the amount of money it brings to the community, the publicity it brings to the college."

Russell sums up the Little I experience, saying: "It's just sort of a tradition. It's the best in the United States."

Chapter 57

The Day President Kennedy Died

At South Dakota State, as with every other campus across America, the start of the 1960s marked heady times for college and university students.

President John F. Kennedy had taken office, ushering in the so-called days of Camelot. The Vietnam War, the Cold War, the Cuban Missile Crisis, the civil rights and feminist movements — all would test the nation's mettle. But not quite yet.

If there was an idyllic time in American life, this — straddling the cusp between the '50s and '60s — was it. Particularly in retrospect.

"When I think about the Kennedy administration," says Terry Nelson,

---

Pictured above, President John F. Kennedy speaks in South Dakota.

class of 1965, "it really was a Camelot. Jackie was a beautiful lady; Jack, a handsome young man, with a lot of idealism. That's where the Peace Corps came from."

Lyle Merriman, also class of 1965, reflects: "The late 1950s were just like 'Happy Days' (the popular television sitcom of the 1970s). We didn't have a lot to be concerned about. Then, we got into the 1960s and we started realizing what was gone."

In just a few short years, Camelot was overrun by the flaws of humanity, both on national and worldwide levels.

Summing up the dramatic and immediate shift, Nelson says: "When Kennedy was shot, idealism went away. (Lyndon) Johnson took over and we got deeper into Vietnam. It was a terrible war. People were getting killed. There was the Gulf of Tonkin incident. Almost in one day, we went from total innocence to the Vietnam War, to death, to reality."

If you were old enough, the assassination of President Kennedy on Nov. 22, 1963, as he rode in a motorcade on the streets of Dallas, Texas, marked one of those instant-recall events. Forty years later, people still remember that Friday in November when they heard the news. The classic funeral footage that followed of Kennedy's casket and a stoic Jackie, flanked by Caroline and a saluting John-John, remain lasting images.

"I was student-teaching in Pipestone, Minn.," says Mary Monahan Broomell, class of 1964. "I was teaching ninth grade and the coordinating teacher was out sick. I had full responsibility for the class. We heard about it at noon, during lunch hour. We heard he was shot. Then at the end of fourth period, they came around and said, 'You have to announce to your class that the president is dead.' It was just rough — one of the roughest announcements. I kind of had to hold it together."

Sandra Rae Henningsen, also class of 1964, says she was in her dorm room when she heard the news: "You just felt numb. A complete sense of shock. I know I was anxious to see if there was anything on TV. The news was overwhelming with sorrow, overwhelming grief."

Henningsen's voice tightens and wavers. "It's even difficult to talk about it today."

Nelson recalls: "They closed the campus. Nothing was going on. It was almost like they shut the lights out. It was a normal college day and then he was shot. By the afternoon, the campus was just like a tomb."

Merriman says he was at lunch when the news started spreading by word of mouth: "I quick finished lunch and went back to my dorm room and turned on the radio. I just listened and listened. I had a 1 o'clock music theory class. I took my portable radio to class and with the teacher's permission, listened. During the class, they announced that he was dead. I announced it to the class. The teacher said, 'Let's go home.'"

Describing the range of emotions, Merriman adds: "First, you didn't want to believe it. ... Then, you were sad, just so sad. We thought, how can this happen in this beautiful country of ours? How can this happen? I can remember just feeling horrible."

For the South Dakota State campus, that particular Friday meant more than the typical start to a weekend.

The military ball — the biggest formal event of the year — was set for that night in the Christy Ballroom. The longstanding tradition involved pomp and circumstance, full military dress for the men, gowns for the women, and big-time bands. The 1963 event, dubbed "Autumn Rhythm," was to feature the swing music of Guy Lombardo and his Royal Canadians.

"The military ball was a big, big event," says Nelson. "I had a date coming from Dakota Wesleyan. I can remember exactly where I was standing. I was in Brown Hall, excitedly awaiting the biggest dance of the year. Then, they made the announcement that Kennedy had died. A lot of us didn't understand the significance right away."

Broomell says: "I think it kind of hit then. Except, when I look back on it, I realize it was the beginning of a whole series of events. Kennedy, (Martin Luther) King, the war. I just look at it as the end of innocence. We were young and innocent; nothing bad had happened. It was sort of a blissful time."

With the ball canceled and completely forgotten, Henningsen says: "we were glued to the television, watching pictures, listening to reports, talking to one another. It was a rude awakening; a hiccup in a life which was very idyllic and filled with optimism. It was a reality check. I think it made us realize there would be trials and traumas we would have to accept in life and move on in a positive manner."

On Sunday, Nov. 24, a capacity crowd filled the State Fieldhouse to pay tribute to Kennedy. The backdrop for the memorial service was a floral blanket of the corsages the men had purchased for their dates to wear to the military ball. Classes resumed the following day. As life returned to the ordinary routine, disbelief continued to hang heavy in the air.

The yearbook reported, "Although they watched the events as they happened, many of the students didn't feel the real impact of what had happened until days later as they crossed the campus and saw the flags flying half-mast and fellow students minus their usual smiles and cheerful greetings."

Nelson says there was some concern in the days that followed about who

Memorial for President Kennedy

A capacity crowd gathered in the State Fieldhouse Nov. 24 to pay tribute to the late President John F. Kennedy. A floral arrangement, made from Military Ball corsages donated by State coeds, hangs on the backdrop.
—Collegian Photo by Don Kerr

Picture taken for the Dec. 5, 1963, issue of the South Dakota Collegian highlighting the memorial held in President Kennedy's honor.

would run the country and whether there was a bigger plot than a lone gunman behind Kennedy's death.

For Merriman and the others, it is much easier 40 years later to put the assassination of the president in perspective.

"It was basically good times until the Cuban Missile Crisis," Merriman says. "That was probably my sophomore year. The big concern had been about the relationship between Cuba and Russia, particularly for college boys. I was on an educational deferment as far as the draft was concerned. We were watching that situation very closely.

"I can still see the newscast, when Russia was sending a missile on a boat to Cuba and the U.S. gave the ultimatum. I can still see that ship making a big turnaround and I remember thinking, 'Oh, phew.'"

In hindsight, Merriman adds, Kennedy's death marked the start of uncertain times and the end of life as people had known it. "Within a year or two, we were engulfed in Vietnam. (Before) you had your daily concerns just like you do now. But, I think the global concerns were much more minimal. Looking back, it was a much better time."

Ironically enough, the remarks Kennedy had intended to deliver to the Texas Democratic State Committee in Austin addressed the very fears and concerns that surfaced in the wake of his death:

"For this country is moving and it must not stop. It cannot stop. For this is a time for courage and a time for challenge. Neither conformity nor complacency will do. Neither the fanatics nor the faint-hearted are needed. And our duty as a party is not to our party alone, but to the Nation, and, indeed, to all mankind. Our duty is not merely the preservation of political power but the preservation of peace and freedom.

"So let us not be petty when our cause is so great. Let us not quarrel amongst ourselves when our Nation's future is at stake. Let us stand together with renewed confidence in our cause — united in our heritage of the past and our hopes for the future — and determined that this land we love shall lead all mankind into frontiers of peace and abundance."

Those words never came to pass. Instead, students at South Dakota State were left to sift through the jagged pieces of a harsh new reality.

Nelson says of the abrupt transition: "This was the '60s. We were very much idealists. With Kennedy's death, I think, we finally realized we were vulnerable."

Ultimately, though, there was nothing to do but forge ahead. After about a week of intense mourning, Broomell says, campus activities slowly but steadily resumed: "We were seniors in college. Life goes on."

Chapter 58

When the College Became a University

"What's in a name?" asked the 1916 Industrial Collegian. Ticking off the list of how students had been addressed by quest speakers — South Dakota Agricultural College, Brookings Agricultural College, Brookings College, Brookings University and State College — the Collegian fumed at the depth of ignorance.

"Perhaps our visitors do not stop to think of our real name," they wrote. "Perhaps they do not know our real name, and yet we cannot believe that our enlightened visitors can be entirely ignorant of the name of an institution which they are supporting. We correct the mistake wherever we see it, but with a population of about six hundred thousand, it will be a long time before every individual in South Dakota can be personally notified as to our real name."

In defense of the state's populace, the school's name had gone through a few changes in its early years, from Dakota Agricultural College to South

Picture taken for the February, 1964 Alumnus showing students Roger Christensen and Pat Dixon and their reaction to the news that State attained university status.

Dakota Agricultural College to South Dakota State College of Agriculture and Mechanic Arts, and finally, to South Dakota State College.

By 1964, the school would undergo one last name change — South Dakota State University. But, the switch would not come easily. In fact, in 1957, when North Dakota State College was pushing to become a university, Collegian editors saw no reason to support the move.

"We wonder why any college would want to change its name after an institution's years of existence," the campus paper weighed in with an editorial. "Surely a large business establishment would not change its name after thousands of persons have associated its products and manufacturing name. This belief also pertains to NDSC. It is unlikely that the institution will benefit by a new title. Publicizing the present name seems more logical."

Barely four years later, the Collegian altered its stance. In the fall of 1961, South Dakota State was one of three remaining land-grant institutions that had yet to change its name to university.

"A name change to university would give a more adequate indication of what type of education is offered here," reasoned a Nov. 22, 1961, Collegian editorial. "The proposed change might also pave the way to State's offering of a bachelor of arts degree."

Harold Bailey, then dean of academic affairs, says it was a natural move to call South Dakota State a university.

"For many years, we had felt we were a true university," Bailey says, explaining the rationale. "We had colleges, even though they were called divisions, and each separate instructional entity had a dean. We had a grad school. We had all the makings of a university without being allowed to call ourselves a university."

By 1963, backers of the name change were mustering support for legislation.

Before the Board of Regents' January meeting, about 2,100 students — two-third's of State's enrollment at the time — had signed a petition calling on the regents to recommend a name change to the state Legislature. The petition drive was sponsored by the men's service fraternity, Alpha Phi Omega.

Sentiment on campus in favor of the switch continued to swell.

"Sixty-five of 68 land-grant schools are now officially termed as universities," argued the Jan. 10, 1963, Collegian. "The college name is now representative of what were formerly called teachers' colleges. By lagging behind, our state is contributing to confusing and chaotic situations, which could easily be alleviated by enacting a name change."

In addition to the technical issues, the Collegian pointed to the added prestige that would come with adding "university" to South Dakota State.

"Unless we are preparing to teach, we will be going out to get jobs and work beside college graduates from universities. We would like to be able to state that we, too, were graduated from a university. ... A name change should also facilitate in hiring and retaining faculty, since prospective instructors prefer to be associated with a university."

Not everyone, however, agreed. Some of the state's newspapers editorialized against the name change, saying that confusion would result from having South Dakota State University and the University of South Dakota. When the deadline passed for legislation in 1963 session, no measures had been filed to address the switch.

Believing that their cause was just, Bailey says, people were frustrated as the fight continued from one year to the next.

"It wasn't until the early '60s that there was real movement in the Legislature," he notes, "but it was countered by the University of South Dakota. They felt there shouldn't be two universities."

In the fall of 1963, State President Hilton Briggs led the charge.

"Montana State College and we are the only two land-grant schools with the name 'college' attached to our titles," Briggs told the Sept. 19, 1963, Collegian. "It appears to us that this is one category in which South Dakota does not have to be last."

Briggs said SDSC was running into roadblocks when competing for potential staff, employment opportunities for graduates and grants and gifts at the national level.

"If your name is such that it doesn't describe your institution," said Briggs, "you find yourself constantly explaining it."

In October 1963, the regents held their monthly meeting at South Dakota State. A few mischievous landscapers saw an opportunity to promote the name-change agenda, rearranging the flower beds at the Medary Avenue entrance to campus to read SDSU instead of SDSC. Physical plant employees quickly replanted the flowers into the proper arrangement.

Part of the debate, according to Bailey, was the "silly argument" that the name switch would cost money to change letterhead stationery and re-mark the SDSC vehicle fleet.

"That came up in the Legislature," Bailey says. "They said it would be too expensive. It turned out to be a big political struggle — the University of South Dakota versus South Dakota State. Just one of the many."

During their October meeting, the regents asked the attorney general's office for a ruling on whether the Legislature had the authority to change the

Headline from the February 13, 1964 South Dakota Collegian.

school's name. Elgie Coacher, then executive secretary for the regents, explained to the Collegian that there was a question whether the change warranted a constitutional amendment. They didn't have to wait long.

Farrar Favors Name Change, reported the lead headline of the Nov. 7, 1963, Collegian, referring to State Attorney General Frank Farrar's opinion.

Speaking to the Campus Young Republicans several days earlier, Farrar had said: "I vigorously endorse the name change. ... We are energetically researching all aspects of the constitution for some way for the Legislature to legally change the name without a referendum."

As expected, USD did not jump readily on the bandwagon. The director of the USD Alumni Association, Tom Brisbane, wrote a letter urging alumni and friends of USD to oppose the name change. He complained that the university title would give State "leverage for expansion" and questioned the cost of two universities.

But in January 1964, Farrar issued a ruling to settle the issue:

"The legislature does have the power to change the name of a higher educational institution of learning in the State of South Dakota to a university or a college, and the Board of Regents does not have this power."

Farrar also pointed out that state legislators had the "duty and the responsibility to secure the advantages of education for the people."

The name-change bill passed both the House and Senate during the 1964 legislative session, but not without an effort by some to call the school South Dakota State University of Agriculture and Applied Science. That amendment ultimately lost out and the name switch went through as intended, becoming effective by law on July 1, 1964. Brookings legislators — Sen. Gordon Mydland, class of 1947, and Rep. John Bibby, class of 1942 — were credited with getting the legislation passed.

Briggs said the bill's legislative success was "an expression of confidence that this institution would continue to provide the finest type of education that is possible under the program on which we operate."

The following fall semester, the admissions office at SDSU reported a record enrollment — 3,938. The figure was 464 more than the fall of 1963.

Chapter 59

The Rules Have Changed

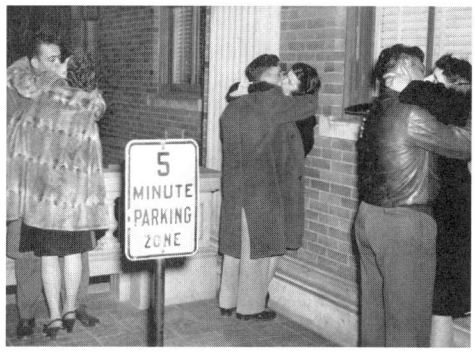

Friday, Nov. 20, 1885, the first girls moved onto campus at Dakota Agricultural College. Within two weeks, a new rule was established — young ladies could not receive gentlemen visitors (except for their brothers) in their room under any circumstances.

It would take 86 years for that policy to fall. And even then, it did not fall easily.

On Oct. 14, 1971, Binnewies Hall became the first of South Dakota State University's nine dormitories to permit visitation.

Weekly visitation totaled 28 hours, which were evenly divided between men and women. Hours on the women's wings were 7-10 p.m. Thursday, 7-11 p.m. Friday, 8-12 p.m. Saturday and 7-10 p.m. Sunday. Hours for the men's rooms were 7-10 p.m. Tuesday, 7-11 p.m. Friday, 2-6 p.m. Saturday and 2-5 p.m. Sunday.

The Oct. 19, 1971, Collegian explained that the drive for visitation began

---

Pictured above, college couples engage in last-minute romance just prior to curfew. This evening ritual became known as "mush rush."

in 1970, starting with approval by the Board of Regents. Binnewies then set up a judiciary body and prepared for a secret ballot vote by the hall's residents. The measure needed a two-thirds approval. Then, the plan was submitted to the residence hall director for review and to the Housing Subcommittee of the Student Affairs Committee for approval. The final version went back to the hall's residents for another vote, which also had to pass by a two-thirds margin.

By current standards, these rules sound dated. But they are nowhere near as severe as in the decades prior to the change.

Jim Marking, class of 1946, and his wife, Carola, class of 1948, find humor today in the rules that governed their years on campus.

"Our curfew was 10:30 during the week and 12 on Friday and Saturday," says Carola. "It was 10:30 on Sunday. There were no curfews for guys."

The men were allowed to visit the women in the common rooms of residence halls. One time, laughs Jim, "Carola was sitting on my lap and the house mother put a magazine underneath her."

Carola adds: "She told us, 'These men are here for one purpose. You be careful. They come in here with their shiny shoes and they've got one thing on their mind — they want to look up your skirt.'"

Carola also remembers the dress code. "My roommate went to play tennis and wore a short skirt or shorts. She didn't change clothes after and when she came in at 10:30, she was grounded."

Most of the girls wore long skirts, even in the winter. Only three or four students had a car.

Bob Karolevitz attended South Dakota State from 1940-43 and then graduated in 1947. He says that with Dean of Women Vivian Volstorff in charge, the guys never thought of breaking the rules by visiting a girl's room. In those years, the curfew was set at 10 p.m.

"When 10 o'clock came," Karolevitz says, "she (Volstorff) came out and jingled her keys and, boy, we all went running. The women went in and the guys went back to the dorm."

Mary Zulk, class of 1967, says the arrival of curfew set off what was known as Mush Rush: "Whether you had to be in at 10 or 11 or 12, you would wait until the absolute last minute, parked in cars, everybody was making out, and the lights would flicker. You'd have one minute to get in before they locked the doors. You would literally be locked out. Although, there were always girls sneaking in through windows."

During her years on campus, from 1963-67, Zulk says women were not allowed to live off-campus.

"When I was there, I was 22, still living in the dorm," she says. "I can remember being 21 and I could go vote for president, but I had to be in at 10 o'clock — 12 o'clock on Friday and Saturday. Sure, we all complained about it ... but you didn't really question it because that's the way it was. I can remember the injustice, that it didn't seem very fair, but I don't remember comparing us to the boys."

It wasn't until the Vietnam War that people started speaking up and voicing opinions, she recalls. No one talked about divorce or pregnancy, and girls didn't play sports. That was why, Zulk says, she became a cheerleader — it was the closest she could get to athletics.

To go anywhere, the women had to sign out and sign back in.

"I remember that I was invited to a formal in Des Moines, Iowa, by a high school friend," laughs Zulk. "My mom and dad had to write letters. ... Vivian Volstorff, the dean of women at the time, she was pretty straight-laced. Kind of from the old school."

Barb Fishback, class of 1972, remembers the sign-up sheets: "There were about 10 questions. Where you were going and with whom, what time you were leaving, what time you were coming back — even if you went home for the weekend. The guys, they had no hours. ... And, of course, there was Mush Rush. Everybody would be making out in the lobby."

By the time she was on campus from 1968-72, Fishback says, the weekday curfew had been extended to 11 p.m. She also recalls the first meeting with her floor's resident assistant: "She said it was a good idea to wear skirts to ball games. That's what girls did. Although, by the end, girls were all wearing jeans, except in the College of Home Economics."

At age 94, Martin Taylor, class of 1932, notes, "There were rules against scuffling in the halls and that sort of thing, making noises and disturbing students who might have been studying."

One of the traditions in the residence halls, says Taylor, was to have your room "stacked."

"You didn't fit into the student body if you didn't have your room stacked — you'd come back and find everything torn apart," he says. "You weren't accepted as part of the group if you didn't have your room stacked at least once. ...

"There also was a well-accepted rumor that if you had liquor in your room, don't leave it there over Christmas vacation because the administration went through your room. If you had some liquor, a bottle might last you for a whole quarter. Typically, it had to be bootleg stuff. The going price was $5 a quart. It was just moonshine-type liquor — you got a quart at the start of

Interesting newspaper headline from the Jan. 19, 1949, issue of the South Dakota Collegian.

the term and it would probably last."

According to a 1949 Collegian article, the housemothers of Wenona, Wecota and Annex — "the homes of the weaker sex of SDSC" — appointed weekly proctors to take bed checks at curfew and make sure everyone was in:

"A very frequent happening is to knock at about four doors and find no one at home. The fifth door usually brings results; ten or fifteen girls are having a gab session and upon seeing the proctor, all try to yell out their room numbers at once, much to the confusion of the proctor. Even more confusing is the two or three strange faces that belong in one of the other dorms, where their proctor is tearing her hair out trying to find them.

"Getting in on gab sessions is only part of the things a proctor runs into — there are haircutting episodes, birthday parties, and sometimes even a room where two 'brains' are studying — it has happened."

As much as the regents and college administrators may have tried to keep the genders apart, shifting trends in the student population sometimes made that policy difficult, if not impossible, to maintain.

In 1962, for example, a rise in the number of women filled the four available dormitories beyond capacity. Consequently, the first floor of Scobey Hall was taken over by women for the 1962-63 school year. The April 12, 1962, Collegian reported the news: "Wardrobes consisting of cocktail dresses and high-heeled shoes will find their place in the closets of Scobey Hall, now filled with ROTC uniforms and western attire, when the school term begins next fall."

The campus paper noted that East Men's Hall previously was run as a coed dorm, but that practice was discontinued in January 1940, when Wecota Annex opened. East Men's had housed both men and women since 1932. To accommodate the women in Scobey, the Collegian noted that draperies, irons and ironing boards were ordered for the entire floor. Preference for the Scobey rooms was based on class rank, with seniors having first dibs. The cost per quarter was $54, compared to the Waneta charge of $72.

That same spring, shortly after the announcement was made about Scobey going coed, the Collegian called for a relaxation of rules in the women's dorms.

"Let's start running our women's housing units like college dormitories rather than like high school boarding houses," the Collegian editors griped. "When freshmen first arrive on campus they are informed they are now young adults and ready to face the world."

However, the editorial pointed out, the list of rules regulating the women's dorms was long and detailed. Room checks were held once a week. No food was allowed on the window sills, beds were made, floors and furniture were dusted, desks were cleared, closets were cleaned and no empty pop bottles were left hanging around. Curfew hours were set at 10:15 p.m. during the week for freshmen and sophomores and 10:30 p.m. for upperclassmen. Friday nights, everyone faced a 12:30 a.m. curfew. Saturday was 1 a.m.

"It seems that by the time coeds are old enough to select a college and a vocation they are certainly capable of keeping their rooms cleaned," reasoned the editorial. "When is a coed to be able to rely on her own judgment? When she graduates at the age of 21 or 22? ... Certainly every college must set up some restrictions, but it does seem that there is a limit. College students are not juveniles and should not be treated as such. It is time for some revision in the college disciplinary code."

The following fall, dorm hours for women continued to stir debate — at least in the campus paper. Housemothers faithfully enforced the curfews, which were not so faithfully followed by students living in the four women's dorms. The female student, according to the Collegian, "must accustom herself to the idea that she is no longer as responsible for making her own decisions as she was in high school. ...

"She must learn that arriving at the dorm on time is more important than seeing the end of a movie, finishing a hand of cards, getting a snack after a dance, or any activity that would take her past the specified hour for that night."

By the spring of 1964, with increased enrollment projected, there was speculation about off-campus housing for women. However, at that time, women were not even allowed to make off-campus visits. That privilege would not come to pass until 1968.

In March 1966, curfew hours were back in the news, with the women making significant strides. The changes included an 11 p.m. curfew for sophomores, juniors and seniors Monday through Thursday — a 30-minute extension. Friday night shifted to 1 a.m. for all classes. Saturday night stayed at 1 a.m. Sunday went from 11 to 11:30 p.m.

As welcome as the later hours were, the sign-out process and prohibition of off-campus visits still rankled the student body.

There was a mass punishment of Pierson Hall's 450 residents in February 1967 after the dorm's sign-out cards went missing. No one was allowed out for one night, but few minded because it was a Monday. The cards turned up the same night, outside Pierson Hall and with a Valentine's card signed "The Mad Sons."

The fall semester of 1967 arrived and the Students' Association Board of Control moved toward allowing women to visit male students' off-campus apartments. Any board action was subject to approval by then-President Hilton Briggs and the Board of Regents. A petition protesting the rule that forbid visitation drew at least 1,000 signatures.

The regents were open to the change. Said the board's president, Charles Burke, "I see nothing wrong with a woman going to a man's off-campus apartment. It is a not a legal issue, but a moral one."

"The (current) regulation is ridiculous," fumed an Oct. 18, 1967, Collegian editorial, titled "Let the Girls In." "It is based on the assumption that women who visit men's apartments engage in sexual intercourse. This is seldom the case.

"And even if the regulation was enforceable, it would not prevent sexual activity. There are, after all, motel rooms and cars. (Maybe some couple will die this winter of carbon monoxide poisoning while upholding the housing office's principle of virtue.)"

On Dec. 1, 1967, State's Housing and Food Service Committee approved the recommended change, but not without debate over how stringent the visitation rule should be. Two amendments designed to ease the restriction for freshman and sophomore women failed. The first measure would have exempted both classes. The second was aimed at just the sophomores.

The Rules Have Changed

According to a Collegian report at the time, Dave Pearson, then assistant to the president and chairman of the housing committee, reminded the students that they were not the only constituency: "The students are a vital public, but we are responsible to a lot of publics, including 15,000 alumni, parents and legislators. We have to be conscious of public mores in South Dakota."

Dean Volstorff also defended the restriction, arguing that women control society's moral standards: "We have to pin our faith on women controlling moral standards if we are going to have any in the future."

The recommended policy stipulated that contractual agreements for visits must be made with landlords and that all visits take place in the "living areas" of an apartment or house. Visits to one-room apartments, therefore, were prohibited.

To be sure, parents did not like the idea women visiting men — on or off campus. A survey asked 1,000 parents whether they approved of women visiting men's dorm rooms. In a resounding 3-1 ratio, the parents said "no."

"This is only the first step in the path of decay of our schools," one parent commented.

Said another: "If they cannot do it or say it in the lounge, it should not be done or said."

A legislator from Mitchell wrote in, "I will terminate my financial and legislative support to State University if the above program is initiated."

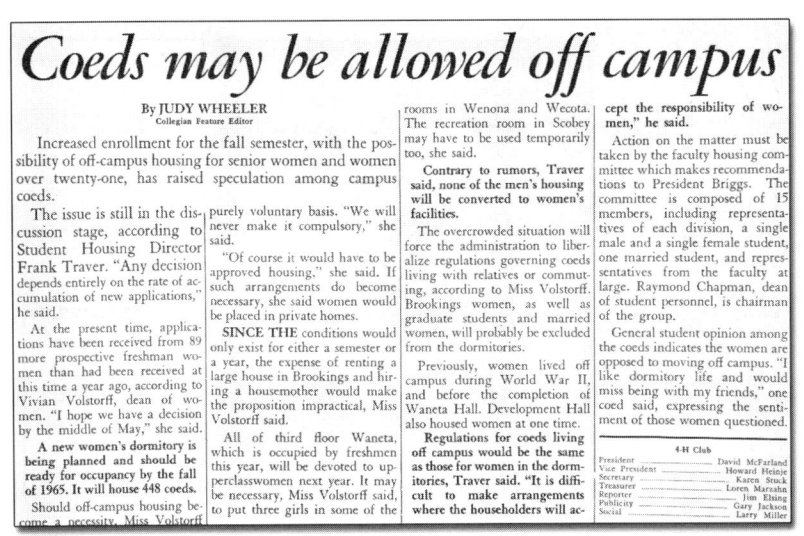

April 30, 1964, headline in the South Dakota Collegian trumpets the possibility that women may be allowed to live off campus.

Despite such strong opposition, women in February 1968 won the right to visit men off campus. Or, at least some of them did when Briggs approved rule revisions. Junior and senior women gained the new privilige of off-campus visitation. Freshman and sophomore women had to have parental permission to do so.

Then, in June 1971, one momentous event radically altered future debates over students' rights. On June 30, 11.5 million 18-year-olds joined the American electorate, effectively making them adults overnight. Whether they were mature enough to handle the shift in responsibility was a moot point.

James O. Pedersen, who was dean of student services from 1970 to 1984, witnessed up close the changing times. He had arrived on campus in 1957 and worked first in admissions. In 1965, he became director of admissions and records, serving in that position until transferring to student services. Pedersen became dean of General Registration and director of the Career and Academic Planning Center in 1984 and worked in that capacity until his retirement in 1996.

"That was the most challenging time," Pedersen says, referring to the early 1970s. "When it changed so that 18-year-olds got to vote, that had huge implications. The university had operated as if it had a parental responsibility — in loco parentis."

The Latin phrase means, "In the position or place of parent." When 18-year-olds became adults, that policy was no longer valid. Students were totally free and supposedly responsible for themselves. That transition was instant.

"But, just because you change the law, that doesn't mean students instantly become mature and responsible," says Pedersen. "They were very interested in the freedom side, but not always in the responsibility side. There were a lot of struggles."

Prior to the change in voting age, residence hall behavior was governed by proctors, who had the right to check rooms and make sure students obeyed curfew regulations.

"What the university believed in," says Pedersen, "was influencing proper behavior until students became an adult. ... Responsible college staff members were not required to abstain from the moral and ethical corrections and directions thought to be relevent to students' needs.

"In reality, there was an expectation that college student affairs staff — especially the deans of men and women — was expected to both control and modify student behavior in conjunction with college rules under the permission of in loco parentis."

Without the in loco parentis authority, Pedersen continues, students began to demand their adult rights. The Vietnam War only added to the complex nature of the times. Pedersen says the era was extremely challenging for the university. One of his dominant memories of the transition to shared control between the adult staff and students was the impatience of students.

They didn't understand, he says, "why there had to be so many committee meetings to decide how and when students could have more control and freedom concerning their out-of-class lives and living arrangements. On the other side were the uneasy faculty and staff who were not willing to give up control until some form of student self-government was in place."

In the fall of 1971, dorm visitation got off to a slow start. Binnewies, as mentioned earlier, was the first residence hall to enjoy the new freedom. The Binnewies rule, which was approved by a campus housing subcommittee, operated on a closed-door policy. Hanson also secured the same status.

However, as other dorms started filing visitation plans, President Briggs informed the housing subcommittee that it could not approve any more closed-door options. Binnewies residents then voted in November — after only one month of visitation — to join forces with Brown and Mathews halls to suspend visitation until an agreement was reached on the closed-door issue.

First, the matter went to the SA's Board of Control, where debate broke out over the University of South Dakota's policy. On paper, the Collegian reported, the U had an open-door policy. But in practice, State students alleged, the Vermillion campus had closed-door visitation.

The regents took up the issue at their Nov. 18, 1971, meeting and passed an open-door visitation policy. Several weeks later, Briggs wrote a letter to deans and residence hall staffs, defining "open door" as being "wide open so all parts of the room are in full view." By the fall semester of 1973, visitation began at most of the nine residence halls on the State campus.

Crediting Briggs with navigating the turbulent waters of the early 1970s, Pedersen says, "His leadership and wisdom had a profound and stabilizing influence during those changing and challenging times."

Once men and women were allowed in each other's rooms, the focus turned to 3.2-percent alcohol beer. In September 1972, a Collegian opinion piece pointed out that students of legal drinking age who lived off campus could drink in the comfort of their own rentals.

"So why not give those people in the dorm the opportunity to drink in their rooms?" the writer asked. "We can go back to our hometowns and sit in the living room with mom and dad and drink, but we are not allowed to do it at school. ... We can walk one block from the dorm to an off-campus dwelling and have a beer with a colleague, but not in our 'living quarters' in the dormitory. How can the regents justify the double standard that they uphold? What are they protecting us from?"

As restrictions eased, the hall staff remained responsible for enforcing rules, according to Pedersen. However, he says, "I remember a meeting with all of the RAs where they exposed the fact that the rules were no longer being followed and the expectation that the university imposed on them to be the enforcer of the rules was no longer valid.

"The challenge to the university was to determine how self-government of students could take place in the halls."

The student code of conduct, complete with violations and consequences, had to be balanced with the individual rights of students, Pedersen says. Students had a right to know the charges against them, they had a right to be heard, and certain rules had to be followed before judgments were handed down.

"We had to go from the university being totally in charge to developing a system whereby indivdual student freedoms were respected," Pedersen says. "The dean of men, Orlin Walder, chaired a committee that wrote the student code. That code is still in place, with modifications. It was the first time that the university had to include students in creating expectations about behavior. Prior to that, the proctors had the rules and regulations book and everybody was to follow the rules. When the students got the right to vote, they also demanded participation in the creation of the rules."

In the spring of 1974, students rallied around the "74 Dorm Reform."

DAKOTA AGRICULTURAL COLLEGE.
Dormitory Regulations.

☞ *Students occupying rooms in the Dormitory must*

1. Keep their rooms neat and otherwise in good order, subject to the daily inspection of the person in charge.

2. Make good, damage to furniture, steam and other fixtures, the breaking of window glass or other damages done, except when those causing the injury are reported.

3. Not drive nails into the wall or put locks on the doors without permission of the proper authorities.

4. Not throw slops or other refuse out of the windows.

5. Not keep or use fire-arms, (including pistols and revolvers, and the cadet musket, swords, bayonets, etc.) in or about the Dormitory buildings.

6. Observe study hours, avoiding all noisy and boisterous conduct which may disturb other students.

7. Not visit the city of Brookings between the hours of seven in the evening and seven in the morning, except by special permission of the Professor in charge.

NOTE.—This rule does not apply to Juniors and Seniors.

8. Act as Floor Marshal one month each term, if elected to the position, and respect the authority of others acting as Marshal, when in the discharge of duty.

☞ Students who do not occupy rooms in the Dormitory are forbidden to visit the same at any time, except by permission of the President or the person in charge of the Dormitory.

A failure to observe the above Regulations forfeits the student's right to a room.

Early dormitory regulations from the records of professor R.F. Kerr. (Courtesy SDSU Archives and Special Collections)

The Rules Have Changed

The campaign consisted of six recommendations aimed at achieving a "new, constructive" dorm attitude:
- That the roles of resident assistants, housing student assistants and residence hall directors be shifted from enforcing regulations to counseling and solving problems.
- That hall governments implement study hours to reduce distracting noise.
- That individuals of legal age be allowed to consume 3.2 beer in their dorm rooms under guidelines and regulations established by wing and dorm supervision.
- That visitation policies be established by individual dorm wings, with designated wings available for those who did not want visitation to be allowed.
- That new campus-wide policies be decided by a committee composed of at least 50 percent students.
- That dorm contracts be decided on a semester basis, with students given the option of whether they want to live with someone of similar or different interests.

At their May 1974 meeting, the regents extended weekend visitation hours to 2 a.m., but delayed action on allowing alcohol in dorm rooms. Two months later, at its July meeting, the board decided to permit the consumption of 3.2 beer in dorm rooms by students 18 and older.

But, there was more to campus and off-campus life than drinking low-point beer and visiting the opposite sex. A student's residence, whether a hall or neighborhood rental, is one of the few constants in an ever-changing landscape of generational shifts and societal trends.

In the spring of 1944, the male students went to war and left behind an empty dorm.

"Tonight the winds sigh and shriek and howl around the imposing, aged, lonely East Men's Hall," wrote Anne Miller in the March 29 edition of the Collegian. "Strange indeed must be this cold darkness that pervades and echoes in East Hall's corridors. ... Silence and inactivity after years of excitement, laughter and youth must be different and almost sad to this old building.

"Since 1919, when our legislature appropriated money to build a dorm to house disabled veterans, until this fall, East Men's had never known a moment's silence."

In its time, East Men's went from freshman boys to a wing for "Aggies," both men and women and an overflow spot for women. From 1929 to 1942, the hall housed a nursery school on the first floor. Then, the Army Air Corps Enlisted Branch No. 3 turned it into a barracks.

By 1947, East Men's was back to life. A Collegian article warned that the residence hall was not the place for the student who liked consistency, routine and privacy: "If you think the Jungle is a busy place, you should spend five minutes counting the faces running in and out of East Men's. Next year they plan on installing stop and go lights."

Dean Volstorff found her job as dean of women equally challenging, including the memorable time she discovered a calf in the women's dormitory lobby. Volstorff apparently heard an odd "clicking" sound one night. Upon finding the calf, she called the night watchman, who came to remove the "cat" after misunderstanding the dean on the phone.

In the late 1940s, the problem wasn't so much visiting girls, but calling them. The Collegian ran a first-person account detailing the trials and tribulations of an attempt to ring up a coed:

"Having selected our candidate from the narrow field of our coed acquaintances, we picked up the phone and whispered to the operator the almost sacred number of Wecota. On our sixth attempt, we got through, and gave the desk girl at Wecota the name of our idol of the evening. We waited, puffing frantically at our pipe, for a few minutes. A voice felt its way out of the phone and said — 'Number please.'

"Not to be easily discouraged we answered, 'Wecota.' Wecota came through with 'Wecota Hall' and the operator waited a few seconds before coming again with 'Number please.' After a few rounds of this we hung up, bafffled, to contemplate the new development."

In April 1958, the Collegian reported on plans to improve the phone system in the women's dorms — a telephone on each floor, totaling three phones in Wenona, three in Wecota and four in the Annex.

It is almost inconceivable for college students today to imagine a time when women had to abide by a different set of standards than men — and not speak out in opposition, or marshal the forces to bring about change.

"It simply was part of the culture at the time," explains Pedersen. "Women were to be protected and men had freedoms that women did not enjoy. ... Even now, as I think about it, I am struggling to try and explain it. That time was so far from where we are now."

The prevailing wisdom in those days also saw the need to protect women from men, Pedersen adds, and there was no trusting the two genders together. "Part of the thinking was that keeping them separate avoided fraternization, avoided illicit sexual activity."

Pedersen credits Volstorff, who served as dean of women from 1932 to 1973, with fostering the slow evolution on campus between the teas and Maypole dances: "Part of her career was to bring about equal opportunity and equal treatment. She was an early women's libber, even though she was very politically smart about this. She knew it was not going to come about overnight."

Sure enough, as the years passed, the restrictions eased. Visiting hours, dress codes, off-campus options, dining services — many changes took place to accommodate students' individual freedoms. The changes have been so substantial, that a look through the 2002-03 Residential Life handbook finds little, if anything, comparable to the rules of 40, 30 and even 20 years ago.

Behavior guidelines are expectations rather than ironclad dictates. Halls are locked not to keep out the opposite gender, but for the safety of residents. Visitation rules permit guests seven days a week, nearly 24 hours a day. The only time you can't have a visitor of the opposite sex in your room is from 2 a.m. to 10:30 a.m. Monday through Friday, and 3 a.m. to 10:30 a.m. Saturday and Sunday.

Pedersen says the issue of visiting paled in comparison to making dorms coed. He recalls, in particular, a 1970 visit with a regents committee in Pierre. The SA president and vice president, Bob Quinn and Mary McEldowney, made the trip with Pedersen. Their goal was to explain some of the merits behind coed halls.

"When we got back, people asked, 'How did it go?' " Pedersen remembers. "I said it was probably similar to appearing before a committee of Congress and advocating the virtues of communism."

Chapter 60

Olivia's Kiss

As a member of the Pershing Rifles, an ROTC group of Army and Air Force cadets, Bruce Olson, class of 1976, often worked campus concerts as part of the security crew.

The Olivia Newton-John performance scheduled for Spring Music Festival on Wednesday, April 24, 1974, started out as the typical duty.

"We'd get the nod to come over, wear security T-shirts and try to keep order," recalls Olson.

In addition to Newton-John, the concert billing included folk rock musician Denny Brooks and El Chicano, the band made famous by its 1970 hit, "Viva Tirado," an homage to a Mexican bullfighter. The event was one of the early concerts to be held in Frost Arena, which had opened barely a year earlier.

Olson says the goal for the security crew was twofold — discourage concertgoers from smoking and from holding up their lighters at the end of songs. University officials were nervous about any damage to the new basketball floor.

Picture from the 1974 Jackrabbit yearbook of Olivia Newton-John during her performance at Frost Arena on April 24, 1974.

"They gave us all a flashlight," Olson says, "but people were not reacting well to getting a flashlight beamed in their face. It was just open revolt."

The security crew backed off and watched. Newton-John, who Olson thinks followed El Chicano as the second act, finished her set and descended the stage to sign autographs.

"She looked great," says Olson. "A lot of people had programs for her to sign, but I didn't have a program. I had a T-shirt. I asked her if she would mind autographing my shirt and I turned around so she could sign the back.

"When she was done, I turned around to say thank you and she gave me a great big kiss on the cheek. She was so radiant. I didn't wash my face for a week."

Bob Roe, class of 1976, says: "I can remember just being mesmerized, kind of awestruck. ... She was the most beautiful woman I think I had ever seen. Of course, it was long before I met my wife."

Dave DeVos, class of 1975, had booked the concert in his student government role of social chairman.

"With Olivia, as I remember it, that was her first college concert ever and first concert ever in United States," DeVos says. "I don't know if that's 100 percent accurate. The night after Brookings, though, she did 'The Midnight Special' show with Wolfman Jack and that jump-started her career."

The 1974 yearbook said Newton-John's performance was her first concert in the United States.

"Olivia brought a little country and a lotta love to America and the crowd could tell: three standing ovations, one at the start, one in the middle, and one at the end," the Jack Rabbit said. "Fantastic."

Newton-John says she does not remember if SDSU was her first show in the States. But, clearly, the campus does hold some memories for her.

"What's the little animal you have associated with your school?" she asks.

She also remembers what she wore — denim bell-bottoms and a floral-patterned peasant blouse with wide-mouthed sleeves — and that she had to change clothes in the locker room.

As best as he can recall, DeVos figures it cost about $1,500 to bring Newton-John to campus. Her popularity had been increasing overseas as she scored a top-10 hit in the United Kingdom with Bob Dylan's "If Not For You."

Listeners in the United States also knew her songs "Let Me Be There," "I Honestly Love You," and "Have You Never Been Mellow." Four years after her appearance at SDSU, in 1978, Newton-John co-starred with John Travolta in the hit movie musical "Grease."

"This (concert) was a big deal for me," remembers Newton-John. "It was very nerve-racking. John Farrar wrote all my songs. He also played the guitar. I was consoling him before the show and he was consoling me."

Part of the stress stemmed from the fact that Newton-John faced last-minute band changes.

"The first band I was assigned was very, very bad," she says. "We had to find another band. We practiced three hours in Minneapolis and then all the way on the bus. It was a Greyhound bus and the toilet didn't work."

Roe says Newton-John put on a great show. As concerts go, though, the audience was small. The turnout of 900 resulted in a $5,000 loss, according to Collegian accounts at the time.

"It wasn't packed by any means," says Roe. "It probably had more to do with the fact that she wasn't a huge headliner. ... Something we had talked about was that it was her first concert in the United States and then she went on to be a great star. That's our claim to fame. SDSU was her first concert. But then, someone said that was not true, that she stopped in North Dakota first. I suppose that's possible."

Wherever she sang first, Olson enjoys his memories: "She was so happy and delighted and thrilled. And, she was just absolutely, incredibly beautiful. The people loved her."

From her vantage point on stage, Newton-John says: "It was a fantastic response from the audience. It was exciting and scary."

Of course, Olson still has the T-shirt with Newton-John's signature. But, he doesn't wear it.

Laughing, he says: "It'd take two of 'em now. Even back then, they ordered large, but they were more like large-small. When I was at 160 (pounds), it fit like a glove. Now, at 220, I could probably pull it on one leg."

DeVos says he has only one regret: "Our stage crew that helped out, we bought T-shirts for them. She asked for a T-shirt and asked for my autograph. Now, I'm thinking I should have asked for hers. Mine, I'm sure she doesn't have that anymore."

Newton-John laughs, "That's cute."

Chapter 61

The Humble Beginnings of Prairie Rep

Thirty-three years after the curtains first opened on Prairie Repertory, there is little evidence of the theater company's humble beginnings.

As was true with other good things that have become synonymous with South Dakota State University — including the establishment of the university itself — Prairie Rep's start was an adventure into the unknown.

Paul Redfield and Joe Habeger, two men not affiliated with State, envisioned creating Prairie Village in Madison. Redfield taught math at Dakota State University and Habeger was a retired railroad man.

"They were all enthused about bringing in the village to Madison," recalls Clare Denton, who had arrived at SDSC in 1956 to work as a designer and tech director in the mass communications department. "They were hauling in churches, hauling in all sorts of buildings, making streets. They got the opera

Pictured above, the Opera House at Prairie Village which once served as a home to Prairie Repertory Theatre. (Courtesy of Raymond Peterson)

house from Oldham. They were really excited about making the village a tourist attraction."

The pair called James Johnson, who was deep into his doctorate studies at DSU and passed them on to Denton.

"They contacted us and we met down the highway for coffee," Denton explains. "They were hopeful to have plays in the opera house. I had a film grant in 1970 and I was out filming. But Judith Zivanovic, she was in the department, and she prepared two plays and took them down to the village.

"There was no floor, just a frame and dirt. The balconies were hanging out over the dirt and they put a platform on top of oil cans. ... People came and sat on planks set on cement blocks."

The following summer, Denton had the idea of doing repertory theater. He had just returned from the University of Minnesota, where he was working on his master of fine arts. The concept of rep theater, as opposed to stock, is that one night you perform one play and the next night you perform another. In the early years, you could buy a season ticket the last week and see all the plays.

The philosophy was that rep theater generated audiences. If you missed a play and there were rave reviews, you could catch it the next time around. With stock, once a play is over, it's done.

"We'd study and have rehearsal every afternoon," Denton says. "We'd start at 4 o'clock and run to meal time. Then we'd rush off, get a sandwich, and come back and do the play. After the audience left, we'd strike the scenery and put up the new scenery."

The early effort, although difficult and draining, was exciting and educational for the students. For the 1971 season, Prairie Rep put on "Harvey," "Three Men on a Horse," "Arsenic and Old Lace," and "The Owl and the Pussycat." The following years were equally ambitious. In 1972, "My Three Angels," "Love Rides the Rails," "You're a Good Man, Charlie Brown," and "The Last of the Red Hot Lovers." In 1973, "The Man Who Came to Dinner," "The Seven Year Itch," "Plaza Suite," and "Two by Two."

The playbills showed the same names from one production to the next. The only thing to change were the roles. When needed, Denton and, when they were hired, Ray Peterson and James L. Johnson, acted as well. So did Denton's two children, Chris and Melissa.

"There were not enough people to go around," Denton explains. "We played bit parts. ... We had a hero in one of the plays who couldn't sing. Ray would stand behind the scenery and sing, and the actor would mouth it. Ray kept singing one time and the guy was doing something entirely different."

The Humble Beginnings of Prairie Rep

The playbill for the 1972 Prairie Repertory Theatre season. (Courtesy Raymond Peterson)

Other times, Mother Nature intervened.

Marie Louise Tesch, class of 1974, was one of the original Prairie Rep members. She laughs at the memories of "Two by Two":

"It was the absolute best rain storm story. 'Two by Two' is about Noah and his ark. There was this huge monologue, where Ron Borstad was on stage for 10 minutes, talking to God. There's this big storm, so someone is backstage making thunder. Well, a real storm started. So we're making our own special effects and then the lights started to flicker. The lights went out, then they'd come right back. The audience would sort of laugh. Finally, the lights really went out for a long time. The roof is leaking. It's raining on stage. We're running around in these little dressing rooms — little triangular rooms — with cups and pans trying to keep rain off the costumes. Ron is on stage. It's raining on the audience. People are holding programs over their heads. The theater has gone dark. It's quiet. Then, there's a big boom and the lights come back on. Ron says, 'Thank you, God.'"

Borstad, class of 1972, says the opportunity for improvisation added to the experience and pushed the young actors into new territory.

"One of the delightful things about the old repertory theater is that we really were in its infancy," he says. "We may not have always been polished, but we'd get to play with the audience."

Another time, says Tesch, there was such a torrential rain during the show that after the performance, the male students had to help audience members push their cars out of the mud in the parking lot.

Creating the sets also posed a formidable challenge.

Denton explains: "We had flats and we had the canvas and muslin, but it was on such a low, low budget. It was stuff we saved up all winter long, repainted and fit together. Set design wasn't designing a set — it was just a matter of you go in and put stuff together. ... We'd bring our stuff down to Madison in open trucks. We'd lose scenery along the way, props were lost."

Tesch recalls: "Oh, yes. I can remember having to stop the truck and walk all over a field and pick up pieces of sets."

Still, it was a wonderful experience for students and faculty alike. The first company did all the scene building as well as the acting. Today, a student might have one or two parts in a whole season of plays.

The lack of money, running water and occasionally electricity built a solid sense of camaraderie.

"We were always coming home sort of late at night from Madison," says Denton. "Oh, and there were hot, hot days down there in the village with the metal roof and no insulation. In that sense, it was wearing."

Worried about the crew, Redfield set up rooms in an old hotel in town for the students. There was no furniture, but they brought bedrolls and sometimes stayed overnight to catch up on sleep.

Tesch, who was 19 when she began with Prairie Rep the summer of 1971, reflects: "That first year, what was so fantastic was that we were just starting out and the people of Madison were so incredibly supportive. We were these poor college students and these people would feed us. We'd rehearse in Brookings, haul our sets down to Madison and we'd get a supper break. I can remember, we'd go to people's houses and they'd feed the entire company."

The audience response to the early days of Prairie Rep was overwhelming. Borstad remembers when he directed "You're a Good Man, Charlie Brown."

"For the evening performance, there were so many people who wanted to see it that we sold out by 2 in the afternoon," says Borstad. "So, we decided to put the play on at 3 or 4 o'clock. Then we gave the cast an hour rest and we put it on again — two performances in one day to a full house. It was an interesting experience, but we said, 'We can never do this again.'"

Between summer seasons, the opera house was vacant. The Prairie Rep crew would return a year later and have to clean all the dirt that had blown in during the winter months.

"One of the reasons that we were not performing in both areas," says Denton, "was that we took almost everything we owned down there. We brought our own lights down, our own dimmer board, everything from State. I think that my first budget was about $4,000 for personnel. I hired four people at $1,000 apiece for the summer."

Under those conditions, he adds, "you had a tendency to run a play two nights and then switch, and then run a play a little longer. ... As the years went by, the company moved a little more toward stock."

Perry Vining, class of 1970, worked for Prairie Rep the first two seasons. "I think I got paid $400 a month," he says. "I did it for Clare; I did it for the thrill of it. ... I directed a couple of plays, acted in others. And, if you weren't acting or directing, you were doing scenery, or lights, or audience."

With the passage of time and the increasing popularity of the program, the cast, stage crew and budget grew. Sets and lighting became more sophisticated and Prairie Rep flirted with stock theater. But, the company stuck to its roots in repertory. Eventually, Prairie Rep brought the plays for a run in Brookings.

Reflecting on the evolution of theater on the State campus and the Madison playhouse, Denton says the changes and success were gradual. Hiring Ray Peterson and then Johnson — making for three full-time staff members — signaled permanency.

"By the early '80s, Prairie Rep was well on its way," Denton says. "Once we had full-time staff, we still hired students to do many things, but scholarships started coming in and we could offer more out of the box office each year."

Prairie Rep always has been a company that lived off its box office, Denton adds, "which has a good aspect and a fault to it. We tried to look at the good side — that it offered students truly a learning experience of what theater is like. It much more closely resembles the chances professional theater has to take. You don't just choose a play because it's an artistically or historically neat play to do. You just can't afford to do that.

"Rep has to meet a payroll, and have the courage it takes to pay the bills. You have to be commercial; you've got to get the audience in. We counted tickets and money at the box office every night to know what we were doing — whether we could buy another ad in the paper."

Johnson, who retired May 10, 2003, after working for Prairie Rep since 1974, compares the theater company then and now. His first summer, Prairie Rep had about 25 performances. There were 21 people in the company, including faculty. The audiences totaled 3,800 people.

"Total expenses came to $16,000, we took in $9,000 in gate receipts," says Johnson, who served as director of State University Theatre and administrative head of Prairie Rep. "We had no funding, no grants, no gifts. A year ago, we performed to 16,100 people. We had 67 in the company, including 12 faculty and staff, and we took in $155,000 in gate receipts. We were right at $30,000 in gifts. Our budget was around $300,000."

The start was meager, but Tesch, to this day, recalls the thrill of getting paid. "I remember distinctly when they had enough money so that each of us received a scholarship of $25."

Tesch says the group had no idea, nor any vision, of what Prairie Rep might become. There was no thought to what the company would become.

"I was 19," she says, laughing. "It was just this great fun. We all thought we were going to go to New York City the next year and open on Broadway."

Says Borstad: "I don't know if we saw that far ahead. We were college kids, seizing the moment."

Vining muses: "When you do stuff like that, you do it to the extent that you love it. You're doing it for the moment. It's wonderful that it survived and thrived like it has, but I don't think any of us dreamed about what it would become. You don't think in those terms at that point in your life."

More than three decades later, Vining finds that his Prairie Rep experience prepared him well for life's work, producing a re-enactment festival in Minnesota with 1,000 participants.

"Because of what Clare taught me," says Vining, "I do what I do today very well. I'm in my 17th year. All that struggle in the heat of the summer and being on those deadlines, having sets fall on your head, forgetting your lines or forgetting a prop — Clare made it fun. He never got too emotional. I guess the best testimony is that the theater is still going after 30 years."

Tesch, too, says Prairie Rep prepared her for life in general. Speaking as she supervised weeding of her garden, she notes, "Everyone who had that summer Rep experience came out of that with the feeling of 'I can do anything.' We painted. We built sets. We did the lights. Everybody did everything.

"In fact, just last night, I was up until 1 o'clock in the morning painting one wall to look like a stone castle. I know how to do that because we painted sets. Get me a sponge and three colors, and I can make a stone wall."

Chapter 62

Dr. Wagner's Marriage Class

R obert Wagner, during his days on the South Dakota State campus, left an indelible mark on both the place and the people through his many and varied contributions.

Wagner's time at State included stints as a graduate student, graduate assistant and professor in the sociology department. He left the department in 1982 to serve first as assistant to the vice president for academic affairs until 1984 and then as president of the university from 1985 through December 1997.

But in terms of making a lifelong impact on students, the ordained minister's marriage class remains without comparison. That Wagner taught the subject for eight years in a manner that captured the attention of thousands

Pictured above, Dr. Robert Wagner addresses students in Rotunda D.

of students, stands as testimony to an educator's greatest gift.

In fact, Marriage 250 was so popular that it was the only class on campus to earn the honor of being featured year after year in the Collegian. No class before — and none since — has achieved such distinction.

Wagner came to teach the class purely as a matter of circumstance. Howard Sauer retired as the head of the sociology department and Wagner was assigned the marriage detail early in June 1974. He spent the summer reviewing textbooks and determining the general course of study.

There was more, though, than pure academics involved. Wagner also faced the challenge of making the subject matter interesting.

"First of all," says Wagner, "I recognized that the subject matter of this course, that this was what you might call a teaching readiness course in the sense that the subject matter could be directed toward the needs and interests of the students at the time.

"It isn't often that you get to teach a course that is especially relevant to the learner. Yet, here was this course, and it could be relevant if you recognized the fact that it is during these college years that students think about mate selection and advanced aspects of dating. ...

"They were beginning not only to date, but also to court. And, sooner or later, they would make a decision as to whom they would want to marry."

Bette Nelson and John Gustafson, both class of 1983, took Wagner's class. They also got married in 1984. Twenty years later, they don't remember any specific words of wisdom. Yet, the couple agrees, Marriage 250 made a lasting impression.

"He was such a good speaker," Bette recalls. "He could have sat up there and said anything and it would have been enjoyable. ... His jacket was always flying out like wings as he was pacing back and forth."

John adds, "Dr. Wagner had a great reputation of being a great teacher. And, there were always rumors that he wouldn't be teaching the class much longer. So that added to the urgency to take it."

A lot of the subjects Wagner addressed, says Bette, were the basic elements. "I think he talked about things like vacuuming and putting music on to make household drudgery more fun. He made us think about things, especially money. I don't remember any specific words, but just things to look at, how you have to work to make a budget and who keeps track of spending. He didn't tell us who should — just that someone should."

Wagner's teaching style was the key to the class' success, John says.

"He always presented the topics in such an easy, off-the-cuff manner," he says. "We weren't being lectured at. It was kind of like having a conversation."

And, adds John, for many young adults, it was a conversation that had not taken place at home.

"A lot of families don't sit down and discuss those things," he says. "It might have been the first exposure for many students."

Margie Fiedler, class of 1977, calls Wagner's class "the best class of my four years."

"It was all the things everyone wanted to learn, but were afraid to ask," Fiedler says. "Sex, marriage, kids, relationships. I think he was trying to actually prepare you for marriage. He really talked about love and infatuation. He was such a man of experience and we were just raging hormonal 19-year-olds. To hear about those real life things — menopause, dealing with children, birth control. It really had an impact."

For Mark Glissendorf, who graduated in 1986, the lessons he learned in Wagner's class still ring true today.

"There are two things that Dr. Wagner talked about that, oddly enough, I have never forgotten," says Glissendorf. "First, he talked about the concept of having in a marriage three checking accounts — the husband's, the wife's and the household's. You had to figure out how much from each paycheck to put into the three accounts."

The reason for the multiple accounts, Glissendorf explains, was for the couple to maintain some degree of financial independence and eliminate potential friction over spending habits. No one has to keep track of who spends more "fun" money, and any gift you give to your spouse truly is a gift.

"He also talked about in a marriage, always needing the approval of your partner," Glissendorf recalls. "He told a story about how his wife, Mary, was gone for a week in Pierre to the Legislature. He stained a door, and when he looked at it, it looked like it matched, and he thought he did a good job. But, it wasn't until Friday night when Mary got home and she looked at it and validated it, that it was. Until that point, he didn't feel like it was completed."

Twenty years later, calling Wagner's class "a gift," Glissendorf says he recognizes those same feelings in his relationship with his wife. "It seems amazing that that story has stuck with me all these years."

Contemplating what made Wagner such a good teacher, Glissendorf says: "He had such tremendous energy. The class was in Rotunda D and the room fit like 400 people. When you grow up in White Lake like I did, population 400, and you're a freshman at SDSU, you're thinking, Rotunda D — my whole town could fit in here. What it takes for one person to command the attention of a room that size …

"He'd be on the elevated stage at the front. I can remember he'd walk to the front of the stage, he'd even stand on the front row of chairs, and evangelize to the class. He never stood still for half a second. You would think that activity would wear you out and be tiring, but it wasn't. It was very natural, just another demonstration of the amount of energy and passion he had for the subject."

On the surface, it may seem silly or unnecessary to teach marriage skills. But, as Wagner aptly points out, when people enter into marriage, they need to take with them the skills, the tools and the understanding that will allow the marriage to be a success.

"What I wanted to have happen was to address those kinds of issues relevant and important to students right then," says Wagner.

The other focus, he explains, is that there is a developmental model that sets forth steps for people to address as they enter into a marriage and the marriage matures. For example, when a couple first marries, it is more important to earn and spend money wisely than it is to learn how to be good parents or plan for retirement. Those aspects will come later.

"There are sequential stages in the life of a marriage in which learning has to take place," Wagner continues. "It was important in class to focus on the early developmental tasks of marriage."

That the class addressed steps students were taking or were about to take, notes Wagner, "was part of the reason that it seemed to be significant to people."

He adds: "Finally, I used this phrase — 'If people are going to succeed in marriage, they had to recognize that marriage is work.' Of course, the romance of a marriage is important. But good marriages are good marriages because the individuals work at it. They are committed to the relationship, committed to the marriage."

To do the work, of course, people need to develop skills and have the proper tools. And therein lies another aspect of Wagner's class: "I thought this course ought to help students discover what those skills and tools are. Like a carpenter. Without skills and tools, you can't build a very good house."

Wagner took on the interrelated subjects of dating, mate selection and marriage. But, instead of a theoretical lecture, he would call all the females in the class to the front of the room.

"That was one of the moments in class that most of the students remember," laughs Wagner. "I would gradually have them sit down based on their ethnicity, their social class, other kinds of characteristics that they would identify themselves with. It was a screening mechanism. When we got all through doing this, there were usually three or four women left standing who

Marriage class gaining popularity

Over 1,000 enrolled last year

BY CANDY JOHNSON
Staff Writer

When students think of sociology, many associate it with innumerable facts, figures and studies.

But Robert Wagner described one of the most popular sociology courses as "a how-to course instead of a straight sociology course."

WAGNER TEACHES MARRIAGE, a course that almost 1,000 students enrolled in last year. He attributed the large numbers of students to the increase in enrollment at State University.

Another reason, according to Wagner, is a feature that Wagner added after the first year he taught Marriage is a film on personal relationships in marriage. He said it used to take four lecture periods to cover the subject, and now the film does it very thoroughly and concisely in one hour.

Wagner sees his class as a tool that students will be able to use when faced with marital problems later on. The class teaches that no topic is too secret to discuss. He said he wants the students to have a vocabulary to use when dealing with problems.

"WITH THE NEW vocabulary and more open attitude," Wagner said, "the students become more aware of the decision-making processes involved in any marriage."

The class is especially practical for engaged couples and newlyweds, according to Wagner. He said, "Marriage helps them recognize problems in adjustment, and helps them face these problems."

Wagner has evidence of the practicality of Marriage class. Graduates who had taken the course have returned, Wagner said. They said Marriage was one of the most important college courses they had taken.

IS MARRIAGE FOR everyone? Wagner doesn't think so. He said, "Marriage is one of the ways people find fulfillment for their creative energies, and one of the ways they see themselves as persons."

Years ago women had to marry to fit into the niche society left for them, he said. A woman's only method of expression was through her husband. "Now with the changing concept of women, marriage is no longer a woman's only access to status," Wagner said.

AND, SINCE PEOPLE are still getting married, this may be a sign that personal relationships are better than ever before, he said.

Is marriage here to stay? "Absolutely!" Wagner said.

Headline from Jan. 14, 1976, Collegian declaring the popularity of Dr. Wagner's marriage class.

could not eliminate themselves."

The goal was to demonstrate mate selection.

Says Wagner: "Finding someone to court and marry is usually the result of a very clear and specified selection process. I think that was a real eye-opener to people, a real breakthrough. It sounds simple, but it's one of the kind of highlight experiences we had."

The exercise also succeeded in taking a class of nearly 400 students in a Rotunda classroom and getting them to interact.

Wagner's class enjoyed spectacular success, particularly when you consider that the course was not required in any core curriculum. When he started, he taught two sections, made up of probably fewer than 100 students. He wound up teaching three sections a year, reaching an annual total of about 1,000 students.

"We figured it out one time that probably 80 percent of the students in the institution took the class," Wagner says.

And, when the class was over, the students took with them what they had learned.

"My wife and I travel a lot," muses Wagner, "and it's pretty hard to go somewhere without someone coming up and saying, 'We took the marriage class and we're still married.' The other thing I found interesting is that there were a number of marriages that did not take place because of it. People said, 'We decided we're not going to continue our courtship because we don't have the kinds of compatibility to make a marriage work.' I thought that was a value as well."

Reflecting on what he tried to accomplish, Wagner says he was not trying to take the love element out of marriage. Romance certainly has its place in a relationship.

"But," notes Wagner, "romance by itself without competence and commitment is not going to make a marriage."

At the same time, Wagner says, it is important to realize that making a marriage work does not require following a prescribed model. Everyone has different methods of making their relationship work.

"Not all marriages are the same," he says. "But good marriages, people work at it. They have the skills and the tools."

Wagner gave his students a lot to think about. Once they got through planning the wedding and the honeymoon, the focus turned to the nuts and bolts. Making the finances work, considering parenting models and ultimately planning for retirement — these topics may not have seemed as relevant as mate selection, but they helped bring home the reality that there was more to marriage than the formal ceremony.

"I think it was a good course," allows Wagner. "But, I was lucky that I had a subject matter that was absolutely relevant to where students were. One of the fundamental concerns of students at the university age is moving out of simply dating."

To teach the course during a period of such significant social change added yet another dimension. The 1970s and 1980s saw substantial liberalization of ideas and traditional gender models, which in turn affected how people interacted and increased the breadth of marriage styles.

"Fundamentally," Wagner reflects, "students at South Dakota State University were more open and tolerant of these changing lifestyles than people of my generation. But, they still believed that marriage was the proper structure for them — to get married and have children and raise a family."

In that respect, the marriage course probably would take on even greater importance and value today. Wagner says people are rediscovering the need for significant relationships even though the traditional models have expanded to include alternatives that were not part of the norm in his teaching days.

Nonetheless, says Wagner, "the need for entering into marriage with competence and commitment is just as great — if not greater — than back in the '70s. Secondly, the need of the right tools and skills, the understanding, that will allow you to make marriage work, is also just as great. Although, some of the understanding, some of the tools and some of the skills would be different. You may have to change what it is you look at."

The entire process continues to be more complicated than in years past, especially when taking into account societal changes, according to Wagner.

Within the last 10 years, there has been a shift toward taking longer at the mate-selection process and marrying later. Part of that is the sense that if you are going to enter into marriage with some kind of financial security, you have to have all the factors in your life established. People are taking longer to complete their education, and it has become increasingly difficult to find a career path.

"A lot of risk factors need to be resolved, and as a result, they're also enhancing and improving the mate-selection process," says Wagner. "If you wait, you have more opportunities to date and know and understand a number of people of the opposite sex. That fine-tunes and develops a sense of awareness. And it gives you a little more rational sophistication in selecting a mate. As a result, marriages are going to be more flexible, more workable. People are going to do better at them."

At the same time, however, the way people look at marriage may sabotage that success. "Marriage is now viewed as a contract by so many people. But, you have to realize that contracts have a termination clause. If it doesn't work out, a contract can always be terminated when it comes time for renewal. ...

"Marriage in the minds of many people is viewed as a contract, which can be terminated, whereas for many of us who were married in other times, marriage is viewed as a covenant, something we entered into for life. The whole idea that no matter what happens, we're in it. We work at it to keep it and save it. That idea is not as predominant today."

Still, some marriages must end. All the tension and agony that can occur when a couple is trying to make a marriage work must be recognized and weighed against the alternatives, says Wagner. "You need to know when a marriage ought to be dissolved and let both spouses go find other paths to happiness in life."

Another fundamental change in marriage, which Wagner applauds, is the shift in traditional roles and boundaries. Although, that also fuels competing needs and demands.

"You can't really talk about marriage today in the same context," he says. "Husbands are no longer the sole provider. Wives are no longer the sole childraiser. Both are involved in work, social activities. Each has career paths, social paths that they need to follow. The things that they need to do together, however, are not always done together. And, their diversions don't allow them both to solely concentrate on the roles they have in their relationships."

And yet, in spite of all the changes marriage has weathered throughout the generations, the sources of marital spats often remain the same: "By and

THE COLLEGE ON THE HILL

large, the fights are not over values — not between one person who values saving money and the other who values spending while they've got it.

"Marriages may break up because of that, but the big fights, the tensions, are going to come over who empties the garbage, who replaces the light bulb. ... It's greatly about roles. Roles, roles, roles. Roles are not as simple as they were. Roles are complicated and multiple. You talk about the soccer mom and the SUV and why you have to have it to haul the kids and all the gear around. And, how to keep your husband connected to his fishing partners and the wife to her bridge club — if she even has time to belong to it."

Does the retired marriage guru have any advice for what at times seems like a bleak landscape? What would he talk about in today's classroom?

"The biggest challenge in the modern marriage," says Wagner, "is trying to sort all that out. How to allow people to be themselves and pursue wonderful diversions and opportunities, while at the same time enjoy love and companionship and a sense of achievement. A sense of partners collaborating together."

Chapter 63

Dance for Dystrophy

Once a year, for nearly two decades, students at South Dakota State set aside their individual aspirations and joined together for a common cause — the Muscular Dystrophy Association.

It was a modest effort at the start in 1972, sponsored by the Intrafraternity Council. Sixty-eight couples started dancing at 6 p.m. Friday, March 17, and didn't stop until midnight Saturday, March 18.

By the time the 30 hours were up, 35 couples had survived. They had danced nonstop in the Christy Ballroom with 30-minute breaks every three hours. For their efforts, the dancers raised $8,000. They also kicked off the legacy of Dance for Dystrophy.

During Dance for Dystrophy's 18-year run on the State campus, a total of 5,270 dancers — with blistered feet from dancing and calloused hands from clapping — raised nearly $530,000 to aid in the fight against Muscular Dystrophy. An additional four years of "HyPER for MDA," a variety night of activities, raised an additional $28,000. Then, in 1994, the SDSU Greek system switched charities to the American Diabetes Association.

Pictured above, SDSU students dance the "Alligator" at the 1978 Dance for Dystrophy event.

Both the success and the appeal of Dance for Dystrophy were contagious from the start. The marathon dance session doubled the amount of money raised by its second year and tripled the amount by its third year.

In 1976, State students set a campus — and national — record. That year, 224 couples raised $35,641.15. State had the highest per capita ratio of $5 per student and the event was said to have been one of the largest campus dances in the country.

As the couple who raised the most amount of money, Pat Wilhelm and Larry Thomas earned the honor to fly to Las Vegas and present Jerry Lewis with the check during his infamous Labor Day weekend telethon.

"I figured dancing for 30 hours would be a challenge and a fun thing to do," Thomas recalls. "So I asked Pat if she'd be interested in dancing with me. We were going pretty serious, so I figured if we could last for 30 hours of dancing …"

Wilhelm, who went on to marry Thomas, laughs on the other extension of the couple's phone line.

"I think a lot of it was the novelty of dancing for 30 hours," she adds. "They made it seem like a big, fun party, and you were doing something for a cause. That was the motivation. You were helping someone else by having fun."

In the days and weeks leading up to the dance, the couple had to get pledges.

Larry explains: "Most of the kids went to other kids for pledges. We started doing that with our friends, but college kids are all pretty poor. So, we decided to go to local businesses and see if they'd sponsor us."

Says Pat, "We also went door to door."

Larry adds: "I don't think anyone had done that before. Things started adding up. We raised almost $1,200 that year. Our dorm (Hansen Hall) also raised the most of all the other dormitories."

The dance, which took place in Frost Arena, began and ended with music by the band Sterling. Nine other bands performed in-between. The live music played a big role in keeping up dancers' energy.

"We sort of ran on adrenaline," says Pat. "They'd play 'The Alligator' and get us rolling around on the floor. You'd get your second wind."

Larry says: "We were numb most of the time. I do remember that time went by very quickly. At first, you were excited. Then, you just went into a numb state. It seemed like from the halfway point on, they started doing things to help increase your adrenaline. There was no slow music. A lot of kids danced in groups with their friends. We invented dance steps just sheer

March 31, 1976, SDSU Collegian announces the success of the recently held marathon.

out of 'Let's do something different.' We probably invented line dancing."

According to the March 31, 1976, Collegian account, many of the dancers used their half-hour breaks to shower, eat and change clothes. Sleeping, however, wasn't advised.

"If you sleep for half an hour, it's worse than if you hadn't slept at all," said Boni Johnson, co-chairperson of the event.

U.S. Sen. George McGovern dropped by the dance that night to congratulate the participants, as did SDSU President Sherwood Berg, Brookings Mayor Orrin Juel and members of the Brookings Chamber of Commerce.

"At the end," says Larry, "it was total excitement, a lot of electricity on the part of all the dancers just for accomplishing such a feat. There were a lot of sore feet. A lot of people had blisters. When they announced the winners — who raised the most — that was sheer excitement."

Pat adds, "It was hard to get to sleep."

Shortly after school resumed in the fall, the pair boarded a plane for Las Vegas, where they met with representatives from other colleges and universities. Once they arrived at the Sahara Hotel, they attended a special reception and received their duties for the telethon weekend. They also had some free time to check out the town.

"For two kids from South Dakota," Larry says, "it was incredible."

To this day, the Thomases share many special memories, starting with the check-in process.

"From my name, they thought I was a boy," laughs Pat. "So they had me rooming with a guy named John. I can't remember where he was from. I said, 'This might be a problem.' They reassigned me to another roommate."

Larry says he and Pat lucked out with their assignment — escorting stars to and from the telethon stage. Pat's most memorable celebrity escort was singer Tony Orlando of Tony Orlando and Dawn fame. The weekend also provided an opportunity to witness a memorable moment in celebrity history.

"It was the first time in 17 years that Dean Martin and Jerry Lewis had seen each other face to face," explains Larry. "Frank Sinatra did that as a surprise — totally unannounced."

Adding to the excitement, Larry still remembers passing Sinatra back stage: "I said, 'Hi, Mr. Sinatra.' And he said, 'Hi ya, kid.'"

Students representing six schools presented checks on stage to Lewis. Larry was chosen simply as a matter of gender equity. Organizers wanted a balance of three girls and three boys.

"It was just really neat," Larry says of the on-camera experience. "The lights go on, the cameras and you kind of go blank. I had rehearsed this little blurb and I actually remembered it."

The Collegian story reported that when Larry gave Lewis the check, he said: "On behalf of my dancing partner, Pat Wilhelm, who withstood me for 30 hours, the 6,000 students of South Dakota State University and the many hundreds of people who gave willingly and lovingly with open hearts, I proudly present this check for $31,000 from South Dakota State University from Brookings, S.D."

Regrettably, Larry says, the Dance for Dystrophy was a one-time experience for the Thomases. They wanted to repeat their performance the following year, but could not because of a scheduling conflict.

"It was a wonderful cause," Larry says. "We loved it — loved everything about it. We were disappointed that we couldn't do it the next year."

As for the Thomases, they got engaged and married. Larry graduated in the spring of 1977 and Pat did at midterm later that year. They have been back to Las Vegas several times since their trip in 1976.

"We've always talked about the telethon and what a super neat experience it was," says Larry. "It's a good thing we were young. After arriving, we hardly slept at all during the whole telethon. Things were always happening. It was like having a backstage pass."

Pat adds, "It's one of the highlights, one of our fond trips together."

For the next eight years, State students continued to dance their way to impressive fund-raising totals. The largest amount — $49,196 — was raised in 1980.

Then, the dollar totals started to drop off until hitting $8,835 in 1990. By then, the number of hours students danced also had fallen — from the height of 30 hours to only three. The nature of the event had changed drastically as well. In 1988, 175 dancers raised $13,699 in 12 hours of dancing. The following year, there were 100 dancers and $9,100 in pledges.

The 19th year, Dance for Dystrophy took place on Saturday, April 7, 1990. The name of the event was switched to HyPER for MDA. Instead of dancing all day and all night, the activities included softball, volleyball and carnival booths. A three-hour dance started at 9 a.m.

Rocky Gilbert, professor emeritus of economics, served as master of ceremonies every year but one during Dance for Dystrophy. He says that cutting back on the commitment led to the demise of the dance. At 30 hours, the event posed a huge challenge to students. The first year, they danced for 50 minutes and then rested for 10 minutes.

"It was that way for 30 hours solid," Gilbert says, "If you make it easy, you kill it. I don't know why, but for some reason, they first dropped it from 30 hours to 24. Right there began its death. You make it just a little softer and it's one step away from that challenge."

For nearly two decades, though, Dance for Dystrophy had a huge impact on people — and not just those who were afflicted with the disease and benefited from the funds raised.

Dance for Dystrophy initiated a significant departure from the typical self-involvement of the college years, shifting students' focus to the greater world around them. The event gave them something to think about beyond themselves and offered a lifelong lesson in reaching out and helping others.

Quentin Schultz, co-chairman of the first Dance for Dystrophy in 1972, says students' overwhelming response to the event surprised organizers.

"I think some people kind of looked at it like a lark, to see if they could last for the whole 30 hours," he says. "For others, it was, 'I can do something for somebody less fortunate than me.'"

Schultz says he participated in the first two dances before graduating. Then, he returned for the 10th anniversary.

"There were a lot of people and it was a lot bigger event," he recalls. "It was more than we had ever imagined. I was surprised to see the size and complexity of what it had turned into."

Most gratifying, though, was that some of the youngsters afflicted by the disease who had attended the dance in 1972 came back in 1982.

"They were in their early 20s," marvels Schultz. "They were a living example of how MDA research (which the Dance for Dystrophy helped fund) had helped increase life expectancy."

Chapter 64

Horatio's

If you attended State in the 1960s and 1970s, chances are Horatio's was a part of your college experience.

Horatio's. Hort's. Call it what you will, no bar by any other name inspires the same sentiments. It was, as the saying goes, the place to be and be seen.

"Hort's," laughs Margie Fiedler, class of 1977. "That was a legend. Horatio's. It was the 18 bar. You'd go when you were 18 and drink 3.2 beer. There was no other alcohol. All the other bars were 21 and over."

As Fiedler put it, Horatio's was the place where State kids of the era socialized. And what a social event it was. "It was packed and loud. It was always packed. There was so much beer on the floor, you'd be sliding all over the place."

And yet, Fiedler adds: "It had a really neat family atmosphere. It was the hangout, the place to be. Kind of like our Cheers bar. ... You'd go to meet

---

Pictured above, a mug bearing the name of a famous SDSU hangout. (Photo courtesy of Eric Landwehr)

friends, even people who didn't drink. We just had fun. And they always had rowdy, live music — good rock 'n' roll music."

Paulette Tobin, also class of 1977, echoes Fiedler's sentiments. Laughing, she exclaims: "Hort's? Oh, my gosh. That was just incredible. It was the place with the biggest dance floor. They'd get live bands. It was just a wild and crazy place where you went if you wanted to find a guy or go dancing. ... I remember doing the dance called The Alligator. I can't believe we ever laid down on the floor."

Tom Yseth, who first managed Horatio's and ultimately owned the place, says the music and beer — although both memorable — were not the main attraction. "The whole thing was to be with people and meet people. It was like a chemistry thing — all these elements, and the one thing that bonded it was the people."

The original Hort's sat in the location that today serves as the west parking lot for the downtown branch of First National Bank in Brookings. Prior to being a 3.2 bar, Horatio's, owned by the Brookings Bowling Corp., was a bowling alley and lounge.

Horatio's, the bar, came to life in 1963, urging coeds in a Collegian ad to visit "The Nation's Finest College Haunt." The establishment offered "pocket billiards specially suited to the feminine taste of distinguished college women, and perfectly balanced Brunswick tables for the sporty college male. ... After billiards, snooker or bowling, relax in the Vulcan Lounge."

Milt Gengler, who still lives in Brookings, says he was brought in to manage Hort's in the early years, when the business was losing money: "They hired jocks to get the college business, but they had too many friends. ... It got to be a hopping place as soon as it opened, but it wasn't being managed."

Turning the business around was simple, says Gengler. "I just was the boss. That's what they needed. Anybody that didn't behave didn't get in."

And, to be sure, everyone wanted in.

"They came from all over," recalls Gengler. "We were full all the time. We had three bars running. We took the bowling alleys out and made benches and seats. They didn't care much at the time what they sat on, just so they could get in."

And once they were in, they drank beer — a lot of it. One year, Horatio's was cited by Sports Illustrated for the most beer consumed per capita in one location. Fred Druin of Brookings drove a delivery truck for Foerster Distributing for 17 years.

"It was a fun place to do a delivery," laughs Druin as he recalls the Hort's stop. "You never knew what volume. We'd haul beer in by the pallet — 49 cases on a pallet, three or four pallets. The kegs were a little risky business. An elevator would have been helpful. The steps were kinda wiggly. I was lucky I never lost a keg."

The 15.5-gallon kegs weighed more than 100 pounds apiece, Druin says. "I took 'em down on a cart, step by step. It was easier to take two kegs at a time, one keg standing up and the other crosswise on top of the first keg."

In 1966, Hort's ran into problems with the dancing on the premises. The Collegian reported: "Obscene dances will be 'out' and bright lights 'in' at Horatio's from now on, pending the outcome of owner Larry Swain's request for a dance license. Dancing in the popular downtown tavern was curtailed Saturday night because of a city ordinance which prohibits the operation of a public dance hall without a special license."

In addition to posting a license, according to the ordinance, legal dance halls had to "employ a (police) matron to supervise the conduct of the participants." The law also forbid "any immodest, suggestive or immoral dances" and the dimming of lights, and it gave police the authority to toss out any individuals found to be intoxicated.

As chronicled in the Jan.10, 1968, Collegian, State students knew just what to do in an emergency. When a power failure hit Brookings at 6 p.m., about 1,300 students headed for the downtown bar.

Yseth arrived on the Hort's scene in 1971. He had just gotten out of the Army, having done a stint after graduating from college. His brother, who owned Horatio's with three other guys, asked him to manage the bar.

"I remember it," Yseth recalls. "It was April 19, the Monday after Easter. We stayed open till school got out. I went back to the Cities. They were going to get rid of it. Well, they called me in July and said, 'We haven't gotten rid of it. Would you come back?' So I did."

Horatio's was purely a college business — open Wednesday through Saturday during the school year. There wasn't much in the way of decor, but then again, as everyone is quick to point out, it was the people who made the place.

Structurally, said Yseth, the front room had a lot of angles to it, featuring several nooks and crannies, along with pool tables and dart boards. The building opened up in the back room, with seating, a set of large bathrooms and a big stage. It's where the bowling alley had been; the raised area where the pinsetters used to be was a like a balcony.

"The bar ran forever, all the way back," says Yseth. "And, the back was full of picnic tables. ... To clean it, we hosed it down with a garden hose and used a squeegee. We could probably get 500 to 700 people in there. On Hobo Day, we opened every exit door."

The back ceiling was done in chicken wire. Live music played Wednesday through Saturday nights. Some people got their mail delivered at Hort's. Others, Yseth laughs, "begged us to tell their parents we were a bookstore."

Certainly, Horatio's was legendary. But, as Yseth discovered, the place was only living up to its name.

According to mythology, Horatius was a Roman hero who saved the early Republic from the Etruscans. In a surprise attack, the Etruscans attempted to capture Rome by crossing a bridge over the River Tiber. Flanked by two comrades, Horatius fought off the enemy until the Romans had destroyed the wooden bridge. As the final supports were sawn away, Horatius ordered his fellow soldiers to return to the Roman banks. They made it, but Horatius had to swim back dressed in full armor. As legend has it, only prayer saved the hero as he dodged enemy arrows and swam across the river.

The connection to the downtown Brookings bar were the wooden planks above the bar. Apparently, Yseth muses, they reminded someone of the Tiber River bridge.

The height of Hort's was during the 18-year-old drinking age. When the minimum age went up to 19, figuring out who was legal and who wasn't posed some difficulty.

"Nineteen were the worst years," Yseth says. "You had to sort through the people. They would come to the door in a large mass and get the carder occupied. As he was looking at IDs, people would be crawling on the ground to get in."

In addition to the lower legal age for drinking, the popularity of Horatio's also stemmed from the fact that many students did not have cars.

"When they came to school," explains Yseth, "they came to school. There weren't a lot of people going home. And, there were fewer three-day weekends. This was their thing."

And then, he adds, there was a time when students were allowed to have beer in their dorm rooms, giving Hort's a brisk off-sale business. House parties were not a problem since students did their drinking downtown or in their dorm rooms.

"After we closed," Yseth says, "which was midnight, then there were house parties."

In 1975, after Horatio's was sold to the bank and Yseth had leased it for a year, Yseth bought the business and moved it to a new location at 419 Third Street, where the NAPA Auto & Truck Parts store is today.

Yseth held onto Hort's until 1978, when Tom Daschle ran for office.

Yseth sold the business to a group of his employees and went to work for Daschle.

"I got it back in 1980, and that was pretty much the end of it," Yseth says. "Whenever they changed the age limit."

Ultimately, the increased legal age for drinking, the construction of a new student union and the opening of a new bar, Friday's, all helped contribute to the demise of Horatio's. When Hort's closed in 1981, Yseth told the Collegian: "Before the Student Union was built, Hort's was the student union and social acitivities center. But when the Union was built, not as many people came down in the afternoon to play pool and have a glass of beer."

Looking back on the Horatio's era, Yseth says "mostly good things happened there." Not the least of which was meeting his wife, Gwen.

Gwen Yseth, class of 1973, started working at Hort's in 1972. Hired by Tom's assistant manager, Gwen says she still remembers the moment she first noticed her husband-to-be and felt an instant attraction. "I can still see it. I was walking in there, and he was up on that little platform. And, I thought, 'Oh my God, this is my boss.'"

The old cliché has it that good matches are made in heaven. Horatio's, however, holds a pretty good record, too.

Brookings attorney Ron Aho, class of 1968, met his wife, Sue, at Hort's.

"December 17, 1966," Aho says without hesitation. "I remember it well. I just happened to be there, and there were some other BHS graduates, some friends of mine. I was talking to them and this girl came up to talk to one of the girls. We were introduced and I followed her back to the dance floor to see if she was with someone else. She was at a table with another girl, so I asked her to dance. And the rest, as they say, is history."

Even for a "pretty straight-laced young man" like himself, Aho says Hort's was the place to go — the only place you could take a date or meet a girl.

"Hort's," Aho says, "when I look back, I see it as the social venue of that era."

Chapter 65

Odds, Ends and Jackrabbit Tales

My, how we have grown
The 1908 Jack Rabbit yearbook compiled statistics on the junior class. Ninety-five years ago, the average height of the boys was 5 feet, 9 3/4 inches. The average girl measured in at 5 feet, 3 inches. The average weight — for the boys, 152 pounds; for the girls, 108.3 pounds.

"Twenty dance much, two dance a little, two dance 'once in a while,'" the yearbook reported. "Most of the others say that they will learn as soon as possible. Twenty play cards quite frequently, two play a little, one plays innocent games, one plays when the folks are not around. Ten do not play. Five do not because they do not know how, two have no time, two do not want to, one would like to; the last desists because his parents object."

On swearing, 13 did when the occasion demanded it. Some of the girls had been heard to mutter "darn it" or "Lordy." Seven smoked regularly and one smoked occasionally — pipes, cigars and/or cigarettes.

Pictured above, Vice President of the United States, Hubert Humphrey, delivers the commencement address to 6,000 people assembled at Coolidge Sylvan Theatre on June 4, 1967.

Hero the Elephant

In addition to students, South Dakota State has a solid track record of attracting a motley collection of animals — both alive and dead.

First and most famous was Hero the Elephant.

On May 15, 1916, the Ortman Bros. Circus came to Elkton and started setting up. Bad weather, however, forced the circus to cancel its performance. While pulling up tent stakes, Hero the Elephant turned on his drunk, abusive trainer and chased him through town in an angry rampage. The men of the town got their guns. A story in the June 1, 1939, Elkton Record reported that it took more than 300 bullets to bring poor Hero down.

"When news of the elephant's death reached Professor (Harold) Miller," recounted the 1918 yearbook, "he saw in an instant a vision of a beautifully mounted skeleton as an addition to the zoological laboratory."

Miller secured permission from the owners and, accompanied by a band of State students, headed for Elkton to bring home the bones. It took the morning just to remove the hide from the 850-pound animal.

In 1963, the then-46-year-old skeleton was sent south to the University of South Dakota at Vermillion.

"We just didn't have any place to put the skeleton, and we felt it better to give it to the University for its new, expanded (W.H. Over) museum than to throw it away," SDSC President Hilton M. Briggs told the May 16, 1963, Collegian.

Cory the Horse

The April 13, 1932, Collegian bid a fond farewell to Cory: "All good things must come to an end, say the philosophers, and so Cory — known and loved by all of State college — passed away last week."

The 38-year-old horse spent most of her life hauling a milk wagon through its Brookings route until she was replaced by the modern-day invention of the milk truck. Her final years were spent pulling the milk wagon from the dairy barn to the creamery.

"There have been many bright spots in Cory's career as a beast of burden," the Collegian noted. "Many times she has been called on to participate in campus activities. Only last fall, with Scabbard and Blade Neophyte Don Kumer astride her graceful back, armed with pop gun and saber, they patrolled campus for hours. She has also served as a mount for Guidon initiates, and for other noted persons, as well as having taken part in numerous Hobo Day parades."

Despite good health, Cory developed swayback, which ultimately led to vertebrae so weak that she could not rise and she had to be humanely killed.

Said the Collegian: "And so State college is mourning the death of Cory, a good and faithful horse. If there are better places for horses than this earth, Cory must be there."

Teddy the Bear

In 1953, a 75-pound black bear cub found in the Northern Minnesota woods joined the "hobo family" at South Dakota State. Aptly named "Teddy," the bear joined a traveling summer show of enthusiastic State boosters, who made appearances at various small-town celebrations to publicize the 42nd annual Hobo Day.

The Oct. 13, 1953, Collegian reported that Teddy also was on hand for a ceremony at the Brookings Airport to inaugurate north-south air service.

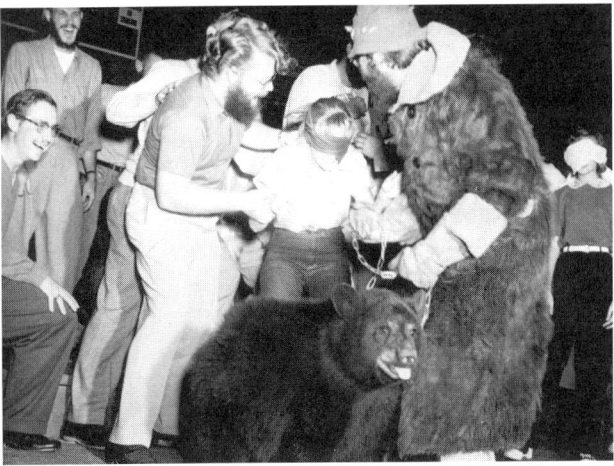
The bear cub, Teddy, participated in a variety of events leading up to Hobo Day 1953.

Teddy was donated to the Hobo Day cause by the brother-in-law of John Hoeke, class of 1954, who found the motherless cub in Minnesota. After Hobo Day festivities, Teddy reportedly was sent to a zoo, but sources indicate that Teddy never made it out of town.

Several giant steps forward for womankind

Amid the fun and frolic of early Hobo Days, there were serious issues to contemplate. In 1915, a group of suffragettes marched. In fact, they were said to be the first organized group to participate in the Hobo Day parade.

In 1931, the state Senate confirmed Gov. Warren Green's appointment of Mrs. E.P. Wanzer of Armour to the Board of Regents. She was the first woman to become a member of the board.

The following year, in June 1932, Genevieve Rose was the first woman to receive an engineering degree from State.

In May 1934, South Dakota State celebrated its first Women's Day. Women wrote and edited the Industrial Collegian and presented the assembly program. There also was a recognition banquet for the Top 10 academically ranked freshman women. All women connected with the college were asked to wear white or pastel colors that day.

And, on March 23, 1972, the Collegian reported that for the first time in 27 years, a woman would be leading the students of South Dakota State. Barb Strandell, class of 1973, overwhelmingly defeated two other candidates in the election for Students' Association president. It was the first time since 1945, when World War II was under way, that a woman held the office of SA president.

Presidential honor

Russell Jensen, class of 1913, swept first place at the national dairy show in Chicago and received his trophy from President Taft.

Ten colleges from the leading dairy states, represented by three-man teams, competed in the event. The 30 men were given 15 minutes to judge individual animals. Jensen placed first individually and his team came in third overall.

"This double victory for South Dakota is the highest kind of a tribute to the character of work done here," crowed the 1913 Jack Rabbit yearbook. "It proves that there is no need for a student to go east if he wants an education and is willing to work for it."

President William Howard Taft is shown presenting a dairy judging trophy to State student Russell Jensen.

When Taft presented the trophy to Jensen, the yearbook reported, "Jensen gripped the presidential hand with both of his own. As the president handed him the cup, he remarked, 'I hope you will fill it many times with mighty good milk.' It was probably the greatest moment hitherto in Mr. Jensen's life."

Strong people, weak coffee

Charles Kuralt, famed CBS reporter, visited the South Dakota State campus during the 1976-77 school year as a participant in the Harding Lecture Series. Brookings left an imprint on the traveling newscaster.

In his book "A Life on the Road," Kuralt reflected on coffee. He wrote:

"West of the Mississippi, travel, if possible, with your own coffee pot. The coffee gets progressively weaker from Illinois westward. My theory for this is that the pioneers ran out of coffee as they traveled west and had to re-use the grounds. Their descendants drew up liking it that way. The weakest coffee in America is served in Brookings, S.D. Some say Salt Lake City, but they are people who have not yet been to Brookings."

Rehearsal for real life

South Dakota State College was considered a pioneer in the field of home economics, or domestic economy as it was once called. The program in the 1920s and 1930s aimed to teach young women "how to manage a home wisely and happily, and how to occupy a fitting place in the community."

There also was training for careers. The Home Economics Practice Cottage offered the opportunity for learning all the necessary skills, including raising a child. Each quarter, six female students moved into the house and assumed various duties.

One of the responsibilities was the "practice cottage baby." The 1928 Jack Rabbit yearbook shows 9-month-old Baby Verba. In other years, there was Baby Sona, Baby Lola and others.

Constance Mark Goodwillie, class of 1938, remembers Baby Fern from her stay in the practice cottage: "We took turns being nurse and cook and laundress. Whoever was nurse took her to school every morning. It was wonderful training."

Eleanor Roscoe, who attended State from 1932-33, says: "We had Baby Arnold. He was from a very large family out in the country and they were very needy. So when this child was born, some way or another Dean (Edith) Pierson knew about this. I don't think he was two or three months old."

From Sousa to Satchmo

South Dakota State always has enjoyed a strong music program. It's only natural, then, that the campus would offer a stage for big-name performers.

In 1928, John Philip Sousa brought his famous band. The so-called

THE COLLEGE ON THE HILL

March King was greeted by record crowds.

In 1955, the great Louis "Satchmo" Armstrong and his world-renowned band performed for two hours before a crowd of 2,100 in the college gym.

Through the years, other performers at State have included Jose Feliciano, Jim Dandy and Ruby Star (Black Oak Arkansas), ZZ Top, Chicago, Dr. Hook and the Medicine Show, Quick Silver Messenger Service, REO Speedwagon, Don McLean, Nitty Gritty Dirt Band, Sugarloaf, the Carpenters, The Chad Mitchell Trio, the Righteous Brothers, and The 5th Dimension.

A bevy of beauties

Throughout the 1940s, 1950s and 1960s, popular male celebrities would be mailed photos of female students and asked to select the Jack Rabbit Queen. One year, the judge was a young Rock Hudson. In 1947, it was noted orchestra leader Vaughn Monroe.

Bob Hope happily did the honors in 1942. He wrote to yearbook editor Warren Syverud, asking if he could join the Jacks:

"I've two good reasons for thinking that I deserve to be a Jack Rabbit: (a) I've been hopping from picture to picture for the last few hours, trying to choose the most beauteous of the beauties; (b) I'd just kinda like to be back there with you so I could sit and drool. Gosh, did you ever see so many pretty girls, except in Esquire?"

Ultimately, Hope selected Rachael Paterson, class of 1942, whom he said was "calm as the night and twice as beautiful."

In 1954, the Feb. 11 Collegian reported: "Eddie Fisher, the No.1 heart throb of America's teen-agers and college girls, served as final judge for the 1954 Jack Rabbit beauty contestants."

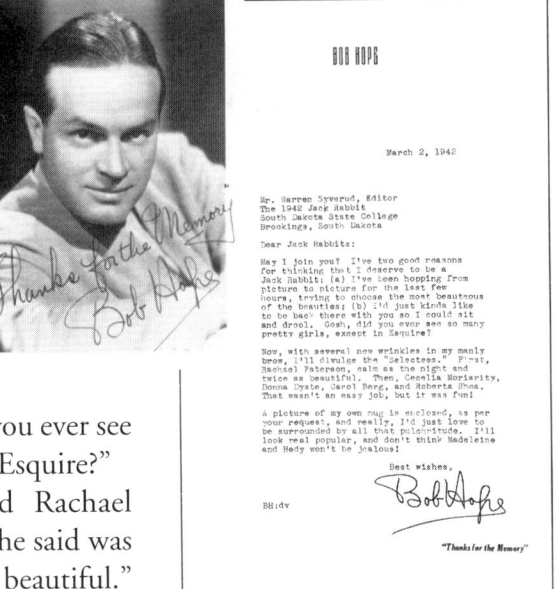

On March 2, 1942, comedian Bob Hope sent this letter indicating his pick of Rachael Paterson, class of 1942, as the most beautiful woman on campus.

Looking over the pictures of South Dakota State coeds, Fisher exclaimed to Jack Rabbit editor Bill McDonald, "A group of real beauties, a real bunch of honeys. It's hard to believe this many beautiful girls came from one school."

Playboy magazine publisher Hugh Hefner did the judging honors for the 1962 contest. The nine contestants that year were first chosen by Paul Jess, assistant professor of journalism, and David Pearson, assistant to State President Hilton Briggs.

Hefner chose Sandra Eaton, commenting, "As you can imagine, I am asked to judge a number of beauty contests every year, but I can't remember one in which the decisions were so hard to make!"

Mass transportation

With no cars and three-quarters of a mile between campus and downtown, Clyde Hinkley saw opportunity knocking and started a bus route in September 1921.

"Mr. Hinkley intends to expand the service as rapidly as the patronage permits," reported the Collegian. "At present, he is making six round trips. Tickets, which sell for 10 cents each or 12 for a $1, have been placed on sale at the book store."

The bus route made three stops on campus — at the Administration Building, the armory and the "girls' dormitory."

Alternative funding sources

Higher education often finds itself in the position of having to scrape and scramble for money. From staff salaries to building and property maintenance, there is never enough to go around. Sometimes, that situation calls for a little creative financing.

The cigarette tax fund paid for the Lincoln Memorial Library, which was built in 1927. The fund also raised enough money to pay for new sidewalks, lights and interior painting of the library. State President C.W. Pugsley said the work would not have been possible without the special appropriation.

The new, wider sidewalks followed the path of older, temporary walks. New lights were installed by the library and others were relocated to provide better sight at night. The library project included the painting of hallways and reading rooms.

Around the world on campus

From 1925-33, night watchman G.L. Bunday managed to walk two-thirds of the way around the world without leaving the State campus.

For eight years, the Sept. 20, 1933, Collegian reported, Bunday walked his campus route to ensure that State property remained unharmed. During that period, he never missed more than 10 nights of work.

"The elderly gentleman walks at least six miles each night, which, if you multiply it by the number of days in a year, is 2,190 miles per year," the college paper figured. "Subtracting the 60 miles State's faithful night watchman missed, in eight years, he has walked 17,420 miles, which is two-thirds around the world."

Holiday traditions

Alumni and Brookings community members alike have fond memories of the annual Christmas choral and orchestra performance of Handel's Messiah, a tradition that began in the early part of the century.

In 1939, professor Karl Theman, head of the music department, directed "a well-drilled chorus of 130 voices, whose quality of tone was extremely good," according to the Collegian. A capacity crowd enjoyed the performance that holiday season.

"The attacks and releases showed many hours of rehearsal," the paper said. "The college orchestra played with sureness and feeling, and furnished a satisfying background for the chorus and soloists."

After the 1954 concert, Theman told the Collegian: "It is interesting to me that these performances improve yearly. They seem to improve from year to year by reason of a carry-over from former performances, which is greater than one might expect, since no one participates more than four times."

Alphabet soup

On Sept. 19, 1934, the Collegian reported a change in the grading system. The old system of E, S, M, I, P and F was switched to the current-day standards of A, B, C, D and F.

"The grading system adopted at South Dakota State College assumes that the fairest and most intelligible record of a student's work is that which indicates his approximate rank in comparison with his fellow students," explained the Collegian.

The Goat's Milk Get-Together

There was a time when every spring, hundreds of State students headed for the country to participate in one of the season's most popular activities — a keg party. Surprisingly enough, it was a tradition that started in 1903.

According to a 1963 Collegian article, Milton J. Matterhorn, head of the horticulture department, rounded up students in 1903 to plant trees on the banks of the Sioux River. After planting 287 trees, some of the boys were sent to bring back kegs for the weary group to sit on.

In addition to the seats, the boys returned with a keg of cold goat's milk — hence the historical reference to the Goat's Milk Get-Together.

Although the tree-planting eventually ceased, the riverside celebration continued. In fact, as the 1963 Collegian noted, keg parties eventually became a year-round festivity.

Speaking of kegs ...

In November 1970, a group of Binnewies Hall boys broke the keg-rolling record.

The 53 residents of Third Floor West rolled an empty 16-gallon keg 292 miles in 50 hours and 25 minutes, besting a record of 150 miles set a month earlier by a group of students from the University of Minnesota-Duluth.

The State crew started the record roll at 6 p.m., heading from Brookings to the Iowa-South Dakota border just north of Sioux City, Iowa, and then back to Brookings.

Chapter 66

Raymond, S.D.

Saturday, March 29, 2003. South Dakota State's women's basketball team was minutes away from winning the Division II Elite Eight tournament — the first national basketball championship for State in 40 years.

An estimated 2,000 Jacks fans were cheering on the team in St. Joseph, Mo. Countless thousands more watched the game on ESPN2 and listened to it on the radio. As the remaining minutes ticked off the clock, the television announcer, in play-by-play narrative, took note of who had possession of the ball — "Sophomore Shannon Schlagel, Raymond, S.D. ..."

The irony of that moment likely was lost on the national audience. Most people don't know where South Dakota is, let alone Raymond, population 81. That Schlagel — a basketball standout of national caliber — hails from a small town in the northeastern part of the state ... well, the dichotomy captures the essence of what South Dakota State University is all about.

Pictured above, the Raymond sign on Highway 212.

R. Adams Dutcher from the 1907 Jack Rabbit yearbook.

In a state where the population of the largest city is 130,000 and the numbers drop off drastically from there, most students arrive on the State campus having grown up in a town like Raymond.

It's not so far-fetched, then, that Schlagel has continued the line of Raymond natives who made a name for themselves at South Dakota State. The tiny community 45 miles west of Watertown also has produced such notables as R. Adams Dutcher and Jerry Lohr.

Certainly, there are differences between Schlagel, Lohr and Dutcher. They were born in different eras and drawn to diverse life paths. Dutcher took to chemistry; Lohr, engineering and farming. Schlagel thinks she will pursue teaching.

Yet, each has left or is leaving a legacy — a permanent, personal imprint — that will carry on for generations to come.

South Dakota State, of course, is the other common denominator, offering fertile ground where individual drive and determination can both take root and take off.

Dutcher played a key role in creating the Jackrabbit mascot and Hobo Day. But his contribution to the lives of others has played out in ways we may never know. Consider Paul Berg, who won the Nobel Prize in chemistry in 1980.

Dutcher was chairman of the biochemistry department at Pennsylvania State College when Berg arrived as a freshman in the fall of 1944. As Berg neared graduation, he faced a complicated dilemma over graduate school offers and sought advice from Dutcher: "He advised me to go where my 'heart' led me."

Berg went back on a commitment to Oklahoma A&M in Stillwater (now Oklahoma State University). Instead, he accepted a late offer from Western Reserve University Medical School in Cleveland, Ohio, to work with Harland Wood, one of the pioneers in the use of stable and radioactive isotopes as tracers for metabolic pathways.

Dutcher, explains Berg, "offered to write to the dean at Oklahoma explaining my dilemma and his advice. I was concerned that Oklahoma would hold me to my earlier acceptance, but quite obviously, Dutcher's intercession was influential as I received a very cordial letter from Oklahoma conceding that I was making the right decision for me."

Berg adds, "As a result, I went to WRU and had a very successful Ph.D. experience, which launched my career."

The Nobel Prize, of course, attests to that. And, for Dutcher to be credited with such an influential role stands as testimony to the now familiar SDSU slogan, "You can go anywhere from here."

Dutcher was born in Raymond on March 28, 1886, to Paul and Susie Dutcher. His first name, in fact, was Raymond. His family moved to Brookings when he was 5 years old. Dutcher graduated from Brookings High School in 1903. He spent the next four years at South Dakota State College and graduated in 1907.

Dutcher stayed on to earn his master of science degree, which he did in 1910, and to teach in the chemistry department. He took a faculty position at the University of Missouri from 1910-12. It was during his time in Missouri that Dutcher witnessed a Hobo Day celebration.

Dutcher moved on to the chemistry department at the University of Illinois, then Oregon State College, the University of Minnesota, and ultimately Penn State.

Jerry Lohr from the 1958 Jack Rabbit yearbook.

As Dutcher earned his master's degree from State in 1910, Jerry Lohr's grandparents, Jake and Agnes, built their farm six miles south of Raymond in Logan Township. In 1916, Agnes Lohr traveled to the World's Fair in Chicago and bought the world champion milking shorthorn cow, which was pregnant at the time. From that one cow, the Lohr family established a herd of registered milking shorthorn cattle.

"We had pretty tough years in the early '50s on the farm," reminisces Lohr, class of 1958. "We came down to State one time to see an artificial insemination program. One of the things my father said that I will never forget was 'Get an education in something else, do something else. You can always come back and farm.' If ever there was a quote that lives in my mind, it was probably that one."

Lohr heeded his father's advice, enrolled at State and pursued a degree in civil engineering. He received his master's from Stanford University, and 45 years later, lives 20 miles from the northern California campus.

In 1965, Lohr and a partner launched a building business. When the environmental movement made it impossible several years later to get subdivision plans approved, Lohr returned to his roots — farming. Instead of cattle or grain, however, Lohr and his partner started a vineyard.

"We bought land for a vineyard in 1971, planted in '72 and '73, and bonded the winery in 1974," says Lohr, who bought out his partner in 1984.

Reflecting on his life's journey, Lohr notes: "It's incredible how much I learned both from growing up on farm and from State that I use on a daily basis. The combination of farming, scheduling, knowing about the soil — that's been the key to our success in the vineyard and the winery."

Lohr, to a generous degree, has returned the favor. From 1993-98, he chaired the "Visions for the Future" campaign, which raised $52.4 million for scholarships, new buildings, additions and extensive renovation projects. Lohr and his wife, Carol, also have established several scholarship funds.

"The challenge now," says Lohr, "is to prove to the state of South Dakota that education is an investment and not an expense. I think that's a huge problem. Every year there's a battle at the Legislature, a battle at the regents, and there shouldn't be."

State is now at a point where the facilities are in good shape, Lohr adds, but there remains considerable work to do.

"We need not only to attract some of the best students from the area, but to retain them here," he says. "We have got to develop a culture here that is attractive to more and more young people. ... A lot of people get educated here, but they go to work in another part of the country. You can go anywhere from here, but why should you? This is a pretty good place to live."

Decades have come and gone since Dutcher and Lohr left Raymond. Yet, growing up in the small South Dakota town remains nearly the same as it ever was.

Shannon Schlagel (Photo courtesy of Eric Landwehr)

Schlagel's parents, Wayne and Jackie, were high school sweethearts. Her mother played one year of basketball at Dakota State. When Wayne's father died of lung cancer in 1980, Schlagel's parents married and moved back to the family farm.

Throughout her childhood, the 20-year-old sophomore says, "My grandma lived 76 feet from our house. Exactly."

The family farms about 2,500 acres and raises about 600 head of cattle and 50 sheep. Schlagel laughs about the grounding experience of returning home for the summer to work on the farm: "Oh man! Running the stinky cattle through the

The basketball hoop on the Schlagel farm.

shoot, I'm thinking 'I play basketball at South Dakota State and now I'm walking through cow poop.' I am probably one of the few girls on campus who can castrate a bull."

Schlagel says growing up on a farm with her younger brothers, Tony and Blake, was an education by itself and helped lay the foundation for whom she is today.

"I think the No. 1 value I learned was that you had to work for everything you got," she says. "There weren't really any days off. I'd feed silage to the cattle, haul buckets of corn or oats to the animals in the barn. I think the one thing I picked up from my parents was the trait of working hard and trying to be the best you could be."

In rural South Dakota, some of life's harder lessons begin early, but country kids learn to take them all in stride. As a kindergartner, Schlagel boarded the school bus at 6:50 a.m. and didn't return home until 5:30 p.m.

"I was the first one on and the last one off," she laughs. "We had a really good bus driver — the same bus driver through sixth grade. Glen Bruflat. He always kept a pretty good hold on us. I kind of sat up close to the front and listened to the stories he told."

Schlagel's first taste of athletics came one summer. There was a shortage of girls her age, so she and two others played baseball with the boys. Soon, her mother started a basketball program.

"Once or twice a week, we'd work on dribbling and passing," she says. "She continued that through third and fourth grade. When I was in fifth grade, she started coaching fifth- and sixth-grade basketball. Once I was in fifth grade, I knew basketball was something I liked. In the summertime, four of us — the Four Farm Girls — we played in three-on-three tournaments."

When Schlagel was in eighth grade, her mother was the assistant basketball coach for Clark High School.

"I'd go with my mom to practice and try and get in, even if it was just filling up water cups," Schlagel says. "Gradually, the head coach let me get in on some of the drills. Then, one day, we were loading up the bus for a game in Milbank. I had two water jugs in one hand, a bag of balls in the other. I was carrying towels. And he says, 'Shannon, go grab your shoes.'

"Well, I had just had junior high practice. I said, 'Oh, did somebody forget their shoes?' He said, 'No. We'll see if we can't get you in a jersey.' Oh man, my heart was racing the whole way up there. I got to play with the freshmen that game. Homecoming of that year, I got a varsity jersey."

The moment when the coach handed her the jersey remains as clear today as when it happened.

"I knew he had one more jersey, and in the back of my mind, I'm thinking, how cool that would be," Schlagel says. "But, I knew I had a lot more work I had to do to get better. Then, the practice before homecoming, he hands me the jersey and says, 'Play JV and you can sit varsity.'"

She grins as she retells the story, still feeling the thrill of realizing her eighth-grade dream. And now, to stake a claim in State history as a member of the team that brought home the school's first national championship in women's basketball — it's a dream come true.

"I'm just ecstatic to be here," says Schlagel. "The band uses the phrase 'The Pride of the Dakotas.' I would say the pride of being a Jackrabbit is indescribable. It's such a great place and the opportunities that are available — to be a part of this is just great."

In wisdom that belies her age, Schlagel ponders the key to her success.

"I think," she says, "never settle for less than what you have to offer. You always have to know in the back of your mind what you want as an individual. Eleanor Roosevelt said, 'The future belongs to those who believe in their dreams.' I think that's very true."

Whether those dreams are big or small, SDSU President Peggy Gordon Miller says it is the school's duty to help students tap into their potential — a responsibility particularly important when young adults often arrive on campus without any experience in the world beyond their small town and little idea of whom or what they can become.

"One of our obligations is to make sure students leave us with the clear understanding and the confidence that they can compete anywhere," she says. "I can remember the first time I went to Ohio State. It was the size of 20 of my hometowns. It took my breath away. But, I lived through the day and went home to talk about it."

Throughout its history, South Dakota State has served as a springboard for an incredible collection of individuals, whether they have been basketball standouts or Nobel Prize winners, industry giants or ordinary citizens. That's no mystery for Miller.

"This is a university that respects talent; that understands that when you find great talent, that you need to nurture that talent," she says. "We aren't afraid of it. One of the real treasures here is that we all still feel an obligation to know our students and respect them enough that we find these talents."

Miller clearly revels in the challenge to prepare young adults from a rural state to succeed in the world that awaits them. Nearly six years into her administration, she says the experience has far exceeded her expectations.

"This is the kind of campus every president hopes to have the opportunity to serve," she says. "It is very easy to work hard for the students and the faculty. Everyone is committed to a larger purpose. ...

"We have to prepare students to make a better world, to create a better tomorrow, to increase their respect for how knowledge can change the world. We want you to come to South Dakota State. And when you come, we're going to change you. We want you to leave us with a broader understanding of the world and a greater sense of your role in it."

Yet, no matter where State students venture, they stay rooted in the South Dakota experience. The small-town connections hold firm, as the strong work ethic takes them however far they want to go.

Schlagel finds family and friends from Raymond and Clark in the stands at nearly every home game, cheering on the Jacks. The diehard support is as dependable as the change of seasons. It boosts her confidence and fuels her drive to succeed.

"I feel honored," she says. "Everybody has been a part of my growing up. If I had gone far away to school, I would struggle without seing a friendly face. It means so much to me to see people I know at each game."

When basketball ends, Schlagel thinks she would like to be a coach or a teacher. Whatever route she takes, she says, "I'd like to go back and give to younger kids what I've been given."

Living away from South Dakota, Lohr appreciates his home state. Perhaps more than others who never leave.

"A lot of people get educated here and work in another part of the country," Lohr says. "But they come back to Clark County."

Likewise, Lohr keeps SDSU close to his heart. "State played a huge role in everything I did and do."

Presidents and Places

The Presidents

In nearly 120 years, South Dakota State has gone from the college equivalent of a one-room schoolhouse to a multimillion-dollar powerhouse of higher education.

When viewed across the spectrum of time, State's growth — from 62 students and a handful of teachers in the first year of college classes to a record-breaking enrollment of 9,952 and 1,775 employees — is breathtaking.

To think of all the internal and external struggles, the political and philosophical debates, the varied views of where State should go and how to take it there — the spectacular success of the institution borders on the inconceivable.

How, exactly, did we get here?

Without question, South Dakota State today represents an incalculable investment of time, energy and finances by thousands of people, from students and parents, faculty and staff to alumni and administrators, regents and legislators, and, of course, taxpayers.

But none of it — neither the good, nor the bad — would have been the

Pictured above, the Great Seal of South Dakota State University.

THE COLLEGE ON THE HILL

George Lilley
1884-1886

Lewis McLouth
1887-1896

John W. Heston
1896-1903

James Chalmers
1903-1906

same without the leadership of 18 individuals. Here, with information gleaned from the SDSU Centennial edition in 1981, is the list of presidents who brought South Dakota State from its inception through more than a century of accomplishment:

GEORGE LILLEY, 1884-86: Hired on June 2, 1884, the 30-year-old Lilley scored the historical feat of being the first president of Dakota Agricultural College. His salary was $1,500. Within two years, regents discovered that Lilley had embellished his credentials. Instead of a doctorate, he held only an honorary degree.

LEWIS MCLOUTH, 1887-96: McLouth, 47, replaced Lilley at the helm of the young college. McLouth came to the Brookings campus from Michigan College. Before he arrived, Stephen Updyke had served as acting president. McLouth's term was characterized by political upheaval and student unrest. The regents asked for his resignation in July 1894, but McLouth did not leave until 1896 when he was asked to hand over his keys to campus buildings.

JOHN W. HESTON, 1896-1903: Heston arrived at State with experience in public schools, a law practice and a college presidency. He is credited with organizing departments, dividing the school year into three quarters, and paying more attention to liberal arts and humanities. However, like others before him, Heston had a troubled relationship with the regents and moved on to become president of the Normal School (now Dakota State University) in Madison.

JAMES CHALMERS, 1903-06: Chalmers came to Brookings from Ohio. A teacher, preacher and administrator, he was well-educated in the liberal arts. More importantly, though, he was well-liked by the regents. But, not by all of them and not for long. Some members of the board tried to put a stop to Chalmers' frequent

The Presidents

Robert L. Slagle
1906-1914

public-speaking engagements, thinking that he was gone too often.

ROBERT L. SLAGLE, 1906-14: That Slagle wanted to come to State from the School of Mines was an impressive feat on the regents' part. Three of the four presidents who preceded Slagle had been fired. Stricter standards during Slagle's administration made it necessary for students to complete four years of high school before entering a degree program. Slagle also oversaw the reorganization of agricultural courses and the establishment of a summer session. He moved on to a position at the University of South Dakota.

Ellwood C. Perisho
1914-1918

ELLWOOD C. PERISHO, 1914-18: Perisho, the former dean of arts and science at USD, brought with him extensive experience in higher education. Perisho's administration oversaw organization of the Extension Department, the designation of a student union building and admission into the North Central Association of Colleges and Secondary Schools.

Willis E. Johnson
1919-1923

WILLIS E. JOHNSON, 1919-23: Johnson was the first State president to enjoy a formal inauguration. His tenure was marked by more rigid academic standards, tightened grading procedures and an increased enrollment by 100 percent. Johnson's administration also was credited with establishing the college bookstore.

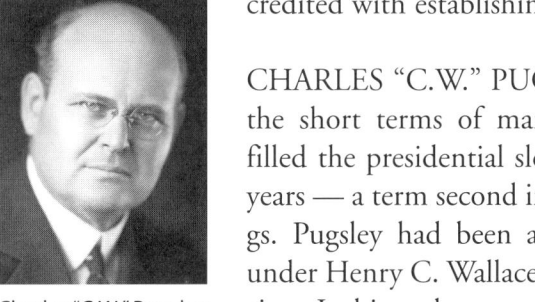
Charles "C.W." Pugsley
1923-1940

CHARLES "C.W." PUGSLEY, 1923-40: In contrast to the short terms of many of his predecessors, Pugsley filled the presidential slot at South Dakota State for 17 years — a term second in length only to Hilton M. Briggs. Pugsley had been assistant secretary of agriculture under Henry C. Wallace during the Harding administration. In his early years, Pugsley oversaw the division of the college into agriculture, general science, home economics, engineering and pharmacy. Enrollment during Pugsley's administration jumped from 698 to 1,376.

George L. Brown
1940

GEORGE L. BROWN, 1940: Brown, when he was more than 70 years old, served as president between Pugsley and Lyman Jackson. A teacher as well as an administrator, Brown also took on acting president duties several times in the life of South Dakota State, his first stint running for five months in 1914.

Lyman Jackson, seen here with Student Body President Paul Hanson '43
1940-1946

LYMAN JACKSON, 1940-46: Jackson was dean of agriculture at Ohio State University prior to arriving in Brookings. Jackson's tenure played out during the difficult years of World War II, which heightened the military presence on campus and increased State's responsibility to the country. From an educational perspective, Jackson oversaw the reorganization of the college into two main divisions — one for four-year programs and the other for two-year.

H.M. Crothers
1946, 1951, 1957-1958

H.M. CROTHERS, 1946, 1951, 1957-58: Crothers, class of 1910, filled in as acting president three times amid the comings and goings of presidents. He served as the Dean of the College of Engineering from 1925-1955.

Fred H. Leinbach
1947-1951

FRED H. LEINBACH, 1947-51: Leinbach was dean of agriculture and head of animal husbandry at the University of Maryland before coming to State. Despite his training, he reportedly resigned four years later because of problems in the college's ag department. Leinbach's brief tenure saw the first hiring of a vice president to

The Presidents

cope with increasing enrollment and the construction of many new buildings. In another first, State's budget exceeded $1 million.

John Headley
1952-1957

JOHN HEADLEY, 1952-57: Faculty concerns over a number of issues greeted Headley when he arrived from his position as president of State Teacher's College at St. Cloud, Minn. He also found himself faced with the agricultural department controversy that had pushed his predecessor out.

Hilton M. Briggs
1958-1975

HILTON M. BRIGGS, 1958-75: Guiding South Dakota State for more than 17 years, Briggs enjoyed the longest tenure in the presidential office. Briggs was beloved by many for both his big heart and straightforward manner. He was tough, plainspoken and focused. Under Briggs, State experienced its largest growth at the time in both buildings and student numbers.

Sherwood O. Berg
1975-1984

SHERWOOD O. BERG, 1975-84: Berg earned the distinction of being the first South Dakota State graduate to serve as president of the institution. Among Berg's goals were efforts to add an international dimension to SDSU and ride the crest of the information age. As the world became more global, Berg saw that many graduates during his time would have opportunities to work in the vast world beyond South Dakota. He wanted to ensure they were prepared and had the necessary tools to be successful.

Ray Hoops
1984-1985

RAY HOOPS, 1984-85: Hoops reigned for a brief eight-month span that ended in controversy. Hoops had high hopes of increasing faculty pay, but wound up embroiled in a mess that involved a faculty member's testimony in the state Senate. According to Hoops, he was told to fire the individual, but he refused. In retrospect, Hoops told the Collegian: "I did what I had to do and I'd do it again a dozen times."

Robert Wagner
1985-1997

ROBERT WAGNER, 1985-97: Wagner attended State as a graduate student and then continued on to earn his doctoral degree. He stayed on as a sociology professor before moving up the administrative ranks. Wagner considered one of his most difficult tasks to be convincing state lawmakers and taxpayers that public higher education was a worthwhile investment. Despite tight fiscal reins, Wagner saw gains in state funding and a huge jump in the SDSU Foundation's bankroll — from $4.8 million to nearly $58 million. In addition, it was during his presidency that the highly succesful Visions for the Future campaign was launched.

Peggy Gordon Miller
1998-present

PEGGY GORDON MILLER, 1998-present: In another entry for the record books, Miller — who came to State from the University of Akron, Ohio — was the first woman to lead South Dakota State. With national experience, contacts in Washington, D.C., and positions on corporate boards, Miller arrived on campus saying she wanted to get to know every student and faculty member. In her six years in office, Miller has presided over continued growth and renovation in campus buildings, a record enrollment of 10,000 students spurred on by the Jackrabbit Guarantee, and the university's plan to move from Division II to Division I athletics in 2004.

The Places

In the beginning, when South Dakota State was new, the campus buildings had generic names based on geographic location — Central, South, North, East and West. But as people came and went throughout the life of the institution, leaving their mark in one way or another, it became customary to honor their contributions by naming a building or room after them.

Today, many places on the SDSU campus bear the name of special individuals. But often times, we pass by those places without any thought given to their namesakes. Here, then, is a listing of campus buildings that carry on certain legacies and a brief explanation of why their name is familiar.

Alvida Myre Sorenson
1924 Jack Rabbit

ALVILDA MYRE SORENSON CENTER: Built in 1980. Alvilda Myre Sorenson, class of 1924, gave generously to her alma mater and earned several honors for her work in home economics and the humanities. The building originally housed the Family Resource and Management Center, operating as a home economics lab area. There also were four apartments in the building. In 1998, home economics moved out and the university police and campus visitors' center moved in.

Harold Bailey

BAILEY HALL: Built in 1994. Harold Bailey served 34 years at SDSU — first as a pharmacy professor and later as vice president of academic affairs and dean of the Graduate School. The hall contains 80 apartments, each with four single bedrooms.

BERG HALL: Built in 1994. Sherwood O. Berg, class of 1947, was the first SDSU graduate to serve as chief administrator of his alma mater. Berg was president

Sherwood O. Berg
1947 Jack Rabbit

Edward R. Binniwies
1917 Jack Rabbit

Hilton M. Briggs

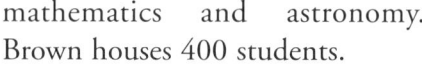
Harold M. Crothers
1913 Jack Rabbit

George L. Brown
1913 Jack Rabbit

William E. DePuy

from 1975-84. Like Bailey, Berg has 80 four-bedroom apartments.

BINNEWIES HALL: Built in 1969. Edward R. Binniwies, class of 1913, was a chemistry professor and director of student affairs. Binnewies worked for the university for more than 50 years and was a member of the first Hobo Day Committee. The residence hall houses 490 students in eight building wings.

H.M. BRIGGS LIBRARY: Built in 1977. Hilton M. Briggs served as State president for 17 years, from 1958 to 1975. The library holds a million bound volumes, periodicals and microfilms with computer access to 500 other research libraries across the United States.

BROWN HALL: Built in 1960. George L. Brown served South Dakota State for more than half a century as president, acting president, dean and professor of mathematics and astronomy. Brown houses 400 students.

CROTHERS ENGINEERING HALL: Built in 1957. Harold M. Crothers was a dean and professor in the College of Engineering. Crothers served as acting president of the university on three occasions. The hall houses the College of Engineering central administration as well as several departments within the college.

DEPUY MILITARY HALL: Built in 1942. William E. DePuy, who was commissioned from the South Dakota State ROTC department in 1941, attained four-star general status in 1973. The building hous-

The Places

Ethel Austin Martin
1916 Jack Rabbit

es both Air Force and Army ROTC departments.

ETHEL AUSTIN MARTIN BUILDING: Built in 1920. Ethel Austin Martin, class of 1916, was a well-known author and distinguished nutritionist. Originally the building housed veterinary science. Since 1999, the building has served as home to the Ethel Austin Martin Program in Human Nutrition.

Guilford C. Gross
1939 Jack Rabbit

GROSS PHARMACY BUILDING: Built in 1980. Located at the south end of Shepard Hall, the building was named in honor of Guilford C. Gross, class of 1939, and former professor and dean of pharmacy. Gross also earned his master's degree from State in 1940 and retired in 1980.

GROVE HALL: Built in 1962. Originally known as Grove Commons, the building was renamed in 1995 and currently houses the Great Plains Water Resources Institute and art department. The name commemorates a walnut grove that once grew in the area.

Grove

HANSEN HALL: Built in 1967. Niels Hansen was a world-famous horticulturist and professor at South Dakota State from 1895-1950. He headed up the horticulture department and was designated as the first plant explorer for the U.S. Department of Agriculture. The four-story coed residence hall houses 440 students.

Niels Hansen
1913 Jack Rabbit

Albert S. Harding
1910 Jack Rabbit

HARDING HALL: Built in 1954. Albert S. Harding is considered one of SDSU's greatest educators. He graduated from State in 1892 and returned to campus in 1897 to teach. Harding served as head of the political science and history department. Today, Harding Hall houses some of the departments of the engineering college.

THE COLLEGE ON THE HILL

Rudolph A. Larson
1913 Jack Rabbit

Abraham Lincoln
Bust sculpted by Gilbert
Riswold, class of 1925.

Hubert M. Mathews
1917 Jack Rabbit

Medary

Edith Pierson
1922 Jack Rabbit

LARSON COMMONS: Built in 1969. Rudolph A. Larson served South Dakota State as college secretary from 1901 until his death in 1959. He also served as treasurer of the Experiment Station. The Commons operates as the dining facility for residents of Young and Binniwies halls.

LINCOLN MUSIC HALL: Built in 1927. The hall has been home to the music department since 1979. Before the Briggs Library was built, Lincoln was the college library. President Calvin Coolidge spoke at the dedication of the library, which honored President Abraham Lincoln for his role in helping create the land-grant college system.

MATHEWS HALL: Built in 1962. Hubert B. Mathews, class of 1892, served as head of the physics department and dean of engineering. Mathews also took on the duties of the first secretary of the SDSU Alumni Association and was a key figure in the early history of South Dakota State. The residence hall houses 400 students.

MEDARY COMMONS: Built in 1965. The dining facility for west campus residents, Medary Commons takes its name from Medary Avenue, which runs directly east of the building. Medary was the name of a small town just south of present-day Brookings. The building also houses the Career and Academic Planning Center.

PIERSON HALL: Built in 1965. Edith Pierson arrived at State in 1919 as an associate professor of home economics. She served as department head and then dean of home economics. Pierson Hall is home to 440 students.

The Places

Charles W. Pugsley

PUGSLEY CENTER: Built in 1940. Charles W. Pugsley was president of State College from 1923-40. Prior to his arrival in Brookings, Pugsley had served as an assistant secretary of agriculture for the U.S. government. Pugsley Center was the student union until 1974. Today, it houses the Information Technology Center, the SDSU preschool, and the communications studies and theater department.

John O'Brien Scobey

SCOBEY HALL: Built in 1940. As the Dakota Territory legislator from Brookings, John O'Brien Scobey secured the city as the location for the new land-grant college. Scobey Hall today is home to a variety of academic departments.

James H. Shepard
1917 Jack Rabbit

SHEPARD HALL: Built in 1965. James H. Shepard, a renowned chemist and professor of chemistry at State from 1888-1918, also served as director of the Experiment Station. The original chemistry building was built in 1929 with a $1.1 million addition completed in 1965. It houses the chemistry department.

SOLBERG HALL: Built in 1901. Halvor C. Solberg, class of 1891, was the engineering professor who introduced mechanical engineering to South Dakota State. Solberg served South Dakota State for more than 40 years and helped develop the state's early highway system. He is credited with plotting the route that ultimately became U.S. Highway 14 from Winona, Minn., to the Black Hills.

Halvor C. Solberg
1913 Jack Rabbit

Stan Marshall

STANLEY J. MARSHALL HPER CENTER: Opened in 1973. The legendary Stan Marshall was director of athletics and HPER department head from 1965 until his death in 1980. Marshall graduated from State in 1950. The building houses offices for the department

THE COLLEGE ON THE HILL

Lawrence, Arthur and Charles Tompkins

of health, physical education and recreation, and Frost Arena, the 8,000-seat home of the SDSU Jackrabbits.

TOMPKINS ALUMNI CENTER: Built in 1976. Brothers Arthur (class of 1918), Lawrence (class of 1923) and Charles (class of 1928) Tompkins donated the money to build the home of State alumni. The 5,000-square-foot facility houses Alumni Association offices, event rooms and a memorabilia library. It stands on the grounds formerly occupied by East Men's Hall. In 1985, the John Ervine Bylander Courtyard was added, including the Aggie Clock Tower that displays the clock faces that once adorned the top of Old North.

Waneta Hall

WANETA HALL: Built in 1960. The residence hall, which houses 320 students, was named after a Yanktonais Native American, who gained fame for his bravery during the War of 1812. The building is connected to Wecota Annex.

Wecota Hall

WECOTA HALL: Built in 1916. The building's name is derived from the Sioux language and refers to the second maiden in a Native American family. The first floor serves as offices and the second, third and fourth floors of Wecota Annex (built in 1939) serve as a residence hall for women.

Wenona Hall

WENONA HALL: Built in 1909. The name signifies the first-born maiden of a Native American family. Built as a residence hall for women, Wenona now houses the College of Education and Counseling and engineering and technology management.

The Places

Woodbine Cottage

Anson Yeager
1947 Jack Rabbit

Ada May Yeager
1942 Jack Rabbit

Gertrude Stickney Young
1909 Jack Rabbit

WOODBINE COTTAGE: Built in 1887. South Dakota State's second president, Lewis McLouth, built Woodbine, which has housed nearly all of the university's presidents. (See Chapter 17.)

YEAGER HALL: Built in 1951. A $2.4 million expansion and renovation of the journalism department building was completed in 2000 with the help of a major gift from Anson Yeager, class of 1947, and his wife, Ada May Yeager, class of 1943. Yeager Hall also houses the Joe L. Floyd Media Laboratory, SDSU print lab and campus post office.

YOUNG HALL: Built in 1969. Gertrude Stickney Young, a pioneer faculty member at State, was a professor of history and English. She authored several books, including a biography of South Dakota State art instructor Ada B. Caldwell. Young was a distinguished teacher from 1907 to 1943, when she was named professor emeritus. Young Hall houses 490 students.